SOLIDARITY AND DEFIANT SPIRITUALITY

RELIGION AND SOCIAL TRANSFORMATION

General Editors: Anthony B. Pinn and Stacey M. Floyd-Thomas

Solidarity and Defiant Spirituality

Africana Lessons on Religion, Racism, and
Ending Gender Violence

Traci C. West

NEW YORK UNIVERSITY PRESS

New York

NEW YORK UNIVERSITY PRESS
New York

www.nyupress.org

References to Internet websites (URLs) were accurate at the time of writing. Neither the author nor New York University Press is responsible for URLs that may have expired or changed since the manuscript was prepared.

Library of Congress Cataloging-in-Publication Data
Names: West, Traci C., 1959– author.
Title: Solidarity and defiant spirituality : Africana lessons on religion, racism, and ending gender violence / Traci C. West.
Description: New York : NYU Press, 2019. | Series: Religion and social transformation | Includes bibliographical references and index.
Identifiers: LCCN 2018021499| ISBN 9781479849031 (cl : alk. paper) | ISBN 9781479833993 (pb : alk. paper)
Subjects: LCSH: Violence—Religious aspects—Christianity. | Sex crimes—Africa. | Sex crimes—South America. | Sex crimes—United States. | Christianity—Africa.
Classification: LCC BT736.15 .W475 2018 | DDC 362.82/92—dc23
LC record available at https://lccn.loc.gov/2018021499

New York University Press books are printed on acid-free paper, and their binding materials are chosen for strength and durability. We strive to use environmentally responsible suppliers and materials to the greatest extent possible in publishing our books.

Manufactured in the United States of America

10 9 8 7 6 5 4 3 2 1

Also available as an ebook

To Jerry G. Watts (1953–2015)

I need you to still be here

CONTENTS

Introduction

The Experiment

In the early twenty-first century, Vice President Joe Biden spoke in Washington, D.C., to a national meeting of Young Women's Christian Association (YWCA) activist leaders committed to supporting victim-survivors of intimate violence in the United States.[1] Displayed on a large screen in the background, their YWCA motto proclaimed the vision of "eliminating racism, empowering women." Biden's speech at the event reinforced an urgent need for reauthorization of the Violence Against Women Act (VAWA), which was caught in a congressional standoff between the House and Senate.[2] He had been the key sponsor of the original bill proposed in 1990, and after it was signed into law in 1994, Biden continued to be a staunch and vocal advocate for increasing government measures to address violence against women and girls.

In this 2012 speech Biden gave witness to an inspiring moral evolution in U.S. public life. He explained that when he first introduced the legislation and decided to press for its passage, he realized that "the single most important thing is for us to have a cultural consensus that this is a God-awful problem."[3] As he spoke, Biden traced the efficacy of the law in over a decade following its enactment. He noted that it "became part of our social fabric . . . part of our political culture," such that "there's a consensus now in America around our daughters, our sisters, our wives, our grandmothers having the right to expect to be free from violent behavior." Even as Biden acknowledged the "sad" fact of the struggle in Congress to reauthorize VAWA, he still boasted that the law had furnished "the redefinition of our culture."[4]

Some of Biden's language tellingly illustrates how racial and religious cultural assumptions can infuse U.S. efforts to stem violence against women and girls. The vice president emphasized the global stature of the United States and the high regard for how we address this particular form of violence. He testified to having personally experienced this attention to our success during his extensive international travel for meetings with world leaders. "They look to us," he claimed. Biden was undeniably sincere in his opposition to gender-based violence. But some of the underlying social values nested in this contention echo an enduring paternalistic understanding of whiteness that often inhabits public expressions of U.S.-American Christianity and national pride.[5] This notion of whiteness denotes superiority but possesses a benevolent attitude rather than hostility toward nonwhites. This attitude of Christian whiteness remained unnamed in explicit terms but subtly present in Biden's description of those who "look to us."

Biden vividly outlined the U.S. missionary role as one in which "we're trying to export this philosophy to nations where daughters and wives are still victimized . . . still suffer unimaginable horrors across the world, so-called honor killings, acid attacks, dowry-related murders, genital mutilation."[6] His approach conveyed a strong moral message about culture and change that assumes that certain religious and racial advantages are intrinsic to the U.S. exporters. The speech stresses antiviolence cultural change in the United States as not only possible but already achieved by us. This is not the case for them. Biden's list of "unimaginable horrors" spotlights the global contrast between "us" and "them." He referenced certain horrific forms of gender-based violence occurring abroad that his predominantly Christian audience was likely to attribute to the non-Christian cultural and religious traditions of those foreigners. As a result, their gender violence was portrayed as intractable, static, and in need of U.S. inspiration to create change in their countries. Moreover, the national populations in which women suffer due to "honor killings, acid attacks, dowry-related murders, genital mutilation" have racial and ethnic identities usually identified by U.S.-American audiences as peoples of African, South Asian, and Middle Eastern descent. In contrast, Biden dotted his speech with references to the praiseworthy, violence-challenging values his Irish Catholic parents instilled in him. His concluding expression of gratitude to the Young Women's Christian Association antiviolence advocates celebrated their efforts with the cherished words of his mother: "You really are doing God's work."[7]

In this book, I too focus on the role of culture in addressing gender-based violence, particularly on religious and racial dynamics. But my starting point markedly conflicts with Biden's view of U.S. achievement of cultural consensus on opposing the violence and the need to globally export the philosophy and values embedded in that cultural consensus. Instead, I experiment with mining resources of activist leaders in other nations to help challenge what I view as a fundamental form of moral myopia within the United States: too much tolerance for intimate violence against women and girls. Deeply embedded cultural support preserves this tolerance, and racial and religious dynamics are often overlooked elements that underpin it.

Settler-colonizers and slave traders initially brought Christianity to this continent, and it is now the religion of a majority (over 70 percent) of the U.S. population.[8] As such, Christianity is implicated in the historical legacy of their violence against colonized and enslaved women and girls and its continuing impact in our society. In striving to end the current problem of gender-based violence, we need a sense of urgency and boldness as we confront the contributing role of entrenched racial and religious values. This confrontation can be energized by the acknowledgment of some of the distinctive features of anti-black racism pervasive in U.S. history and contemporary culture and further mobilized by the capacity to recognize how those distinctive racial features often work together with heteropatriarchal values dominant within Christianity.

Too little attention to this entangled cultural imprint can undermine otherwise compelling feminist scholarly and activist proposals for the kind of systemic shifts necessary in criminology, public health, and other arenas of public policy that address the violence. When feminist public policy analyses neglect racial and religious values, they leave intact those basic moral understandings within local community life that uphold our current culture of permission for the violence. Similarly, critical theorists of race may recognize how the commodification of bodies in racist logics and practices of white supremacy, colonialism, and Orientalism have helped to globally organize varied forms of gender-based violence thriving in the Americas and elsewhere.[9] But the violence is usually discussed with insufficient accompanying consideration of the peculiar Christian religious values that have saturated and supported those logics and practices in many Western societies.

Foundational feminist scholarly investigations of Christian religion have been devoted to assessing the damaging consequences of Christian heteropatriarchal traditions and institutional practices for victim-survivors of intimate violence and abuse. This literature has considered how communal values sustained through church regulations, rituals, leadership, scriptures, and theologies have helped to justify gender-based intimate abuse and violence, especially for male perpetrators who target females.[10] What many of those discussions often leave unspecified, however, are the residual distorting racial cues that carry white supremacist messages embedded in Christology, theological metaphors, and scriptural interpretations.[11] The ways in which these racial cues enhance gender-violence-supporting elements of U.S. Christian religious and civic self-expression need further critical amplification.

This kind of siloing—typical of scholarly approaches to gender, race, and religion—can undercut the conceptualization of more systemic responses to gender-based violence and reproduce similar myopic cultural assumptions as those found in public conversations by well-meaning leaders such as Biden. We desperately need daring moral imaginations to ignite more culturally nuanced understandings and reject self-congratulatory satisfaction with our inadequate remedies.

This book experiments with an uncustomary method of intercultural inquiry and engagement of multiple geopolitical sites as points of reference. It draws on the perspectives and experiences of anti-gender-violence activists in South America and Africa to inform efforts to end intimate violence here in the United States. This approach is intended to disturb the reflexive quality in U.S. nationalist and cultural consciousness about gender-based violence that retains a built-in opacity—a collectively constructed protective membrane infused with specific forms of heteropatriarchal Christian religious and white supremacist values. To participate in such disruption, the ideas I develop embrace a transnational Africana perspective that relies on an experientially based method of analysis. While critically engaging the unique global political status and influence of the United States, the transnational perspective unfolds as I describe my encounters with activist leaders of African descent that occurred over the past several years in Ghana, Brazil, and South Africa, as I interviewed these leaders about their work to end violence against women and girls. Highlighted in the discussions are varied expressions of anti-black racism in their contexts and aspects of their Christian, Muslim, or Candomblé religion that are relevant. The focus on how our struggle against intimate violence in the United States might be informed by some understanding of their work requires scrutiny of the political challenges that this kind of transnational and intercultural learning entails. Since gender-based violence takes so many forms, the discussion here is mainly limited to rape within heterosexual marriage and other types of male-perpetrated domestic violence against women, sex trafficking of women and girls, and the targeting of lesbians for rape and murder.

Even though what now seems like profoundly unyielding polarization and cynicism in politics and religion in the United States can easily lead us to an even more solidified resignation to the prevalence of intimate violence, this book is about hope. It stubbornly focuses on a hope-filled vision in tandem with ideas about actual practices to end gender-based violence. It locates that hope by engaging in a process of learning from encounters with activists abroad.

Rape Tolerance in American Cultural History

Invoking a transnational Africana lens as useful for understanding U.S. cultural tolerance for the sexual assault of women and girls is unusual, conceptually risky, and likely to prompt a degree of skepticism. For U.S.-Americans, our self-understandings can foment this skeptical response based, in part, on a view of our own moral exceptionalism learned through the claims of leaders like Biden about our relationship to other places in the world, especially Africa. Indeed, this racially informed sense of moral exceptionalism is a treacherous feature of gendered historical amnesia. It functions as a vital element in the collective erasure of how intimate violence against women and girls has been condoned within certain aspects of U.S. culture and history.

Anthropologist Sally Engle Merry has described how dedicated international state leaders and human rights activists discuss culture in their deliberations on international strategies to stop gender-based violence. Different from Biden's boastful identification of U.S. culture as a global symbol of progress, Merry explains how, in international human rights meetings she has attended, "culture often refers to traditions and customs: ways of doing things that are justified by their roots in the past."[12] Especially in U.S.-based discussions of localized forms of violence against women and girls that occur around the globe, derogatory, racialized connotations may be attached to the use of the term *culture*. Understood primarily as the unifying notions of nation, ethnicity, and religious identity, culture is routinely acknowledged in global conversations as a core problem in the production of gender-based violence. But there is, as Merry describes, "a whiff of the notion of the primitive" and an assumption that "culture more often describes the developing world than the developed one."[13] Within the dominant mind-set of white settler states such as the United States and Canada, only certain populations are regarded as mired in a cultural trap of replicating religious and racial/ethnic traditions and customs from the past that reinforce violence against women. Those groups are usually assumed to be racialized (read nonwhite), primitive others, most often located in communities in the Global South, descendants of African slaves, or recent immigrants from those societies to the United States and other Global North states.

Religious and racial/ethnic customs rooted in our past yet still alive in current cultural patterns, and still bolstering violence against women and girls, should be approached in a new way. In actuality, we should acknowledge those persistent harms as endemic to the views of the dominant actors from dominant groups who have so fundamentally shaped the mainstream history and culture of the United States. Indeed, a major impetus grounding the international focus given here is the influential presence of sexual violence, racism, and religion in American history. This endemic triumvirate so formative in U.S. cultural identity inevitably shaped the questions I brought to Africa and South America. Clues about the nature of the moral beginnings of cultural support for intimate violence against women and girls are found in the intercultural encounters at the birthing of this continent as the Americas. Patterns of tolerance emerged from the culturally and legally sanctioned rape of enslaved African women and Indigenous Native women by Christian European men starting from the sixteenth century.[14] These culturally rooted patterns also formed in intraracial male sexual and physical violence against women and girls by European Christian settlers that was sometimes met with religious approval, and sometimes punished as shameful behavior.[15] Any prohibitions on gender violence among European Christians (intraracial violence) coexisted with the seeming cultural normalcy of their acts of interracial sexual assault.

This rape history offers a sobering account of the Christian legacy passed down from Euro-American forefathers. It is a more precise moral recollection than the examples U.S. teenagers might be assigned to study in school, such as Massachusetts Bay Colony governor John Winthrop's 1630 "City on a Hill" Puritan vision, which saw the colony's mission in the Americas as creating a "truly Godly society."[16] However, the cultural acceptance of sexual assaults of enslaved Africans and Indigenous women by colonists in early America should be understood as impacting modern American moral sensibilities as profoundly as Winthrop's Christian mission theology or European philosophers' ideas normally seen as foundational. For primary moral sources of American political identity, this rape history ought to be recognized as rivaling influences such as English philosopher John Locke's 1689 treatises on individual rights, equality, limited government, and religious tolerance.

The same moral corrective should be applied to other history lessons on, for instance, the iconic status of colonial leader and third U.S. president Thomas Jefferson. To appreciate Jefferson's importance in shaping U.S. ideals, teachers ordinarily direct students' attention to his elegant articulation of the moral impetus behind the founding of the nation. Alongside of his 1776 Declaration of Independence assertion, "We hold these truths to be self-evident, that all men are created equal, that they are endowed by their Creator with certain unalienable rights; that among these are life, liberty, and the pursuit of happiness," is the fact of his rape of his young teenage black slave, Sally Hemings.[17] Both of these historical truths represent equally authentic illustrations of the moral values Jefferson helped standardize. If acknowledged at all, the fact that Jefferson, at about age forty, was a child rapist of his black slave has come to be regarded as an ordinary occurrence that reflects normalized sexual relations for so many white male slaveholders within his historical context. More often, this fact simply disappears within the customary valorization of Jefferson as the quintessential anti-colonial national hero who crafted culturally foundational language about how human freedom and equality were endowed by our Creator. Note that with the invocation of the Creator as part of these iconic words Jefferson penned in the Declaration of Independence, a religious, or more accurately, a divine imprimatur is also attached to the rape tolerance tradition currently embedded in U.S. society.

No matter what their racial or ethnic origins might be, all U.S.-Americans inherit this collective legacy of hypocrisy. This heritage contributes multiple, enduring strands to the fabric of our current moral formation. It contains throughout a vital religious certainty of God's abiding providence on the side of both violence-perpetrating slaveholders and alleged pacifiers of supposedly wild Indians. For historical perpetrators and contemporary students of history alike, religion (specifically Christianity) has most often helped to cloak a history of heterosexual sexual violence in a supposed righteous purpose.

While it is necessary to point out how the routine intimate violence against African and Native women was seamlessly woven into the history of early American religious and moral habits, contemplating those actual encounters can be an emotionally fraught activity. But we must engage the embodied and emotional dimensions of these historical violent encounters if we are to interrupt the cultural process in which abstract moral principles from colonial American history are enshrined as a normative legacy.[18] Embodied sensory and emotional responses reflect core experiential elements of racial encounters, religious practices, and, of course, sexual assaults and exploitation. Embodied sensory and emotional experiences such as smells (of cleanness, purity, soiledness) and fears (of the racial other, of God, of the perpetrator or threat of his assault) play a pivotal role in one's social and spiritual perceptions and can help to morally discipline one's responses to the other in the encounter. Stubborn refusal to ignore the role of the affective, therefore, assists in constructing resistance to the moral numbness that permeates collective denial of the significance of intimate violence in U.S. cultural and economic history.

Pale-skinned men's bended knees forcefully split apart the naked, brown legs of women: taking, using, hurting those women's bodies. In the case of African slaves, pale-skinned men claimed that they owned those legs and the rest of the women's bodies and minds as well as the babies that came out of their bodies regardless of the conditions surrounding conception.[19] There may be some hesitation about summoning such realities because it is difficult to rule out the possibility that, for some readers, our recollection of these details of past humiliations could provide a degree of pornographic titillation. It seems too dishonest, however, to consider this history and omit any reference to the embodied wretchedness of many Native and African women's experiences of those violent encounters. Nor should the religiosity surrounding these assaults be relegated to the background. For example, after many of the enslaved Africans were converted to Christianity, even their souls (human spirits) were understood as belonging to someone else, a god-man, Jesus Christ. Their human owners characterized this notion of how they now belonged to God as conversion to Christ. Christian conversion increased the market value of the dark brown bodies for the business of human trafficking.[20]

Christianity mattered in other ways too. Pale-skinned male perpetrators and supporters of the violence justified their brutality through their authorizing savior Jesus Christ, whom they believed called forth a superior Anglo-Saxon (or Anglo-Norman) race to fulfill their manifest destiny in the Americas.[21] Presumably, in their regular Christian practice of prayer and the receiving of communion during worship services, some knelt on the same bended knees privately used for assaults as they publicly, ritually affirmed their property rights as God's blessing. For a few, religious authorization of their supposed sacred mission to subdue inferior races might have forestalled any guilt as perpetrators and/or collaborators in the rapes and other forms of violence against African and Indigenous Indian peoples. But I am not certain.[22]

The success story of the overarching global capitalist project of the U.S. economy rests on a past deeply informed by intertwined, mutually supporting elements of Christian religiosity, white European superiority, and heterosexual sexual violence. Simply put, the narrative of U.S. success is situated in a part of the globe where colonial control by Catholic and Protestant Europeans proliferated for centuries in the mainland and island economies of the Americas. The middle region of the northern mainland of the continent, initially controlled by a few thousand (mostly) impoverished British Christian settler-colonialists, was transformed into an independent, wealthy nation peopled by hundreds of millions of European, African, Indigenous/Native, Latin American, or Asian descent, and their variously mixed progeny, ruled by democratically elected government leaders. This transformation was due, in part, to centuries of a Christianity-justified slave economy and theft of Native lands. Therefore, built into the U.S. historical narrative that charts socioeconomic and democratic success are millions of African women, many used as breeders and then separated from their progeny. Sometimes, they were raped. But almost all of them were used to strengthen the U.S. political economy through their bodily reproduction of enslaved workers.[23]

In this collective historical narrative, we find both a specific cultural logic of acceptable heterosexual sexual violence and commodification as well as individual stories about cultural icons such as Jefferson. This perspective provides an anchor for the cultural lens I brought with me on my quest for insights about contemporary responses to violence against women and girls. In essence, religion, mainly dominant expressions of Christianity, and anti-black racism played a crucial role in the global history that helped develop U.S.-American cultural tolerance for rape on this continent. It is imperative, therefore, to consider how religion and anti-black racism might also play a role in repudiating that acquiescence. Exploring the possibility of global resources that spark recognition of the global connections that have contributed to the history of religiously sanctioned anti-black racism might further creative and meaningful antiviolence responses in the United States.

Although I focus on anti-black racism in this book, rape tolerance also figures prominently in the history of racism against Native American peoples.[24] Rape and racism also continue in the present to combine as significant factors for Native American women, especially those who remain within the territory of Indigenous tribal nations. Native American women experience some of the highest rates of sexual violence (when compared with non-Native women in the United States), and non-Native men overwhelmingly perpetrate these assaults.[25] The struggle for visibility and justice persists for Native women who have been sexually assaulted. For example, in the 2012 political debate over VAWA's reauthorization that was the occasion for Biden's speech, there was a major effort in the U.S. Congress to block prosecution under VAWA of non-Native men who rape Native women on tribal lands.[26] My focus on anti-black racism, therefore, only partially captures the contours of the racist legacy in the politics of U.S.-American rape culture tolerance.

In its consideration of discrete cultural dynamics related to race and religion, the political approach in this book could be metaphorically encapsulated as a desire to render intimate violence homeless. Ever since this violence took up cultural residence in the Americas centuries ago, its poisonous tentacles have been lengthened by a host of social inequalities and related forms of economic exploitation. What conceptual tools are needed for this eviction process? Caribbean feminist transnational theorist M. Jacqui Alexander's notion of decolonization helps us to conjure them. Alexander describes colonialism and slavery as "twin companions" with legacies in the psyches and material realities that have produced the current racial, economic, and gendered hierarchies with which we now contend in the Americas.[27] The work of decolonization, she insists, is the project of all on the American continent no matter what country of origin they might claim.[28] Social hierarchies and belief systems that insist on innate superior human traits of some and innate inferior human traits of others serve to rationalize intimate violence against those deemed inferior. This culturally supported rationalization prevails across varied forms of the violence. It might exist in the interpersonal violence of husband against wife; intimate assaults by state representatives, such as the police or prison guards, against those over whom the state gives them authority to monitor; or the murder of a transgender woman on the street by a heterosexual stranger.

Decolonization offers a congruent analytical starting point that builds on the linkage of past to present geopolitical patterns and brutal or exploitative one-on-one assaults to wide-ranging cultural collaboration in the violence. This paradigm of geopolitical linkages and social collaboration undergirds this study of transnational antiviolence concepts and activism. It is a fundamental point of departure that centers on the need for thinking, feeling, and acting to refute the violence of the willful, nonconsensual taking of another. Historically, the nation-state racist politics of colonization together with its twin companion chattel slavery can be described as coercively taking up residence in someone else's home or taking them from that home. The significance of the gender-based violence component (sexual violations and exploitation) of these coercive acts cannot be adequately studied without confronting the colonial aims in the history of the Americas that congealed around asserting power and control over home cultures, land, and bodily freedoms and defining the elements needed in decolonizing countermeasures.

To intrinsically lend support to a specific, gendered notion of decolonization requires close attention to systemically connected moral values. They thrive within the web of interrelated cultural support for gender-based violence found in criminal justice, health care, religious, and government legislative and regulatory institutions that shred the respect, trustworthiness, hope, and safety that these institutions ought to reliably provide their constituencies in the civil society they call home. Drawing upon multiple national Africana homes of activist work assists in the conceptualization of decolonizing resistance to such home-bound cultural processes of moral decay.

Constructive forms of spirituality that are not necessarily religious, though they can be, also need to be methodologically incorporated. They ought to be recognized as providing a means by which to devise a response to the saturation of moral sensibilities that violence-condoning values in this colonial/chattel slavery cultural history deliver. As Alexander explains, "since colonization has produced fragmentation and dismemberment at both the material and psychic levels, the work of decolonization has to make room for the deep yearning for wholeness."[29] In the case of gender-based violence, decolonization aims to restore wholeness to the individual human spirits of victim-survivors preyed upon by embodied violence and its attendant forms of social humiliation and betrayal. But decolonization must also be conceived as a restoration project that appreciates the need to instigate a steadfast, society-wide sense of yearning for wholeness. Restoring societal wholeness is critical in the face of the fragmenting and dismembering moral harm that our history of cultural denials, protection, and sustenance of intimate violence has created. The spiritual import of this kind of collective yearning retains an intangible quality, making it difficult to find suitable language and strategies to depict its power.

Decolonizing Method: Narrative Writing and Activist Research

Decolonizing goals ought to be reflected in corresponding decolonizing methods—their design, tools of analysis, and execution. The pursuit of activist ideas that promote expansive, daring moral imaginations demands similar means for discovering them. Because of the staggering consequences for the lived realities of women and girls, a discussion of the goals and methods of activist responses to the violence should be explicit and concrete. In its focus on analyzing how my encounters with activist leaders in Ghana, Brazil, and South Africa might usefully engage the challenge of ending gender-based violence in the United States, this book presents an embodied methodological commitment to decolonizing goals. As stated above, the transnational nature of this focus involves resistance to the racialized and heteropatriarchal Christian values that American colonialism and chattel slavery helped to shape. But it also necessitates resistance to those values reproduced in newer, current forms of global neocolonialism and human trafficking, which continue to contribute to and uphold gender-based violence. A decolonizing method consistent with these goals ought to incorporate some form of transnational praxis. Feminist transnational gender theorists Richa Nagar and Amanda Lock Swarr argue in their "working definition" of *transnational feminism* that it must "interweave critiques, actions, and self-reflexivity so as to resist a priori predictions of what might constitute feminist politics in a given time and place."[30] In accord with this definition, I have sought to craft a critically self-reflexive, transnational, black feminist praxis within each step of my research and writing. Instead of a standard participant-observer research method, this interwoven theory-praxis approach has meant relying on a hybrid collection of research methods and included some uncomfortable risks about the outcome.

I include storytelling as a method of writing about my research. In social science literature, the paradigms it builds upon have been variously called feminist autoethnography, storytelling sociology, portraiture, and black feminist performative activist ethnography. In religious studies, the blended subfields that inform the method found here range from storytelling ethnography and world religions to studies of religious and societal practices that represent conversations between ethnography and Christian theology and ethics.

At its most basic level, the narrative approach reflects my activist stance regarding gender-based violence and the need for antiracist resistance to it. My approach is steeped in an epistemological tradition that is, as feminist anthropologists Christa Craven and Dána-Ain Davis have framed it, concerned with feminist activist ethnographers "connecting their research to broader social justice efforts."[31] In probing supports for violence against women and girls that are embedded in notions of race/ethnicity, gender, class, sexuality, religion, and nation, my investigation exhibits characteristics of the activist feminist research Craven and Davis identify. These cultural markers do not merely intersect but rather blur together. Within each culturally distinctive geopolitical context, they offer imbricated moral messages that work together efficiently to buttress the violence, leaving behind the expected fixed and boundaried characteristics of such identity categories. The view that an exclusively discursive window allows for examining these cultural processes will not suffice. A storytelling approach generates more possibilities for the depth and intensity of my learning about these cultural processes to emerge and allow others access to them. When sociologists Ronald J. Berger and Richard Quinney describe the narrative turn in social inquiry, they explain that "in storytelling sociology, the writing is part of the research process. [It] encourages writing that experiments with different forms of representation and seeks engagement with the world beyond the academe."[32] The style of writing and the choice of research subject matter cohere in this approach akin to the ways that goals and method must. The storytelling approach interwoven throughout this text experiments with representing the politically complicated process of engaging activists in the world beyond the academy that I call home and considering what it means to value their ideas.

As I craft analyses of my encounters with the leaders I interviewed, I must critically acknowledge that I am part of the story. All scholars and researchers, whether they admit it or not, make subjective choices that interpret the subjects we study. In critical feminist research methodology, there is general agreement that this choice comes with particular responsibilities. Psychology theorist Michelle Fine and education theorist Lois Weis helpfully define them in discussing their own feminist qualitative research assumptions. "We, as critical ethnographers, have a responsibility to talk about our own identities, why we interrogate as we do," they assert, "what we choose not to report, on whom we train our scholarly gaze, who is protected and *not* protected as we do our work."[33] For instance, I repeatedly explore questions about my status as a Christian U.S. citizen throughout the book with a focus on the connections between my individual sense of religiosocial identity and varied institutionalized expressions of U.S. Christian, political, and economic global paternalisms and neocolonialisms. This approach requires grappling with how some combination of those linkages may undermine the decolonizing gaze I intend to bring to my African and South American encounters with Christians and non-Christians.

However, my Christian faith background may also have constructively influenced my exploration of Africana intercultural dynamics as a potential resource for communal ethical insights about responding to the violence. Particular stories of one ancient Palestinian Jewish leader, Jesus of Nazareth, and of the other Jewish leaders who were his followers infuse the core of Christian theology and practices of the Gentiles who constitute the contemporary global Christian church. Most of us believe that common moral lessons are discernable from the details of biblical stories about how specific ancient Jewish leaders negotiated stratifications within their own group as well as permeable boundaries with other groups in their ancient Mediterranean community settings. The negotiation of intercultural moral understandings could be considered an inherent component of all gospel-rooted expressions of contemporary Christianity.[34]

As a major cultural influence found in the places I travel, Christian religion arises as both a part of the problem of cultural support for male-perpetrated intimate violence against women and girls and (sometimes) a helpful resource for countering it. An accurate depiction of my encounters with Christian and non-Christian activist leaders must acknowledge my own biased desire for a Christianity with a greater capacity for countering the violence than for supporting it. The evidence in both directions contributes to the evolving understanding of spirituality in this text. Similarly, I try to maintain a keen awareness of the racial filters I bring and how they impact my understanding of both the racial/ethnic classifications and social discrimination described by the antiviolence advocates I met in Africa and South America. I strive to shed or at least confront my parochialisms, similar to admissions by Henry Louis Gates in his travelogue investigation of blackness in Latin America (though his project is unconcerned with violence against women).[35] In his discussion of Brazil, Gates explains that previously whenever he "heard the word *race*, only images of black people in the United States came to mind . . . *race* was a code word for black people, and for their relations with white people in this country."[36] Responsible confrontation of such racial/ethnic and religious predispositions demands ongoing critical disclosures about the process of analysis.

An unpredictable and creative dimension lies in the exercise of this responsibility. Some scholars of religion comment on the necessity for unconventional forms of writing and inductive methods of research because they are particularly appropriate for inquiries that highlight religion and culture. In his essay "Between Biography and Ethnography," world religions and anthropology scholar Michael Jackson calls for novel forms of academic writing and interdisciplinary thought.[37] It must be produced, he argues, by those who find "orthodox ways of describing and analyzing the world do not do justice to the experiences involved," especially in relation to religious, cultural, or social identity.[38] These cultural facets of knowledge are generative precisely in their instability and intersubjectivity and invite description and analysis that can convey these exact characteristics.[39] To communicate these dynamics I focus on the kind of listening, cultural translation, and solidarity that can make possible meaningful transnational connections among non-U.S. activists' responses to intimate violence and ours in the United States. Something happens in that process which in turn transforms the process itself. The intercultural dynamics of encountering and trying to learn from these remarkable individuals shook me up—irrevocably, in mind, body, and spirit—and it is that profound sense of transformation that I claim as an essential aspect of the intercultural listening, translation, and solidarity building needed to invent Africana approaches to defy gendered violence in the United States and elsewhere.

The challenge of waiting for discoveries to emerge involved an anxiety-producing, unpredictable quality that however uncomfortable was essential for the inductive purpose of my encounters with interviewees. The inductive method, a common approach in ethnographic research, relies on what can be learned from a specific situation or experience that is part of a larger web of cultural signifiers. Christian theology and ethics scholars Christian Scharen and Aana Marie Vigen describe a method of inquiry where ethnography and Christian studies in theology and ethics intersect. "The researcher assumes the posture of a learner," they explain, "who wants to be taught rather than that of an expert who possesses the crucial theory for analyzing what is going on or what is real."[40] This learner posture can help undercut the presence of imperialist and racist assumptions regarding cultural permissibility of gender-based violence in Africana settings abroad. Alongside being a willing learner, I would add, is the need for some indication of "what is going on" in the posture one brings to the encounter. It must include firm antiracism and antiviolence commitments in relation to issues of violence in one's own context.

The learning posture is also pertinent to the process of appreciating religious and spiritual details in activist responses to gender-based violence. The unique claims activist adherents make about their religion's ultimate truths can be revealed—or one might say learned—only through attention to particular "embodied habits, relations, practices, narratives, and struggles," as Scharen and Vigen state.[41] Some elements of mystery that believers claim as part of those truths will always remain elusive. Yet these qualities of religion and spirituality related to truth claims and the embrace of mystery have methodological significance. They underscore the generative qualities of understanding oneself as a researcher who does not already possess truths she has previously decided ought to be applied to the situation, including those embedded in her own religious beliefs and beliefs about other religions. An open-ended, indeterminate investigatory posture can also advantageously blend with the questioning of one's cultural prejudices that a decolonizing mode of inquiry demands. Allowing oneself to be vulnerable is intrinsic to maintaining this posture.

The narratives framing the analysis reveal my vulnerabilities that include uncertainties, hopes, blunders, awakenings, and commitments. I reference my U.S. cultural biases and personal impressions of the individuals and places I visited and admit my unresolved questions each step of the way. A degree of uncertainty functions like a kind of methodological talisman warding off the hazards of arrogant claims about having definitively captured the knowledge of the Africana activists and scholars. This quest generated an unrelenting sense of vulnerability with regard to these kinds of pull-back-the-curtain, candid disclosures about the details of researching. Because I was raised in a rather staid New England subculture of the United States, I have always been somewhat reserved when it comes to publicly sharing information about myself. This reticence persists even under the current pressure of the ascendency of unceasing self-disclosures through social media. So, part of the difficulty I faced in experimenting with this approach was the extent to which it was so personally ill-fitting. I delight in the warm cocoon of privacy as a coffee lover savors a hot, freshly brewed cup of her favorite blend. Most of my academic training, moreover, regards emotional distance as a standard barometer of credible scholarship. Therefore, normally, I would reflexively edit out of my text any trace of personal sentiment.

As feminist anthropologist Ruth Behar has described in *The Vulnerable Observer*, there are many analytical pitfalls to avoid when incorporating self-disclosure.[42] In this pioneering feminist autoethnographic text, Behar integrates her personal stories with those of Cuban villagers she interviewed about death and loss in their lives. Behar reflects on these same themes in her own family life together with an account of the evolution of her Cuban American identity. She offers guiding insights on exposing the self, explaining, "Vulnerability doesn't mean that anything personal goes. . . . It has to be essential to the argument, not a decorative flourish, not exposure for its own sake."[43] Avoiding self-exposure for its own sake is a principle I readily affirm. But again, concession to my own uncertainty may be in order when judging whether or not I succeeded in omitting all decorative flourish and incorporating only self-descriptions essential to deeper understandings of antiviolence strategies.

Because I utilized translators when I met with activist leaders in Brazil, language translation became a necessary part of my method in that setting. This represented another methodological risk related to the authenticity of transnational and intercultural communication about antiviolence strategies. Language translation makes one vulnerable to inaccuracy and miscommunication of cultural nuance. I relied upon the combined assistance of two black feminist activist-scholars as translators, one U.S.-based and the other a local resident of Salvador. The U.S.-based translator served in a primary role, especially for my English to Brazilian Portuguese questions, and the Brazil-based translator frequently assisted her in translating some of the interviewees' Brazilian-Portuguese phrases into English. We all shared an intense interest in understanding issues of gender, sexuality, race, and religion, but there was a considerable gap in our ages and formal relationship with the academy. I was much older and a university faculty member; they were young adult scholar-activists with recent advanced academic degrees.

Feminist theorists of research methodology rightly criticize traditional qualitative approaches that treat the translator as a technical, controlled, and concealed part of the process. Indeed, language translation issues in intercultural research helpfully reflect broader challenges and opportunities.[44] I repeatedly acknowledge the presence of my translators in the Brazil sections of the book. The methodological inclusion of a narrative approach allows for depictions of the role of these translators in my interactions with interviewees and others in the local Salvador setting. Rather than a problem to be hidden from view, tricky issues of translation—language and cultural—provided a rich reserve of ideas for drawing out the details of valuing interculturality. The narrative stresses imperfections in our communication and lingering questions as sites of learning. Also, note that in all three settings the burdensome difficulty persisted of navigating status, privilege, and deference attached to me, as well as scorn, hostility, and annoyance in some reactions to me, as an English-speaking U.S.-American. However, the harms of the violence and the potential power in intercultural and transnational activist solidarity in antiviolence spurred my unhesitating rejection of any kind of guilt-ridden, hand-wringing paralysis as an adequate response to this burden.

Also illuminating my narrative approach were several sets of dialogical norms: aesthetic and empirical, intuitive and counterintuitive, interpersonal experience and theoretical writings. A narrative approach has to incorporate an appreciation of the aesthetic. Far from being a segregating, distinctive emphasis, this appreciation involves bridge building, creating connections with other more concretized facets of research that are sometimes positioned as modes of inquiry at odds with the aesthetic. Few have captured this dynamic as acutely as black feminist sociologist and education theorist Sara Lawrence-Lightfoot. Her method, which she calls "portraiture," deliberately seeks "to bridge aesthetics and empiricism and appeal to intellect and emotion . . . to inform and inspire and join the endeavors of documentation, interpretation, and intervention."[45] In addition to my insistence on incorporating these combined categories, I also seek to bridge the aesthetic and the ethical in my discussion of transnational intercultural encounters, particularly in the emphasis on religious and spiritual resources. At their best, religious and spiritual beliefs and practices nurture the conjoined aesthetic and ethical dimensions of human sensibilities and capacities. Methodologically, when exploring strategic responses to gender-based violence, the aesthetic and ethical work together in a way that furthers the analysis. The aesthetic (for example, recognition of subjective experiences of spiritual harm and healing related to intimate violence) joins with the ethical (for example, reflecting on how to galvanize the collective moral will of communities in a sustained commitment to end such violence). The aesthetic and the ethical can cooperatively participate in an embrace of what may be identified as counterintuitive in order to produce antiviolence conceptualizations that "join the endeavors of documentation, interpretation, and intervention."

The counterintuitive provides an indispensable analytical vehicle because of its disarming capabilities. Lawrence-Lightfoot stresses the benefits of the counterintuitive particularly when the "identity and voice" of the researcher are so centrally positioned. "One might even say that *because* the self of the portraitist is so essential to the development of the work, the portraitist must be that much more vigilant about identifying other sources of challenge to her or his perspective. The counterintuitive must always be present even as the portraitist takes full advantage of the intuitive."[46] In antiviolence analysis that is the focus here, even the desire to take full advantage of the intuitive will require a simultaneous deep suspicion of it. The realm of intuitive knowledge possesses some of the most dangerous and powerful factors operative in racial ideologies and religious beliefs and practices that lend support to the violence against women and girls. To actively oppose moral cues that nurture the violence through those intuitive cultural sensibilities, therefore, necessitates reliance on the counterintuitive. Identification of counterintuitive resources can contest intuitive judgments that devalue the personhood of black women and girls and contribute myopic barriers to ending the violence against them.

In slight contrast to Lawrence-Lightfoot, rather than create a portrait of another person or institution, I incorporate intuitive and counterintuitive lenses to describe my initial encounters with activists. If regarded as any type of portrait, it is a portrait of intercultural dynamics in motion. Those dynamics become the data for this project. Said differently, the overarching aim here lies within the content of my engagement with the leaders and their community settings rather than in an ethnographic portrait of them. Emphasizing the dynamics of my encounters does not reflect an ethnographer's typical concern with comprehensively representing the lives and voices of her interviewees. Rather, the dynamics of the interpersonal encounters I describe hold in themselves powerful lessons about politics and culture in decolonizing antiviolence work.

The violence itself can be understood as a crucial guidepost for this methodological focus on the intuitive and counterintuitive lessons that such interpersonal encounters can yield. Acknowledgment of the violence of intimate, interpersonal violence so necessary for conceptualizing an adequate response to it represents not only a significant emotive impetus for generating concern, but also an analytical resource for strategies. The physical, emotional, cultural, political, and spiritual characteristics of the violence summon heightened attention to the prospect of a method that entails learning from different and often uncomfortable interpersonal encounters with leaders.

After your lover hits you in the face, for instance, the stinging pain of encounter lodges in your flesh and your spirit. Soul-wrenching, indelible memories may remain of the pounding sensations of a rapist's invasion of your body's openings. Waves of shock, betrayal, shame, and powerlessness may wash over you during a sexual assault and in subsequent reoccurring flashbacks. A wide range of unheeded lessons about needed social change are taught by the interpersonal details of this intimate violence by your interactions with loved ones, acquaintances, colleagues, professionals sought out for help, or by-stander strangers. Moreover, lessons about the needed responses also reside in the destructive (intuitive) racialized social messages about worth and dignity that may be thoroughly enmeshed in the emotional and spiritual consequences of such gendered assaults.[47] The psychosocial and spiritual experiences for women of intimate sexual and physical attacks perpetrated in the majority of cases by men can provide a sickening but unflinchingly honest depiction of the moral ethos generally seen as normal in U.S. society.[48] Discussions of how to alter that moral ethos must not avoid the political lessons those realities of vulnerability hold. In addition, the challenge of counterintuitive learning requires defiance and engagement of conventional Western Christian paternalisms and racist disdain for regarding global leaders of African descent as a starting place for advanced antiviolence ideas that are also needed in the United States.

The exploration of public responses to gender-based violence takes into account multivalent destructive means the violence utilizes and functions as a methodological catalyst. My encounters with leaders hold potential for teaching truths about how to *jointly* recognize and shift deeply rooted gendered mores that sustain the violence. What might encounters with activist leaders reveal, for instance, about how to appreciate the spiritual power required to sustain shared resistance to the violence? Distinctive forms of truth can be found in those encounters that are unlike the ones in scholarship that claim detachment from the fluid, dialogical realm of subjective experience that, in actuality, human thought always inhabits. The results illustrate both limitations and inspiration.

Emotional and embodied elements of learning must also be incorporated in the description and analysis. Black feminist ethnographer and performance theorist D. Soyini Madison pays detailed attention to this method in her study of women's activism in Ghana.[49] Her study included a Ghanaian activist leader, Patience (with whom I also met), whose work focused on religiously instigated abuse of girls and women. As Madison aptly encapsulated with regard to this sensory aspect, "the researcher embraces the emotions and sensuality of *what* is being described and *how* it is being described through highlighting, sometimes redescribing, the remembered textures, smells, sounds, tastes, and sights rendered through story and performance."[50] Here, such an embrace takes place not only in relation to the activists I encountered but also strangers in each local setting, whether among the members of the crowd gathered at the beachfront in Salvador or in the streets of Accra.

I interweave theoretical insights mainly from feminist, Africana feminist, womanist, and queer studies with discussions of my encounters with activists. These sources help to illuminate political and historical issues of race, ethnicity, religion, and sexuality relevant to gender-based violence in each setting. Rigid boundaries between theory and practice are deliberately breached as these scholarly sources are incorporated. Madison again helpfully articulates a rationale for this integrative aspect. In the interplay of theory and narrative accounts of interviews, the role of theory for a researcher is a way "to defend the complexity and dignity of the multiple truths and paradoxes below the surface but holding the surface in place."[51] The paradoxes and multiple truths about each setting inevitably constitute more than I can convey within the constraints of this project. Theoretical discussions and scholarly studies, such as Madison's combined performance theory and ethnographic examination of Ghanaian women's activism or Erica Lorraine Williams's black feminist ethnographic analysis of sex tourism in Salvador, Brazil, represent crucial anchors. They assist in mapping the expansive breadth of the moral terrain that questions about addressing and ending specific forms of gender-based violence inhabit.

The presentation of the narratives about my meetings with activist leaders in Ghana, Brazil, and South Africa reflects the limitations of this format, such as selectiveness about which stories to tell (every single encounter contains many), and as always, the stories are unfinished. Nevertheless, the act of forming the narratives functions as an example of an empowering activity that allows for participation in locating and defining hope and defiance.[52]

Parameters and Organization

There are also certain choices made here about what to include concerning activism, race/ethnicity, gender, and religion in such varied global settings. To collectively excavate each of these cultural portals for insights, the following discussions of them will hold in common an unwavering emphasis on antiviolence. Readers seeking evidentiary descriptions of brutal rapes and intimate partner beatings of black Africans, black South Americans, and black U.S.-Americans and how they coped in the aftermath will be disappointed. Rather than the testimony of women victim-survivors and family members of those who have been murdered explaining the experience of victimization, activist leaders abroad who focus on responses were deliberately chosen as interviewees. These leaders work in NGOs (nongovernmental organizations), government agencies, religious organizations, grassroots groups, scholar-activist networks (including academic institutions)—some inhabit combinations of these locations.

I highlight particular aspects of these leaders' antiviolence activism, especially its relationship to religion and local racial and ethnic categories, over others. These selective descriptions represent needed limits placed on an inquiry with international scope. What seems like a vast geographic and cultural territory to investigate actually becomes a more limited concern featuring certain antiviolence examples. In the cities I visited, I found versions of a cultural history of rape, for instance, involving religion and race/ethnicity that have intriguing resonances with the United States. My discussion of this connection varies according to each context where I conducted interviews—in the cities of Accra, Ghana; Pietermaritzburg, Johannesburg, and Cape Town, South Africa; and Salvador, Brazil, where there is a high concentration of African descendants. I discovered some of the ways in which combinations of Christian religion and anti-black racism were significant pacifying factors supporting European colonial dominance in all of their regional histories. In Ghana and Brazil, in particular, colonial and transatlantic slave trade histories directly connect with the socioeconomic development of the Americas. Sexual coercion and assaults of black slave women are incorporated in that shared history. Although the details of these historical, sociopolitical patterns that involve anti-black racism and European Christianity help shape present cultural attitudes, my discussions focus on the recent past and delve into activist resistance to gender-based violence in contemporary societies, specifically in the early twenty-first century.

Undoubtedly, more reflective attention could have been given to the distinctive character of Christian colonial influences in each setting—Catholicism in Brazil, varying Protestant missionary movements in Ghana, and Anglican and Dutch Reformed churches in South Africa. Moreover, the brief references to black U.S.-American Christianity fail to sort out the traditions of African American churchgoers who may be part of Presbyterian, Pentecostal, African Methodist Episcopal, Metropolitan Community Church, and other faith groups. The nuances of how each group cultivates and resists gender-based violence deserve further investigation. I found sufficient challenge in a religious and spiritual focus on mapping the terrain of how those concerns emerged from my encounters with activist leaders, but I readily concede that even more in-depth religious considerations are still needed.

Throughout this book, the central concern remains on placing examples of my U.S. cultural vantage point in dialogue with elements of each setting in which I met activists and the ideas that were most relevant to those encounters. A general comparison of the overall nature and extent of the gender-based violence and activist resistance in each country falls outside the scope of this project. The challenges of, collective organizational responses to, and individual activist vocational journeys in relation to gender-based violence have, of course, continued to evolve beyond my snapshot encounters with the leaders. Even in terms of specific forms of the violence, I am neither tracking responses to the exact same problem across all three countries nor comparatively investigating their responses to the same problems that exist in the United States. The political situations within each of the three international settings provide a cornucopia of gender-justice activism intent on systemic change. Of course, I am able to recognize the seriousness of the issues related to the gender-based violence they seek to address, in part because of similar ones in the United States. These commonalities appear to verify the global nature of the problem of male-perpetrated intimate assaults on women and girls, but rejecting easy generalizations about such commonalities is both an essential goal and a core method in my interrogation of it. I aim for a sharply critical awareness of how certain U.S.-American cultural assumptions about its basic (universal) dynamics can foster imprecise assertions about the ubiquity of male-perpetrated gender violence. This view can too easily collapse into partial acceptance of its inevitability, everywhere. I also eschew the goal of merely tracking the traits gender-based violence retains across global contexts that resonate with what I already know about how it manifests in the United States. To search for sameness in the nature of violence across global contexts undermines the capacity to learn something unfamiliar or unexpected about how to address it.

Myriad U.S. activist efforts to end gender-based violence could be placed in dialogue with similar efforts found abroad. However, the arguments in this book bypass the worthy task of exploring existing U.S. activist-generated responses that include a range of social services, shelters, hotlines, legislative advocacy, women's self-defense resistance, media campaigns, and other initiatives by both religious and nonreligious nonprofit groups. Instead, the discussion centers on addressing the unwieldy cultural and systemic maintenance of gender-based violence, especially related to religion and racism, against some of the most stigmatized and marginalized women and girls. Its antiracist assumptions are deeply informed by similarly oriented U.S.-based gender approaches. For example, black feminist public policy theorist Beth Richie studies a combination of systemic factors in the violence against acutely socially marginalized U.S. black women. She finds them in "as much danger as ever, precisely because of the ideological and strategic direction the antiviolence movement has taken," related to issues of criminalization.[53] Richie argues that persistent forms of racism in white feminist antiviolence activism together with some of the leaders in communities of color who continue "to refuse to pay sufficient attention to gender inequality" make an explicitly antiracist response to such instances of victimization imperative.[54] Even though creative U.S. efforts to surmount it exist, this too frequent double bind of political neglect particularly vulnerable women and girls face supports a transnational approach that might reveal vantage points useful for conceptualizing alternatives.

The meanings of gender vary within the activist responses to gender-based violence that I encounter because they reflect the localized cultural understandings pertinent to the forms of violence under discussion. The meanings of gender have evolved in relation to ongoing sociopolitical developments in the regional contexts of the activist leaders and the history of global relationships impacting those regions. An adequate conceptualization of decolonizing antiviolence resistance and restoration challenges long-standing patterns of gender hierarchies and gender definitions that help fuel gender-based violence in each setting. In this text, the meanings of gender that receive attention have been shaped primarily by antiviolence understandings about the perpetuation of gender-based violence that the activists convey together with relevant insights from gender-justice theorists. As I learned more about the activist work of some of the leaders I met, I explored the necessity for and parameters of more expansive gender definitions. I was challenged, for example, to reexamine what kinds of critiques of sexist Christianity are needed in response to more masculinized gendered self-expressions of gender-nonconforming community members. More clarity about how culturally assigned gender categories are defined and contested enables more accurate recognition of the cultural sanctions for gender-based violence and the capacity to envision the political transformations needed to end it.

As with gender, assumptions about the meaning of religion steer away from universalistic views unencumbered by particular experiences of it and definitions relying on an exclusive deference to so-called great world religions. My concern here in exploring the role of religion is in emphasizing power relations and practices over metaphysics, symbolism, doctrines, and philosophies. Unfortunately, there is a temptation among secular gender justice activists to neglect the impact of internal power relations and practices of religious groups. Secular antiviolence activists too often view those traits as merely hopeless generators of fanatical commitments to hierarchical, exploitative, and homophobic values that fuel gender-based violence in multiple forms. This destructive impact is then mistakenly cordoned off to the domain of a supposedly culturally confined space of religion. Yet, irrefutably, religion comprises core values utilized for everyday moral decision making by much of the world's populations. Even if one is not a religious adherent when victimized by misogynistic violence and/or advocating on behalf of others who have been victimized by it, the social presence of religion and the moral and political influence of its adherents still affect one's plight and/or advocacy agenda. As already noted, for Ghana, Brazil, South Africa, and the United States, the historical legacy of European Christian colonizers has had an enduring impact on populations across religious and nonreligious groups.

Other cultural factors also function like a form of religion in their capacity to generate loyalties and conformity that assist in regulating harmful gendered intimate behavior. They include expressions of civil religion or nationalism, capitalist beliefs in free markets and commercialization of every facet of life, as well as long-standing ethnic/tribal traditions. The violence-tolerant moral perspectives of these religiously cherished influences overlap and compete with the moral messages about intimate violence within globally dominant religious traditions such as Christianity and Islam.

My analysis is deeply influenced by liberationist Christian critiques of Christian theological traditions. This branch of contemporary Christian studies assumes that liberationist Christian conceptualizations of religion and society can dynamically contribute to activist understandings of antiracist, feminist, and peaceful cultural values. This assumption was moderated and complicated as I encountered some leaders whose antiviolence commitments emanate from the non-Christian religious perspectives of Islam, Candomblé, and Indigenous African religious traditions. The ability to perceive the nuances of those commitments involves reliance upon a capacious Africana studies approach to religion. It resonates with the perspective offered by Christian social ethicist

Emilie Townes when arguing for a "womanist dancing mind" scholarly framework. According to Townes, this mode of conceptualization presumes the need for a broad cultural map of "Africa, the Caribbean, Brazil, the United States (South, North, East, and West)" as well as a wide array of religious traditions including Christianity, Islam, and Candomblé.[55] The degree of relevance and concern with religious traditions varies according to the antiviolence strategies and proclivities of the leaders encountered.

Several practical and organizational choices offer further illustrations of the selectiveness incorporated here. I do not tell the stories of my encounters in the order in which they took place. I traveled to Ghana, Brazil, and South Africa in a series of short trips over a period of several years. The duration and sequencing of the trips were dictated by a variety of logistical and financial considerations. In an effort to offer the most coherent account of my visits to each country, I group them thematically rather than chronologically. I present meetings and interactions that occurred over the course of several days or several trips in a condensed format that does not necessarily reflect the order in which they occurred or the actual length of the conversations and interactions. I chose my interviewees using a modified snowball sampling approach that began with developing connections with scholars and activists in each setting. Although each meeting yielded valuable lessons, I include only a small sampling of my meetings in each country. The group meetings I cohosted (with local leaders) and one-on-one interactive interviews I conducted during seven brief trips (of two to three weeks each) were unevenly spread out over seven years.[56] In sum, participants in the group meetings and one-on-one interactive interviews numbered approximately one hundred eighty. The recorded one-on-one interviews totaled seventy-five, lasted about two hours, and usually took place in the offices of the leaders. In some instances, I conducted additional follow-up meetings, informal conversations, and meals with respondents.

The process of intercultural learning is highlighted in the following chapter sequence. The narrative deliberately unfolds gradually by presenting realizations that require patience with the tensions they generate. The tensions are neither subverted nor superficially resolved. The opening chapters in the first section launch an exploration of the meaning of intercultural learning about antiviolence strategies by focusing on the basic task of listening to the insights of the leaders with whom I met. After introducing some of the religious and political issues that characterize U.S. resignation to the occurrence of violence against women, the remainder of this section describes my encounters in Accra, Ghana, following the passage of that nation's first national domestic violence law (2007). I briefly introduce the setting, including references to rape in the history of that West African region's role in the transatlantic slave trade and relationship to U.S.-African American slave ancestry. The main concern in the first section is to explore contemporary activist responses to sexual abuse and domestic violence, especially the issue of marital rape in heterosexual marriage. To differing degrees, I incorporate discussions of Islam, Christianity, and Indigenous African religious tradition. The ideas that emerge exemplify some of the ways in which the activist leaders have grappled with local cultural mores in order to create systemic change. Reflections on the role of culture lead to considerations of potential racist stumbling blocks and dismissals when trying to convey to a U.S. audience the benefits of learning from black African strategies for confronting gender-based violence.

The second section incorporates interviews with Brazilian activists in Salvador, Bahia, and foregrounds the thorny issues of comprehending and translating the unfamiliar in interreligious and intercultural engagement. An overarching question in this section is this: how does one avoid distortions when translating foreign political innovations and spirituality into more familiar categories for the sake of making meaningful connections with and garnering lessons relevant to U.S. contexts? I note the distinctiveness of the Brazilian context, especially the ways in which Brazil's prominence as a port of entry for transatlantic slaves in the Americas influenced Salvador's contemporary racial makeup. I encounter the secretive world of Candomblé, an African-based religious tradition some of my interviewees practice. Brazil's highly developed institutionalized responses to gender-based violence contrast with the less coordinated federal government responses in the United States. Yet there are also similarities between the responses in the two countries such as a central reliance on police and the criminalization in poor communities. The racial dynamics involved in sex tourism and trafficking in Brazil are revealing for defining the harm that gender-based violence encompasses. Besides the racially nuanced activist responses sex tourism and trafficking require, this border-crossing form of sexual exploitation points to the transnational connections in the Americas that must be attended to when envisioning comprehensive U.S. antiviolence strategies. My encounters in Brazil highlight the ways in which intercultural learning and activist resistance to violence involve vulnerability as well as holistic engagement of mind, body, and spirit.

The third section focuses on how intercultural interactions with South African activist leaders and examples of social movement building strategies hold potential for transnational solidarity in opposing multiple forms of sexualized violence, including the targeting of lesbians for assaults and murder. In particular, it conceptualizes how leaders crafting responses to this violence use defiant Africana spirituality as a resource. As with the local settings in the other sections of the book, I introduce the South African context with an emphasis on the role of racism, including their unique classifications of coloureds and blacks. South Africa's recent history of freedom struggle against apartheid is most germane here because of their post-apartheid constitutional clauses addressing freedom and equality based on gender and sexual orientation. This section of the book explores questions about the timing of when and how solidarity-building practices are incorporated in social movement responses to sexual assault. The South African post-apartheid setting provides a fertile arena for intensively examining social movement ties between anti-black racism and gender violence. This synergy comes into vibrant focus within the political work of South African activist leaders who oppose both in a coordinated fashion. My encounters in this context instigate an exploration of the concrete meaning of defiant Africana spirituality in spontaneous street responses, grieving rituals, public witness, and other organizational practices. My envisioning of how certain leadership practices function as acts of defiant spirituality draws from examples of both South African and U.S. leaders and activist-scholars.

The final chapter corrals common themes in the insights and lessons acquired from the array of leaders and places included in the book. With religion, spirituality, and antiracism as the focal points for the kaleidoscope of ideas gleaned throughout, it dwells on the process of how defiant Africana spirituality births hope for border-crossing solidarity. The chapter outlines methodological characteristics of defiant Africana spirituality that enable hope for ending the violence. It also offers particular cautions for U.S.-American Christian participation.

My analytical discussions reference legal remedies and other responses to the violence in the cultural contexts of my interviewees together with related dynamics in the United States. I frame and juxtapose those examples and insights gleaned from gender justice theorists with stories about eating unfamiliar food, communicating through translators, chatting with taxi drivers, trying to grasp the unfamiliar, deep wells of spiritual resources of the leaders, and other daily cultural negotiations. This kind of theory-practice analytical approach is intended to be suggestive of how the building of nonviolent gender relations is characterized by untidy, interactive everyday endeavors. This approach decidedly opposes the correlative ordinariness in the sexual violence of the early history of transnational intercultural encounters in the founding of the U.S. nation in the Americas. It demonstrates how decolonizing goals might sprout from discrete, imperfect interactions and analysis that highlights religion and spirituality in activist efforts to address the violence. This method also relies upon a degree of unpredictability in the quest for insights that offer alternatives to the degrees of cultural permission given for wives to be beaten and raped by husbands, girls sold and sexually exploited by adults, lesbians targeted for rape and murder, and other gendered intimate assaults on body, mind, and spirit.

PART I

A Thirst for Truth-Telling

From the United States to Ghana

1

Constricted Religious Responses

I can recollect a winter evening at home when I was agitatedly muttering to myself while poring over news clippings. It was a typical moment early in my quest for more ideas about antiracist and religious responses to gender-based violence and for unconventional methods of discovering strategies to end it. I looked at the face of the African American girl pictured in a faded clipping from my local newspaper and felt a wave of deep sadness.[1] The girl's face in the news photo contorted with anguish and flowing tears as she turned away from the open casket where the body of her mother, Monica Paul, lay. The daughter was surrounded by family and friends at Christ Church, a large, predominantly black, nondenominational church in Montclair, New Jersey, a racially integrated, affluent suburb of New York City. Paul had been shot to death by her former intimate partner, Kenneth Duckett.[2] The black heterosexual couple had shared a home together for several years but were separated when Duckett killed Paul after she took out a restraining order against him. The murder occurred inside the Montclair Young Men's Christian Association in close proximity to their four-year-old son, who was attending his swimming lesson, and directly in front of their eleven-year-old daughter, whom the newspaper photographed at the funeral.

Mounting frustration surpassed sadness as I continued to skim through several other news items describing this tragedy. The articles about Monica Paul resided with a collection of other newspaper and magazine stories on incidents of intimate violence against black women in communities around the United States. The articles spilled out of bulging folders lying on my desk and the floor around it. Overstuffed manila folders containing hundreds of these clippings sat in stacked piles on the floor. I had intended to scan them all someday when there was enough time and add them to my collection of electronic files on violence against black women.

The clippings revealed disturbing cultural patterns surrounding this kind of gendered violence in the United States. One news article about Monica Paul's murder and funeral mentioned the comforting message of the funeral sermon.[3] This section of the article drew my attention partly because I have spent the past several years teaching seminary students who are preparing to be Protestant ministers. My reaction to accounts such as this one referencing the funeral sermon was deep dissatisfaction even though I had not been there. I was less concerned about the sermon's content than the exclusive role of the minister as a soothing resource in the aftermath of the tragedy. Under what circumstances, I wondered, might religious leaders play a different, less reactive role in response to the problem of a husband's violence against his wife? Instead of stories about ministers easing the pain of grieving victims, I wanted more examples of ministers contributing ambitious violence-prevention strategies. Religious leadership should work toward creating a world in which no grieving families require consolation after a husband's intimate violence escalates to a wife's murder.

In addition, too many cultural dynamics linked to the politics of race and religion in the United States inveigh against concern for ending the varied forms of intimate violence threatening black women's lives. They can contribute to a cultural malaise, if not capitulation to the ongoing presence of the violence. Sometimes, those dynamics subtly play out in otherwise constructive community work focused on combating anti-black racism and nurturing deeply rooted African American religious commitments. Alongside of Christianity's dominant cultural influence, non-Christian religious traditions and spiritual practices may also offer mixed moral messages to U.S. black women victim-survivors. The combined religious and racial dynamics that foster many peculiar forms of violence toleration in the United States readily adhere to other contributing factors offered in the popular media that the public imbibes on a daily basis. Ultimately, I decide to explore for how to conceptualize bolder critiques of these patterns by seeking out transnational perspectives, starting with the ideas in antiviolence values and methods of activist leaders in Accra, Ghana.

U.S. Cultural Problems That Demand Response

Studying my news clippings that night in my home reminded me that for religious leaders and others trying to address gender-based violence, the topic of race introduces an array of stumbling blocks related to U.S. intercultural conflicts and competition. Any evaluation of religious and other communal responses that draws attention to black women's experiences must take into account regressive politics of race. Unfortunately, antiviolence advocates who want to create sympathetic responses to intimate violence by black men against black women can unwittingly foster gradualism. They may find it prudent to start with a focus on translating the significance of black women's particular victim-survivor experiences in more universalistic terms that represent them as general, society-wide concerns that cut across all cultural groups. The impulse to take time to provide such translations of black women's experiences of violence usually rests on a strategy of developing one-size-fits-all public understandings and responses. Some advocates prize this kind of approach as more broadly efficacious for achieving policy changes for all women victim-survivors precisely because it prioritizes gender commonalities and minimizes, brackets, or erases cultural and racial particularities. In a contrasting but equally problematic approach, discussing the blackness of victimized black women like Monica Paul might serve to isolate them and consequently attenuate concern among those who identify as non-blacks of Hispanic or Latin American descent, Asian Americans, Indigenous/Natives, Pacific Islanders, whites, or racially mixed members of U.S. communities.

In a twenty-first-century context of an increasingly racially and culturally diverse U.S.-American society, religious and nonreligious advocates require advanced abilities for negotiations of intercultural and interracial realities. Such skills enable leaders to muster the empathy, solidarity, and activism necessary to incite greater public intolerance for gender-based violence. In order to truly galvanize the public and generate a sufficiently broad response, leaders must invoke a sense of a shared, immediate crisis of violence as well as directly confront the deep polarization, denial, and confusion about culture and race that exist.

Additionally, violence terminology matters for the mobilization of public concern by advocates and scholars. Terms such as *interpersonal violence, domestic violence, intimate violence,* and *gender-based violence* offer slightly different emphases for categorizing the patterns violence assumes. *Interpersonal violence* is an umbrella term for the varied patterns of emotional, physical, and sexual abuse perpetrators inflict on their victims (whether the perpetrators are familiar to the victims or not). *Domestic violence* magnifies the abusive behavioral patterns exhibited in an offender's abuse and violence within an intimate partner or romantic relationship.

I most often apply the terms *intimate violence* and *gender-based violence* in a coordinated fashion, sometimes interchangeably, in order to stress the range of dynamics these terms encompass. *Intimate violence* refers to various forms of physical and sexual assaults committed within intimate relationships as well as sexual assaults by less familiar acquaintances or by strangers. Even when the perpetrator is a stranger, the sexual nature of the attack renders the violence intimate. The context of intimate assaults is wide-ranging and may include childhood sexual abuse by your family member, physical assaults by your adult intimate partner, or sexual harassment by a prison staff member in a housing unit where you are incarcerated. The term *intimate violence* highlights how the violence is experienced by women and girls who are victimized, not how the perpetrator behaves. The term points to the fact that the violence is so very intimate in part because its destructive capacity can be so comprehensive—assaulting a girl or woman's body, mind, personhood, and spirit.

The term *gender-based violence* calls attention to the ways in which gender expression is a key aspect in the targeting of women and girls. It highlights how violence thrives on widespread cultural assumptions about appropriate gender behavior that often reflect constricted binary and heteronormative criteria. In this way, for instance, violence or the ongoing threat of violence helps ensure conformity to heteropatriarchal norms while feeding on social devaluation, stereotypes, and stigmas often attached to black women's sexuality in the broader culture, especially that of poor black women.[4] The emphasis on the gendering of the violence in the use of the term *gender-based violence* therefore highlights a link between vulnerability to male violence and the politics of sex/gender expression for black women in their varied communal settings. Besides a link to the intimate nature of sexuality when one is sexually assaulted, the use of the related term *intimate violence* also signals a refusal to neglect the insidious impacts that may lurk in one's spirit and emotions during and in the aftermath of the multiple forms of assault and abuse mentioned above. Those effects represent violations of trust, human dignity, and spiritual wholeness that can accompany the sexual and other bodily assaults of black women victim-survivors. The combined implications the two terms illuminate offer guideposts for responses to the intimate and cultural politics of the violence. Of course, when contemplating any such response one must be mindful of the intricate ways in which issues related to black women's racial identities permeate their experiences of abuse and violence. And it is important to note that the impacts never occur in an identical, assembly-line pattern as if every black woman had the same personality, emotional makeup, family background, socioeconomic status, or experience of skin color prejudice.

My focus on male violence against black women fits into a broader landscape of patterns of gender-based violence in the United States. Gender-based assaults routinely occur in the lives of women and girls across sexual orientations, gender expressions, and gender identities. Men also victimize other men and boys. Women perpetrate intimate violence, although in much lower numbers than men, against both men and women. Women sometimes victimize their intimate partners within their same-gender intimate relationships.[5]

National statistics from the early twenty-first century document instructive trends about how gender matters in the frequency of gender-based violence—at least for reported violence. For example, the Justice Department studied what it called nonfatal intimate partner violence including rape, sexual assault, robbery, aggravated assault, and simple assault committed by a current or former spouse, boyfriend, or girlfriend. The report indicated that the rate of intimate partner violence somewhat declined for females from 2000 through 2005 and then held steady from 2005 through 2010.[6] Also holding steady statistically was the fact that females made up the majority—four out of five—of those victimized by nonfatal intimate partner violence.[7] The fact that females constituted 70 percent of those killed by intimate partner violence held steady from 1993 through 2007.[8] The Centers for Disease Control and Prevention issued a 2010 National Intimate Partner and Sexual Violence Survey stating that almost 20 percent of all women (across all racial groups) in the United States had been raped in their lifetime. During just the preceding year of the survey, approximately 1.3 million women were raped in the United States.[9] In general, most studies have found that black females experience intimate partner violence, rapes, and sexual assaults at higher rates than white females.[10] The problem documented as "domestic violence fatalities" affects women from almost every racial/ethnic background, but evidence suggests that black women are disproportionately affected.[11] Black females are four times more likely than white females, for example, to be murdered by a boyfriend or girlfriend.[12]

Aspiring church leaders and other community leaders who might be resources for victims and their friends and families should be aware of how many women experience an attempted or completed rape and of how frequently restraining orders that women take out against intimate partners are violated. Before deciding to offer counseling to couples, for example, religious leaders need to know that in the majority of cases in which a heterosexual intimate partner was murdered (no matter which partner was killed), the man physically abused the woman beforehand.[13] Leaders serving black communities ought to be especially cognizant of how frequently black females killed in both single-victim and single-offender incidents are killed by a spouse, intimate acquaintance, or family member.[14]

Not surprisingly, Monica Paul's murder embodied several of these broader patterns—her husband had abused her, and she had obtained a restraining order against him before he murdered her. Paul's murder was also only one in a rash that year of similar incidents—six resulting in eleven deaths—in my region of New Jersey.[15] The term newspaper accounts have frequently used to refer to such killings—*domestic fatalities*—is grossly inadequate. Why not *domestic murders* or even *femicide*, which are more precise?[16] Femicide refers to the misogynist targeting of women by abusive husbands, boyfriends, or sons-in-law, and by stalkers, male serial killers, or perpetrators of massacres.[17] As feminist scholar-activist Ann Jones pointed out in her aptly titled study *Next Time She'll Be Dead*, even the term *domestic violence* is a "euphemistic abstraction that keeps us at a dispassionate distance, far from the repugnant spectacle of human beings in pain."[18] None of these terms satisfactorily accounts for the ways in which the violence is culturally informed. In describing the murders of hundreds of women in Juárez, Mexico, for example, feminist Christian liberation theologian Nancy Pineda-Madrid prefers *feminicide*. In her view, feminicide more accurately captures the systemic nature of that violence and how it is "rooted in structural inequalities that render some women and girls acutely vulnerable."[19] As Pineda-Madrid rightly explains, the nature of the violence is deeply informed by particular forms of socioeconomic vulnerability as well as the cultural and geopolitical location of women and girls. The language used to name violence must reflect these cultural and political ingredients before we can conceptualize adequate responses to address it. Intercultural understandings and communication skills are in turn indispensable for sharing those responses with one another across varied cultural and geopolitical settings.

As noted above, black women are disproportionately represented in so-called domestic violence fatalities.[20] But more common are male-perpetrated domestic violence incidents in which no murder is committed. In the early twenty-first century in New Jersey, for instance, the state police reported about seventy thousand domestic violence offenses per year.[21] And what should be especially troubling for those of us who identify as Christian, these assaults occur most frequently on Sunday evenings—a day that in a country culturally dominated by its Christian majority is ostensibly designated for honoring the religion's custom of a weekly celebration of its communal rituals and symbols. Although no direct causal link exists between the Christian Sabbath and elevated violence rates on that day, the apparently comfortable coexistence of a high rate of male violence against women in their domestic settings on Sundays arguably communicates a subtle message of moral tolerance. At the very least, the confluence signals that a needed message about violence and gender is missing from Christianity's powerful moral influence on society.

Monica Paul's news clipping was only one of the many stories contained in multiple "to be scanned" folders on my floor—stories revealing painful violence inflicted within varied intimate relationships of African Americans across socioeconomic class groupings. One headline described "relationship violence" between heterosexual black college student couples. "Kira Johnson still becomes tearful," the bold print inset on the page declared, "when she recalls the incident eight years ago when her college boyfriend held a gun to her head threatening to end her life because he feared she was about to leave him."[22] In another article, the *Washington Post* portrayed the anguished face and closed eyes of Aarolyn Mills, the daughter of black 1960s U.S. civil rights movement hero and Baptist preacher James Bevel. Mills had bravely broken the silence and testified how Bevel had sexually preyed upon his daughters for many years, for which the court finally convicted him.[23] In still another, *Essence* magazine described an epidemic of domestic violence (including many femicides) in one of the nation's wealthiest black suburban communities. Close-up photographs in the article portrayed the open-eyed and expressive faces of a woman and her daughter beneath the caption "A Survivor's Tale: Set on fire by her estranged husband, Yvette Cade, has miraculously survived and committed her life to encouraging others in abusive relationships."[24] We should honor, study, and celebrate how each of these women responded to intimate violence with individual expressions of courage and self-empowerment. Yet there is also an overwhelming need for more dynamic community support and justice activism systemically working to prevent intimate violence from occurring at all and therefore lessen—or maybe even someday eradicate—the demand on so many victim-survivors to defend themselves so bravely.

The mounds of paper files in folders that documented the violence were scattered in an unruly mess on and around my desk waiting to be scanned. While wanting to escape to the distraction of mindless television or my favorite popcorn snack, I settled instead into inertia and staring outside. The setting sun was invisible behind ashy-white winter clouds that threatened more of the icy rain we'd had earlier in the day.

Inadequacy of Insular Black Religious Responses

A common response of diligent antiviolence advocates is to call for greater awareness by religious leaders of the nature of the epidemic of violence against women and its impact on black communities. But increasing awareness can never be an adequate primary goal for ending violence against women and girls. In part, due to religion's importance in many black communities, certain religious responses play a unique role as incubators for the violence. Analyses by religious leaders about black communal moral life that seek to balance celebration of black religious life with some admission of the problems within it deserve our wariness. This approach has the potential to bolster complacency about gender-based violence. Attempts to balance public affirmations of the virtuousness of black communal religiosity with acknowledgment of the need to offer private forms of comfort to victim-survivors within those communities may compound suffering. Victims can be tormented by the experience of being attracted by the allure of receiving comfort and support from black religious leaders and institutions but then having to cope with their public moral equivocations about the significance of this problem for the whole community. Equivocations may be subtly communicated in the difference between the expression of outrage and threat to communal wholeness leaders convey about white racist violence against black men and about abusive black men's violence against them. This unique, institutionalized capacity for succor and betrayal linked to one's racial, gender, and spiritual identity illustrates a peculiar means of participating in black women's victimization that religion possesses.

When surveyed, African Americans consistently identify as more religious than the U.S. population as a whole.[25] Even those who are unaffiliated with a specific religious group, particularly black women, tend to indicate that religion and spirituality play an important role in their lives.[26] In their study of black church responses to domestic violence, social work scholars Tricia Bent-Goodley, Noelle St. Vil, and Paulette Hubbert point out that "African American women are more likely to turn to their faith community and extended family first before reaching out to formal providers, such as social workers, law enforcement, and health professionals."[27] But the insular understandings of race and institutional religion held by some of those family members to whom the women turn for help can lead them to give detrimental messages instead of solace to the women searching for support.

For example, womanist Christian pastoral care scholar Stephanie Crumpton cites the testimony of a black woman, Cirene, who had been repeatedly sexually molested and raped as a child by an older male family member.[28] As a teenager, Cirene admitted her deep feelings of depression to her mother and asked about the possibility of getting therapeutic help. Her mother responded by asserting that black people did not need to go to therapists: "We got the church. We got God; so, no."[29] There may have been particular reasons for her mother's antipathy to psychotherapy, including perhaps a lack of information about its benefits.[30] But the comment illustrates a traditional theological view that opposes, or perhaps even fears, the replacement of God and church as a source of sustenance with nonreligious authoritative sources. The racialized dimension of the "we" in this response may have been fed by broader intracommunal attitudes that claimed a need for blacks to maintain private, contained social spheres, such as black faith communities seen as offering a shielding boundary that provides respite from the control and close scrutiny of whites. Maintenance of this sphere may be seen as a protective communal necessity for coping with the prevalence of anti-black racist attitudes that normalize white dominance in U.S. society.

But such responses to abuse and violence centered on privacy that supposedly grants refuge from white control can deepen the anguish of women victim-survivors by discouraging them from seeking any outside help and resources they truly need in the aftermath of assaults. The responses can nurture anguish and shame by attaching a self-sacrificial black racial loyalty obligation to Christian moral and theological obligations to sacrifice self in a manner also demanded of them by their allegiances to their faith communities. This combination fosters false, burdensome expectations from God, church, and community that black women victim-survivors should exclusively look inward to their black faith communities in order to receive help.

Yet many Christian black women and girls who have been victimized and the family members to whom they turn for help still regard church leaders as primary, trustworthy resources. It would thus be a mistake to dismiss the value of assisting religious leaders in acquiring specific knowledge and skills to aid victimized women. Yet the systemically transformative potential of those efforts remains uncertain.

A communal response that solely emphasizes religious leaders' attainment of more knowledge about the occurrence of violence and better counseling skills could be easily sabotaged by myopic sociopolitical assumptions if they are left unchallenged. Commonplace cultural disincentives militate against utilizing those skills once leaders have developed them. As noted earlier, gender-based violence against black women is, by definition, supported by broad cultural values that teach conformity to heteropatriarchal and inflexible gender binaries, which unfairly limit women's self-expression and equality. Collusion exists among sexist Christian religious practices and traditions, U.S.-American forms of anti-black racism, and other cultural sources in generating violence-supporting mores. They work together in supporting the subversion of black victim-survivors' safety and freedom for the sake of other obligations and loyalties. A communal response that focuses on increasing awareness, knowledge, and skills to address intimate violence must offer guiding, strategic interventions that challenge religious and sociopolitical values that subjugate women. There must be some way to provoke more strategies that encourage clergy to listen carefully to the truths that black women and girls tell about their victimization and to confront the lies that black male perpetrators tell about their actions in order to resist accountability.

Responses to the violence that focus on educating and training clergy often include seismic omissions of political considerations that can substantively undermine worthy goals for raising awareness. Troublingly, education-oriented communal responses frequently ignore the negative ramifications on status and credibility that religious leaders may confront within their traditional religious institutional cultures when they do make radical changes in their practices and teachings in response to intimate violence against women. In a tradition as steeped in patriarchal norms as Christianity has been, there are subtle (and not-so-subtle) penalties for dissent from values that sanction gender violence and concomitant rewards for enforcing conformity to those traditional values. Strategic omissions of attention to social penalties and rewards constitute either a naïve approach or a duplicitous one. In short, "without faith-based leaders' desire to address domestic violence," as Tricia Bent-Goodley and Dawnovise Fowler report in their study on religion and domestic violence in three African American communities, "training curricula and further research will be useless."[31] In another study also co-authored by Bent-Goodley, when a group of African American clergy reported their unequivocal belief that there was a need for heightened concern about domestic violence and abuse within their faith communities, a majority of them also admitted that the church did little to prevent such abuse and violence.[32] There must be attention to how one ignites the will to counter the gender violence tolerance embedded in sexist cultural messages ranging from ancient religious traditions to contemporary racial politics. Religious leaders must find willful countercultural courage not only to respond to violence crises after they occur but also to act to prevent them from occurring in the first place.

Harmful or ineffectual responses to gender violence are not confined to indifference generated by a lack of education, awareness, or will to address it. Far too many U.S. religious leaders serving communities across racial and ethnic groups have yet to be persuaded to desist in their practice of giving life-endangering advice to victim-survivors. One study, for example, found that most clergy continue to recommend joint counseling to couples when domestic violence occurs, even though doing so creates the risk of dangerous retaliation by the abuser against the abused as a result of what may be shared during the sessions.[33]

Some religious messages directly received by black women victim-survivors support their private internalization of the impacts of the violence and direct them literally to remain in situations where they are subject to further abuse and violence. Those who seek help from clergy are sometimes "encouraged to submit to the male leadership in the house" in accordance with scripture, as culture and gender scholar Venita Kelley reported in her study of African American women's experiences of domestic violence in Lincoln, Nebraska.[34] Kelley found that clergy counseled women to stay with their abusers and that some even blamed women, especially those seeking divorce, for their situations.[35] In another study of black women and intimate partner abuse, sociologist Hillary Potter pointed to reports by Christian interviewees about "being told by pastors to remain in the relationship and 'work things out.'"[36]

Christian leaders' disregard for the further endangerment and suffering of women who have been abused is exhibited in multiple ways. Sometimes church leaders and counselors instruct women victim-survivors of intimate violence to just pray harder for deliverance from their suffering or for the abuser to change, to bear their cross like Jesus did, to stay married to their intimate partner abusers because divorce is a sin, or to practice forgiveness of their sexual molesters or rapists by forgetting about the assaults without demanding any public form of accountability from those offenders. Such messages comport with repeated gendered assertions from black community leaders about the black community's unifying priority to protect black men from police violence and harassment in the context of widespread racist criminal justice practices.[37] Antiracist activist leaders frequently identify black men as the primary targets of and those most injured by white racism. This black community priority enables the sacrifice of activist attention to the threats from black men's intimate violence toward black women and further isolates black women's suffering at the hands of black men from communal concern.[38]

The triumvirate of sexist Christian church theological and pastoral counseling messages, black leaders' political messages about black racial solidarity requiring support for "truly endangered" black men, and abusers' coercive methods contain disturbingly close parallels and overlaps. The various combinations and permutations of these three narratives result in a unique form of moral and spiritual assault.[39] When the responses church leaders and counselors offer victim-survivors include these woman-sacrificing themes, they can suffuse an abuser's self-justifying logic with sacred moral authority. For black women seeking help, these church responses aid in maintaining a sense of confusion about the costs of their vulnerability to abuse and violence and their right to escape it.[40]

An extreme version of this moral and spiritual harm lurks in instances when a male pastor is himself a sexual abuser of women in his congregation. In such situations, in addition to the women who are directly victimized by the pastor, the church's response will likely be inadequate for victim-survivors (of other abusers) in need of support in that abusing pastor's faith community. An overall church ethos that normalizes autocratic black pastoral leadership and abuse of power contributes hospitable conditions for pastoral sexual misconduct. Black church settings that permit only men to become head pastors or speak from the pulpit while women compose the majority of congregants enhance conditions for exploitation. In their study of black clergy sexual misconduct, Christian pastoral leadership scholars Anson Shupe and Janelle M. Eliasson-Nannini depict particularly egregious examples, including one in which a Texas pastor was convicted of drugging then sexually assaulting multiple women in the congregation.[41] Shupe and Eliasson-Nannini point out a dire need for the debunking of the "awe of ecclesiastical office and pastoral person" that assists in allowing such predators to thrive.[42] Moreover, in some black church initiatives to support strong black manhood in their communities, the reinforcement of strictly bifurcated gender boundaries can allow predatory leaders to perpetrate abuse while simultaneously fostering the church community's unresponsiveness to the women they victimize.[43]

Some leaders of prominent black churches do publicly utilize their pastoral authority to oppose intimate violence against women. Yet sometimes, even such public messages of support offer subtle manipulations that undermine their reliability and overall message. This problem is especially evident when a pastor's public rhetoric of antiviolence is accompanied by aggressive public pressure by the pastor on the spiritually depleted and physically assaulted victim-survivors in the congregation to spend their financial resources on supporting that church pastor. Few nationally influential male pastors of black churches have so intently seized upon the problem of sexual abuse and domestic violence perpetrated against black women than Bishop T. D. Jakes, a Texas-based black Pentecostal megachurch pastor and millionaire entrepreneur. Jakes initially preached a sermon titled "Woman Thou Art Loosed" at a 1993 national Pentecostal gathering, after which he launched an enterprise that generated tens of millions of dollars. Jakes transformed the major themes of the sermon—women's experiences of abuse and violence— into a best-selling novel, a blockbuster movie (in general audience theaters), a stage play, a cookbook, and a music CD. The topic became the focal point for a series of biannual national conferences that attract tens of thousands of (predominantly black) women to whom Jakes also sells these products.[44]

Jakes has vocally supported women's equality, publicly opposed sexual and domestic violence toward women, and actively promoted the church as a healing resource for victim-survivors.[45] Yet he also has explained that women were created by God to be "receptacles," "receivers," and helpers of their men while men were created to be providers, protectors, or covers for women.[46] In his book *God's Leading Lady: Out of the Shadows and into the Light*, as he discusses preventative measures for sexual and domestic abuse women may face, he advises them to "be careful" and "watch out."[47] Failing to exercise such caution, "like Tamar," for instance, a biblical character who was raped by her brother, Jakes warns women that "you could be left trembling and muttering to yourself, 'Why didn't I see this coming?'"[48]

The focus by Jakes on hyperindividualism, self-help, and maintaining a stringent heterosexual gender binary helps maintain a communal homeostasis that is too tolerant of violence, especially because of the manner in which he asserts women's responsibility for preventing or stopping it. His Christian logic problematically places the onus on women to stem the proliferation of intimate violence by encouraging them to spiritually look inward and find ways to learn to behave outwardly as more careful, more chaste, more feminine "receptacles." Their receipt of such encouragement appears to be directly linked to their purchase of more of his books, sermon recordings, and conference registrations.

Even when church leaders such as Jakes condemn the violence and champion women's equality, their matching emphasis on women's responsibility to avoid being victimized undercuts their antiviolence message. In addition, messages from church leaders such as Jakes about how the inadequacy of their femininity may contribute to their victimization are echoed elsewhere. Prevalent racist stereotypes in the broader culture represent black women as too loud, too aggressive, or in some other way supposedly lacking desirable feminine traits that their idealized white women counterparts manifest. A comfortable stasis is provided for the violence by constricted, unyieldingly binary gender norms in Christian moral understandings of sin and virtuousness that require conformity. Rigid gender assumptions enable gender-based violence to flourish when left not only undisturbed but sacralized in core teachings by black Christian faith community leaders who describe blameworthy expressions of femininity. Faulty models of Christian community response in which the victimized woman has to share some of the responsibility for the fact that she was victimized protect perpetrators from accountability for their abusive and violent behavior.

To adequately address religious and spiritual issues for black women victim-survivors, religious and spiritual communal responses are needed that reach beyond the standard roles of Christian leaders and institutions as well as traditional theological understandings. Spiritual needs should be seen as incorporating a longing for connectedness and affirmation that does not merely focus on a powerful deity that one worships. Religious and spiritual needs most relevant to the communal responses discussed here include meaningful, caring connections to other people, mystical connections to ancestors or beloved relatives who have died, and a sense of communal or familial belonging that includes their unequivocal affirmation of one's individual worth. The varied means for nurturing these social aspects of spirituality are wide ranging from supportive, electronically communicated messages from one's network of friends and acquaintances to embodied participation in collective rituals artistically invoking the sacred through music or dance, and many others between and beyond.

Starting with the individual experiences of spirituality and religion for African American women victim-survivors of intimate violence, Crumpton's womanist pastoral care analyses adeptly point to the complexity of their communal religious relationships. She describes, for example, how in the aftermath of intimate violence such as battering or rape, "some Black women may need to mourn the loss of the Black church."[49] One woman in her study, Octavia, found an exploration of Buddhism, Catholicism, and Islam meaningful after she was gang-raped.[50] Although most African Americans who strongly affiliate with religious organizations identify themselves as Protestant Christians, an active minority belong to other traditions, such as Islam. Approximately 20 to 30 percent of U.S. Muslims identify as African American.[51]

Like Christian African American women, Muslim African American women report destructive as well as supportive responses from religious leaders and communities in the wake of intimate assaults. Womanist religious historian Debra Majeed presents a case study about the harmful effects of a mosque community's keeping of secrets and protection of an abuser.[52] The example featured an African American woman convert to Islam who was battered by her husband, a devout leader at the mosque. When the woman, Khalidah, sought "help from local Muslim leaders, they informed her that intervention required her husband's permission. Although he refused their mediation, they continued to permit him to instruct other Muslims in issues of marriage and daily life."[53] Like the Christian pastors' endangering advice, this form of institutional response exacerbates religious and spiritual harm to a victim-survivor. It creates a kind of encircling, impermeable wall of indifference to her suffering that fuses together her abuser's sense of entitlement to victimize her with authoritative understandings of women's submission from her faith community's leadership.

In contrast, in her qualitative study of battered black women's use of religious organizations to exit their abusive relationships, Potter found that the Muslim women experienced more satisfactory responses than the Christian women. In many instances, however, satisfactory responses still relied upon paternalistic forms of protection from internal community structures. After a battering incident with her husband, for example, when one woman contacted her mosque's "security faction," composed of several men, the men escorted her abusive husband from their home. Another formerly abused black Muslim woman explained that Muslim men "take care of their own . . . instead of calling the police, all you need to do is call your Wali. . . . Call him and all the Muslim brothers will come and handle the individual."[54] In this approach, the faith community was responsive to the woman's request for help and offered an immediately effective end to the violence, at least in the short term, as long as none of the men who were on call to respond was the woman's abuser. But it illustrates another crisis-oriented strategy handled purely on an individual case basis. This type of strategy provides a means of retreat into a private religious world where crisis intervention remains constituted by a communal reliance on gender binaries. The men who are on call perform prescribed gender roles as protectors and the victimized women appear to be dependent on their responsiveness.

The limitations of church- and mosque-based black communal responses send frustratingly contradictory messages about the process of emancipation from gender-based violence. In many instances, they remind black women victim-survivors not to stray too far from the confines of community resources identified as their own, that is, linked to their racial and faith identities. Responses of their own faith communities hold out the promise of an affirming sense of belonging but not freedom from gendered notions of blameworthiness and submission. The underlying conceptualization of community response in these approaches leaves black faith communities quagmired in a primary self-understanding of guardianship. At best, they are custodians of endangering gender norms and an assuaging influence in the midst of the emergency or aftermath of male abuse and violence. At worst, they function as enforcers, making anguishing, self-sacrificial, dependent practices or protection of black male abusers morally standard requirements of faithful black women victim-survivors. Even well-intentioned and well-trained leaders can be afflicted by a crisis of imagination to move beyond such responses. There seems to be a shortage of visionary capacity or will to conceive of a role more focused on prevention strategies.

Too often lacking in the responses of religious leaders is a conceptual aptitude for taking into account the politics of anti-black racism and gender norms in a manner that fully breaks with communal habits that support and subtly perpetuate the violence.

Anti-black racism is an important instigator that helps make inwardly directed black communal religious responses seem necessary. Fears of white control or stereotyping judgments can influence leaders to try to maintain private black religious space that bolsters black racial solidarity rather than unconventional interpretations of tradition and public advocacy that challenge black male abuse of power and of women. Capitulation to those fears constitutes surrender to cultural attitudes and practices that uphold white racist permission for sacrificing the safety and well-being of black women victim-survivors. Anti-black racism is therefore implicated in black religious and spiritual responses that offer a protective communal shield for intimate violence and its perpetrators. This manifestation of racism creates an a priori boundary that regulates the available space for black religious visions and activist dismantling of gender-based violence against black women and girls. Since the development of moral and spiritual imagination constitutes a central aim of organized religious traditions, this accommodation curtails the considerable antiviolence contributions that religions could offer.

For reasons that include the hypervisibility of blacks as symbols and targets of racism, anti-black racism affects the attitudes and practices of all members of the broader U.S. society. Therefore, further contemplation of these and other religious connections to anti-black racism may hold potential clues for addressing the prevalence of the gender-based violence shared, but in distinctive forms, across varied ethnic, racial, and national group backgrounds. Additionally, the troubling patterns related to black faith community responses to intimate violence certainly do not thrive in a cultural vacuum. They are informed by broad-based, dominant U.S. cultural values that continue to foster tolerance of intimate violence against women and girls no matter their race, religion, or socioeconomic status. And nowhere are those values more evident than in U.S. popular culture.

Popular Culture Violence and Launching a Quest for Alternatives

The evening I sat at my desk surrounded by newspaper clippings was only one episode in a long saga of moody agitation. Those moments helped propel me toward more experimental methods for considering alternative antiviolence approaches. That evening when tempted by the urge for microwave popcorn or mindless television, TV seemed like a better diversion. But that idea faded quickly. An escape into the worlds of network or cable television would likely generate a renewed wave of frustration. Indeed, many programs magnify some of the same troubling aspects of black religious responses to gender-based violence—notably, the emphasis on self-scrutiny by victimized women. Experts responding to the voices of real-life victimized women can be heard on pseudo-therapy and tell-all talk shows that reach millions of viewers on a daily basis.[55] As sociologist Nancy Berns explains, "whether these shows feature the pop psychology of hosts like Dr. Phil or Oprah or outside 'experts,' the same message is given to guests and to the viewing audience. Victims need to wake up, reclaim their power, acknowledge how they are allowing themselves to be abused."[56] This individualized narrative of self-empowerment found on talk shows and other media venues, Berns rightly argues, does make the problem of domestic violence more visible. But it also helps limit public awareness by leading them to favor counseling for victim-survivors as a remedy over "any changes in structural and cultural factors that foster violence."[57] Through such talk shows on mass media television, the U.S. public has become well rehearsed in reductive narratives that place full responsibility on women victim-survivors for addressing the violence through self-empowerment.[58]

Popular programming helps to illustrate other harmful aspects of U.S. cultural responses. Television shows commercialize repetitive images of specific forms of both violence against women and gun violence in factual and fictional representations. Real-life stories render disturbing, dramatic portrayals of the violence.[59] Haunting images repeatedly flash on the screen in news magazine reenactments of women's murders most often by loved ones and acquaintances in their local communities. True-crime "reality shows" depict police officers answering domestic violence distress calls made by frantic low-income women, mainly in inner-city neighborhoods. News stories regularly feature celebrity cases frequently of black athletes and music stars physically abusing women.[60] When available, images of this violence against individual black women saturate the coverage by mass media news outlets and Internet media sources.

In U.S. mass media, both factual and fictional stories often feature gun violence. A considerable amount of gun violence is included in fictional media depictions of criminal acts and crime fighters. One study found that the gun violence portrayed in PG-13-rated films had more than tripled in the first twenty-five years after the ratings system was instituted in 1985.[61] And in the real lives of U.S. residents, there are more killings and suicides by firearms than in any other Western industrialized nation.[62] Sociology and public health scholars debate whether there is any direct causal connection between fictional media violence representations of gun violence and actual incidents.[63]

Guns play a prominent role in real-life U.S. domestic violence femicides and other, nonfatal acts of domestic terror men perpetrate against women known to them.[64] One study shows that gun violence is the leading cause of death for black men and boys aged fifteen to thirty-four, and the second leading cause of death for black women and girls the same ages.[65] Overwhelmingly, most black women who are victims of femicides that involve firearms are killed by black men known to them.[66] In the wider cultural climate in which this violence occurs, insufficient public will and political leadership exist to create national public policy that stems gun violence. Large U.S. audiences continue to feed, seemingly insatiably, on gory news stories about gun violence as well as fictional representations of it on television.

In the dominant moral ethos of the United States, television programming constitutes an influential communal response to gender-based violence. Its ongoing barrage of messages about violence against women can easily dull one's sense of urgency about the need to create change. Popular television programming serves up varied grotesque images of violently victimized women together with diligent, racially integrated teams of law enforcement characters that single-mindedly pursue justice on behalf of the victimized and almost always catch or kill the perpetrators.[67] Whether through fictional characters or real lives on display in newsmagazine shows, these commercially profitable images make intimate violence against women seem like fascinating entertainment.[68]

Mass-media producers exhibit ever-increasing cleverness in blurring lines between real criminal assaults covered by news reports and fictional crime dramas. They not only aid viewers in lumping them all together as a similar form of entertainment but also convincingly represent the adequacy of law enforcement responses. Media portrayals of violence can be construed as constructing a kind of belief system for the public that resembles the ways that traditional religions discipline their believers. Media studies researchers Michael Morgan, James Shanahan, and Nancy Signorielli point out, "as with religion, the social function of television lies in the continual repetition of stories (myths, 'facts,' lessons, and so on) that serve to define the world and legitimize a particular social order."[69] Because violence has become such a staple source of entertainment in this medium, television programming can be understood as a powerful moral mechanism ensuring that acquiescence to its seeming normalcy remains intact.

The late twentieth-century rallying cry of feminist scholar-activists (including myself) about the need to "break the silence" no longer adequately captures the cultural milieu of the twenty-first century. The crevices of our moral sensibilities about gender-based violence are crowded with media images publicizing it, fictional crime fighters addressing it, and advice giving by supposed experts counseling women on how to stop tolerating it. Sensationalized chatter in social media circulating around particular incidents in the news, crime drama episodes, and graphic images from news headlines also add trivializing or ineffectual sounds of concern to our moral ethos. Cumulatively, all of these media responses help reinforce a cultural belief that no major problem of intimate violence exists that is not already being discussed and therefore presumably attended to.

My own sense of a need for a startling awakening to fresh perspectives that differed from frustrating media and cyclical religious responses would not relent. It drew me toward a preoccupation with seeking out bold black women activist leaders in non-U.S. settings. I suspected that in the particularity of lived ethics and advocacy found in their activist leadership could be found deep wells of knowledge about resistance strategies as well as courage to transform impeding cultural mores in their settings. Anti-black racist values in the United States and elsewhere foster disdain toward the idea that peoples of African descent might serve as rich resources for advanced thought. Especially appealing to me was some kind of action that disavowed this racist projection of black human capacities. More than just a reaction to white racism, an inquiry with an emphasis on reaching outward could perhaps spur unconventional thinking. It might help in conceptualizing resistance to cycles of inwardly directed black community religious responses and U.S. cultural values that entrapped victim-survivors and fostered communal tolerance of the violence.

Eventually, after a long period of debating the merits, I challenged myself to move as far out of my comfort zone as I could bear, immersing myself in the role of learner rather than teacher. From friends and colleagues I learned about leaders who shared my interests and might be willing to meet with me. On short trips outside of the United States, I began by interviewing community leaders and activists whose work addressed gender violence against black women and girls. I began with a less organized itinerary than I had hoped for but a compensating desire to allow spontaneous learning to occur.

I traveled first to the West African country of Ghana, which at the time had recently passed a comprehensive national law to address domestic violence.[70] In light of this legislative success, I sought out Ghanaian activist leaders who had worked in the movement to pass this law as well as other leaders involved in combating gender-based violence. This national legislative approach differed from that of the United States, where no permanent federal law forbids violence against women. As the Biden speech exemplified, the federal law that does exist, VAWA, requires political leaders to fight for its reauthorization every five years.[71]

To start the process of breaking open basic barriers in the intercultural task of learning from the antiviolence work and context of Ghanaian activist-leaders, I began with religious leaders. As I sought their views on their national and local faith community strategies, I thought that gathering information was my chief reason for meeting with them. Only later would it become evident how much the slow, politically charged process of recognizing them as antiviolence resources would matter.

Seeking Leaders in Ghana: Useful Cultural Dislocation

After arriving in Accra, I met my taxi driver, Fiifi. I had contacted him ahead of time with the assistance of a coworker at my university, a U.S. relative of Fiifi's. Although his slightly graying, short black hair told me he was about the same middle age as I was, he spontaneously assumed a fatherly concern about my safety. In what seemed a bit overly protective, for instance, he guarded me when I exchanged U.S. dollars for Ghanaian cedis. Then he helpfully reminded me to get a receipt when I started to leave without one.

I sat in the front passenger's seat and looked out of the window of his black and orange taxicab at the bustling city. Accra had a population of over three million people. I noticed the beautiful colors of the clothing at the outdoor market stands and tried to guess which ones were made of Kente cloth, a well-known Ghanaian textile containing intricate, bright color patterns often worn in Ghana for ceremonial occasions. Imitations of this cloth are sold in the United States and are frequently part of the décor in homes of African American families who celebrate Kwanzaa during the December holiday season.[72]

At almost every major traffic light in Accra dark brown-skinned women stood with all kinds of food to sell, including fish, meats, and grains. They balanced high piles on their heads and offered their goods to potential customers seated in cars waiting for red lights. In the bright hot sun, teenage boys and girls combed the same territory, selling newspapers, small containers of water, and colorful handkerchiefs. At each traffic light, groups of sellers descended upon our cab. "There are no jobs," Fiifi told me, answering a question I had not asked. I nodded.

Fumes from the congested morning rush-hour traffic wafted into the car from buses, taxis, private cars, and motor bikes. Occasionally, a goat or two also crossed a busy intersection. I marveled at how the goats safely navigated the traffic as they crossed from one side of the street to the other. The fronts of most of the small shops we passed announced the seemingly ubiquitous presence of Christianity and its comfortable relationship with capitalist entrepreneurship. Shop signs displayed names such as "God's Time Is the Best Artworks Shop" and "Praise the Lord Beauty Salon." These Christian signs were absent in the Muslim sections of the city that I visited.

Christians constitute the majority (over 50 percent) of Ghana's population.[73] Outside of a sizable group in Accra and other cities in differing regions of the country, the largest segment of the Muslim population lives in the northern regions of Ghana. Muslims, predominantly Sunni, represent approximately 15 to 18 percent of the country's population.[74] Adherents of African Traditional Religions make up the smallest religious group in the nation.[75] Ghana maintains a concertedly secular state and has done so since it gained independence from British colonial rule in 1957.

Ghana was the first sub-Saharan African nation to achieve independent status, an event celebrated by many African American activists and scholars. There is a long tradition of African American scholars and activists traveling to Ghana to learn from Ghanaians; some even repatriated there. In the wake of independence, an impressive group of black Americans from the United States attended the 1957 inaugural celebration of Ghana's first prime minister, Kwame Nkrumah. The group included political leaders, such as civil rights activist and Christian minister Martin Luther King Jr. and his wife Coretta Scott King, political scientist, diplomat, and 1950 Nobel Peace Prize winner Ralph Bunche, congressman and Harlem's Abyssinian Baptist Church pastor Adam Clayton Powell Jr., and social activist and founder of the first predominantly black national labor union, the Brotherhood of Sleeping Car Porters, A. Philip Randolph.[76] Lucille Armstrong (wife of jazz trumpeter Louis Armstrong) had also been part of the group. The couple had just visited Nkrumah during Louis Armstrong's international 1956 Goodwill Tour.[77] Vice President Richard Nixon led the U.S. delegation alongside official representatives from over seventy other nations.[78]

Of direct relevance to my interest in gender-based activism were the connections forged between U.S. and Ghanaian activist women leaders during that period. African American Christian feminist activist/scholar Pauli Murray, for example, went to Accra to teach U.S. constitutional law to a fresh crop of constitutional lawyers for the fledgling postcolonial, democratic African state.[79] And an unprecedented activist collaboration between African and African American women had occurred in this city in 1960. One of the first conferences to be held in the new nation focused on and gathered together "African Women and Women of African Descent" where not only Murray but also Christian civil rights activist Anna

Arnold Hedgeman participated.[80] Later, Hedgeman would be the only woman on the planning committee for the 1963 March on Washington.

I sat there in Fiifi's borrowed cab a little over fifty years after those activist meetings in the immediate aftermath of Ghana's independence from British colonizers and more than two hundred years after the European transatlantic slave trade legally ended. I stared at the Ghanaian faces in the streets and neighboring cars. My emotional reaction to being in the black African city was intense: relaxing and disorienting at the same time. I moved among them, a socially awkward foreigner with lingering uncertainties about how to achieve my goals. Yet, oddly, the decision to seek out antiviolence activists in Ghana felt just right.

A deeply violent history connected West Africa to the political economies of the United States and Europe featuring the collusion of Christian religion in the sexual assault of black women. Over twelve million Africans crossed the Atlantic to ports in the Americas; millions more started out as cargo on the ships but could not survive the horrific conditions onboard. But in the days before the journey even began on those Christian European slave ships travelling from Africa to the Americas, sexual violence became a part of the torment for some of the enslaved African women and girls.

In the southern Ghana coastal communities of Cape Coast and Elmina, castles remain where African slaves had been kept. From the fifteenth to the eighteenth centuries, European colonists stored their human cargo in separate male and female dungeons. They were loaded directly from the dungeons onto ships bound for Brazil, the Caribbean, and elsewhere in the Americas. Even the architectural design of Elmina castle reminds modern-day tourists of the normalcy of sexual assault for its former slave inhabitants. Elmina was built by the Portuguese in the 1400s, taken over by the Dutch in the 1600s, and acquired by the British in the late 1800s. Daily, crowds that often included African Americans visited Elmina castle's historic dungeons, balconies, and stairways. One narrow back stairway that visitors could climb was reserved for female slaves selected by the resident governor to rape. The enclosed stairway led up to his private bedroom, where each one was sent after being bathed, fed, and temporarily clothed in a dress.

The chapel of the European slave traders stood in the center of that castle. Christian scripture adorned its wall and memorialized the Christian blessing of the violence and human trafficking that took place there. It should be noted that the Europeans exported almost twice as many men as women African slaves.[81] Still, the haunting presence of those raped African women looms in this Euro-American history of human trafficking. Female experiences at the castles prompt other considerations of gender, such as its role in the process by which certain populations came to be captured by Christian European traders. The slaves held at the castles were usually kidnapped and sold to Europeans with the collaboration of some of the local black African men.

In a poignant account of her search for her slave ancestors in Ghana, African American studies scholar Saidiya Hartman gives examples of how the Portuguese collected slaves to bring to Elmina. She describes "girls or women between the ages of ten and twenty" who were sometimes ferried to Elmina from trades made with the king of Benin. Hartman explains how the Portuguese had the "right arm seared with the cross" to mark the slaves as the property of the sixteenth-century king of Portugal.[82] In this form of human torture, the cross of Jesus Christ literally signified white European entitlement to own black African bodies. Religion was a part of the lives of those involved in slave trade in many other ways as well. Indigenous slavery among the Akan in the kingdom of the Asante in West Africa and among North African Muslim communities as well as other African groups was thoroughly enmeshed with the European slave trade business. A significant number of Muslim slaves brought to the Americas from those northern communities retained their Islamic religion for as long as they could.[83]

In some debates among African Americans, the fact that Africans collaborated with Europeans in obtaining slaves to export to the Americas represents an especially problematic aspect of an already painful history.[84] Both dishonesty and honesty about acknowledging this history could potentially impede the building of relationships between contemporary West Africans and African Americans. Some West African male collaborators did play a heinous role in assisting the European slave traders in obtaining Africans for European transatlantic slave trade in human commerce that then fed the system of chattel slavery in the United States for several centuries.

The wealth-generating European slave trade together with the Euro-American-controlled system of U.S. chattel slavery birthed national and racial/ethnic identities as well as the version of the religion to which I now belong. Yet the outward-oriented perspective I sought would be undermined if one's understanding of this West African coastal nation were frozen in the past. The significance of its history must not be limited to its role in shaping my individual cultural identity or to a sentimentalized re-creation as the idyllic motherland of "my people." Living Ghanaian activist women leaders are shaping societal responses to gender-based violence in their contemporary nation. In past centuries, too many duplicitous foreigners had already come to this African land they named the Gold Coast and thereby aided in initiating globalized patterns of anti-black racism. In turns, the Portuguese, Dutch, British, and Germans had invaded the region in search of gold, slaves, colonial territory, and supposed heathens to convert to Christianity. Through military coercion, unscrupulous trading practices, and Christian catechisms they made its peoples and environmental resources a means to their own ends. I wanted to chart a dramatically different path when seeking their knowledge and insights, and I wrestled with the question of how to appropriately ask them to share it with me. In getting started, the interplay between mundane travel challenges and conceptual assumptions about this endeavor was illustrated in a couple of my brief, initial meetings.

Rudimentary logistical arrangements were needed to contact the antiviolence activist leaders. I needed to reach an activist-scholar named Fatimatu N-Eyare Sulemanu. Religion faculty members at the University of Ghana, Legon, with whom I had met when I first arrived, referred me to her. I discovered that I could not make contact with her (literally) because the cell phone I had purchased for my visit did not work, although "Africa" had been listed as a place where the telephone would function. Of course the African continent covers more than eleven million square miles and includes over fifty countries in which over one billion people reside. This routine label description highlighted the weaknesses in utilizing the term *Africa* (a European invention) as a prism for a meaningful cultural understanding of local communities and nations.[85] White supremacist constructions of African homogeneity were embedded in references as commonplace as the very name of the continent on which I was standing.

After giving up on the supposed global cell phone from the United States, I purchased a local Ghanaian phone and card. This easy and inexpensive solution presented other difficulties. Unaccustomed to the number of digits their telephone numbers required, I kept thinking that I needed to add more numbers, or ignore some of them, but which ones? An audiotaped voice informing me that the call could not be placed kept stopping me from getting through. Finally, to my delight, a hurried-sounding woman's voice interrupted the ringing sound with "Hello."

Fatimatu N-Eyare Sulemanu was one of the leaders of the Federation of Muslim Women's Associations in Ghana (FOMWAG). On the telephone, she kindly agreed to see me after I offered a brief introduction of myself and what I was seeking. She did not respond by telling me that she needed to consult her calendar and get back to me, as I would have done if contacted by a stranger in the middle of my busy workday. At her invitation, we met at the Islamic Education Unit later that same day after she had completed a few tasks of her own.

As we spoke, Sulemanu stressed access to education for women and girls and the efficacy of the Federation's structure in allowing strong local participation by women and girls throughout the country. The Federation created a space for victimized women to voice their own concerns about the violence they experienced and to support one another in creating the changes they needed. Space for the emergence of grassroots voices and leadership was a theme she repeated, making emphatic gestures with her dark-brown hands and square-shaped fingertips. Sulemanu had included this point in an essay about religion and gender issues in Ghana that I would later read. "Many Muslim women may not be found at the top of political leadership," she wrote about their nation, "but at the grassroots they are a force to be reckoned with."[86] Local needs of Muslim Ghanaian women shaped the breadth and complexity of the Federation's work.

Rabiatu Ammah, the president of FOMWAG and a senior religious studies scholar at the University of Ghana, Legon, has written extensively on Islam and violence against women in Ghana. In one article, Ammah expresses concern about early marriages forced on girls and the consequent subjugation of the girls in those marital relationships, which sometimes included male violence. She has reported on a Federation grassroots session in a rural area where Muslim girls "complained bitterly that despite having learned a trade and being ready to establish businesses of their own, their families refused to sanction their decision and insisted rather that they should get married first."[87] Ammah argues for an even more vital education and advocacy role on behalf of the rights of women and girls in Ghana's Muslim communities.

In our brief face-to-face time, Sulemanu conveyed the spirit of the Federation's work in a way that my readings about it could not capture. She punctuated her main points with an earnest, "You see, Traci." She explained the necessity of a broad-based sociocultural and political approach. She commented on the kind of grassroots organizing, critiques of sexist interpretations of the Qur'an, and broad social change cumulatively needed to stop marriages forced on girls too young for it, genital circumcision, battering of wives, and rape of girls and women.[88] Her commitment to systemic organizing helped to make plain how much the resilience of gender-based violence depends on the diffuse nature of its many forms and the cultural permissions to which the violence is attached. She described the collective organizing of Muslim women, programs of education and support throughout every age of their life span, and simultaneous multiple points of focus on gender violence.

The religious antiviolence activism Sulemanu and I discussed aroused a sense of exciting possibilities. However, the dominant cultural ethos in the U.S.-American context, where public attitudes and state practices perpetually stigmatize Islam, would likely hamper appreciation for the Ghanaian approach she had shared with me. State surveillance of Muslim faith communities, for instance, and anti-Muslim fear-baiting rhetoric proffered by elected Christian state leaders are pervasive. Between 2010 and 2012, Christian politicians embraced this tactic in state legislative bodies in Oklahoma, Alabama, Arizona, and several other states.[89] They invented a nonexistent threat in their attempts to add legislative bans on the use of Islamic "Sharia law" by officials in their states.[90] As gender justice scholar-activist Ruksana Ayyub has argued about the impacts of the hostile twenty-first-century climate on South Asian American Muslims, they feel "scrutinized and under siege . . . [and] the worst affected were the victims of domestic violence, for it became even more difficult for them to speak out and seek help."[91]

My encounter with Sulemanu created an opportunity to contemplate Muslim women's leadership in Ghana as normative for thinking about community responses to gender violence. It could perhaps crack open the antiviolence conceptual space to which I was accustomed. Contemplation of this Ghanaian perspective decentered the moral limitations imposed by religiopolitical factors ranging from U.S. anti-Muslim state politics to well-intentioned black church and African American mosque crisis responses to abused women. Its interjection of a religiopolitical starting point disconcerting to that moral ethos could provide a refreshing catalyst for conceiving of transformative antiviolence social change.

Admittedly, I still found certain familiar starting points a comforting default position when interculturally exploring religious strategies to end intimate violence against women and girls. I experienced a sense of this security, for example, when I met with a Ghanaian pastor and community leader. I settled back in my chair feeling at ease as she spoke about the Christian religious perspective we shared.

"Last week was Christian home week, and the focus was on rape," explained the Very Rev. Helena Opoku-Sarkodie, Methodist clergy and director of religious programming at the state-run Ghana Broadcasting Corporation (GBC).[92] She described the importance of ongoing education on sexual violence against women and children in the local church where she served as a pastor while also maintaining her position at GBC. Opoku-Sarkodie used her pastoral authority to teach about the problem. In blunt discussions with parents and other adult family members, she explained to them that "people who rape their little girls are people they know. It is okay to trust somebody because the person is supposedly a Christian brother but at the same time, you need to be careful."[93]

As I listened to Opoku-Sarkodie in her GBC office in Accra I was impressed by her calm presence and candid style. She had no trouble matter-of-factly pointing out to her parishioners that what they believed to be true about the trustworthiness of members of their faith community simply because they shared the same faith may not be so. In a sense, she introduced doubt as a healthy preventative measure. For the protection of their children, parents in a Christian faith community must cultivate it. The doubt they needed was not of their God, of course, but in the trustworthiness of those in their own community, those who shared their same religious faith. The perpetrators "may claim to be Christians," Opoku-Sarkodie continued, illustrating for me how she cautioned her parishioners, "but then they come to your house just to win your trust" while targeting your children for abuse.[94]

She addressed the question of how to recognize an authentic, trustworthy Christian. Although her caution emerged from instructive counsel on preventing child sexual abuse, it has wider religious implications and holds potential for spiritually nurturing mindfulness about what it means to seek seclusion and safety in Christian faith communities. Churches ought not be understood as private clubs with memberships open to prescreened safe individuals. Instead, they should be Christian faith spaces that encourage the risk of constructive engagement with others by deliberately, communally, developing antiviolence consciousness and practices.

Opoku-Sarkodie's next point abruptly cut short my initial easy identification with her Christian church leadership and understanding of the challenges she faced. She described how a man in his late sixties had responded to her antirape teaching in the church. In discussions with her, he had explained that he thought that when "you sleep with these underage girls it gives you a free bowel movement."[95] In Opoku-Sarkodie's critical understanding of this situation, the man was "buying into myths" and some of "his contemporaries who do those things do them because they claim that 'it helps you to have free bowel movements.' And at their age, who doesn't want to have free bowel movements?"[96]

I must have looked surprised.

"I know. I thought it was weird. I'd never heard that before," she reassured me.[97]

I cringed inwardly about my initial expression of surprise. I had mistakenly assumed that the man's claims were a version of some African cultural myth that may have sounded strange to me but was probably known to her. I had to confront the possibility that even my own reactions could be influenced by anti-black African racist stereotypes. Racist stereotyping permitted a knee-jerk association of a bizarre rationalization for sexual abuse within the nebulous category of African cultural myths rather than appropriately identifying the bowel movement excuse as another idiosyncratic justification of abuse invented by offenders.

In her church, Opoku-Sarkodie's pastoral response had included hosting forums with doctors who could dispel myths by teaching facts about physiological problems older people may experience with their bowels. She had also taken steps to build a closer rapport with girls in her church that would allow them to feel free to confide in her if they had been abused. She wasted no time on denial or hand-wringing laments about the presence of perpetrators in the faith community. No prudishness on the subject of bowel movements stopped the process of addressing this problem. The church response provided straight talk about the wrongness of some of the older men's views on sex with girl children together with other strategies to change attitudes that normalized assaults. The faith community took responsibility for debunking the perpetrators' justifications for violence. Shame was attached to the perpetrators of the abuse rather than the girls they victimized. Opoku-Sarkodie's response sent a public signal to the entire faith community that the sexual assaults were indefensible while fostering an alternative, community-wide, antiviolence sensibility.

This approach resonates with the vision cast by Ghanaian feminist religious studies scholar Rose Mary Amenga-Etego when she identifies churches as especially well-suited for creating effective interventions against gender-based violence. A helpful corrective for stereotypes outsiders (like me) might impose, the foundational assumptions for Christian intervention incorporate a role for varied, authentic cultural understandings. "The Ghanaian Church, like her counterparts in other parts of Africa, needs to reflect upon issues of violence from their plural religions, traditions, and culture," Amenga-Etego has written. "This calls for serious practical reflections on each situation within specific contexts to arrive at the needed solutions."[98] Churches provide a distinct ethos wherein cultural plurality of their members can be a springboard for holistic and practical responses. Other Ghanaian women activist leaders and scholars I met reiterated her point about the significance of addressing cultural plurality in religion-based responses to the violence against women and girls.

The approaches of Christian Ghanaian activist-leaders prompted questions about whether comparable forms of church intervention were applicable in the United States. Consideration of strategies for simultaneously attending to a plurality of cultural backgrounds, drawing from commonly held Christian faith traditions, and the formation of alliances with Muslim and other non-Christian groups does seem relevant for churches that are serious about addressing widespread sexual abuse of U.S. children by their fathers, brothers, uncles, teachers, neighbors, and others known to them.[99] In each of these roles, the influence of distinctive subcultural mores helps define how children are supposed to respond to adults and matters for effective U.S. religious antiviolence responses, whether in a nondenominational Pentecostal congregation in Georgia, Mormon congregation in Utah, Lutheran Church Missouri Synod congregation in Minnesota, Fellowship of Affirming Ministries congregation in California, or others. Recognition of regional cultural and political differences linked to sectarian ones is as crucial for designing religious responses as attention to the ethnic and national backgrounds of immigrants (one in eight U.S. residents) who are most often publicly identified as representative of cultural plurality in local communities.[100] But treating ethnicity, national origin, and religious beliefs like static, impermeable, and monolithic categories in social policies and analyses addressing sexual abuse and violence can also create obstacles. Even if the existence of cultural pluralities in the United States were categorized as an innate font of resources for the reconceptualization of approaches to antiviolence, these possibilities remain largely unearthed in most local communities, including among church organizations.

Undeniably, the plurality of traditions, religions, and cultures in Ghana differs from the U.S. context. Political strategies to engage them would therefore differ as well. Collectively, the activist perceptions and methods of activists like Sulemanu and Opoku-Sarkodie illustrate for me the kind of momentum for which I have thirsted. These two Ghanaian activist leaders focused on how to release the unique capacities of religious communities to stem gender-based violence by ferreting out misogynist biases in their traditions and practices. They centered their religious communal processes on prevention. The Christian pastor-community leader Opoku-Sarkodie galvanized her faith community through public and family conversations that unabashedly reviewed myths and facts regarding the threat of sexual violence against girls and took steps to help them recognize the threat and prevent it. Unlike some of the more troubling frameworks in some U.S. religious responses to African American women, Ghanaian Christian approaches that I encountered did not rely for its primary means of redress on private counseling or public advice forums in which experts told women victim-survivors to stop being so disempowered. Similarly, the Muslim organizer-scholar Sulemanu focused on antiviolence prevention by coordinating women-led, women/girl-supporting grassroots education networks. Her activist approach fostered engagement with the Qur'an and multiple tough issues of inequality and abuse of girls and women. It did not rely on male religious authorities for permission to address crises of abuse. Participatory approaches of both leaders contributed to my greater understanding of how systemic religious intervention anchored in communal accountability conflicts with the individualistic moral assumptions currently found in some U.S. religious approaches. Not all of the ideas I discussed with Ghanaian leaders were directly relatable to U.S. cultural values—nor did I expect them to be. Ghanaian approaches to intimate violence have little bearing, for instance, on certain major cultural factors linked to U.S. gender-based violence, such as the high U.S. tolerance for gun violence evident in the case of Monica Paul and so many others.

It was the border-crossing element that lay at the heart of how this method of connecting with and listening to particular black West African women leaders spurred systemic thinking about the role of religion and racism in intimate violence against African American women. The stories and context of the Ghanaian leaders provide clues for recognizing that in order to disrupt systemic tolerance of violence trends in the U.S. cultural context, we must consider how contemporary moral patterns are rooted in and were initiated within particular racist historical relations. The global history of anti-black racism and sexual violence against black women fostered in the colonial transatlantic slave trade links the United States and Ghana. That shared history featured Christianity's role in routinizing complacent moral attitudes about sexual violence against black women. At the Elmina slave castle complex, the spatial proximity of the chapel to the bedroom where Christian European traders raped African slave women provides a structural demonstration. It is a symbol of how rape tolerance was compartmentalized within influential foundations of global Christian mission and capitalist commerce. This historical compartmentalization assisted in how sexual violence in the broader U.S.-American society became morally integrated as one, albeit an unfortunate one, among other enculturated habits. Christianity-authorized compartmentalization has therefore actively participated in narrowing moral sensibilities and responses and the formation of a kind of built-in cultural numbness to the harmfulness of the violence.

The content of the encounters with activist-leaders seemed to open up moral space to confront cultural and religious impacts of this legacy and defy the politics of compartmentalization that has served the interests of gender-based violence and anti-black racism so well. The encounters retained a vulnerability to the pitfalls of misread cultural cues or uncomfortable questions still to be probed about who may legitimately identify authentic cultural and religious values in need of transformation. Could cultural outsiders as well as insiders do so?

2

Authentic Cultural Values

Dorcas Coker-Appiah, executive director of the Gender Studies and Human Rights Documentation Centre, told me "it all started" with her involvement in a U.N. meeting on human rights in Vienna in the 1990s.[1] She made it clear to me that she needed to begin our conversation by explaining the origins of her current antiviolence work. Excited to meet Coker-Appiah in her office in Accra, Ghana, I sat across from her fidgeting with my gadgets and notebook. Each time I had asked local advocates and scholars working on gender-based violence for suggestions of leaders in Ghana I should meet, she had repeatedly come up as a key "auntie" of the movement. With papers scattered on her desk, a pen in her hand, and a blinking cursor paused in the middle of a document on her computer screen, she looked up and studied me, peering over the top of her glasses. She was obviously busy, but her composed, attentive demeanor conveyed a genuine interest in my visit. The NGO chief administrator smiled, extended her hand, and offered a warm and reassuring greeting.

Christian Ghanaian activists like Coker-Appiah negotiate certain claims about what constitutes authentic and inauthentic expressions of cultural values, including religion. These competing notions arise in the context of activist efforts to stop two different forms of heterosexual sexual coercion of women and girls, one related to domestic violence and one related to indigenous religious practices. Comments by activist leaders elicit possible comparisons with the violence women and girls face in U.S.-American communities and how cultural and religious claims can impede attention to it. The details of my interactions with these leaders illustrate the methodological impossibility of separating what is learned from how learning occurs. My narrative account of these meetings carries forward a steady drumbeat of discomfiting tensions. They inevitably surround a process of taking in new knowledge about antiviolence strategies while one is displaced from what is culturally familiar.

Coker-Appiah's work was significant in helping to lay the groundwork for passage of Ghana's 2007 domestic violence bill. "I'm a lawyer by profession and I'm a member of the International Federation of Women Lawyers," Coker-Appiah told me.[2] Her vocational identity holds a deeply rooted sense of international solidarity on issues of gender and social change—connections that drew her to her Gender Centre leadership role. During our meeting, she recounted her participation in women's rights activism in U.N. forums during the 1990s, which catapulted the feminist activist drive for international recognition of violence against women as a human rights violation.

The United Nations held its first world conference on women in Mexico in 1975, followed by Copenhagen in 1980, Nairobi in 1985, and Beijing in 1995. The international community's concern with legal protections addressing violence against women slowly evolved during this period. The U.N. General Assembly passed the Convention on the Elimination of All Forms of Discrimination Against Women (CEDAW) in 1979, but it contained no specific reference to violence against women. [3] In 1993, the General Assembly adopted the Declaration on the Elimination of Violence Against Women (DEVAW) and named three types of violence against women as specific areas of accountability for member states: violence in the family, communal violence, and state-perpetrated violence.[4] Through these international arenas, activists had succeeded in transforming the issue of domestic violence against women from a private, individualistic concern into a matter of international law. Most U.N. member states have pledged their support for these declarations. Ghana has been a participating, ratifying nation since 1986. Although U.N. declarations do not hold the power of sanctions, they still do important policy work, as South African human rights legal theorist Bonita Meyersfeld has explained, by requiring states "to report on the status of women's rights in their country."[5] As with most U.N. human rights initiatives, unfortunately, the United States has steadfastly refused to sign any declaration on the elimination of violence against women. U.S.-American political leaders have recoiled from participation in CEDAW, citing supposed U.S. exceptionalism from the gender violence problems with which the convention is concerned as well as a purported threat to U.S. sovereignty and U.S. cultural values related to family and motherhood.[6] In one of many explicit appeals by national leaders to defend

U.S. culture from the threat of CEDAW, a powerful U.S. senator, chair of its Foreign Relations Committee, Jesse Helms, entered the fray. Helms charged during a public debate about CEDAW's ratification in 2000 that it could even bring about "abolishment of Mother's Day" in the United States.[7]

Filled with inspiration after attending the 1990s global forums, Coker-Appiah amended the registration form at her legal clinic in Ghana. Together with her colleagues they decided to add "just a simple question that said, 'Are you ever beaten by your spouse or your partner?' And then I became really astonished at the answers that we were receiving," she said. The women's responses confirmed the widespread existence of domestic violence. It was just the beginning of the meticulous documentation of the problem by Coker-Appiah and her team. They conducted a nationwide research project on domestic violence and published the results.[8]

The research team's strategy comprehensively engaged society—from state agency bureaucrats to local tribal leaders—as a means of confronting the conjoined realms of culture and politics. After conducting the national research study, the Gender Centre also undertook a pilot program that involved police training and sensitization together with community discussions on the root causes of the violence. They waded into topics like patriarchy and polygyny. The more she spoke about the high level of community involvement the research demanded, the more obvious its galvanizing impact across local communities became. When I asked her about it, she told me that they had, of course, met resistance. According to Coker-Appiah, some local community leaders who were "in denial as to the existence of the problem" would "say 'Oh, this is not a problem for us. This is a problem that you educated women want to invent.'" As she made this last comment, unwavering determination poured out through her words and manner. As I listened, I could not help wanting to absorb it.

Coker-Appiah had accepted the challenge of proving what she knew to be true about the presence of the violence. As a consequence, she had to defend herself against the charge that her formal education transformed her into a woman who made up stories about her community. By referring to her as one of those "educated women," her critics linked her to an entire class of women they saw as manufacturing problems that did not exist. Her account of this experience enables our recognition of how the creation of new gender myths could serve as a tool in upholding the violence. New, discrediting myths about women activist leaders who tried to end the violence held in place old myths about its nonexistence as a problem. If one was kept busy with justifying what kind of woman one was to convince critics of one's trustworthiness it distracted from the work of trying to reveal the truth about how often women and girls were sexually and physically hurt by trusted family members.

Coker-Appiah lost neither her sense of humor nor her focus as she described her conversations with opponents. When advocating for the passage of the domestic violence bill, she would ask her opponents: "Would you allow something like this to happen to your daughter or sister?" After pausing to reflect on that point, she explained, many of their attitudes shifted. "Once you get them to think about how it's something that could happen to somebody who is close to them—not their wife. Their wife is not close to them," she remarked half-jokingly and then chuckled. My laugh of agreement came out in an awkward snort. I related to her humor through my familiarity with U.S.-American pop-culture stereotypes of heterosexual wives as the "old ball and chain" or "henpecking nags" where emotional distance from one's wife was, half-jokingly, seen as crucial for a husband's maintenance of sanity in heterosexual marriage. The moment was also a reminder that the kind of ironic humor Coker-Appiah demonstrated in talking with me could be an effective cultural tool in thwarting the normalcy of the violence by poking fun at the attitudes that upheld it. Humor often also played a crucial part in preserving the sanity and stamina of antiviolence activists as well.

"So, the long and short of it is," Coker-Appiah said, underscoring with her tone the end of both her description and the time she had for meeting with me, "it took us six years to get that bill passed."

Later, I had a chance to gather another perspective on this work from Audrey Gadzekpo, a scholar-activist School of Communications professor at the University of Ghana, Legon. I learned more about the long journey activists had traveled during their final push to get the domestic violence bill passed. Gadzekpo had been another active member of the coalition that worked to get it passed. Marital rape had been one of the most contentious issues the coalition's opposition raised.[9] Gadzekpo described how one political opponent in the government—the Minister for Women and Children's Affairs, who happened to be a woman—referred to the bill's criminalization of marital rape as one of the "non-Ghanaian cultural aspects of the bill."[10] The public uproar surrounding the issue of marital rape became one of "the toughest things to deal with," Gadzekpo confided.

Gadzekpo and I met in her spacious and comfortable campus office. She offered me a bottle of water from her mini-refrigerator. As I glanced inside the refrigerator when she reached for a bottle for herself it looked like I would be rudely taking her last one, I declined, saying, "No thank you." "Are you sure?" she encouraged. Before she sipped hers, she placed the other bottle near me, hoping I would change my mind. I could not have foreseen that later, when I returned home, I would regret my seemingly banal response: "No, I'm fine, thank you. Please go on. What happened?"

Continuing, Gadzekpo explained how the news media had helped inflame an already politically tense situation. "There was never a clause in there [the bill] on marital rape. What was in there," she contended, was the assertion "that it was important in the context of the bill to repeal a portion of our penal code that allowed for [sexual] force within the context of marriage." Grimacing with displeasure as she relived the turmoil, she said that "the media decided there was a 'marital rape clause'" and their repetition of that phrase created "a certain tone of debate" that was particularly acrimonious.

The debate converged around the issue of what constituted cultural authenticity. In a later analysis, Ghanaian feminist scholar A. Adomako Ampofo described the public comment Gadzekpo had mentioned to me by the Minister for Women and Children's Affairs.[11] "By constructing the issue in cultural terms," Ampofo criticized, "she [the government minister] appealed to essentialist notions of so-called 'authentic' and 'pure' African identities, reducing a discussion about women's well-being, indeed women's very lives, to one of cultural relativism."[12]

I heard yet another perspective when this subject came up in a much later discussion I had with a pioneering Christian Ghanaian feminist religion scholar-activist, Mercy Amba Oduyoye, who had been present at many meetings surrounding passage of the bill.[13] In her view, the assertion that there was no such thing as marital rape in authentic Ghanaian cultural traditions was false. "I told opponents," Oduyoye said, with the same ire she described having felt during that confrontation surfacing in her tone, "of course this is a problem that has been known in our culture. There is even a word for marital rape in Twi, 'mmonnaa,' that when translated into English means: 'jumping on a sleeping woman to have sex with her' (woman equals wife). There are even specific sanctions against it. If it occurred, the wife was to report it to her family or to the [tribal] queen mother." Oduyoye's point demonstrated an additional critical perspective on incorporating indigenous cultural traditions besides merely rejecting its sexist components that supported the violence. In Oduyoye's approach, cultural tradition could sometimes be invoked as a powerful antiviolence rebuttal to certain opponents who claimed to be the exclusive guardians of authentic cultural practices.

Questions of truth, Ghanaian cultural self-expression, and gender violence swirled around each other at the core of those marital rape debates. To listen and ultimately learn from the experience of Ghanaian scholar-activists requires a grasp of what was at stake in these interlocked issues. Yet, as a non-Ghanaian U.S.-American outsider, I had to acknowledge my inability to ascertain what kind of public policy directly concerned with sexual coercion in marriage could faithfully represent Ghanaian cultural traditions. When I had pressed her on how the contents of the Ghanaian legislature's bill could possibly be "non-Ghanaian," Gadzekpo explained further.

Some political opponents argued that if the domestic violence bill specifically outlawed marital rape, it would "lead to the breakdown of families because, women, who didn't want to have sex, could then just claim that their husbands had raped them."[14] In this logic, wives were assumed to be liars. For some opponents, upholding "authentic" Ghanaian culture seemed to require the assumption that wives could not be trusted to be truthful about rape by their husbands. Like the "educated women" that critics of Coker-Appiah had referenced, the veracity of wives was suspect.

During what Gadzekpo called "a long hard fight," she too had advocated passage of the domestic violence legislation. Her comments were instructive on the contested cultural claims related to a married woman's right to tell her husband "when she wants to have sex" and presumably refuse him when she does not, without fearing he might force her to submit to his desire. They highlighted the benefits of open public discussion on sexual violence and sexual consent within heterosexual marriage. Such a public discussion could provide an opportunity to examine the meaning of consent—what it looks and sounds like—within heterosexual marriage. Outlawing marital rape meant confronting what was for some a culturally acceptable definition of marriage as a site of unquestioned male heterosexual sexual privilege where husbands can coerce wives into sexual relations. Opponents of the bill were apparently threatened by the idea that would enforce, instead, a view of heterosexual marriage as defined by an egalitarian sexual relationship between both the male and female partners.

Activist leader and attorney Angela Dwamena-Aboagye explained to me that proponents of the bill faced an uphill battle against the idea that "a woman who has agreed to be married can't say when she wants to have sex."[15] When I met with her in Accra, Dwamena-Aboagye was director of the Ark Foundation, a major service and advocacy organization that focuses on violence against women and children in Ghana.[16] Through this organization, she had been a strong proponent of fostering a coordinated community response toward ending gender-based violence. The organization worked hard at antiviolence education with local opinion makers, especially church pastors to whom so many victimized women initially turn after experiencing abuse. As she explained to me, "the church is powerful" in Ghana, and "most women will listen to what their pastors say."[17] Alongside their training efforts, the Ark Foundation was dedicated to implementing and monitoring the bill's provisions in the aftermath of its passage. As we spoke about the relationship between local cultural traditions and domestic violence, Dwamena-Aboagye expressed optimism about the extent to which real antiviolence change, albeit gradual, was taking place.

The deep spiritual roots of her Christian commitment helped propel the ongoing leadership that continuation of this forward momentum required of her: "I take a lot of comfort from knowing that God wants me to do it. And so at the end of the day no matter how frustrating it is, I comfort myself with a lot of scripture."[18] Her frustration stemmed, in part, from some pastors she knew utilizing that same Christian scripture to convince abused wives to return home and submit to their abusive husbands. Instead of letting herself be stalled by the conundrum of how these religious leaders could use the Christian Bible she so cherished as a tool of such harm for the population whose violent victimization she sought to stop, there appeared to be a seamless correlation for her. Her own readings of Christian scripture formed an energizing resource to counter their endangering advice as well as other cultural forces fueling the violence against women and girls.

The Ark Foundation, which Dwamena-Aboagye helped found in the late 1990s, established the first shelter for battered women in Ghana. I found this pioneering achievement deeply inspirational and hoped to meet and learn from its staff members. When I asked if the shelter was located in Accra, she told me in a firm but friendly tone, "We don't disclose the exact location, I'm sure you know why." I nodded vigorously. Of course I was familiar with such safety precautions. I had previously served on a board of directors of a shelter in the United States. I felt embarrassed about my mistake, and wished I could delete it from our interactions. I worried that it may have appeared to her as if I disregarded the safety of Ghanaian battered women. She seemed unperturbed, however, spent additional hours talking with me, and recommended other leaders I might contact in the city. I discovered that sometimes it is possible to be intent upon listening for what one does not know, to strive to be open to the disconcerting accompanying effects of unfamiliarity while listening, but in the process, unintentionally, lose track of what one knows quite well. Doing so, again inadvertently, can undermine the integrity of the woman-affirming values driving the very project of intercultural listening to antiviolence strategies.

Lessons on the role of religion and culture instructively echoed off each other throughout my conversations on heterosexual marital violence in Ghana. When I had been in her office, Gadzekpo had pointed to several underlying cultural assumptions in the rhetoric of their public debates on marital rape. When referring to a common cultural view of a man as head of the household with certain claims on a woman, including sex whether she liked it or not, Gadzekpo stressed the role of religion in shaping that view. With a deliberate cadence, she remarked, "I know that our cultures have been complicated by our colonial history and Christianization."[19] As she stressed the plural form when she referred to Ghanaian cultures, it seemed important to her that I recognize the complex multiplicity of cultural identities in Ghana. European colonial Christianity and U.S. missionary Christianity had too often taught a monolithic notion of "African culture" and posited it as synonymous with backwardness in need of Christianization and civilizing European and U.S. forms of education.

For Gadzekpo, the specific cultural context of attitudes about gender and marriage offered an avenue for crafting resistance to the gender violence. In an article on antiviolence activism, she had argued for more investigation of how their experience in Ghana under British colonial rule had "reinforced notions of female subjugation and the acceptance of violence against women and children."[20] From her vantage point as both scholar and activist, Gadzekpo saw the need to confront the damage that the legacy of (the white racism of) colonialism had wrought through its (Christianized) teachings affirming sexist gender relations. Not an exercise in merely assessing the impact of prior historical conditions, the primary focus should be on dismantling multiply rooted cultural patterns that have supported and continue to allow male-perpetrated intimate violence against women and girls.

Gadzekpo's caution has wide implications. The cultural positioning of formerly colonized nations demands scrutiny even within such hardwon human rights efforts as CEDAW (U.N. Convention on the Elimination of All Forms of Discrimination Against Women). As U.S. cultural anthropologist Sally Engle Merry argues, with its references to harmful cultural practices, the declaration could reproduce historic colonial paternalisms in seeking "to move ethnically defined subjects into the realm of rights-bearing modernity."[21] She points out the political understandings that may infuse such documents where "modernity defines what counts as tradition" and a binary distinction is created such that "these terms subtly juxtapose modernity with savagery and locate culture in the domain of the latter and civilization in the former."[22] Similarly, in most Western-dominated worldviews, Christian religious traditions could also escape a primary association with harmful cultural practices.

Christianity has been equated with civilized modernity in spite of its teachings on rape. Christian morality heralded in the colonial project of civilizing Africans incorporates scriptural messages with highly problematic views on gender and intimate violence. Biblical scriptures contain metaphoric images of God as a husband abusively punishing his adulterous wife in a manner that included sexual humiliation and ownership (Hosea 2).[23] Scriptural commentary on rape can be found within the cultural imprint of European Christian traditions that were not only complicit in colonial paternalisms in Africa but also foundational for U.S. Christian theologies. There is a long history, for instance, of ancient and medieval scriptural interpreters who offered guidance on the topic of a husband allowing other men to rape his wife in commentaries on Judges 19.[24] Some medieval Christian leaders theologically justified the willingness of the husband in this passage to subject his wife to a gang rape so brutal that it resulted in her death by depicting her as an adulterous sinner deserving of such punishment.[25] Here, the wife was deemed more than suspect. This medieval interpretation of scripture labeled her as guilty of being a sexual cheat without any evidence in the actual text. Christians must not leave uninterrogated this kind of long-standing history of Christian traditions sanctioning a husband's patriarchal rights to sexually abuse his wife or allow other men to do so. A critical focus by Christian leaders about Christian sanctions for this form of gender-based violence (heterosexual rape of wives) might help undermine covertly racialized narratives about an exclusively civilizing and modernizing impact that Western European Christian cultural influences brought to Africa as well as the Americas.

Eventually, the reference to marital rape in Ghana's domestic violence bill was dropped to ensure its passage. Though they did not withdraw their support for the amended bill, advocates did register their disagreement with this deletion. In an open letter protesting this change in the legislation, they pointed out the nineteenth-century origins in British colonial rule and common law of the so-called marital rape clause in Ghanaian criminal codes.[26] Coalition members declared that "Ghanaian women have come too far to be tied to the dictates of a colonial relic."[27] With this strategy, the activists named the dilemma of having to negotiate a white racist European colonial past as an obstacle to women's freedom. And they simultaneously leveraged the public's disdain for that past as a tool to support the legislative action they sought for stopping the violence against women. The objectionable wording in the penal code that allowed marital rape was removed less than a year later in an unrelated legislative process updating the penal code.[28]

When I left Gadzekpo's office, I paused, perching on a low concrete wall. Noticing ordinary campus spaces, including the university bookstore, library, dormitories, and department offices, was relaxing, like the embrace of an old friend. Then, my glance fell warily on one of the ever-present Ghanaian lizards puttering around next to me and I quickly stood. The small lizards were not harmful. But I decided to continue to reflect on some of the questions raised by my meetings by walking around instead of sitting down, even though it was a blazing-hot sub-Saharan day. The analyses Ghanaian activist leaders had offered me about national debates on whether tolerance of male coerced sexual intercourse in heterosexual marriage was authentically part of Ghanaian cultures prompted my further reflection on the U.S. cultural context and my cultural position as listener.

The activist women leaders I had encountered thus far leveled their cultural self-critiques with ease. Their approach produced a longing in me for similarly intense public discussions in the United States on the topic of rape within heterosexual marriage. Public debate about gender roles, violence, and sexual morality was apparently a crucial step toward developing wider consensus on moving forward on comprehensive, nationwide legislative change to address this form of sexual violence. Their debates provoked questions about how cultural values ought to inform U.S. federal policy outlawing sexual violence against women within heterosexual marriages. Like its Ghanaian counterpart, U.S. law is rooted in British common law, and the marital rape exemption in both countries can be traced back to Sir William Hale's 1736 declaration "the husband cannot be guilty of a rape committed by himself upon his lawful wife, for by their mutual matrimonial consent and contract the wife hath given up herself in this kind unto her husband, which she cannot retract."[29] Current laws regulating marital rape in the United States vary from state to state. Some do not distinguish between marital rape and nonmarital rape. Others allow for the prosecution of marital rape but only under limited circumstances or with extra requirements imposed on the victim-survivors, such as shorter time limits for reporting than were required of those victimized by stranger rape or acquaintance rape.[30] As legal theorist Jessica Klarfeld explains, "even in states that do not have these increased requirements, successful prosecution of marital rape cases is still extremely difficult."[31] The moral message sent by these uneven regulations of marital rape in the U.S.-American context seems to be that marital rape can be tolerated under certain circumstances.

The Ghanaian activist context sparked consideration of the particular question of how one might identify authentic U.S. cultural values linked to marital rape and confront them in order to stop the assaults from occurring. In a discussion of inadequate Christian pastoral responses to marital rape, U.S. feminist, religion scholar Carol Adams begins with the role of transnational cultural mores. She cites differing responses to an anthropological account of supposedly tolerable amounts of violence including the rape of women in a remote South American village. Adams compares the responses they received to that study with U.S. concern for the problem of marital rape and argues "that this disparity in interpretation—in which some people minimize the significance of violence while others see sanctioned cultural violence—is true for our culture as well."[32] What are the current, authentic, and "sanctioning" U.S. cultural values about a husband's right to have sexual intercourse with his wife regardless of her wishes? What are inauthentic ones? How should a range of transnational immigrant cultural realities related to marital rape be incorporated into whatever understandings are seen as authentic U.S. cultural values?[33] What kinds of cultural myths prop up the inconsistent state-by-state regulations of marital rape or disregard for such inconsistency? In our religiously plural but Christian-dominated society, what about Christian religious teachings and practices related to gender within our history? How might chattel slavery and colonization of Indigenous peoples be culpable within enduring cultural patterns that contribute to the permissibility of heterosexual marital rape?

The rhetoric contained in highly publicized U.S. debates in the late twentieth and early twenty-first centuries about marriage rights has subtly reinforced the permissibility of heterosexual marital sexual violence. Harsh exchanges have taken place about what should be considered a culturally appropriate and morally exemplary definition of marriage in an array of political and media venues. Although rape was certainly not mentioned in these debates, heterosexual sexuality and rigid oppositional gender roles are at the heart of the repeated spurious appeals made by some to cross-cultural or transhistorical cultural norms in the true definition of marriage. Starting in the late 1990s, state legislators and courts in the United States became embroiled in fierce struggles over same-sex marriage. During that time, twenty-nine states passed state constitutional amendments and six states banned same-sex marriages. Thus 70 percent of the nation had for over two decades focused considerable political energy and financial resources on marriage laws.[34] Religion had certainly been present in almost all of those cultural debates.[35] The views of homophobic Christians—politicians and church leaders—frequently received media attention when those state laws were enacted.[36] The maintenance of patriarchal authority through heterosexual marriage could be heard in some public claims about supposedly authentic traditions of marriage they sought to preserve. For example, the *Washington Post* noted that one African American former civil rights leader and current urban pastor opposed same-sex marriage and advocated for only heterosexual marriages in black communities: "Don't tell my young women that they do not need a man."[37] Such assertions diverted concern for young black women's primary entitlement to safety and autonomy. Furthermore, the insistence of Christian anti-gay rights' activists that the moral, Godly, and legal understanding of a marital relationship rests fundamentally upon the couple's heterosexuality minimizes the suffering of those U.S. wives whose husbands have physically battered, emotionally abused, raped, or murdered them. Assertions of the intrinsic virtuousness of sexuality within marriage as vested in its heterosexuality, rather than the egalitarian, loving relations of a couple, protect patriarchal privileges of husbands that include marital rape.

In Ghana, serious public discussion about sexual coercion within heterosexual marriage occurred in the period prior to enactment of their domestic violence law. These conversations included an array of perspectives on whether or not their cultural values supported it. Opponents of the proposed law struggled with women's rights activists over how national legislation should address this form of rape. I did not agree with the Ghanaian legislature's decision to exclude a prohibition of it from the Ghanaian domestic violence bill. But the neglectful treatment in my U.S. national context of this form of gender-based violence in heterosexual marriages enabled appreciation of the significance of even instigating a public dialogue on it.

While striving to learn from the work of these gutsy Ghanaian women activist leaders, conversations about their public debates on marital rape made me especially cognizant of being a cultural outsider. The process required some filtering of the information I was learning through my U.S. so-called developed-nation cultural lens. I wanted to convey insights from my encounters with these activists with U.S. audiences. Problematically, skewed popular perceptions of Africans often cloud the U.S. lens when receiving information about Africa.[38] U.S. mass media news reports about African nations can reinforce a sense of U.S. superiority in the public mind with coverage that tends to feature failed states devolving into violent political chaos, dire health epidemics, or natural disasters that permanently destabilize the lives of its residents.[39] Hollywood adds to this impression with popular fictional films that with few exceptions depict everyday African life as solely focused on contending with cruel dictators who wantonly torture and kill their citizens, genocides motivated by tribal animosities, and devastating civil wars exacerbated by the struggle to obtain valuable natural resources.[40] Images of the haunted eyes and emaciated bodies of black African babies also bombard audiences in Christian charity appeals carried on U.S. television and other venues. For casual observers, the African continent appears to be an undifferentiated mass of wall-to-wall sad, malnourished, orphaned black children. To share certain aspects of what I was learning in Ghana could possibly foster distorted views of Africans too. I had to consider whether it was best to omit any statements I had heard about how marital rape was a problem rooted in Ghanaian cultures, albeit deeply European colonial and missionary Christianity influenced cultures. If the recounting of their political battles over marital rape could be used to add further support for racist stereotyping of black Africans and inaccurate generalizations, it would be a shameful betrayal of the leaders I had met.

Taking a break from reflecting on my meetings, I lined up to have lunch at the university's cafeteria. Students seated at tables were eating a range of foods available for purchase, including chicken, rice, soup, and fufu (a dietary staple in this region of Africa made by vigorously pounding starchy vegetables to a doughy consistency). Not an adventurous eater, I chose plain rice and fried plantains. When trying to follow the route of other diners in picking up utensils, I was not sure if I pulled my fork from the basin that held clean ones or soiled ones and did not want to ask.

After sitting down, I began talking with a friendly young student across from me. As my fork pushed the food around, I noticed she was eating her lunch of fufu with her fingers. I considered imitating this common practice but decided against it. We had an animated chat about her university studies, and I shared a little about myself. She gave a patient, knowing nod when I informed her that I was a new visitor in the country. My U.S.-American-accented English had long since given me away.

"You do not like our food?" she finally blurted out after watching the aimless motion of my fork scattering food on my plate. "Oh, you see my, I," my unconvincing response began, "my stomach is a little upset." This was partly true. Later, I imagined the disapproval of surrounding students in the crowded dining hall as I wastefully disposed of my food. In reality, they were too preoccupied with eating their own lunches and chatting with friends to notice me. I purchased a soda and quickly exited, keeping my head down and eyes averted. The next meal would work out better, I thought to myself, dialing Fiifi to ask him to please come pick me up at the university.

Listening involved far more than opening my mind to comprehend the words Ghanaian activist leaders spoke. More active listening was required. Only a definitive breakthrough, cracking deep layers of psychic bias tied to what was familiar to me, could achieve openness to the plurality of cultures and multiple roles of religion the activists had described. In short, the task of transforming arrogance, ignorance, and apprehension into engaged, unguarded listening would involve a radical surrendering and expansion of known social categories and perceptions. It demanded a far more wrenching process than merely contemplating fresh ideas about community responses to gender-based violence.

Undoing Cultural Support for Violence

We retraced our route a few times, but when Fiifi and I could not find the office of International Needs Ghana, I worried about arriving late or missing my appointment altogether. When driving to meetings, confusion frequently arose about the correct street address. I never received directions that resembled what I expected—there was no "turn left on Main Street, after three blocks turn right on College Avenue." Information supplied by the leaders with whom I had an appointment or their support staff was usually somewhat general such as "we're near Ridge Hospital and Scripture Union block." When I relayed this limited information to Fiifi, his patience baffled me. Often, he would take the telephone for additional instructions. Sometimes, we continued to circle around and had to call back. Fiifi spoke to the person assisting us in one of the many local languages (usually Twi, I think). I could not help with the new directions unless he translated, further delaying us. This trial-and-error process required me to trust that we would eventually arrive where we wanted to go—not unlike my overall quest.

Finally having arrived at the International Needs Ghana office, I sat down, relieved. Posters on the walls grabbed my attention. Smartly for-mulated and professionally designed, they surrounded me on all sides with a variety of messages about the urgency of opposing intimate vio-lence. I stood to get a closer look. Offered in a series of cartoon sketches, the first frame of one poster featured a nicely dressed adult black woman sitting at a desk. She was taking money from a leering black man in sunglasses with his pants slipping down in back, low enough to allow his white underwear to peek into view. "How much am I paying for the little girl?" he asked, leaving no doubt about what he was purchasing. A girl could be seen in a back room seated on a bed apparently clothed in only a bed sheet. In a later frame, the woman was looking glum be-hind gray prison bars that she clasped with both hands. A tall, authorita-tive male police officer stood nearby. All of the characters were drawn with beautiful copper-brown skin. The poster's bold print underscored the point to the viewer: "Children Are Not Sex Objects. Don't Abuse Their Rights." Why, I wondered while studying it, had the culpability of an adult woman collaborator been so highlighted in a crime of male-perpetrated sexual violence? On another poster, the colorful sketches featured a shirtless gleeful black man who seemed to be preparing to sexually assault a fearful small child. Off to the side in the next frame of the poster, the same man was pictured behind prison bars dejectedly sticking his head out between them. "You will go to jail for sexual abuse," the bottom of the poster read. If circulated in the United States, a poster with this image of a black man would likely be received by many in black and brown communities as an incendiary racial slur. Why was it more acceptable here? The poster campaign was a reminder of how certain divergences in the racial histories and politics of each place fundamen-tally tailored public responsiveness to public campaigns about gender violence.

I met with Patience, then head of the gender programs at International Needs Ghana.[41] She greeted me, and I followed her into a conference room where we sat at a large table. In the ensuing conversation, her tenaciousness about confronting tough issues reminded me of Rev. Opoku-Sarkodie. Patience was also a Christian, but her focus on religion was not on Christianity. She had a low-key, gentle style, not to be mistaken for a lack of determination about achieving her goals.

In response to my questions, Patience described how a major aspect of her work at this Christian-based NGO involved the liberation of women who had been enslaved as young girls due to the practices of a non-Christian religion.[42] Some leaders, though not all of them, perpetuated these practices as part of traditional African religious practices centered on the Troxovi.[43] Troxovi shrines were located mainly in the predominantly rural Volta region of Ghana. These shrines also existed in the neighboring countries of Togo and Benin. In Ghana, harmful gender practices of abusing girls and women were officially outlawed in the 1990s but continued covertly afterward in several locales.

Shrines of many differing African Traditional Religions were scattered all over the landscape of rural Ghana, but Troxovi shrines were mainly found among the Ewe people. Before reforms occurred, girls as young as five years old could be given by their families to the priest at a nearby Troxovi shrine to atone for an offense that an adult family member had committed. Besides forced labor without payment, the girls often suffered sexual violence by the priests as they grew up and sometimes bore their children.

Though her focus had not been on religion, when black feminist theorist D. Soyini Madison had written about Patience's liberation work based on extensive participant observations, Madison noted the changes in these Troxovi shrine practices over time. As Madison described, after years of joint reform work by activists and traditionalists, "some of these shrines remain for religious worship, but in several cases, the girls and women are no longer being sequestered or abused. However, there were some areas where Trokosi girls and women were still being violated."[44] Valiant activist efforts had been crucial for generating broad public concern about the enslavement of the girls and women at some of the shrines and helping it be named as a problem that should be stopped.

Improvements had been achieved, but only as a consequence of painstaking negotiations by leaders.

Patience brought considerable "on-the-ground" experience in creating this change. She spoke about her starting assumptions for this interfaith work and carefully outlined some of the nuances. Her manner and words cautioned me against making quick, simplistic judgments. The politics of religion in Ghana sometimes surfaced in a tense rapport between Christians and Traditionalists. Constructively building this rapport had been a delicate process. Negotiations related to the shrines and their treatment of women and girls epitomized an opportunistic moment for animosity to arise between Christians and Traditionalists.[45] Patience explained her foundational view: "There are so many forms of religion, and I just happen to be a Christian. That doesn't mean that I condemn other people's religion. I will not do that. I am a Ghanaian, and I love my culture as a Ghanaian."[46] With this comment, I once again became keenly aware that there were subtleties in what she intended to convey that I could not fully decipher. At the same time, her linkage of nation, religion, and cultures evidenced a provocative and complex texture I wanted to explore. It incorporated a shared Ghanaian communal sensibility that blurred what was regarded as "other people's religion" together with what she claimed as her own culture.

Later I also considered whether the phrase "I am a Ghanaian, and I love my culture as a Ghanaian" tumbled from her thoughts out into the space between us in part because a U.S.-American sat across from her. In that moment, the African in my African Americanness held little salience for either one of us. Her comment embraced her cultural and national identity in a way that seemed most relevant for a conversation about her work with a non-African foreign visitor. She omitted any insider references to those ethnic identities such as Akan, Ewe, or Ga that were so significant in Ghanaian history and politics and mattered in her work with the shrines. Additionally, she might have been so firm in asserting her love for Ghanaian culture in response to local criticism of her group's work from Traditionalists and others in public narratives about authenticity and loyalty that were known to her but unfamiliar to me.[47]

Patience described the conditions of enslaved girls and women at the shrines. The knowledge and intensity she displayed reflected many years of work on their behalf within this minefield of interfaith negotiation. She gave details about the Troxovi tradition as well as the respectful stance required of her to engage it as a Christian leader. Patience's own attitude bore witness to this general stance toward the religion even while she indicated the position of the girls and women caught in an abusive practice she clearly did not respect.

Simple escape from the shrines back to their homes was not a viable option. "Your family will not receive you back," she said, "because you'll bring back the curse onto the family and they will begin to die. So, they want you to be there [in the shrine]. You are serving as a kind of . . . you are there to protect them, spiritually." She did not ridicule the community's beliefs as merely misogynist myths with a destructive impact on women and girls. Patience implored me to take seriously the beneficial intent of the religious practice, explaining how it had become a means for the shrine to enforce a sense of responsibility among community members toward one another. Patience described a religious practice in Ghana where the exchange value of girl children involved restoration of family honor and did not entail the monetary purchase of children. Yet, the details of her ideas and activist leadership provided fertile ground for exploring their connections to how public concern is formulated about other contemporary forms of slavery that are cash-based.

In the United States where the illegal buying and selling of children for sexual exploitation routinely occurs, there are campaigns to try to stop it. In calls for more responsible public attitudes to help eradicate the enslavement of women and girls coerced into sex work, the themes of nation, religion, and race/ethnicity are also present but tied together in a manner quite different from the ways in which Patience had described the traditions of the Troxovi shrines in Ghana. One area of difference lies in the relationship between religion and pride in their nation as expressed in her activism against this form of modern slavery.

Current U.S. public conversations about sex slavery frequently reference the history of the European slave trade of Africans. Government leaders and anti–sex slavery activists alike utilize general public agreement on the immorality of U.S. involvement in the transatlantic slave trade history.[48] In his book *A Call to Action: Women, Religion, Violence, and Power*, former U.S. president Jimmy Carter began his chapter on sex slavery and prostitution by mentioning his own nineteenth-century family history, which includes a great-great-grandfather who owned "several dozen" African Americans in the South and great uncles who fought for the Confederacy. Carter concluded this brief historical account by noting that the cessation of the ravages of the Civil War brought "a sigh of relief from both sides that the time of slavery was over."[49] This is, at best, an overly generous characterization of the Confederate view of slavery at the end of the Civil War, at worst, a complete misrepresentation of the economic practices that the South preserved.[50] This point nevertheless lays the foundation for his central argument condemning the current pervasiveness of slavery involving the sexual exploitation of women and girls. He addresses both domestic and global contexts. The same historical link was also mentioned as the former U.S. president, over ninety years old when the book was released, appeared on a popular television talk show to promote it. He articulated his determined opposition to the global problem of violence against women. But then he claimed, "slavery is a worse problem now than it ever was in the nineteenth century."[51] This claim grossly underestimates the significance of U.S. legal protections that maintained chattel slavery as a bedrock institution of U.S. economic and social life in the nineteenth century.

Former investment banker turned activist Siddharth Kara, a staunch anti-trafficking advocate, declared similarly to Carter that "the time had come to tell this story," in his exposé *Sex Trafficking: Inside the Business of Modern Slavery.*[52] Kara recounted his attempts to interview modern sex slaves. When introducing the section on human trade in the United States, he explained, "individuals from every corner of the world are trafficked to the 'land of the free, and the home of the brave,' where they are treated no better than Africans who arrived on slave ships two centuries ago."[53] For Kara and others the current existence of sex slavery within our nation is a shocking phenomenon when contrasted with the conventional image of U.S.-American culture as a propagator of freedom. In other words, Kara assumed that most people believe that no one in the United States was still treated like those enslaved Africans had been. And, he asserted, it would be appalling for the public to find out that such treatment persisted. A form of religious belief is at play here too.

For U.S. citizens, a tradition of civil religion nurtures worshipful allegiance to an understanding of our nation as imbued with exceptional moral identity. Civil religion construes certain cultural beliefs, behaviors, and institutions as positive contributors to the social order.[54] This should not be confused with other, more traditional forms of world religions. There is, however, some overlap between Protestant Christian religious culture and common narratives of civil religion expressed in the United States. Sociologist Robert Bellah has been one of the strongest proponents of the idea of a deeply embedded U.S. civil religion. Bellah argues that the normative core of American civil religion can be found in statements about this nation being conceived in liberty and dedicated to the equality.[55] He points to such claims in President Abraham Lincoln's Gettysburg Address delivered during the Civil War as a prime example. For scholars like Bellah as well as other believers within the populace, the United States is a place where political freedoms are uniquely cherished.

It is precisely this kind of religiously held conviction that reverberates throughout public discussions on how to address the problem of currently enslaved sex laborers. As one U.S. senator proclaimed in the early twenty-first century, the struggle against sex slavery represents "another war to protect American ideals and principles, a war against an old evil—human trafficking and slavery . . . that this nation fought a bloody war to destroy."[56] Civil religion present in the senator's comments asserts pristine "American ideals and principles." The moral trajectory projected by U.S.-American antislavery narratives steeped in this religiously held belief demands closer examination.

When well-meaning anti–sex slavery advocates seek to garner supporters with reminders of the exceptional ways in which freedom and equality have been valued in the United States, they may be fostering another kind of slavery denial and effectively erasing the significance of centuries of chattel slavery in our history. They reinforce a notion that although slavery occurred here for centuries, it did not reflect our authentic cultural values. Disappearing from this latter narrative (exemplified in the senator's reference to the Civil War) were millions of Americans in eleven states who seceded from the nation and waged war in part to preserve the right to own black slaves as part of their American identity. The "sigh of relief" at the ending of slavery cited by President Carter also serves to illustrate this kind of erasure. It incorporates a specious freedom-loving narrative in which the entire nation—northerners and slave-owning southerners alike—universally came to recognize the immorality of slavery at the end of the Civil War. Arguments that link "human trafficking to transatlantic slavery," as U.S. feminist theorist Julietta Hua observes, make "possible the rewriting of U.S. history of racial discord and exploitation into a national mythology of progress toward pluralism, equality, and liberty."[57]

To ignore resilient historical patterns of racist animus and inequality contravenes the freedom and human flourishing that girls and women currently sexually enslaved in the United States rightfully deserve. Mostly fueled by broadly accepted stereotypes and unfounded fears, several states enacted particularly harsh anti-immigrant policies that augment similar federal initiatives.[58] These policies are likely to continue to plague, for example, trafficked immigrant Latinas even if the women do somehow manage to gain their freedom from the predators who sexually exploit them and economically profit from their labor.[59] The women's race/ethnicity and immigrant status may allow them to be viewed by the public as sacrificable. One qualitative study documenting the experiences of trafficked immigrant women reports on "kick down the door" raids by law enforcement officials, including those who supposedly focus primarily on anti-trafficking rescues.[60] When compared to other women (mostly of Asian and Eastern European descent), Latinas who were discovered in these raids experienced the greatest number of arrests and detention, typically for prostitution, and were very seldom asked if they had been trafficked.[61] These criminalized Latin American women have hybrid African, European, and Native American racial/ethnic heritage as a result of European colonialism. They become captives to racist and xenophobic politics that cultivate dubiousness about their entitlement to both citizens' and human rights.

Patience and I existed within uncannily reversed yet parallel moral universes. In her self-description, love for her Ghanaian nation and culture begat activism to end sexually exploitative religious practices. In the U.S.-American national context, anti–sex slavery advocates often reverently referenced as their inspiration a U.S. civil religion I find wanting. When calling for a critique of newly spawned iterations of what are in fact long-standing racist U.S. values, I urge a counternarrative to many contemporary slave liberators in my context. The national values those liberators championed are problematic precisely because they are riddled with the hypocrisy present within dehumanizing rape-tolerant values from the transatlantic slavery era. These historically rooted U.S. values are implicated in the resilience of current forms of human trafficking and may be found in certain criminalizing official responses to victim-survivors. Racist values obfuscate the vulnerability of the sexually entrapped women and girls, such as those from Mexico and impoverished communities throughout Latin America. But in asserting such a counternarrative, I risk being seen as *failing* to love my nation. I could appear to be guilty of this sacrilege because I deliberately refuse to recognize my nation's cultural values of freedom and equality as the most authentic ones, as so many anti–sex slavery advocates and others touted.

To ensure the freedom of the women trapped at Troxovi shrines in Ghana, Patience and her colleagues had engaged in a slow, deliberate process of building consensus. The liberation they had achieved for thousands of women occurred with hard-won agreements from the families who placed them in the shrines as children, local community leaders, and the priests at the shrines in charge of the girls and women. "What we are advocating for is children," she stated imploringly, "innocent children, being sent to slavery. They have not committed any crime."[62]

Patience and her colleagues provided intensive, long-term therapeutic support as well as vocational training programs for the liberated women. She spoke about how the liberated women testified about the abuse they had endured and how long it took the women to internally understand themselves as free human beings. It was difficult for me to relate to her firm commitment to a stance of respect for the good intentions found in this religious tradition with certain gender practices she opposed. But then, her motivation inhabited an identity space that I could not share: "I am a Ghanaian, and I love my culture as a Ghanaian," she'd said.

Patience's human rights approach represented one among several formulated by leaders in Ghana who believed in holding religion accountable in their activist struggle. Many other leaders there shared that same commitment to a movement for wide-ranging social change to end all forms of gender-based violence. As the Ghanaian Christian feminist religion scholar mentioned above, Mercy Amba Oduyoye, has written, "To a large extent, Christianity and traditional Ghanaian religious cultures support each other in the negative attitudes and practices that harm women. However, we know that if critically appropriated they can become positive forces in women's lives. . . . There is a need for gender and antiviolence activists to engage with, and target religious and opinion leaders, including male and female church leaders and pastors, traditional priests and priestesses, as well as traditional rulers."[63] Oduyoye's analysis aptly encapsulates how the approaches of leaders I had met identified religious leadership and specific cultural understandings as key to ending gender violence. Additionally, a resolute spirit clearly discernable in my encounters with the Ghanaian lawyers, academics, and religious leaders also inhabited the methods they employed. But the exact contours of this spirituality and how to learn from it could not be summarized as succinctly as their methodological emphasis on culture.

This first step of listening to the critical cultural appropriations of the Ghanaian leaders I had met surfaced unexpected implications for the practice of intercultural learning about antiviolence strategies. I had anticipated and found an expanded capacity to gauge cultural dissimilarities underlying U.S. and Ghanaian responses to gender-based violence. Less predictable was how consideration of those differences could shake loose a critical view of U.S. cultural proclivities for passivity about muted political responses to U.S. gender-based violence. The discussions in Ghana demonstrate how certain claims of cultural authenticity can be used to elude systemic forms of antiviolence accountability. For example, learning details of the work of activists like Coker-Appiah casts a spotlight on the U.S. evasion of and fears about being subjected to international accountability. The Ghanaian activist leadership also provokes consideration of which authentic U.S. cultural values contribute to a stubbornly enduring neglect of uniform federal laws outlawing marital rape.

Public assertions by U.S.-American leaders that maintain the sacredness of racially informed narratives of publicly cherished freedom and equality earn the designation of our most authentic U.S. cultural values. However well intentioned, those narratives can augment broad cultural commitments that sanctioned slavery in the past and tolerate it in the present. Repetition of these racialized civil religious beliefs about our core virtuousness impedes the naming of entrenched racist and ethnocentric attitudes that we must confront in the ongoing project of abolishing slavery and sex trafficking. Reiteration of narratives claiming the overriding authenticity of freedom and equality values upholds public recalcitrance about implementing more systemic antislavery interventions. It fashions a U.S. civil religion that can be especially costly for women from Latin America who are trafficked into the United States and coerced into sex work.

My interpersonal experiences in this Ghanaian context also revealed evasions (of new knowledge about foreign culture), erasures (of valuable antiviolence knowledge familiar to me), and fears (of exposing knowledge that invited further racist stereotypes). These evasions, erasures, and fears hovered in and around my one-on-one intercultural exchanges with Ghanaian antiviolence leaders. They undermined possibilities for even contemplating intercultural and transnational solidarity. At the same time, in a helpful way, the pernicious, violence-supporting societal impact of evasions (of systemic protections of heterosexual intimate violence), erasures (of historical knowledge of patriarchal gender patterns in amalgamated cultural legacies), and fears (of educated women) also came to the surface. Deliberate reflection on the antiviolence social change strategies discussed in my encounters with Ghanaian activists usefully unravels these threads.

Religion continually plays a morally authoritative function as it partners with definitions of national and racial/ethnic group identities. This partnering creates a litmus test for what constitutes ethical expressions of gender and sexuality and what upholds supposedly authentic cultural values. The resulting narrow criteria for normative values can hinder religious scrutiny and opposition to gender-based violence. Nevertheless, my meetings with Ghanaian activists also draw attention to religion's capacity to change and adapt. The legacies of a violence-supporting history of colonial Christian morality coexist alongside of contemporary freedom-authorizing moral values in the work of Christian and Muslim women activist leaders for systemic antiviolence measures. There remains a constant struggle to determine how to leverage the powerful capacity of religion to thwart violence rather than hide its harmfulness by normalizing its occurrence within cultural traditions of Ghana, the United States, and elsewhere.

The experiential dynamics of my conversations with leaders in Ghana held more lessons on antiviolence methods. Grateful for the stories they had chosen to share, I took in as much as I could. I had not found all of what I originally sought, but had productively engaged their ideas, courage, and persistence. Active listening proved daunting but crucial for enabling my ability to learn from their imbricated religion-culture-politics approach to ending the violence. The kind of openness that I needed for this learning to be possible required uncomfortable moments of cultural disorientation. Ironically, this destabilization stimulated deeper levels of inquiry about how to incorporate critiques of cultures and religion within activist resistance to intimate violence against women and children. Whether reflecting on Rev. Opoku-Sarkodie's communal confrontation of a perpetrator's myths justifying sex with little girls or the political significance of having public debates about heterosexual marital rape, encounters with culturally and politically unfamiliar strategies were helpfully provocative. The experience of dissonance held potential for unleashing truths that could be deployed for opposing tolerance of the violence.

Unexpected modes of unleashing such truths can open up more recognition of how dangerously misleading it can be to prize only culturally familiar, inwardly directed, religious communal responses. The history of transatlantic slavery that the Ghanaian setting invokes offers a unique counterperspective, particularly for Christians. The specter of the slave castles looms in the background, containing memories in its rooms and compartments that reflect the companionable coexistence of sexual violence and the Christian religion of the European captors. This history contains a painful reminder for U.S. African American Christians—and indeed all other Christians—about the tradition's historic participation in teaching compartmentalized societal values and about the nature of lived Christianity. The history of European and Euro-American enslavement of Africans exposes as mythical any notion of Christian religious space as intrinsically respite space from anti-black white racism that could also be equated with safety from sexual violence for women and girls of African descent. A proven malleability to be formed by such racist violence resides in Christian theology and practices.

Similarly, encounters with contemporary black African women leaders in Ghana possessed a capacity to perhaps deflate any idealized African American notions associating exclusive and authentically black Africana communal space with inherent restorative qualities in response to gender-based violence. The insistent nature of their activism in the black African context of Ghana is a clarifying indicator that such a pristine cultural space does not exist. Vigilant antiviolence activism is still necessary. Moral values bequeathed from colonial British common law (fundamentally influenced by Christianity) that mitigated against, for example, a comprehensive ban on husbands sexually assaulting their wives continue to permeate attitudes in the national politics and cultural landscapes of the United States and Ghana.

The act of entering into discussion with Ghanaian activist women leaders offers guideposts for how to invoke the American-African-European shared slave trade legacy of violence within contemporary antiviolence concepts and strategies. Most U.S. scholars and activists concerned with this history rightly focus on sexual violence against African slave women and their treatment by their captors as objects and property.[64] An added vantage point for analysis of resistance to this legacy emerges when we also make central the views of these contemporary African opponents of gender-based violence. When activist Ghanaian gender justice leaders are recognized as authentic knowledge bearers, decision makers, and interpreters of religious tradition, interactions with them offer a springboard for criticizing racist and religious patterns embedded in U.S. practices related to gender violence. Engagement with their ideas and participatory practices can simultaneously acknowledge and challenge the misogynist morality given expression in colonial European cultural and religious values and commercial slave trade practices. It generates a dissenting moral imperative for intercultural negotiation and critical appropriation of nonviolent gender equality in religious and cultural life and might function as a seedbed for even broader societal changes. But this imperative is perceivable only if religious, legal, and other cultural legacies commodifying women's sexuality and distrusting their witness about male violence are soundly repudiated.

I began the journey home at Accra's bustling Kotoka International Airport. On the other side of the last security checkpoint I hoisted my two heavy pieces of carry-on luggage onto each of my shoulders. Suddenly my legs weakened and wobbled beneath me. My head felt dizzy. I was starting to have trouble taking a normal breath. Thinking that a drink would help, I purchased a soda with the last of my Ghanaian cedis. My shaking hand mainly succeeded in splashing soda on my chin and shirt. The room started to fade into what seemed like a lovely black, moonless night. I sank toward the floor. "I'm sorry. I'm fine," I apologized unnecessarily to strangers who rushed over to assist me. Eventually, some of them, also preparing to depart on my flight, pushed me to the gate in a rolling office chair. I begged a dubious airline staff member to allow me to board.

Much later, I was lying on a thin mattress in the local hospital near my home in New Jersey still stubbornly asserting, "I'm fine, really." I had ended up going directly to the hospital upon my arrival because of a repeat health episode at New York's JFK International Airport. When reviewing my lab test results the doctor at the hospital asked about my intake of liquid and solid nourishment over the past few weeks. I responded with a sullen shrug. It would not have been truthful to suggest that I had consumed little nourishment during my time in Ghana. I had feasted upon the ideas of the leaders with whom I had spoken. As I lay there, I chose to interpret my temporary weakened state as a dramatic somatic recommendation that I incorporate more holistic, embodied sensibilities in any future investigations of activist responses to intimate violence against women and girls.

In the New Jersey hospital, the medical staff quickly restored me to normal hydration. While waiting for additional routine medical tests, I became embroiled in a heated argument with my male nurse, a West African immigrant. It began when I mentioned having returned from Ghana. With a delighted smile that exuded pride in his native region of West Africa, he asked why I had gone. I enthusiastically recounted stories about the women leaders and issues they championed, including an end to marital rape. When he responded, we instantly disagreed. I opposed his claim that intimate violence against women was an innate cultural problem in Africa, albeit a minimal one, that could never be solved. In a pitying tone, he indicated that an African American like me could not possibly have a true understanding of matters such as intimate relations (he avoided the word *rape*) between a husband and wife in Africa. He then began to witness to me about his Christian faith, emphasizing biblical instruction on how God created man as superior to woman. With my last bit of strength, I pushed my body up and leaned forward. I argued against his understanding of Christianity and pointed out how it could support violence against women and girls. "Against mothers, sisters, daughters, nieces," I added for emphasis, my voice louder than appropriate for a hospital. He paused and relented a tiny bit as he mentioned his little daughters at home and his desire for them to be treated well in their marriages to men when they grew up.

I had not consciously chosen to use Coker-Appiah's strategy as I named categories of family members he might feel "close to." Yet it had been an effective way of adding helpful tensions to the subject of appropriate gender relations within authentic Christian faith. I would like to think I had simply internalized the wisdom the leaders had shared with me. Yet Coker-Appiah had described a strategy she employed within her own national-cultural context on another continent. If I was going to borrow it for my discussions with people in the United States such as this nurse, shouldn't I have made some adjustments? I had not anticipated those convoluted dynamics of interethnic black encounters within the U.S. context where the meaning of black Africanness was routinely stereotyped as perpetually morally and socioeconomically wanting and its association with Christianity as morally vindicating. Social rewards and penalties of Christianity that abetted anti-black racist lies about black human moral worth had to be taken into account and confronted. More attention was needed to how to create effective translations from one context to another in pursuit of transnational learning about religion and ending gender-based violence. Moreover, an interrogation of distinctly African diasporic perspectives on crafting antiviolence responses to violence against black women could not result from encounters with black African leaders in Ghana.

My head drooping with fatigue, I mumbled to the nurse who was no longer present, "I'm ready to leave now, must get going."

PART II

Translating Knowledge

Between the United States and Salvador, Bahia, Brazil

3

Vulnerability

Ahead of me, I saw a tall, circular wall. While contently breathing in the mild, warm morning air of Salvador, Brazil, I strolled over to it. A brilliant, sunlit sky rested overhead.

The size and shape of the structure reminded me of an above-ground circular pool that one might see in the backyard of a lower-middle-class U.S. suburb. Except, unlike the perimeter wall of an above-ground pool, this structure was high in the back, low in the front, and about six inches wide. The back half of this round wall rose up almost as tall as I was then sloped downward toward the front where I stood. The front part of the enclosed circular wall stood only about a foot from the ground. Not a recreational space at all, this was a round religious structure made of concrete—its exterior painted a shiny ocean blue, visible from afar. The glossiness of the round wall's bright-blue exterior was matched by its spotless and shining white interior. The sacred floor space in the center was an unpainted, pristine light-gray concrete.

This structure represented part of the religious traditions of Candomblé. I encountered it during my first few hours in the predominantly black South American city of Salvador, where I engaged in daily cultural and language negotiations. They further emphasized the challenge of adequately translating ideas from one context to another and how that matters for conceiving activist transnational understandings that counter gender-based violence. In meetings with activist leaders in Salvador, concern about how women's vulnerability to violence was linked to racial and class stigmas became a repeated theme that represented a touchstone for their advocacy. Several of the leaders had been involved in implementing Brazil's 2006 Maria da Penha gender violence law and other related public policy measures.[1] Their work included outreach education to victimized poor black women, organizing black domestic workers vulnerable to workplace sexual harassment and assaults, promoting enforcement of the law, and participating in grassroots advocacy that enabled victimized women in poor communities to access state services under the provisions of the law.

Each approach I encountered evokes comparisons to related forms of vulnerability for black women victim-survivors in the United States. The gender politics of state intervention were dramatically different, while the racial issues did not seem to be as dissimilar. Yet, verbatim translations between the political or phenotypic racial understandings I brought to Salvador and what I found there frustrate more than clarify the analysis. In addition, a concern for women's vulnerability to violence compels appreciation for human embodiment and holistic, restorative understandings of it when constructing frameworks for gender violence resistance work. My experiential reflections on embodiment in this Brazilian setting encourage consideration of how spiritual and bodily awareness might contribute to that work.

Religious Legacies That Spur Black Women's Activism

The morning I stopped in front of the circular structure, I studied the objects on the floor of the walled-in space. Upon closer inspection, I decided that rather than a backyard swimming pool, the structure bore a stronger resemblance to a miniature ice-skating rink or the concave section of a skateboard park, only with the addition of sharply sloping perimeter walls. I kept trying to translate what I saw into something familiar, as if that would help to explain the structure's significance in its community. A variety of gold, white, and silver vases had been placed all around the inside concrete floor, some containing wild flowers and others empty. The careful arrangement of the vases made it obvious that this was a holy, sacramental space.

"It represents a boat," Sandra dos Santos explained in Brazilian Portuguese.[2] She was an Afro-Brazilian organizer with a state-sponsored community outreach project to local black women, part of the implementation of the Maria da Penha Law. As in Ghana, I had come in the wake of the passage of sweeping national legislation on gender-based violence. But unlike in Ghana, here in Brazil I met with leaders who were focused on implementation and assessment a few years after this groundbreaking law had been enacted.

"It commemorates the African women who brought the religion," Sandra remarked, as I continued to stare at the structure.[3] My friend and colleague from the United States, Nessette, translated Sandra's Brazilian Portuguese for me. Nessette was an Afro-Puerto Rican queer studies and anthropology scholar from New York City. The work of translation and networking that she and Salvadoran activist and community organizer Erica Rocha provided made it possible for me to meet with Sandra and many other black women leaders in the region. The city included vibrant governmental and nongovernmental activist leaders concerned with varying forms of gender justice policies. Enactment of the 2006 Maria da Penha Law was largely due to the strength of grassroots feminist activist efforts. The law and its related governmental infrastructure represented one of the most comprehensive national strategies to address violence against women in the Americas.[4] Sandra's spiritual and work commitments exemplified the unique combination of how issues of race and religion mattered in grassroots activism to ensure implementation.

As Sandra spoke, we stood together on the grounds of the *terreiro* (temple) of Da Casa Branca (also known as Ilê Axé Iyá Nassô Oká), which is located in Salvador, a northeastern port and capital city of the state of Bahia, Brazil. Bahia is one of the largest states within Brazil as well as a major cultural center for Afro-Brazilian life, populated by a higher percentage of blacks than any other state in the nation. This *terreiro* to which Sandra belonged was one of the many Candomblé community houses scattered throughout the city.[5] Candomblé is an African-based religion widely practiced in Salvador that often attracts large crowds of local working-class and poor people to its ceremonies. Casa Branca was considered to be the first Candomblé *terreiro* in Brazil, established in the nineteenth century, and according to their tradition, three African women were its founders.[6]

Candomblé is a West and Central African Yoruba–based religious tradition, also influenced by elements of popular Catholicism, Kardecist Spiritism, and ritual practices of some of the Native peoples of Brazil. In her study of the nineteenth-century origins of Candomblé in Bahia, U.S.-based historian of Afro-Atlantic religions Rachel Harding points out that a wide range of indigenous African traditions figured in its formation. The Vodun of the Dahomean Jejes, the Inquice and ancestor traditions of the Congo-Angola Bantus, "and even, evidence suggests," Harding wrote, "some aspects of the Islam of the Hausas, Yorubas, and other Sudanese Muslims" have contributed to the religion's contemporary iteration.[7]

The diverse origins of Candomblé's religious tradition reflect the colonial and transatlantic slave-trade history of the Americas. About 40 percent of the millions of Africans captured and bought as property by Europeans were shipped to Brazil. Consequently, the area received a larger concentration of African slaves than anywhere else in the Americas. Most originated from West and Central Africa, including present-day Ghana, as well as Angola, and from Portuguese colonies throughout Africa.[8] When scholars note the significance of South American ports such as this one in Bahia in the transatlantic slave trade, they provide a more accurate understanding of the slave trade than those who focus exclusively on North America. Understanding the sheer numbers of African slaves who arrived in ports like Salvador expands the focus commonly taught in U.S. grade-school history lessons that feature the seventeenth-century arrival of slaves in Virginia.[9] A history of slavery in the Americas that includes Brazil, where three to four million Africans had been shipped beginning almost one hundred years earlier than the several hundred thousand who would begin to arrive later in what is now the United States, highlights the stunning breadth of the trade and reminds us of its larger impact on the entire hemisphere.[10]

Multiple traditions of Christianity promoted, sustained, and rationalized the slave trade. As early as the fifteenth century, the Vatican granted Portugal and Spain official approval "to invade, conquer, crush, pacify . . . and to reduce their persons to perpetual slavery" in West Africa.[11] In the history of slavery in Brazil, Portuguese Catholicism played a prominent role in normalizing the obedience of slaves to their masters. Political scientist Anthony Marx notes that for most of this history, the church in Brazil "saw no contradiction in allowing slaves to be baptized at the same time as they were branded."[12] In the North American slave trade, British Protestant Christianity played a key role in the conceptualization of slavery as it emerged in the British colonies and in the United States after it won its independence. As historian Winthrop Jordan explains, because seventeenth-century Protestant Christianity integrated English patriotism with their definition of what it meant to be "normal and proper," it aided British colonizers in pejoratively depicting the supposedly contrasting attributes of the Africans they encountered.[13] For the English, Jordan explains, "to be Christian was to be civilized rather than barbarous, English rather than African, white rather than black."[14] In U.S. history, the influence of English Protestant Christianity provided a cultural container for recognizing phenotypic and cultural differences that justified the permanent enslavement of blacks.

Because of its dominance across the American continent, European Protestant and Catholic Christianity provided the moral compass guiding societal values related to sexuality and marriage as well as economic relations, including the ownership of slaves. Local laws that governed slavery in American contexts—across the continent—featured the regulation of access to and ownership of black slave women's sexuality, bodies, and progeny. When comparing the differing degrees of brutality in North and South American slave practices, scholars routinely reference the rape of black women and speculate about whether or not they willingly participated in miscegenation.[15] To better understand the cultural and economic foundations of slavery in the Americas as well as its contemporary legacy requires a grasp of how a conjoined moral web of Christian religion, anti-black racism, and sexual access to black women enabled the totalizing forms of racialization that helped to make it unique.[16]

In the twenty-first century, Brazil has the largest population of persons of African descent of any nation outside of sub-Saharan Africa. Its population also has a long tradition of generating vibrant political, artistic, and intellectual discourse contesting anti-black racism in the Americas. Opposition to racism has been an integral part of the politics of Brazil's late twentieth-century women's movement.[17] The gender violence work of black women activists such as Sandra has occurred within a wider context of an intense recent history of social equality movements. As Kia Lilly Caldwell, scholar of black women's studies in Brazil and the United States, describes, the black women's movement in Brazil gained momentum during the 1970s and 1980s as the struggle to end military dictatorship and increase democracy took hold.[18] Leaders of the black women's movement arose within both Brazil's black and feminist movements during this period.

The black women's manifesto first presented at a feminist Brazilian women's meeting in 1975 insisted on the interrogation of racialized histories that sublimated the sexual violation of black women. This history often remained unacknowledged in popular cultural narratives that celebrated Brazil's racially hybrid population as evidence of its supposed nonracialism and racial democracy.[19] As Caldwell explained, "by unmasking the gendered aspects of racial domination and the racial aspects of gender domination, the manifesto also highlighted black women's victimization by long-standing practices of sexual exploitation."[20] Although black women leaders were active in these movements elsewhere in the country, such as São Paulo and Rio de Janeiro, Salvador was an epicenter for them.[21] The gender-based antiviolence organizing by current leaders has been nurtured in this culture of black women's political action.

Salvador teems with evidence of past and present as well as local and global forms of racial and sexual politics related to human exploitation and commodification. Artifacts in history and art museums represent the slave past.[22] One can visit the dungeons beneath the city's major tourist market (former site of the Customs House) where enslaved Africans were kept in quarantine upon their arrival in the city during the period of European colonial rule. A more consumerist energy also abounds, invigorated by contemporary European and U.S. tourists. The city features a typical Latin American or Caribbean coastal tourist scene with hotel beaches and lots of shopping and street vendors, bars and restaurants, poor people begging for money, and taxi drivers looking for customers. Like other Latin American and Caribbean destinations, Salvador is also a magnet for sex tourism.

While visiting Casa Branca I noticed that it was close to a busy city street filled with buses and taxis. There were many shades of bronze and ebony skin tones among the local Bahian residents I observed walking on the sidewalk. They bore evidence of the racial and ethnic mixtures that resulted from their history of interracial sexual assaults by European slave owners and colonists as well as consensual sexual encounters among Europeans, Africans, and indigenous peoples. In the sounds of the Brazilian Portuguese I heard Afro-Brazilians speak were similar reminders of the cultural assimilation of African slaves to the dictates of European domination. Oddly, I had never thought of my own English language in this same way, that is, as evidence of an African accommodation to the cultural dictates of British European dominance.

When comparing anti-black racisms in the United States and Brazil, the prospect of erroneous judgments about racial inequalities in Brazil lay in wait for U.S.-American observers if the U.S. context was treated as the standard experience of racism. Black U.S. scholars had been contrasting the form and growth of anti-black racism in Brazil with the United States for almost a century.[23] In his 1942 study "The Negro Family in Bahia," pioneering African American sociologist E. Franklin Frazier paid particular attention to the role of Candomblé in shaping gender norms among "Negroes" in Salvador. Frazier optimistically asserted "in the absence of race prejudice, such as exists in the United States, the increasing mobility of the Negroes accelerated the mixture of races."[24] Undoubtedly, Frazier's positive view of Brazil's racial politics pivoted on his comparison to the United States, which was home to public lynchings of blacks, strictly enforced racial segregation in the South, and a racist denial of black voting rights. Frazier may not have fully comprehended the repression of the political rights of blacks in Brazil. The widespread racial hybridity of the population appeared to Frazier and many other scholars as signaling an absence of racial prejudice. Yet this supposed lack of racial prejudice did not translate into political and/or economic equality for blacks in Brazil.[25] Frazier found, as have other scholars who have continued to compare anti-black racism in Brazil and the United States, that some Brazilians who identified as black, mulatto, or white have disputed the idea that racism has been as serious a problem in Brazil.[26] Many Brazilians across all racial groups still hold this view.

Nevertheless, Frazier's 1940s view of race prejudice provides an illustration of the difficulty of interpreting the cultural meanings of racism across national borders. A rigidly singular, literal translation could too dramatically narrow its meaning and unwittingly attenuate the ability to perceive it outside of one's own context. What would it mean to recognize "the existence of multiple culturally and historically specific racisms," as Caldwell asserted in her study of black women's movements in Brazil and the United States?[27] I reveled in the challenge of sorting out such cultural translations that the Brazilian setting demanded. Translation was vital to my quest for transnational intercultural learning that focused on ending gender-based violence and discerning the influence of racial and religious narratives in that work.

Translation was integral for sharing ideas and solidarities across nation-state boundaries that might spark emboldening insights for resisting gender-based violence in the United States. As feminist Latin American studies scholar Sonia Alvarez has explained, "translation is politically and theoretically indispensable to forging feminist, prosocial justice, antiracist, postcolonial/decolonial, and anti-imperial political alliances and epistemologies."[28] A political science scholar of contemporary women's movements in Brazil, Alvarez has argued for an understanding of the "processes of translocal translation" in which meanings of race, class, sexualities, and genders are interrogated.[29] In short, translation holds an intrinsic capacity to build relational bridges and reproduce local knowledge.

Truthful cultural translations, therefore, may enable the conceptualization of useful political linkages that can function as building blocks for antiviolence solidarity. Relational ingredients, such as trust, candor, openness, empathy, and shared political commitments, provide fuel for truthful translations. In particular, "processes of translocal translations" could build interculturally informed moral understandings of black women's intrinsic equality, worth, and dignity in support of ending gender-based violence. Of course, conversely erroneous or distorting translations could impede this antiviolence solidarity strategy. An emphasis on appropriate and adequate translations is indispensable when highlighting the role of religion. Painstaking interpretative translations of scriptural and spiritual texts and traditions play a guiding role in religious and spiritual gender-based activism. Indeed, almost every interpersonal exchange that occurred while I was in the Brazilian setting underscored the risky process of cultural translation and its necessity.

Our visit to the Casa Branca religious community was made possible because Sandra was a member, and I felt privileged to have her as our guide on its grounds. She interpreted the traditions in response to several of my questions, but some information she could not share. On the *terreiro* grounds sat a slightly larger than life-sized statue that looked like a shapely mermaid—brown-skinned, bare-chested, and seated on a white platform, a golden crown on her head. Her hands gestured as if she were teaching. In Candomblé, the *orixá* (deity/spirit/saint/mediator) Iemanjá was known as the spirit of the sea and of motherhood. I did not comprehend the gendered religious significance of this statue for the members of this Casa Branca community.[30] Yet there was something about the statue. The combination of staring at it and talking with Sandra about her work with victimized women and her religious beliefs invited contemplation of how religion, spirituality, and an affirmation of black women's embodiment might occupy the core of an antiviolence religious response.

The Candomblé religion includes many male and female *orixàs* and is deeply committed to honoring the spirits of the community's ancestors. Initiates undergo rigorous preparation of mind, body, and spirit. The details of most Candomblé rituals could not be revealed to me by its practitioners, even when I asked about them directly. Candomblé rituals and symbols include many layers of meaning incomprehensible to outsiders such as myself. Even the smallest religious icons I noticed, such as the miniature colorfully beaded snake on the outside wall of the house, contained symbolism indecipherable to me. Similarly, I could not understand the meanings of the drumming, chanting, and spirit possession I observed during the Candomblé ceremonies open to visitors.

Most of the Candomblé leaders were black women, including Casa Branca's *mãe-de-santo* (highest spiritual leader), whom I met. Candomblé is not merely a religious phenomenon—it has also occupied a position of major cultural and political significance in Bahia. It was popularized in Carnival street celebrations for tourists, and local tourism bureaus proudly touted certain public ceremonies as attractions for visitors.[31] Some local evangelical Protestant Christians publicly castigated the tradition.[32] Historically, especially during the early twentieth century, the police in Salvador enforced periods of extreme repression of Candomblé.[33]

For adherents and the crowds of local community members who attended its events, Candomblé had black political significance. In a summary description of how this religious tradition carved out a space of political and cultural resistance for Salvador community members, Rachel Harding has explained that "Candomblé provided a means of remembering and (re)creating an identity of value and connectedness—to Spirit, to a pre-slavery past, to ancestors, to community."[34] It held religious values that explicitly supported a self-affirming black identity that confronted the history of anti-black racist repression. The predominance of women's leadership within its organizational practices demonstrated black women's agency as a normative value.

Earlier in life, Sandra had spent several years as part of a Catholic convent community but then had decided to leave. Now, after over seventeen years of a deep commitment to Candomblé, she was an experienced and revered practitioner within the tradition. Sandra also held a government job as a community organizer working on the prevention of intimate violence against women and girls. She coordinated outreach efforts not only in this city but also throughout the state of Bahia by traveling to small neighborhood groups in an attempt to help poor black women learn about the Maria da Penha Law. Later, I saw some of the stacks of materials she had distributed, including state-issued pamphlets, postcards, and posters. Many featured photographs of black women. One poster declared: "Somos donas da nossa voz, nosso corpo, nosso historia. Muhleres Negras: por uma vida sem violência!" (We are the owners of our voice, our body, our history. Black Women: for a life without violence). And below this slogan the poster indicated that it was sponsored by the "Campanha Pelo fim da Violência contras as Mulheres Negras Na Bahia" (campaign to end violence against black women in Bahia). The words of the campaign encouraged contemporary black women with an indirect reference to a past when ownership of their bodies that included sexual exploitation had been the norm. Black women were galvanized in this mass media campaign against domestic violence through an affirmation of their capacity to create a counternarrative to that history of societally sanctioned devaluation. The posters offered a truth-telling and defiant public reference to their political identities that was intended to affirm and bolster those same capacities in black women who found themselves amid the personal turmoil of intimate violence.

In addition to hosting regular meetings of a support group for women in her own neighborhood, Sandra traveled tirelessly from community to community distributing information about the law and related services available to victimized women. Her religious devotion directly connected to her work addressing violence against women. As she explained, "I believe it was really Oxum, my Orixá, who prepared this space for me to be working today in my work place while I'm a state employee but also my space of activism."[35] The government work seemed to be more of a temporary means to an end, while her antiviolence activism would remain constant. She spoke of a "mystical" component that allowed her to pursue her antiviolence outreach commitment to "the poorest women, the poorest people [who] don't have access to the state's infrastructure."[36] Racial discrimination and class marginalization seemed to be inseparable in her view of the obstacles encountered by the population of abused black women with whom she worked. Specifically, Sandra's emphasis on the mystical cohered with her concern for the dire material conditions of poverty that compounded their desperation. This congruence of deeply held mystical commitments and concerns about unfair material realities also attached itself to her drive to expand the outreach of the state and the accessibility of its services to the women. In short, there was a productive confluence of concern with the mystical, the material, and state responsibility in the assertiveness of her activism.

When we walked around the grounds of the *terreiro* during our first meeting, Sandra pointed to the luscious green plants and trees surrounding the "boat" that I had seen as I had initially approached the *terreiro* and statue. She commented, "It's peaceful like Africa." For Sandra, this understanding of peacefulness derived from her religious tradition seemed to be a primary motivation in helping defuse violence against women and girls. The idea of peacefulness that Sandra invoked commemorated an intangible African heritage and at the same time occupied a specific kind of tangible space and place. The space, filled with plush plant life, appeared to give witness to the need for an intentionally nontoxic natural environment as a resource in this work of countering the toxicity of intimate, deliberately inflicted human cruelty.

When Sandra matter-of-factly asserted, "It's peaceful like Africa," I could almost sense it too. At least, I thought so. In Brazil, I began to reckon with the degree to which my own goals contained spiritual dimensions. It was a gradual process of reckoning since I was not certain how to translate my own Christian faith and spiritual longings. The concern with violence that antiviolence commitments demanded intrinsically tested one's hope and spirit. And the Brazilian Bahian space and meetings with activist women leaders made palpable the potential for the kind of politically enmeshed spirituality so crucial in the work of addressing soul-splitting violations and betrayals of gendered violence.

The markers of Bahia's ties to Africa and the history of slavery that created those ties were not merely a means of recollecting the past in the spirituality at the *terreiros*. Those Africana markers also had complex, ongoing significance in the present. They permeated the broader ethos of the city, ranging from its museums to the self-understandings articulated in their politics. Scholars, especially anthropologists, have debated the degree to which one finds authentic African roots in Bahia, especially in Candomblé.[37] In addition to anthropologists, tourists also come seeking those roots. But because of my focus on gender-based violence I wanted it to be clear to my hosts that I was not one of those black U.S.-American "roots tourists" to whom Latin American studies scholar Patricia de Santana Pinho disparagingly refers.[38] Pinho decries U.S. black visitors who project a circumscribed view of Africa onto the Bahian ethos, a projection that insists "on an ethnic homogeneity of the slave contingents who arrived in the Americas." In addition, Pinho writes, they participate in "glorifying the persistence of Africanisms per se, as if they could possibly have a life of their own," without the contemporary descendants who re-create and manipulate culture for their own benefit.[39]

Even when I thought that I could grasp what Sandra meant when she described the *terreiro* as "peaceful like Africa," Pinho's cautionary insight about Africanisms applied. I needed to bring a critical cognizance of Sandra's reference to Africa as only imagined and of the agency of the leaders of the *terreiro* in re-creating it. This critical consciousness must nevertheless acknowledge, as Harding noted, the power in the imagined for Candomblé believers and the power they derived from an Afro-diasporic notion of shared community and connectedness to an African preslavery past.[40] A critical consciousness of the constructed idea must not deny the ways in which even an imagined Africa was still a real force that Sandra (and others) identified as a religious grounding for her political activism and daily work on gender-based violence.

I glanced back at the statue. Sandra's Candomblé beliefs emanated from Yoruba and several other African cultural and religious traditions that were definitely not my own. Yet I wondered what it would have meant for my understanding of spirituality and sexuality had I grown up in a religion where a beautiful brown-skinned topless woman was depicted as a symbol of what was considered most sacred. What difference had it made to me that instead the God I had learned to worship while growing up was depicted as a handsome white man with a deeply sun-tanned body, blue eyes, and brunette hair that always looked freshly shampooed? He, too, was often represented in Christian art as topless, but only as he was tortured and executed by the Roman state. I did not know how or if those violent, gendered images of a white God-man Jesus might have influenced my current interests in gender-based violence. Before immediately dismissing my questions as too idiosyncratic and having no certain answers, I had to acknowledge that my encounter with Candomblé had summoned these political and Christian theological questions. I lingered in front of the statue as Sandra approached. With a twinkle of pride in her smile, she explained that the statue had been a generous gift to their Casa Branca community. Then a grimace overtook the smile as she whispered her ambivalent response to the statue's long, straight black hair and blue eyes.

Salvador birthed complicated manifestations of Africanness that bore a resemblance to some of the anti-black political and cultural values in the United States. We may gain more insights about such transnational resonances by examining in closer detail antiviolence activist responses that have emphasized the need to attend to particular circumstances of vulnerability for Salvadoran women of African descent.

Domestic Violence at Work

Creuza Maria Oliveira's office was a short distance away from Casa Branca. We arrived by taxi. Oliveira was about five feet three inches tall—several inches shorter than myself. She had a beautiful dark-skinned face surrounded by shoulder-length, neatly arranged, kinky, curly black dreads. As I had learned was customary when first meeting someone in Brazil, we kissed each other on both cheeks.

Oliveira, president of the Federação Nacional das Trabalhadoras Domésticas (National Federation of Domestic Workers), also exchanged greetings with my colleague-translator Nessette, and Erica, my Brazilian host who had arranged the meeting. We sat down in a spacious community room within the small building that housed the headquarters of the domestic workers union. Soon after we began our discussion a few of their members walked into the room and explained that they needed the space. They were in the midst of a training program that required the room's media equipment to watch a film together. Vacating the community room to allow the Federation members to use it, my group piled into Oliveira's small office.

The Federation advocated for the women's rights as domestic workers and coordinated educational and support services for its members. In Brazil, domestic workers number well over six million and most are women, black, and undereducated.[41] Some scholars have estimated that as many as one in three Afro-Brazilian women have worked as a domestic servant.[42] Only a small percentage of all women domestic workers were unionized, and most members of this union were black.[43]

The significance of the domestic workers union for understanding antiviolence work in Brazil was multilayered. It made evident certain gendered legacies of the history of the enslavement of blacks in the Americas. Many of the captured African women who first came to Brazil had worked as domestic slaves. Many of their female progeny worked as domestic servants after the emancipation of slaves occurred in Brazil in 1888. The organizing for workers' rights waged by the union's contemporary black women domestic workers built upon a long history of struggle for black women's freedom from exploitation in private domestic quarters. The Federation's activist emphasis on stopping domestic abuse by employers contributed a distinctive aspect to any general formulation of the kind of resistance to domestic violence that was needed in present-day Brazilian society.

By contrast, in the late twentieth century, *domestic violence* became a standard term utilized by U.S. women's rights leaders to identify the patterns of behavior that constitute intimate partner abuse and violence in heterosexual relationships. But this definition failed to adequately capture the many characteristics that male-perpetrated violence against women in domestic settings can assume. As my discussion with Oliveira would attest, when applied to heterosexual male-perpetrated intimate violence, the term needs a broader definition beyond pointing to the abusive patterns of husbands or live-in boyfriends. Concern about the types of domestic violence experienced by poor black and brown women throughout the Americas must incorporate the conditions encountered by those who work in domestic settings. Their very livelihood has required them to navigate intimate areas of the living spaces inhabited by their employers and guests such as bedrooms and bathrooms. These intimate spaces also include temporary living accommodations, such as hotels. The workers' sociopolitically disadvantaged status, which is already shaped by racial, ethnic, and class stigmas, combines with their routine vulnerability to sexual harassment and assault in private domestic quarters. This dangerous combination has served to normalize little regard for women harassed and assaulted while performing their duties in low-wage domestic cleaning and caretaking jobs.

The highly publicized 2011 case of Nafissatou Diallo in New York City demonstrated the political precariousness and vulnerability to danger for women domestic workers in the U.S.-American context. Diallo was an African immigrant and asylum seeker from Guinea, a former French colony in West Africa. She worked as a hotel maid in the luxurious Hotel Sofitel in Manhattan. Diallo reported that she had been sexually assaulted by a naked man who emerged from the bathroom after she had entered his room to clean it.[44] The case received worldwide media attention due to the identity of the accused perpetrator, hotel guest Dominique Strauss-Kahn, who was at the time an influential French politician and managing director of the International Monetary Fund (a position he would resign amid wide press coverage of this incident). After he was arrested and shown to be the source of semen found at the scene, he claimed that a consensual sexual encounter had taken place. In several news accounts, the press attacked Diallo's character and credibility. These largely unsubstantiated attacks seemed to guide public reactions toward placing Diallo on trial rather than her attacker.[45] As feminist psychology theorist Michelle Fine noted, Diallo was accused of "prostitution, having HIV/AIDS, being undocumented, lying about her taxes, having unsavory friends."[46] Citing Diallo's lack of credibility as a victim, prosecutors ultimately decided not to allow a jury to even hear her complaint about being sexual assaulted in that hotel room.

The intertwined links to European, African, and American continents in the details of this case heightened the relevance of a transnational intercultural lens for antiviolence analysis and collaboration.[47] The incident illustrates the political insufficiency of strategic approaches to gender-based violence within the United States that do not possess some degree of transnational consciousness. Yet unlike most of the maids in hotels and private homes in the United States and other places in the world that are economically dependent upon exploited immigrant labor, the overwhelming majority of domestic workers in Brazil are native-born women.[48]

The president of Brazil's domestic workers union was polite and welcoming as I sat in her office and described my interests and questions. Her attitude toward me was also cautious and appraising. She told me that she had met others from North America who "come down here to get something from us" for their various projects. She voiced several pointed questions of her own—asking me why I was there and what benefit it would have for her work. I felt as if I was experiencing a sampling of what a formidable advocate she must have been on behalf of union members. Oliveira's initial response to me was like a helpful splash of cold water on my face. There would be no romanticized, unearned black woman solidarity in this conversation. The privileges of U.S.-American citizenship, class, and status that I brought markedly contrasted with the lives of the women she stood for and with. Those privileges could not be hidden. Creuza Oliveira would not allow it.

In reply to her questioning, I explained as best I could the longings and hopes that had brought me there. The moments that immediately followed were uncomfortable. I stole a glance at my local host who had placed her activist reputation on the line by bringing me here. I could not detect any hint that Erica was embarrassed by me. Her activist-scholar's instincts were perceptible, and she maintained a placid and attentive facial expression. The awkwardness of those moments only deepened my desire to learn more about Oliveira's leadership. However, my silent struggle to assuage her suspiciousness of me persisted throughout the visit.

"This is the work that most black women do here,"[49] she told me. Often it is the only work available to them. And the obstacles to organizing domestics are considerable. She pointed out that their cause was not one that white Brazilian feminist activists have typically championed. Oliveira assumed (correctly) that I had read about the robust late twentieth-century women's movement in Brazil. I recognized that she wanted to alert me to some of the everyday racial realities of the movement and the racial assumptions in the ways in which it is typically chronicled. She assumed that insights about the lives of black women domestic workers might not have been available in the academic accounts of Brazilian women's activism with which she associated me. More than language barriers and separate nationalities, the chasm of class differences continued to subtly appear between us as she inquired about what I knew about the women's movement there. I could bridge the gap only perfunctorily.

Oliveira described the intense process of negotiating with the country's legislators. Her group lobbied them for better public policies aimed at improving working conditions for domestic workers. Outside their role as public officials, some politicians were, as *patrónes* (employers), simultaneously participating in the day-to-day demeaning treatment that the workers faced. As Oliveira explained, these men were among those who benefited from the exploited labor of domestics in their homes. In a manner that few other women's rights groups encountered, the Federation's activist work had to interrupt a forceful adhesion between the political leaders' protectiveness of their intimate home lives, their self-interests, and their public service commitments as policy makers. These legislative dynamics incorporated degrees of racist paternalism that are also present in the relationships between most Brazilian domestics and their employers. As Latin American scholars Patricia de Santana Pinho and Elizabeth Silva have attested in their analysis of race issues confronting black domestic workers in Brazil, "the association between whiteness and authority is visible in the daily interactions between maids and their employers . . . embedded in the performances of blackness validating the supremacy, command, and superiority of exercising whiteness."[50]

Not coincidentally, the stronghold of white supremacy has also been operative in barring legislative protections for the rights of domestic workers in the United States.[51] In 1935, the comprehensive U.S. National Labor Relations Act (Wagner Act) excluded domestic workers in order to win the votes of white southern Congress members who did not want their black maids to have basic labor protections.[52] Comprehensive federal protections for these workers have yet to be added to U.S. federal laws, though there have been ongoing state-by-state fights for such rights in the early twenty-first century.[53] In 2012, for example, some major victories were achieved in New York State.[54] Yet, that same year, a supposedly liberal Democrat was responsible for a setback in the most populous U.S. state (over thirty-five million residents), California, when Governor Jerry Brown vetoed the enactment of a domestic worker bill of rights. Activists had defeated business leaders' aggressive opposition to it and attained hard-won passage by their legislature only to face the governor's veto. Some of their disappointment over that veto was undoubtedly fueled by the not unreasonable expectation that their chances would be better with the ostensibly left-leaning governor.

Brown's predecessor—right-leaning actor-turned-politician Arnold Schwarzenegger—had previously been elected to two terms as governor. Just before leaving office, Schwarzenegger had publicly confessed to an extramarital sexual relationship with his family's long-term Latina immigrant (Guatemala-born) housekeeper-administrator. Schwarzenegger fathered a child with her and then failed to acknowledge the child for fourteen years as she continued to work for the family. There was no allegation of violence or sexual harassment by the housekeeper-assistant Mildred Baena. Schwarzenegger explained in his autobiography that this was the only time during his marriage that he "had anything going with someone who worked for me" and that he had the housekeeper continue "working in our home because I thought I could control the situation better that way."[55] The California domestic worker bill of rights rejected in 2012 by Schwarzenegger's successor (Jerry Brown) had included protections as basic as adequate sleeping conditions for live-in domestic workers.[56] Governor Brown eventually relented and signed a statewide domestic worker rights law in 2013.

A precise translation of the position of *patrónes* Oliveira described did not fit this U.S. context of political leadership and labor rights. But there were some analytically useful connections. The intimacies of male heterosexuality did seem to conflate with racial/ethnic hierarchies of privilege in the maintenance of control of a domestic employee within the governor's (Schwarzenegger's) home life. And it was soon proven that the political rights of all domestic workers were captive to the exercise of authority by those who held this state office. Workers could be vulnerable to the capriciousness of how the political and personal arenas combined for such government chief executives and then possibly affected the determination of the workers' legal rights.

"What about the church?" I asked Oliveira. As part of my preamble to that question I had mentioned my disgust with the "go home and pray harder" response to women's domestic violence victimization. I noted that too often some U.S. clergy offered this kind of response. I wanted to delve into her activist's perspective on how church and clergy addressed the abuse domestic workers confronted. Oliveira was Baptist in a country with an overwhelmingly Catholic religious population. At that time, megachurches connected to the United States as well as the influence of Brazilian-based Protestant evangelicals and Pentecostals were spreading rapidly in Brazil. Some of their leaders expressed an intensifying Christian hostility to Candomblé, especially certain aggressive Protestant evangelicals.[57]

Oliveira shook her head and gave a brief dismissive reply to my question. In her view, in most churches the combined politics of race, gender, and poverty that she and the women in the Federation challenged in their advocacy work were taboo subjects. According to Oliveira, church leaders usually relegated the concerns of the domestic workers to the realm of social problems and thus were not the spiritual ones to which the church attended. Oliveira offered a critique of Christian religious disengagement from the political conditions surrounding Afro-Brazilian domestic workers' exploitation. The spirituality normally identified with Christian practices reeked of irrelevancy to the women's lives. In her assessment, "the church," at least when I invoked it in my question to her, did not share the same goals regarding poor black women's empowerment that the Federation championed. Still, I wondered about Christianity's central messages about redemption and salvation most likely preached and taught by Protestant evangelical leaders there. Wasn't there some aspect, in Oliveira's view, that could translate into an embrace of the Federation's vision? Some liberation theologians did. In her treatise on women's embodied experience of evil, Christian Brazilian feminist theologian Ivone Gebara included the exploitative treatment of Brazilian domestic workers among the key concerns Christian salvation theology must address.[58] But I did not pursue these theological issues with Oliveira. A quest for useful Christian theological notions veered from her activist priorities and distracted from the ideas about creating political change that she was urging me to grasp.

As they persevered against the considerable obstacles Oliveira had mentioned, they—the Federation, its supporters, and like-minded social movement colleagues—could also count some successes. She told me, for instance, about the passage of 2006 national legislation on labor conditions for domestic workers, with specific guarantees such as a right to a day off each week and vacation as part of their salary package.[59] In addition, like several of the leaders whom I had met in Ghana, Oliveira retained a deep investment in the broader international context of her work. She referenced her ties to similar organizations in other South American countries and the strategic knowledge sharing that occurred among them.

It was essential to Oliveira that I realize how the violence black women domestics faced from their employers was psychological, sexual, and physical. All three aspects were involved. "Total," she repeated for emphasis. This violence was extremely difficult to uncover and combat, she said, because it took place in an extremely private setting, with clear imbalances of power and status. Oliveira had helped found the Federation in part because of her own experiences. She began working as a domestic when she was nine or ten years old. Tears began to trickle down her cheeks as she described how she too experienced violence as a very young domestic worker: all three forms. "All of them," Oliveira stressed, letting the tears flow. Nessette lovingly hugged her. Reaching an arm around Oliveira's shoulders, she allowed a respectful silent pause before translating the words for me. Oliveira's employers told her that she must be obedient to them as if they were her father and mother.

Translation of her words was not altogether necessary. I could sense what she meant about the comprehensiveness of the violence. I could intuitively decipher why she was so committed to assessing, naming, and confronting imbalanced power dynamics like those between her and me or between the *patrónes* legislators and black domestics in her organization. Painful firsthand experiences of how intimate violence hinged on power and control thoroughly informed her leadership and ignited her defiance of rules that maintained the conditions of inequality. Oliveira's method for creating social change relied on her keen appraisal of the obstacles as well as her international networks. Both nurtured her vision and pursuit of the human rights to which women domestic workers are entitled. And her group engaged in multiple shrewd forms of joint disobedience. One might even describe the defiance as a kind of spiritual unity resulting, in part, from their shared vulnerability. It provided collective support for countering the exploitation of the domestic workers' vulnerability in their isolated household settings. This spiritual unity was not rooted in institutionalized religiosity, but resembled it. In the face of inescapable vulnerability to intimate abuse and the frequent experience of it, this spiritual force I perceived as underlying the Federation's work offered members a connection to a larger, supportive whole that was politically aggressive on their behalf.

Later, I reflected on the power of Oliveira's witness to her "human rights work," as she identified it. The meeting evoked questions about what it would mean to have this same language in public-sphere popular discourse in the United States. For instance, if network local television news programs referred to incidents of domestic violence as human rights violations, how might it assist in altering public perceptions of this abuse? The discussion with Oliveira also instigated imaginative ideas about possible transnational connections for local U.S. domestic violence shelter staff, rape-crisis hotline coordinators, labor organizers of domestic workers, and religiously based activist leaders. If feasible, might there be utility and support found in routinized conversations with their international counterparts on their antiviolence strategies and commitments to antiracism? Might there be a way of even including some kind of affirmation of nonreligious spiritual transnational solidarity in such resource sharing? More specifically, what if activist leaders opposing gender-based violence in Guinea, France, and New York had been able to collaborate on a strategy to protest the New York City prosecutor's refusal to bring Diallo's complaint against Strauss-Kahn to trial?

The relevance of the Federation's focus on black women's empowerment held additional, provocative import for the U.S. context. It prompted questions about whether awareness of anti-black racism in U.S. labor history could be empowering to ethnically diverse domestic workers now struggling for their rights across the United States. How might current workers' rights activists utilize knowledge of the anti-black white racism in policies blocking federal protections for domestic workers dating back to the 1930s? How could this racial knowledge constructively contribute to analysis of the struggles of Latina and Asian American immigrant domestic worker activists already combating popular xenophobic anti-immigrant attitudes on multiple fronts?[60] No doubt to some of them, anti-black racism may not seem relevant to their struggle to bring attention to issues such as sexual harassment and assault of the mainly (new) immigrant workers in domestic work settings. But the historical imprint of anti-black white racism in the initial structuring of the barriers impeding their receipt of basic labor rights was still manifest. U.S. domestic workers have continued to endure some of those same historical political obstacles as they battle for comprehensive federal legislation like the Brazilian domestic worker rights law. This labor rights history also served as a potentially inspiring reminder of the legacy left by groups of domestic workers who had resisted in earlier U.S. labor movements.[61] In Brazil, the Federation's commitment to black racial empowerment invited contemplation of how to embrace the significance of anti-black racism and activist struggle against it throughout the Americas. Their example churned up a host of intriguingly pregnant questions about how a similar commitment to black racial empowerment could be claimed as a resource that fuels intercultural solidarity in woman-affirming social change movements in the U.S.-American context. Could it be as politically useful in the United States as it was in Brazil to support antiviolence and domestic worker activists in the United States who claimed widely ranging nonblack transnational cultural backgrounds?

Later that evening, my young adult host-translators tried to persuade me to go out to hear a Brazilian hip-hop band and join with them in the dancing. "This is a local Salvador band! You have to come," Erica said. Unlike me, my hosts seemed to have no need for a rest at the end of a long, intense day. The concert was held at one of the main downtown beach venues.

"I'm really sorry but I can't go. Besides," I said smiling, "I'm a terrible dancer. I don't have any sense of rhythm." They did not seem to notice my attempt at humor, playing off of the stereotype about all black people having natural rhythm. This humor was perhaps culturally confined to a U.S. racial milieu. "I'm sorry. I can't go," I repeated. In fact, I needed to organize my notes about the meetings. I really did not have time for a beach party.

But in response to their insistence my resolve eventually broke down, and I ended up joining them. When we arrived at the beach it was packed mainly with tourist youth, but some local young residents were there too. I enjoyed the familiar, blaring hip-hop beat of the music and bounced my head to its rhythm, but I did not try to dance.[62] After spending some time with my hosts, I wandered toward the water away from the crowd gathered around the band on stage. Taking off my sandals, I let my toes play at the edge of the ocean and watched the last of each frothy wave melt into the sand. Lights from the concert stage and nearby street illuminated the ocean waves and the children playing in them. Surrounded by a gorgeous black sky with a few stars in it, I let the cool water massage my feet and then my ankles as I moved farther into it. I was glad I'd made the last-minute decision to wear a swimsuit under my shorts and shirt. The ocean felt like heaven. I was reminded how spirituality can inhabit sensuality and that tactile spirituality has the potential to help counter the impact of violence. From the bondage of the humiliation of sexual assault, spirituality offers a mind-freeing, body-affirming countersensation.

The waves washed over my body rhythmically, gently, one after another. I did not care that I was the only adult shrieking playfully as the water sprayed and crashed against the shore around me. A small, thin girl of about eight with caramel-brown skin was playing nearby in the water. She came over and began talking to me. As I explained to her that I did not speak Portuguese, her eyes widened and she grinned at the sound of my funny accent poorly pronouncing such simple Portuguese words.

All at once she scooped up a big splash of ocean water and pushed it toward me and laughed. Her immediate, easy acceptance surprised me as she beckoned her younger brother over to come and meet me. When he entered the water, I glanced at the shore for a protective, wary parent, but the two of them appeared to be on their own. The little girl tried to imitate my body surfing, and I saw that she did not know how to swim. Without any warning, she jumped on my back for a ride, her bony fingers tightly clasped around my neck. I giggled with her and flapped around in the water for a while. When her little brother wanted a ride too, I happily obliged.

I soon wanted to swim on my own and used sign language to indicate to my little friend that she and her brother were not to follow me into the deeper water. I was not sure she understood. She looked like she was going to try to follow me. I paused to figure out how to communicate nonverbally the real danger of serious harm. I needed to find a way to convey her vulnerability to harm by something that looked and felt so nurturing and could be so pleasurable and fun. Of course, even for confident swimmers there are still times when raging waves powered by strong currents can render one helpless.

Policing and Governmental Responses

Taped to the office wall in the police station were small Polaroid squares showing women's bodies photographed at varied camera angles. For the women in these photographs, the danger they faced might have resembled the unforeseeable danger that resides in the depths of the nurturing, pleasurable ocean. Most likely, when these women first became romantically involved with the boyfriends and husbands who turned out to be their abusers, they did not imagine they risked harm. At some earlier point in their relationships, most of the men had probably represented a nurturing and pleasurable human connection in their lives. The photographs comprised close-up views of burned, bruised, cut, and bleeding bodies. Most but not all depicted dark-brown-skinned faces, arms, legs, thighs. Three photographs documented one case in which an abuser had badly mutilated a woman's nipple. One showed the breast with a mutilated nipple. Adjacent to that image was one of the woman's other breast, which appeared to have been scarred from an earlier mutilation. In a third photograph, the woman's solemn face stared at the camera as she clutched her raised blouse, exposing simultaneously both injured breasts with their mutilated nipples.

Over a hundred photographs of women's bodies were set against the unifying background of the wall's clean, off-white painted surface. The photographs documented violence that was brutal, horrific, and painful. I wanted to know what had happened to the men who committed these acts of violence. I needed to be certain that they had been held accountable. But perhaps it was appropriate only for other Brazilians to demand such accountability, not those, like me, who were neither long-term residents nor citizens.

The snapshots blanketing the wall were located in Tânia Mendonça's office. Not unlike Oliveira, Mendonça was dark-brown-skinned, solidly built, and small in stature. Upon meeting her, one immediately understood that she was a no-nonsense police official. Her office was part of Brazil's unique system of "women's police stations" that concentrated on violence against women, with a special unit called the Delegacia Especial de Atendimento à Mulher (DEAM). This type of policing was first created in the mid-1980s in response to feminist activist demands. Similar women's police stations were elsewhere in this region of the world, such as Ecuador, Nicaragua, and Peru.[63] In Brazil, these police units increased in function and importance through the implementation of the 2006 Maria da Penha Law. In addition to the police stations, the law provided for a nationwide special court system, codes for stricter sentences, women's shelters, and access to free legal advice. Over four hundred women's police stations were located all over Brazil when I visited. With their exclusive focus on domestic violence, these police stations showcased a kind of seriousness about the need for a systemic, nationally coordinated governmental approach to violence against women. A response wholly unlike those that elected U.S. leaders contemplated, even those who are genuinely concerned about the problem.

The Brazilian federal government also sponsored and funded battered women's shelters throughout sections of their country. In the United States, by contrast, financial support for battered women's shelters usually requires persistent fund-raising efforts by boards of directors and supporters. These volunteers often include women members of religious faith communities who take up the mission work of seeking resources to attend to the varied needs of the shelter seekers, such as housing, legal services, medical attention, and emotional and spiritual support. This volunteer work in the United States is not unlike the service offered by clergy of providing meaningful funerals for grieving family members of women murdered by their intimate partners. In the United States, largely voluntarily funded local shelters, though desperately needed, consign faith groups to a remediating role between society and the problem of intimate violence. The groups offer help only after assaults occur. In this way, through their voluntary contribution, religious community members are in the position of complying, albeit unwittingly, with the entrenched belief promoted by liberal and conservative leaders alike that caring for the victimized women is primarily a private-sector responsibility for nonprofit, nongovernmental groups. This belief has been further bolstered by a mistaken yet prevailing view of intimate partner violence and abuse as predominantly a problem of a narrow sector of the population, poor women of color, already too easily viewed paternalistically as appropriate objects of private mission work.[64]

These attitudes are accompanied by the reality of the insufficiency of available services. Public policy researchers Radha Iyengar and Lindsay Sabik have pointed out racial disparities in their comprehensive national study documenting the shortage of U.S. domestic violence services.[65] Because of resource constraints for those who request these services, poorer areas and "areas that have predominantly black or Native American populations" appear to have many more unmet requests for help than more affluent communities.[66] Impoverished, abused women thus often find themselves simultaneously isolated by abusers, racially stigmatizing public attitudes, paternalistic charities, and a lack of choices of organizations from which to seek help. Meanwhile, well-intentioned religious volunteers participate unwittingly in the cultural normalization of public neglect of gender-based violence in the priorities of government spending and the broader U.S. political economy.

The content of my discussions of the Maria da Penha Law in Brazil resembled the overall theme that also arose in relation to the work of Ghanaian activists on the passage of their national domestic violence law. Their society-wide efforts raise the foundational moral issue of how a national investment in change was expressed governmentally. Their legislative accomplishments make more evident how the politics of and deliberate moral choices within U.S. social policies can help maintain the vulnerability of so many women and girls to gender-based violence. Even a brief introduction to Brazil's extensive federalized initiatives to address violence against women, including funding for sheltering victimized women, created a sharp contrast, representing a polar opposite perspective from the predominant U.S. cultural and political inclination against any expansion of collective fiscal responsibility for caregiving. A conservative budgetary climate had dominated U.S. federal public policy since at least the social spending cutbacks President Ronald Reagan launched in the 1980s. This U.S. crowd-pleasing goal of "reducing big government" does not allow time or space to begin a debate on the federal government's responsibility on the scale of the gender violence initiatives in Brazil. As U.S. feminist public policy theorist Mimi Abramovitz has argued about a more recent economic downturn, in the wake of the 2008 economic collapse, women were disproportionately negatively affected by aggressive attacks on spending on public-sector services and jobs on the state and federal levels.[67] As one example, throughout the early twenty-first century, dramatic spending cutbacks in state courts have meant less courthouse security and delays of up to several years in court proceedings, including domestic violence cases.[68]

Notoriously, in 2011, the Topeka, Kansas, city council almost defunded the criminalization of domestic violence because the cost of prosecuting domestic violence cases was too high.[69]

Regarding the goal of more effectively enlisting the power of the state, there are some unique U.S. characteristics that were not mirrored in the state culture Brazilian activists confronted. For instance, U.S. military spending outpaces that of any other nation in the world, and the expense of perpetual war must be incorporated in any thoughtful consideration of how to make violence against women a budgetary priority.[70] Acknowledgment of perpetual war spending again underscores the unavoidability of a transnational perspective for U.S.-American antiviolence activists. Aggressive U.S. commitments to interminable international war campaigns and widespread military bases have helped generate more sexual exploitation of and violence against women and girls abroad—many of whom are the poorest in their communities.[71] This exploitation has thrived alongside the ongoing epidemic of sexual violence within the ranks of the U.S. military, constituting a pattern of what feminist political scientist Cynthia Enloe terms the "militarization of rape."[72] To neglect this pattern of militarized sexual violence and exploitation in foreign relations would undercut the integrity of a simultaneous expression of a national moral will to end gender-based violence internally within our local communities—that is, if such a moral will were to exist.

I had a chance to learn more about the role of the state in Brazilian gender-based policy from an official key to implementing that policy. Seated in front of Mendonça, I had the opportunity to ask the coordinator of the entire investigative unit in one of Salvador's violence against women *delegacias* a host of questions about what Brazil had accomplished.[73] "How big is your staff? Are there male police officers as well as female ones? How do you deal with the problem of victimized women who change their minds about pressing charges against their abusers? Besides domestic violence, what is the range of violent offenses against women that you handle? What is the ratio of stranger-rape cases to known-assailant cases that you see? Do your laws include domestic violence within lesbian intimate partner relationships? If so, how many of these cases do you see? Are they treated in the same manner as the cases of heterosexual couples?"

Mendonça patiently responded. She carefully described the origin of these police stations in long, hard-fought battles by activist women during the 1970s and 1980s.[74] Mendonça seemed to represent what Salvador-based feminist scholars Cecilia Sardenberg and Ana Alice Alcantara Costa called "participatory state feminism" of women leaders in Brazil.[75] This type of feminist leadership was certainly not free from state co-optation, nor did it escape the tension between the state and feminism. Nonetheless, Sardenberg and Costa argued, participatory state feminism "made it possible for feminists to take a greater part in the formulation and monitoring of public policies that respond to women's demands in building a more equitable society."[76] This officer's attitude of affirming the women's movement was incongruous with what I expected from the police. When proudly identifying herself and her police work with Brazil's women's movement, she referred to her duties as a product of feminist struggle.

Without hesitation, Mendonça also listed the challenges and shortcomings of the gendered police system. Based on her long experience in Salvador, for instance, she cited a past statistic of over nine thousand cases filed in one recent year—many more cases than they could handle.[77] Overall, she was proud of what they had accomplished but recognized that they still had much more to do in order to be as effective in stopping the violence as she would like.

Mendonça personally led us through a tour of the facility. When we came to the area where some of the male perpetrators were housed, bunched together in small jail cells, I had not anticipated my reaction. Mendonça proudly, insistently pointed to the prisoners. But I hung back, creating an awkward moment with my refusal even as her assertive demeanor and rapidly moving dark-brown hands beckoned, directing me to step closer.

I could not see what Mendonça saw. She knew the stories of their victims' suffering. She could directly connect them to those snapshots of victims on her office wall. She could see the product of her team's investigative work. The very existence of the DEAM jail cells represented the formal mechanism of accountability that her feminist commitment had helped develop for over twenty years.[78] Glancing quickly in their direction, I did not pity these black men accused of or sentenced for perpetrating violence against women and children. But nor did I experience the catharsis I desired. Instead, I felt a sense of deep, angry sadness as I thought of the story each man likely represented of criminal, deliberately inflicted pain. The permeating sadness I felt was matched by my discomfort with staring at those black male bodies as if they were an exhibit in a Brazilian museum.

Women's police stations and other aspects of the expanded federal government intervention under the Maria da Penha Law exemplified the results of feminist activism. This comprehensive national law had served as an anchoring, galvanizing focus for a wide array of activist leadership, especially for generating public antipathy to gender-based violence. But I am not sure that Brazil's expansion of state power through an increased criminal justice apparatus provides a model for addressing violence against women in the United States. This kind of knowledge may not be translatable to the U.S. context and perhaps should not be.

In particular, the emphasis on criminalization in the Brazilian law cast doubts on the merits of that approach for impoverished U.S. black women, for example, who were already subject to hazardous state interventions in their economic and family lives. Beth Richie, a U.S.-American black feminist social theorist, has trenchantly articulated these hazards. She is one of too few activist/scholars committed to analysis of antiracism in the United States who, while acknowledging the mounting problem of the mass incarceration of black men, focuses on the plight of assaulted and abused black women.[79] Richie proclaimed the current climate for the most socioeconomically disadvantaged black communities to be a "prison nation." With this naming, she referred to the stranglehold produced by a combination of factors including increased criminalization, aggressive law enforcement, and the undermining of civil and human rights such that "women of color are more likely to be treated as criminals than as victims when they are abused."[80]

Certain socioeconomic and racial cautions must be applied if we are to earnestly contemplate possibilities for relying on a radically enhanced and creative state response to violence against women in the United States. Currently, state intervention varies dramatically in the lives of U.S.-American community members in accord with their socioeconomic class and racial/ethnic background as well as their immigration status. In particular, women in low-income black and brown communities are routinely victimized by not only the abusive practices of state agencies that provide social services but also police and immigration officials.[81]

When reflecting on my visit to the women's police station, I was not sure how to incorporate comprehensive and accurate comparisons between the rampant police violence that was also regularly leveled against members of low-income black communities in Brazil and the violence by parallel state officials in the United States.[82] To make useful comparisons for transnational learning across these contexts compels listening that attends to the correct features of the state apparatus in the Brazilian context. The identification of analogous criteria for effectively addressing gender-based violence—such as how racism systemically allies with the intimate violence that the activists took on—merely constitutes a starting point in mapping the state, religious, historical, and other foundational cultural influences.

To reduce the approach described by the activists I encountered in Salvador to a singular reliance on the increased policing stipulated in the Maria da Penha Law would be grossly inaccurate. To narrowly concentrate on governmental institutional practices and leaders would neglect the role of ongoing nongovernmental activist work in forming and reforming community responses to the gender-based violence. It would also omit what was perhaps the hardest to translate yet most important lesson to learn: the fundamental courage-spirit of their movement.

In one of the low-income neighborhoods of Salvador, I learned more about how enforcement of the Penha Law worked from the grassroots perspective. My colleague-hosts, Nessette and Erica, and I followed two community leaders up a steep hill into their neighborhood. Low-income communities in Brazil like this one are sometimes called *favelas*, often translated to mean slums or shantytowns. I met two women activists, Jacinta Marta and Taveres Leiro, who described how their group addressed violence against women within their own neighborhood. They exposed their deeply critical view of the Maria da Penha Law and the many ways it failed to render the assistance it had promised.[83] Speaking with them helped place the work of the state I had glimpsed at the *delegacia* into a broader syncopation of community responses. The women's police station represented one chord in a larger movement, albeit a major chord, but one, as I would learn from Marta and Leiro, that was in need of ongoing, modifying, activist engagement.

As I followed these leaders, the muscles in my calves and thighs burned. We headed up the narrow street at what seemed like an angle pretty close to vertical. Brazilian *favelas* are known to be high-crime neighborhoods usually rampant with drug-related crime controlled by ruthless violent gangs. But somehow I did not feel apprehensive. I did feel physically challenged to keep up with the rapid, determined pace of the women activists leading the way. They were very light-tan-skinned women whom I guessed were in their early forties. They did not seem to notice the steepness of the hills as they rattled off information about the area without any sign of breathlessness. They said they had limited time to talk with me because of a busy schedule that day. The narrow street we climbed was mostly deserted. I noticed one man milling about on the porch of one of the small homes crowded together on the narrow street. He seemed to be staring in the direction of the activists but then slowly turned his head, looking away from the two women with a sour expression spreading across his face as if he smelled something truly foul.

The meeting space where Marta and Leiro led us consisted of a large room in a small concrete house. Their building seemed to have been carved directly into the earth of the steep hill. A government sign on the exterior indicated that this was a community space where support for the prevention of HIV and AIDS could be found. As we began to talk together the leaders became impatient with the tortoise pace of my elementary Portuguese and asked if I could just use the translator to save time. I hid my disappointment because I had thought, apparently mistakenly, that I had been communicating fairly well.

Their sixteen-year-old group, the Women's Collective of Calafate, focused on confronting violence against women through advocacy, such as protests against the state's ineffective implementation of the Penha Law. They offered direct assistance to neighborhood women seeking to escape from and survive the immediate crisis of intimate violence. In multiple ways, they were on call twenty-four hours a day for the women of their community. Marta and Leiro stressed that they were "a self-educating, self-organizing group." With no "external people like social workers or psychologists; we organize ourselves, just women from the community," they stated emphatically. They gave details of the day-to-day realities of abused women's lives to which those who crafted the law had not given consideration and that impeded access to state services the law had created.[84]

Marta and Leiro voiced quite a few criticisms based on their "on-the-ground" experiences of supporting women. For instance, many women could not afford the transportation costs to get to the distant police stations and therefore did not file complaints when they needed to. "There ought to be vouchers" for transportation, Marta and Leiro asserted. They also commented on how officers were poorly trained and that follow-ups on complaints took too long, months or sometimes even a year. They told specific stories about how components of the law meant to offer protections for violence against lesbians failed to do so. In addition to their on-going women's support groups, the Collective routinely launched protests to government officials about the inadequacy of the services even while continuing to assist women in accessing those services.

Members of the Collective and other activist leaders had participated in a 2010 comprehensive study to evaluate Brazil's governmental services, titled "Domestic Violence and Women's Access to Justice in Brazil."[85] Stipulations in the original law required this kind of evaluation and accountability. Among the six cities studied, the report noted that some of the highest percentages of problems in the implementation of the law had occurred in the predominantly black Salvador area. Many of those women, for example, expressed that they had received little guidance or information when filing their complaints.[86] Salvador also included some of the lowest percentages of women who could affirm that they knew how the law operated.[87]

Additionally, other critics of the law rejected its foundational premise about the urgency of addressing gender-based violence. Part of the criticism of the policy by conservative Brazilian political leaders had directly referenced religion. Quoted in the "Access to Justice" report were certain problematic and pervasively taught Christian ideas about morality and gender that lent support for violence against women. A Brazilian judge was among those cited as referencing Christianity to help criticize the law. This judge was from another more southern area of Brazil and had apparently strongly resisted implementation of the Maria da Penha Law. He argued against its supposed discrimination against men, pointing out both that "human disgrace started in Eden: because of women" and that "Jesus was a man."[88] This kind of religious posturing echoed similar ways in which conservatives sometimes utilized Christianity in U.S. policy debates on gender issues and the law. In one widely publicized instance during a federal election cycle, a Christian nominee for the U.S. Senate from Indiana, Richard Mourdock, asserted his opposition to legalized reproductive choices for women that included abortion. He commented that if "life" results even from "the horrible situation of rape," then it is "something God intended to happen."[89] His political advocacy of gender restrictions in the law that included God's use of gender violence to enforce them demonstrated a remarkable dexterity in the maintenance of rape culture in U.S. public life.

In the Christianity-dominated cultural contexts of both the United States and Brazil, such violence-supporting public rhetoric serves as a general reminder of the readily available gender-based moral gravity that this religious tradition offers to the political opponents of women's rights activists. The role of Christianity in the moral conflagrations within the national politics of Brazil is complicated. It has been a source of some of the most creative forms of feminist liberation theology, including innovative black Christian centers in Salvador. Yet the wider field of women's rights activists had clearly proceeded without relying upon the Christian religion to summon a Christianity-derived, egalitarian, woman-affirming notion from its believers to create national policies that address gender-based violence.

Activism that constructively pursued an explicitly gendered form of justice functioned through cumulative strands of mobilization. Feminist activists had played a key role in initiating public policy that expressed a national moral will for viewing gender-based violence as intolerable in their civil society. State agents, some identifiably "participatory state feminists," implemented the law. Others, like Sandra dos Santos, rooted in her Candomblé faith, delivered the news of its resources as one aspect of her faith-driven antiviolence commitment. Community activists like Marta and Leiro who responded to immediate struggles of abused women monitored the policy's efficacy on a daily basis. They also contributed the political labor of organizing targeted local protests. In the "Access to Justice" report, feminist scholar-activists comprehensively evaluated the extent to which the law's implementation fulfilled its original mandate. Even in the disagreements between participatory state feminists and activist-academic feminist critics of state failures, a shared commonality of purpose held. They insisted on making the state accountable for its responsibility to reflect a collective moral consensus against domestic violence. And their strategy for accountability fundamentally (though not exclusively) featured an elaborate national policy criminalizing this violence.

Quite dissimilar to the gender-based criticism made by Christian religious conservatives in their context, feminist critiques of the policy by scholars such as Cecília MacDowell Santos pointed to the problematic implications of the policy's dependence on narrow gender assumptions.[90] Some feminist critiques debated the necessity for engineering gendered responses to the violence. Others criticized the entire system of women's police stations as founded on an essentialist conceptualization of gender that perpetuated erroneous assumptions that were dangerous for abused women seeking help. This state-sponsored policing strategy assumed that, for instance, women police officers would be intrinsically more sympathetic to abused women than male officers would be—an assumption that was not always true. The gender expectations implicit in this strategy could make the women seeking help even more vulnerable to abuse by policewomen rather than receiving the state protection to which they were entitled.

The female gender identity of the two community activists sitting across from me had a profound significance for their work as well. Their gender contributed to the riskiness of their daily witness. At one point, the discussion turned to the subject of the dangers they faced from neighboring violent male drug dealers who had repeatedly threatened their lives. The dealers did not like the way the Collective relentlessly supported women in their community who wanted to leave their male abusers. In response to my questions about these risks, Marta and Leiro exchanged glances with each other and uttered a humorless laugh.

After our meeting ended, I watched as they receded back into their neighborhood. They briskly walked away, heading farther up the sharply inclined narrow road. Their bodies propelled forward in a determined motion. Their hands moved as they consulted and talked. Again, I marveled at their spirited gait, traveling uphill as if its steepness was nothing for them to surmount.

The inspiring encounter with Marta and Leiro gave rise to considerations about a way of defining blackness that focused on actions. The meaning of black identity might stretch beyond assumptions linked to skin color, cultural values and relationships, and sociopolitical history that have been key to forming the boundaries of U.S.-American racial classifications. Instead of merely relying on such familiar U.S.-American assumptions about defining race, how could the meaning of blackness be expanded to embrace the type of activism to which Marta and Leiro gave expression in their lives? Admittedly, the linking of Marta and Leiro's example to this redefinition involves translation to a U.S. racial worldview.

Blackness represented a political touchstone in discussions with other gender violence activist leaders who tellingly reiterated the need to acknowledge the role of broader political contours of anti-black racism in Brazil. There were obvious racial disparities found, for instance, in statistics on the uneven implementation of the Maria da Penha Law in poorer black neighborhoods. Therefore, for many of the activists I met a distinctive black survival power had to be vitally inflected in the gendered work of addressing the violence there. In their tenacious grassroots leadership Marta and Leiro demonstrated their commitment to this integral task as they concentrated on emancipating black women from violent male control in their neighborhood. Their work teaches us how black power can reside in gendered freedom of women from the intimate violence of men and from racially discriminatory, negligent state responses.

Transnational intercultural learning from the Salvador activists can amplify certain knotty details of creating space for cultural translations that further antiviolence work in the United States. Reflecting on the anti-black racism emphasis of Brazilian women domestics at the Federation might be a useful catalyst for probing understandings of blackness in antiracism organizing among immigrant domestic laborers in the U.S. context from multiple racial/ethnic/national backgrounds who are similarly vulnerable to sexual exploitation. On the one hand, the determination of Brazilian activists who galvanized national moral will to enact federal antiviolence policies and then their monitoring of the implementation of those laws ought to be translatable to the U.S.-American context. Doing so could expand U.S. moral imaginations, which have traditionally low expectations for a meaningful state response to violence. On the other hand, these lessons might not be translatable to the U.S. context precisely because our moral imaginations are so diminished by our customs of prioritizing the U.S. war economy and tolerating abusive forms of state power targeting women (and men) in black and brown poor communities. When a state obsessively asserts its privilege and impunity, it increases women's vulnerability to assaults both domestically and abroad, especially within and surrounding U.S. military bases.

The theme of vulnerability that arose in these discussions can contribute to a conceptualization of antiviolence that takes seriously the spirituality of activism. In Brazil, this spiritual impetus relates specifically to the gendered, bodily vulnerability of women, which in turn can serve as a collective resource for countering sexual and domestic forms of gender-based violence. The spirituality I experienced there pulsated with social movement perseverance that had taken shape in direct response to the privatized humiliations of bodily assaults. In Salvador, the memory of black victimization and survival of forced servitude that routinely included such assaults fed their resolve. Rather than a focus on a perfect or invulnerable deity usually associated with religions, this nonreligious spirituality is characterized by an adaptable chain of imperfect yet persistent responses to women's vulnerability to intimate violence. Leaders pursued just relations in societal structures and holistic restoration out of a loyal concern for one another's vulnerability.

Simultaneously, in Salvador the distinctive religious spirituality embedded in the Candomblé tradition has also led practitioners such as Sandra to recognize and attend to women's vulnerability to gender-based violence. It is not the kind of spirituality that encourages a universalistic indifference to sex/gender politics in everyday exchanges, especially intimate ones within our shared living spaces. Nor does it make allowances for willful amnesia about the particular circumstances of racist injustice in their history. Rather, a fierce hold on the details of such politics and historical memories has been embedded in the tradition and enabled a kind of decolonized spirituality. As this Brazilian setting illustrated, spirituality can lend vitality to the task of forging ahead with antiviolence ideals that take on the challenges of creating a wholly different kind of racial history in the future.

4

Precious Bodies

"The majority of victims are black . . . and it's kind of, there is this image of black women in Brazil, being black and being hot and being ready for sex. That's something that the tourists come here for—for black women more often," said Débora Cristina da Silva Aranha, a white English-speaking Brazilian activist.[1] I met her in the offices of the NGO Winrock in the city of Salvador.[2]

Aranha was the coordinator/chief administrator for Winrock's Salvador office. This NGO was housed in an office building several stories high in one of the more upscale neighborhoods of Salvador that I had visited so far. Winrock is a U.S.-based international development organization. Its beautifully typeset, written in English, and glossily illustrated literature described its programs in Brazil as offering "innovative training programs to raise awareness and promote safe behavior for women at risk of being trafficked."[3] Aranha had initially explained to me that their group focused on the abuse of children in the form of trafficking. In an attempt to document the problem, they collected data on child trafficking in Bahia.[4] Their work in Salvador, where the majority of the population is Afro-Brazilian, revealed the vulnerability of girls and young women of African descent to sexual exploitation, particularly by some tourists.[5]

The strategies of activist leaders I had met earlier that focused on disrupting women's vulnerability to abuse and violence in their domestic work and home lives differed from the global dynamics of vulnerability with which these leaders had to contend. Winrock and others concentrated their attention on antiviolence responses to sexual exploitation by strangers that black women and girls encounter in public life as a result of sex tourism. My discussions with these NGO leaders provoke consideration of the complicity of contemporary forms of Christian religious influence in the exploitative practices of sex trafficking and sex tourism. Certain Christian moral understandings of sinfulness and normative sexual expression can contribute judgments that calibrate whose gendered bodies among the economically marginal in the local population are seen as precious and whose are not. Such judgments render the supposedly good intentions in Christian anti-trafficking commitments hollow and misleading. But resistance to Christian sexism expressed by a Christian activist NGO leader I meet in Salvador provides an example of the generative fuel that a Christian critique of Christian moral assumptions about gender and sexuality can provide for anti-trafficking activism.

My conversations with activists at the NGOs also foreground some of the ways in which anti-trafficking goals and strategies must account for transnational cultural values related to racial status and consumerist desires. Aranha's assertion with which I began this chapter names the pivotal role of outsiders' perceptions of "black women in Brazil [as] being black and being hot and being ready for sex." Thus, in this particular form of activist antiviolence work, whether it is in the desire for freedom by trafficked women and girls or the anti-traffickers' desire to set them free, the racialized moral goals and perceptions at stake are inherently transnational. A conceptualization of sexual violence related to sex tourism highlights the role of existing transnational ties between the United States and Brazil and evokes similar concerns with regard to other popular U.S. tourist destinations. The topic of sex tourism adds to earlier parallel linkages yet another dimension of reflection on transnational connections related to issues of race and religion in gender violence activism. Instigated by my encounters with these Salvador NGO activist-leaders, this discussion brings into sharper focus the need to address the ethics of how desires should be controlled in border-crossing antiviolence approaches. Consideration of these dynamics begins with a focus on defining and understanding the role of coercion in sex trafficking, particularly in sex tourism.

Desire and Coercion: Definitions

Traveling with my hosts, Nessette and Erica, we arrived by bus for my appointment at the Winrock office. They were teaching me how to take the city buses, and when we started out I had readily joined them and the bustling crowd of city dwellers preparing to board. Following along in the long line of adult Bahians engrossed in getting to their destinations, I had pushed through the turnstile on the bus. I was unaccustomed to both the turnstile and the collection of fares at the back rather than front of the bus. I double-checked to make sure that I handed over the correct number of Brazilian reals as I paid my fare. I could get a better sense of everyday community life while riding on a weekday morning bus and therefore felt less like a tourist than I did when we rode in taxis. Tourists doggedly pursue a nonstop mission to fulfill their desires to consume local sights, cuisine, wares, activities, and even knowledge. For some reason, riding on the bus nudged me toward suspending the tourist impulses inhabiting my own senses. If only for a few minutes, I allowed the vibrating hum of the bus and salty air of the port city to lull me into closing my eyes, leaning my body back on the seat in a slack repose, and halting my fretting thoughts. A state of contemplative, eyes-closed, bodily stillness might have been counterintuitive for an international visitor, especially for one with my focus on encounters that would illuminate ideas about how best to participate in active struggle. But maybe the counterintuitive stillness I claimed for those few minutes helped summon the psychospiritual awareness required to cultivate a desire to communicate rather than consume. I am not sure.

Salvador, Bahia, is one of Brazil's major tourism destinations with millions of international visitors each year. It is the most popular destination in the northeastern part of the nation.[6] Indeed, Brazil has put considerable resources into developing the tourism industry in Bahia, specifically targeting U.S. visitors.[7] It was hardly happenstance that so many U.S. black tourists were there to explore varied expressions of African cultural roots.[8] One *BBC* reporter who interviewed the Bahia tourism secretary noted that tourist officials were directly targeting "the African-American market and they hope it will help Brazil as well as the visitors."[9]

In the anti-trafficking NGO office, Aranha amicably pointed with her head to her black coworker sitting behind me and said, "Let's just bring Leide into the conversation because she is very much into the black movement here." I nodded in agreement and turned to say hello to Leide Manuela Santos, a tall, thin, dark-brown-skinned woman who had been quietly sitting at her desk in the back of room, behind the table where I sat with my two host-translators and Aranha.

"Yes, there is an issue of fetish of black women" and how tourists view their bodies, "but there is also their economic vulnerability, much more than white women have," Santos stressed when she joined the conversation.[10]

I leaned toward her with a facial expression that I hoped conveyed attentiveness. With my body language, I was trying to let Santos know that I understood the gravity of her point even though she and I were dependent upon translation of our words as we spoke to one another. Economic and racial relationships constituted a place in the conversation about the vulnerability of girls to sex trafficking where Santos wanted to tarry.

While discussing anti-trafficking work in Salvador, I encountered slightly different nuances for defining the nature of the violence than I had presumed I would. As do most U.S.-based gender justice scholars and activists, the Salvador NGO leaders distinguished between sexual abuse, sex trafficking, sex tourism, and sex slavery. Among feminist scholars, religious advocates, and international policy makers, debates are ongoing about how to define the nature and extent of the coercion each of these categories involves. But I was not convinced of the degree to which the task of constructing finely tuned distinctions among the illicit, sexually exploitative practices behind these terms mattered for the basic goal of supporting the human dignity of black girls and women targeted for exploitation. As my exchanges with leaders in Salvador helped demonstrate, however, details do matter for gauging the complex amalgam of the agency and victimization around which NGO activists design their social change work and advocates formulate their policy goals.

In one example of how even the definition of vulnerability is contested, Brazil-based researcher Julie Lima de Pérez pointed to the 2000 U.N. Trafficking Protocol.[11] The protocol refers to *trafficked persons* as those who face threat, force, coercion, abduction, fraud, deception, and abuse of power or of a position of vulnerability. Lima de Pérez analyzed how this protocol established the "abuse of a position of vulnerability" as one of the means used to identify trafficked persons. She argued that this idea "has been misappropriated in the context of human trafficking, particularly in the case of trafficking for sexual exploitation," and could be used to constrain migration or even travel for leisure, "particularly of women who are seen as (potential) sex workers."[12] Ironically, in attempts to prevent the sexual exploitation of women and girls that occurs in sex trafficking, a focus on recognizing their vulnerability can foster their coercion. Some analysts like Lima de Pérez have warned of organized responses that include coercive preventative policy measures that are intended to protect the vulnerable but in actuality may restrict their freedom of movement. Vulnerable girls and young women may wish to travel abroad for a wide variety of reasons. Targeting them in well-intentioned media campaigns in which anti-trafficking NGOs caution them about the dangers of traffickers and sex tourists, anti-trafficking messages actively try to curb their desires to travel.

In her critical analysis of anti-trafficking NGOs in Bahia, U.S. anthropologist Erica Lorraine Williams asserted, "The specter of sex tourism has created a situation in which Brazilian women of African descent who want to move beyond national borders are not only discouraged because of the 'risks and dangers' of trafficking but are also automatically seen as suspect."[13] Local anti-trafficking activist leaders had to devise strategies that weighed vulnerability, desires, and coercion in a precise calculus that avoided any complicity in treating the girls as the suspects similar to the traffickers and tourists who wanted to sexually exploit them.

As she discussed the vulnerability of girls with me, Aranha delineated a distinction between the sexual abuse and trafficking of children: "trafficking is a very specific form of sexual violence."[14] Certainly, children are emotionally and physically abused when they are sexually exploited. But her organization was not focused on what is traditionally understood as child sexual abuse: "something that happens within the community or home, with close relatives or neighbors."[15] Instead, in Winrock's work in Bahia they understood sex trafficking as the business network that utilizes coercion and deception to move human beings around the country usually from rural to city areas or around the globe from city to city and sell them as commercial sexual products. In the global business of sex trafficking, the United States was more often a destination country than a country of origin for merchandised women and girls. But in Brazil as well as the United States, the trafficking that occurs is both internal to the country as well as international.

Sex tourism often involves international travelers as perpetrators of sexual exploitation and is not synonymous with sex trafficking, which always involves some wider network. However, some sex tourists do access an established business network through sex tourist clubs in order to set up their exploits in the countries they plan to visit.[16] Sex tourists tend to enter into one-on-one contracts for purchasing sex either for a one-time encounter or sometimes for longer-term arrangements. Although these sexual purchases usually occur in the foreign locale the tourist is visiting, in certain cases they also involve moving the "purchase" back to the tourist's home country. In what is termed *sex slavery*, a practice that very often operates in collusion with sex trafficking, sexually exploited persons are trapped in a kind of debt bondage to their supposed owners and have to pay through delivery of sexual services until or unless their freedom can be purchased. Aranha mentioned that during their data collection on sex trafficking in Bahia, they had heard of a price as high as thirty thousand dollars per female victim-survivor.

Sexual coercion demands activist attention whether it occurs within broad sex trafficking networks, individual instances of sex tourism, or extended periods of sexual enslavement, and regardless of whether a child, youth, or adult is exploited. In this organization's work in Bahia, each instance has usually involved a coercive commodification of how certain bodies of African descent are seen as gendered. Individuals who sexually prey upon girls often target the most vulnerable populations, particularly those who live in socioeconomically marginal communities. Deception is a primary tool for predatory and coercive sexual invasions of girls. To recognize this sexual commerce as a form of gender-based violence requires an understanding of the varied coercive means that are operative.

But in listening to Aranha and Santos, it became evident that a definition wholly centered on sexual coercion is insufficiently comprehensive for capturing the fundamentals of the violence against the mind, body, and spirit that trafficking involves. The slow, measured pace of my discussion with Aranha and Santos differed markedly from my rapid interactions with the two activists in the *favela*. Aranha and Santos slowly enumerated the circumstances of individual girls with whom they had worked in order to clarify how broader systemic factors contributed to their victimization.

Santos kept drawing my focus back to the consequences of economic vulnerability for poor black women and girls and stressed that this was the most fundamental problem that needed to be addressed. "It's because of all of the things the black woman lacks from the time she is a child, and sometimes, also the issues in her own family," Santos said, incorporating the racialized dimension of the harsh economic realities that mattered. "They are driven away from their homes because it is not a safe place. Sometimes, they are abused, so they turn to the streets," Aranha interpreted. She made clear how the desperation produced by the experience of sexual abuse inside a child's home allied with the goals of sex traffickers seeking vulnerable and desperate children.

"And these young women, they go out in search of what they consider other opportunities. She may think she comes out profiting from selling her body," Santos continued. Her words, "She may think she comes out profiting," were startling to me. Santos's depiction of victimization belied the typical image of a female victim of trafficking as frozen in helplessness and awaiting rescue.

Too often, widely agreed upon definitions of sex trafficking include presumptions of total helplessness on the part of those victimized. Purportedly, only a complete lack of conscious will when one's body is prostituted to men for money or "gifts" merits compassion and proves one's worthiness of rescue. In sex trafficking, like other forms of gender-based violence, the degree to which coercion is recognizable rests upon culturally informed definitions of authentic vulnerability of the victimized. In the U.S. context, Christian views of sexuality and gender deeply informed this understanding of sexual victimization that is also embedded in other cultural and political anti-trafficking perspectives. The conditional compassion for trafficked girls and women in these Christian-based U.S. perspectives reflects assumptions about sex, vulnerability, and coercion incompatible with the perspective Santos articulated.

Mores of dominant Protestant Christianity are such a normalized, mainstream aspect of U.S.-American culture and politics that it can take effort to identify any of their distinguishing features within anti-trafficking efforts. As U.S. Christian ethicist Yvonne Zimmerman has explained in her detailed analysis of religion and U.S. anti-trafficking policy initiatives, "concern about sexual exploitation and sexual propriety that is expressed with regard to an issue like human trafficking must be understood not just as [U.S.-]American beneficence but also as indelibly Protestant and as expressing Protestant sensibilities."[17]

Protestant sensibilities have been given expression by a range of U.S. anti-trafficking policy makers and advocates, some of whom religiously identify as Christian while others are secular state officials. Zimmerman argues that the underlying Christian Protestant values framing the conditionality of their compassion are evidenced, for example, in their emphasis on sexual regulation that equates sexual freedom exclusively with heterosexual marriage. As she rightly criticized, it is problematic when U.S. leaders link eradication of trafficking to a view of trafficked persons as in need of "redemption" or "a Savior."[18] Anti-trafficking efforts driven by one's desire to be a redeeming savior for a trafficked person maintain an erroneously individualized lens for understanding how trafficking is perpetuated and thus for how it can be eradicated.

For some conservative Christian U.S.-based anti-trafficking groups, heterosexual marriage constitutes the precise form of redemption that sexually trafficked girls need.[19] In this logic, heterosexual marriage for individually trafficked girls and women provides a rectifying sexual response for the supposed taint of the fornication that was forced upon them. Marriage constitutes a religiously informed heterosex-regulation response and assists in narrowing an understanding of the scope of trafficking in a manner that excludes crucial factors the Winrock leaders identified as key to the endurance of trafficking, such as how racist objectification helped drive the desire to sexually exploit girls.

Aranha supplemented the point Santos had begun about how some of the girls who were trafficked thought about the need to escape their poverty. "The girls want to be able to buy goods," she stated, "they want to have a cell phone, they want to have clothing, they want to have things."[20] As if feeding me bits of bread to help me follow the trail of insights they were offering about the economic factors trafficking involved, Aranha provided concrete illustrations of Santos's point. They called attention to the lure of specific commercial goods that symbolized the better life and freedom the girls craved.

As they offered details, I sought to retain my grasp on their definition of violence. There is a sacralized U.S.-American commitment to cherishing the commercialized appetites of neoliberal capitalism that makes it difficult for me to fully recognize their depiction of the violence of trafficking. My upbringing as a U.S.-American means that I have been indoctrinated into the supposed societal good of perpetually stoking consumerist longings for heaping amounts and varieties of foods, the latest fashionable clothing and shoes, home fixtures and furniture upgrades, the newest versions of cars and new car options, the most updated electronic media device attached to your fingertips or wrist, and other insatiable longings. At the beginning of the twenty-first century, a U.S. president had even recommended consumerist economic activities as an important remedy for a grieving, fearful public in the wake of the historic national tragedy on September 11, 2001.[21] I needed no translation on this point about how a constant drive for the acquisition of commercial products—supposedly goods—was understood as a means for bettering one's life emotionally, spiritually, and materially. This was a basic and primary social value within neoliberal capitalist societies as well as in our interdependent global economic lives. However, my encounter with the Brazilian activists generated a fresh realization of how the stoking of this primary drive could provide a razor-sharp weapon for sex traffickers and sex tourists seeking children and youth.

Consumerist values are sometimes directly featured in anti-trafficking goals. For some U.S. anti-trafficking advocates, revitalizing capitalist free-market values in the lives of those who have been trafficked represents an invaluable, liberating response. In an essay on Christian ethics and human trafficking activism, U.S. Christian ethicists Yvonne Zimmerman and Letitia Campbell discuss this approach, citing the views of Kevin Bales, a leading U.S. activist opponent of modern slavery and human trafficking, as an example. They point to Bales's support of neoliberal capitalist responses championing the goal of helping freed slaves to become consumers.[22] Here, the task of assisting those who had previously been sexually trafficked to participate in the free market as consumers is represented as enabling the kind of freedom that can sustain them in the aftermath of enslavement. Defining freedom from human trafficking in terms of a deepened commitment to free-market consumption and expanded consumerist desires starkly conflicted with the analysis of Aranha and Santos. For these Salvador NGO activists, the violence of human trafficking underscored the manner in which the relentless, systemic production of insatiable consumerist desire could both fuel the vulnerability of the girls and equip those who wanted to sexually exploit them.

In a contrasting perspective, Protestant moral assumptions sometimes comfortably merged with neoliberal capitalist free-market values in U.S. anti-trafficking efforts. U.S.-based feminist studies theorists Elizabeth Bernstein and Janet Jakobsen critically point to unusual alliances between Christian Protestant evangelicals and secular feminists in their embrace of a free-market approach to sex trafficking: "Evangelical as well as secular feminist groups have increasingly committed themselves to this approach, no longer framing the problem of human trafficking in terms of broader dynamics of globalization, gendered labour and migration . . . but rather as a humanitarian issue that global capitalists can help combat."[23] Bernstein and Jakobsen skeptically appraise a conjoined Christian evangelical internationalist and secular anti-trafficking activist view of participation in entry-level jobs as freedom for trafficked persons.[24] They note how the recent emphasis of evangelical Protestants and secular feminists runs counter to earlier concerns expressed by antiglobalization activists who had protested unacceptable sweatshop conditions for low-level workers that proliferated in neoliberal capitalism. As the desire to save sexually trafficked persons becomes indistinguishable from, for example, a desire to create a steady pool of unskilled and low-paid workers for private industry, traditional divisions among anti-trafficking activists dissipate. Liberal and conservative, secular and Christian, feminist and antifeminist could all seemingly converge in their acceptance of the redemptive capacity of the market. A Christian mission and redemption narrative lends forceful moral language and symbolism to the overall meaning of anti-trafficking endeavors in this problematic synergy that hides exploitative free market consequences.

Entitlement of Gendered Bodies

In the politics of consumerist desire that saturates so many responses to sexual trafficking, explicit racial dynamics are tied to market economy concerns and also thrive beyond them. Distinctive harmful racial attitudes, such as longings for white racial entitlement, must not be neglected when considering transnational forms of sexual violence and exploitation. Certainly, Aranha and Santos explained, traffickers exploited the dreams of the girls for international travel and made false promises about helping them become well-known singers and dancers. But Santos, in particular, also wanted to make it clear to me that "trafficking was one of the sicknesses of racism."[25] In her view, racism is not merely one factor that needs to be considered alongside other contributors to the exploitation of the trafficked girls. Rather, understanding trafficking will enable a better understanding of racism.

Aranha contextualized vulnerability to the racist dynamics of trafficking in terms of a lack of many social supports to which children should be entitled and also of their longing, in many instances, for a safe place away from abuse at home. "There is this image of the foreigner, the man coming from abroad, that he would be a prince that would save their lives . . . sometimes a white man coming, with blue eyes, coming from abroad," Aranha described, "so they fall in love with this man, tourist, but actually some of them are traffickers."[26] Santos concentrated on internal black community dynamics: "There's the issue of bettering the race."[27] She spelled out her view of the perspective of the girls, bluntly stating that to them "black men don't have economic stability. . . . [It is a] possible step up in life because white men, just by being white men, already represent so much in society."[28] Her comments brought attention to the question of what role unearned white privilege and status might play in how white male tourists were perceived. The assertion made available a microcosmic analysis of trafficking that marked what was usually left unmarked: the omnipresence of systemic white racist values. They helped maintain the vulnerability of the girls to exploitation.

Yet I was uneasy with the description of the girls in this discussion. First, it seemed to misleadingly presume that all victimized girls are heterosexual.[29] Second, when limited to scrutinizing the racial illusions of the girls, our discussion seemed unjustly one-sided. This focus could too easily be interpreted as a victim-blaming caricature of the girls. In her critique of NGO campaigns against sex trafficking and sex tourism in Bahia, U.S.-based anthropologist Erica Williams pointed out how these campaigns often simplistically "depict Brazilian women of African descent as not only naïve but also eager to use transnational ties to foreigners as a 'get-rich-quick' scheme."[30] If the girls and women are depicted as schemers trying to gain economic advantages, they lose the credibility of their victim status and are portrayed as blameworthy even in the messages NGOs try to craft as public warnings for them about the dire consequences and risks posed by sex traffickers and sex tourists.

But I do not think that Santos and Aranha intended to uphold a victim-blaming indictment of the morality of the girls. They had a decidedly nonjudgmental attitude about the aspirations of the girls and insisted upon attributing subjectivity to them—a subjectivity that comprised neither unencumbered agency nor totally helpless victimization. The dignity and worth in the moral subjectivity they assumed about the girls with whom they had spent so much time incorporated a full range of social longings, desires, dreams, immaturity, maturity, keen survival instincts, and inadequacies. This understanding of their subjectivity sidestepped a standard individualistic, victim-agency dichotomy that was routinely debated in analyses of violence against women. Instead the leaders were mapping out a decidedly antiracist definition of what it meant to combat sex trafficking and sex tourism in their activist work. The vulnerability and coercion of the trafficked girls that activists had to find strategies to fend off was found in transnationally imbibed white racist values and desires for the conferral of white racial status.

Even when we acknowledge the influence of white racism in the girls' desires for social status and how that ties directly to their sexual exploitation, a focus on judging the self-image or aspirations of the girls remains. This focus is deeply unsatisfactory because it hinders an adequate grasp of the extent of the role of transnational white racism in helping to perpetuate sexual exploitation. Male tourists' sexual and social motivations are pivotal. Issues of race and social status are often at play for the self-image of the male tourists as well. U.K.-based sociologists Julia O'Connell Davidson and Jacqueline Sanchez Taylor studied sex tourists in a variety of popular destinations (especially in the Caribbean) and offered observations relevant to Bahia. Davidson and Taylor note that for some white tourists, "sex tourism can also be understood as a collective behavior oriented toward the restoration of a generalized belief about what it is to be white: to be truly white is to be served, revered, and envied by Others. For black [U.S.] American male sex tourists . . . a sense of Western-ness and so of inclusion in a privileged world" is affirmed.[31] Their study illustrates this latter view with comments from a U.S. African American male sex tourist whose visits included Brazil among other countries in Latin America and Asia.[32] He pointed to the status, cooperation, and deference he was accorded when utilizing U.S. dollars instead of the local currency to bring the "girls" he wanted into his hotels.

This example of a heterosexual African American tourist from the United States illuminates a harmful element lurking among the meanings of racial inclusivity, one that reflects the realities of hierarchical racial privileges. Here, the longing for generative black racial connections could not be further from the pursuit of a sense of belonging to a self-affirming global Africana community of color. Instead, a perpetually unappeased desire for entitlement seems to prevail, a yearning for publicly conferred worth that matches the worth accorded U.S. whites, and this U.S.-based black racial desire can travel to the foreign site. And sexual exploitation of the brown and black girls who reside there may be seen as a means to its attainment.

Sexual and racial desires of male tourists were also sometimes a central driving force when they sought out Candomblé *terreiros* as a local attraction to visit. As Williams found in her study of sex tourism in Bahia, "the realm of the sacred is not left unscathed in the transnational touristscape of Salvador, where eroticized blackness is situated as the valued ideal."[33] Some tourists across racial and national groupings as well as sexual identities and orientations devour the sense of entitlement the touristscape offers to participate in the eroticizing of Bahian blackness. In my discussion of the role of religion with the anti-trafficking activists at Winrock, Santos had immediately mentioned Candomblé and the need for attention to the sexual exploitation of men by tourists that also occurred there.[34]

Gay male sex tourists sometimes targeted gay male Candomblé adherents for exploitation. In one example, Williams describes a meeting with a Candomblé priest who was a black gay political activist in Bahia. He denounced the ways in which sex tourism sometimes infiltrated their spaces of worship.[35] He told her about gay foreign tourists he had met, "who were interested in exploring Candomblé not for spiritual reasons but rather because they identified it as a 'black space' where they could encounter their 'objects of desire'—black men."[36]

In my discussion of religion with the Winrock activist leaders, when we focused on Christianity, Aranha offered another reminder of how the systemic crafting of sex/gender vulnerability supports the violence of trafficking. She pointed out how "sometimes we see that religious—some—religious groups will discriminate or deny that gay people and transsexuals are just as human as other people."[37] She observed how such devaluing religious values and practices deliberately increase the social isolation of "gay people and transsexuals" in Bahia, which, particularly for those already economically marginal, increases their vulnerability to exploitation by predators. Religious culpability is also apparent in routine Christian beliefs that reserve superior moral status and divine approval for binary gender constructions of maleness and femaleness. Intolerance with the blurring of socially ascribed gender role boundaries is complicit in tolerance for the abuse and exploitation in this form of gender violence against LGBTQ local community members. Christian faith traditions too rarely engage in the violence resistance work of equipping their believers to celebrate an entitlement to equal regard for transgender and gay identities as a standard aspect of how gendered self-expression and sexual identities are incorporated in Christian theological anthropology.

Aranha stressed that "the most vulnerable groups are the transsexuals who are really, really marginalized here in Brazil."[38] Apparently, some perpetrators of exploitation and violence targeted persons exhibiting a combination of socially ascribed characteristics of maleness and femaleness. In short, it was clear from her description that transsexuals have been targeted because they are transsexual. During my meetings, I found that most Brazilian LGBT rights activists and antiviolence activists use the term *transsexual*, while in the United States similar activists use *transgender*. In each context, the activists undoubtedly perceive some differences in what each term means. Issues of language translation can hamper a satisfactory understanding of such linguistic and cultural nuances. Nevertheless, a deeply disturbing parallel political reality of targeted victimization exists in both contexts. Assaults and murders of transsexuals and transgender women of African descent seem to abound with a singular viciousness in both the United States and Brazil.[39] Analyses of gender-based violence must not gloss over the consistent, particular form of misogyny that this gendered targeting of transgender women reveals.

We need to better understand the details of how religion fosters gender violence and exploitation through its public denials of a basic entitlement to bodily safety, equal rights, and human flourishing for gay, lesbian, transgender, and transsexual members of local communities. Religion's impact, however, is never uniform. One Salvador activist I met told me that she knew transsexuals who had experienced sex trafficking and/or sexual exploitation by strangers as well as rejection by their own families but had found a welcoming home within certain Candomblé communities.[40] In other instances, the very struggle against repressive religious ideas about gender and sexist practices by its adherents represented a meaningful step in creating a resilient commitment to anti-trafficking work. I glimpsed such resilience in Isabella Santos de Jesus, a young woman staff member I met at another NGO focused on trafficking and sex tourism. Unlike Aranha and Santos, Santos de Jesus focused on prevention strategies.

Santos de Jesus explained how her anti-trafficking activist leadership had been a means of liberation from church-enforced gender norms. In her twenties, with sparkling, smooth, deep copper-brown skin and a calm, professional manner, Santos de Jesus spoke to me in the Salvador, Bahia, offices of CHAME (Centro Humanitário de Apoio à Mulher; Humanitarian Center for the Support of Women) and described its work as preventing trafficking in women and sex tourism. Her job included a range of tasks, from management of financial accounts to community project design and workshop leadership.

Santos de Jesus became especially animated as she described preventative anti-trafficking workshops with children that she had helped lead. They took place mainly in local schools. In those conversations with the girls about trafficking, they had mentioned the humiliation of enduring police suspicion and harassment supposedly for their protection. Santos de Jesus also related stories about girls who had traveled abroad for domestic jobs and instead became imprisoned by their employers. "But prevention, for me, that is the most important work."[41] Her workshops at the schools stressed women's empowerment. "We work on the issue of gender, first, gender and patriarchy," she said.[42] Then, in a seamless transition, she also described her own journey of empowerment.

Santos de Jesus had been actively involved in an evangelical Christian church where she suffered under its restrictive, sexist teachings. She explained that her church taught that "the woman always had to be submissive to the man."[43] Church leaders had forbidden her to go to college because she was a woman. To them, it seemed, to become an exemplary moral example of a female-gendered body, the development of her mind had to be truncated. But, she told me, "I was a rebel in the church."[44] With a defiant flash in her eyes, she told me that teaching about the gender violence of trafficking enabled her to recognize the "institutional violence of the church." Then she offered a concise summary of her core ethical drive as an anti-trafficking activist: "I had the right to dream, that I could in some way empower myself, that I could do much more for other women . . . and that I could be the owner of my own life."[45] Rebellion against repressive gender enforcement in church settings translated into entitlement to dream. Her rebellion meant creating change for girls and women that would make them less vulnerable to traffickers.

As Erica, Nessette, and I left the CHAME office, we walked down the busy street trying to figure out whether we would take a taxi or bus back to Erica's apartment. There was an infectious quality of hopefulness in the ways in which Santos de Jesus's example of rebellious Christian faith was lived out in preventative activist conversations with girls. Her rebellious Christianity had resonated deeply with my own spirituality and added a slight, unconscious spring to my step as we walked away. Yet I knew the qualities that had resonated so strongly with my own commitments had to be held together with helpful feminist critiques of how the inadvertent consequences of the work of NGOs, sometimes called "NGOization," mute the strength of local movements.[46]

Cumulatively, the visits with the anti-trafficking activists in Salvador triggered a reminder of how any assertion of social entitlement to dream, desire, travel, study, and engage in spiritual and religious practice had to be attached to black female bodily entitlement instead of an eager, colonizing regard for them. Said differently, an antiracist conceptualization of entitlement ought not be fed by transnational desires to sexually consume or save their bodies. Attention to the struggle against the exploitation that occurs in sex trafficking and tourism also expands one's imagination when defining gender-based violence. It enlarges the foundational notion that rightly assumes men target women because of the diminished status that accompanies their social identity as women and thus increases the possibility that men can exploit and assault women with impunity. This standard idea fails to reflect the variegated role of gender in the gender-based violence of sex trafficking and sex tourism.

In sex trafficking and sex tourism, the politics of desire attached to exploitation reveal a fissure in exclusively binary definitions of gender assumed by many traditional conceptualizations of gender-based violence. Crucial, but only partial, truths can be found in the definition of gender-based violence that views socially ascribed differences between males and females as granting permission for the harmful acts, coercion, and deprivation of freedom.[47] My discussions with activists and leaders in Salvador revealed how, as cisgender and transgender black girls and boys were exploited, multiple, intersecting expectations infused the targeting of them for exploitation by sex tourists and traffickers. To imagine and create strategies for ending these forms of violence, the definition of gender-based violence must incorporate multiple gendered forms of targeting as well as multiple gendered rebellious assertions of mind-body-spirit wholeness and dignity. The strategies must boldly assert the preciousness of gendered bodies socially marked by queer, fluid, and nonconforming gender identities and erotic blackness.

Disregard for the preciousness of the personhood of those victimized, such as the targeted girls, youth, and transsexual adults of African descent in Salvador, sabotages a meaningful antiviolence response. Few factors figure as heavily in generating disregard as a reliance on the controlling power of certain fixed social and economic norms. Fixed gender mores inflame the perpetrator excuses for the violence and popular indifference to it. In similar ways, fixed and hierarchically ordered notions of racial status lend support to sexual exploitation. And anti-trafficking conversations with Brazilian activists spark awareness of how religious values that are complicit in generating restrictive narratives of victimization and freedom are also intertwined with fixed, virtuous understandings of transnational consumerist and neoliberal market values. In the nexus of desires at issue when crafting sufficiently nimble anti-trafficking responses, transnational consumerist values cannot be separated from transnational black racial desires for social status and white racist objectifications of blackness. Resistance strategies to counter them beckon recognition of subjectivity beyond the relegation of bodily identities to the status of receptacles for satisfying one's sexual, racial entitlement, or salvation mission desires.

Admittedly, I had found it uncomfortable to learn the complex details from Aranha and Santos about the material and status desires of some of the individual girls and youth exploited by traffickers and tourists, together with the racial politics surrounding all of them. If some subset of the exploited girls made deliberately opportunistic economic and racial calculations about what selling their bodies might bring, it left room for them to be judged unsympathetically. Cultural translation in transnational solidarity should not require suspension of judgments about what constitutes exploitation. But the approach of these activist leaders demanded that I pay attention to the subjectivity of the girls, including their own reflections on their plight—reflections undoubtedly informed by an array of devaluing social messages. In other words, this kind of violence involves a slow, protracted process of social dehumanization, not reducible to isolated incidents of intimate assault. Here the unhurried, consuming power of gender-based violence takes the form of racialized socioeconomic entrapment. It cultivates a commodification of one's sexual selfhood in the expedient, deliberate conversion of hopeful dreams and longings into a means for commercial sexual transaction using the dreamer's body. Recognition of each young person's subjectivity or consciousness defies the caustic process of exploitation that occurs in sex tourism and trafficking.

The Brazilian activists' approach challenges the utility of sympathetic, and even empathetic, responses if those responses require black girls to internalize unself-conscious helplessness to legitimize their victimization. Reliance on empathy might be expected or even seem necessary to spur intercultural concern by those outside the direct circumstances of sex trafficking and sex tourism in Salvador. But empathy may be unproductive for creating lasting change to stem sexual violence.[48] Empathy is too conditional and restrictive because it requires identifying oneself with the suffering of sexually exploited persons of African descent, as if that suffering was something one could try on like a borrowed coat. In this traditional notion of empathy, one successfully identifies with the suffering through one's imagination, thereby making the exploited, suffering person seem worthy of help. Unfortunately, conversely, an inability to empathize renders the individual unworthy of help. Instead of using this unreliable quality of empathy as a basis for antiviolence activism, my exchange with the Brazilian activist leaders points to the need to passionately recognize that the circumstances of exploitation are intolerable.

* * *

It was my last night in Salvador. When listening to the Brazilian activists, I had experienced both exhilaration and challenge to my very core. An activist domestic worker union leader, a Candomblé practitioner advocate of the Maria da Penha Law, a feminist jailer at the police station, and anti-trafficking critics of Christianity had made the terminology of domestic violence and gender violence vibrate for me with expansive meanings. These leaders did not seem intimidated by goliath forces of global economies fostering gender violence and providing lenses for reading sexual domination through racial categories. Those forces anchored the gendered violence against domestics who were employed in private homes, against wives and girlfriends living in *favelas*, and against transsexuals on the street. The activist strategies of changing racist perceptions of intimate coercion had been manifest both in formal agencies (governmental and nongovernmental) and in small neighborhood groups, sometimes primarily organized for protest and at other times centered mainly on support.

The challenge of formulating bridges between lessons learned through my interactions with Brazilian activists and the U.S. context of gender-based violence continued a theme that had emerged with my Ghanaian interviewees. In Ghana, I wrestled with how to describe what I had learned from black Africans about countering violence when I returned home without reinforcing well-worn pernicious stereotypes of inferior, brutal Africans. The quandary had forced me into an awkward, off-balance position, unsure of how to decisively move forward with translating their insights. In Brazil, I grappled with how to confront the ways in which well-known sexualized stereotypes of Brazilian women of African descent represented pleasurable tourist attractions for people back home to consume on their vacations or through the media. Those images were not readily accepted as a contributing factor in U.S.-perpetrated transnational gender-based violence. I had been pushed even further off-balance than I had in Ghana by the perpetual challenge of translating Brazilian Portuguese alongside the task of accurately perceiving the cultural and political substance of what I heard in Brazil. In Ghana, cultural translation had seemed an inescapable, fraught aspect of the kind of listening needed to even envision solidarity with black African activists. The literal necessity for language translation in Brazil presented a continual reminder of the productive, ethical necessity for cultural translation in conceptualizing and achieving antiviolence goals.

In diverse geopolitical situations in which violence has been fed by deep historical roots of intercultural conflict, cultural translation could be embraced as a political resource, not an encumbrance. In her discussion of Jewishness as a resource for peaceful, antiracist cohabitation in Israel and Palestine, feminist philosopher Judith Butler argues for the indispensability of translation in furthering that goal and finds potential for transformation once we push past assumptions about how the ethics and politics of translation involve only constraints, not possibilities for growth. "On the one hand," she writes, "one might assume that translation is assimilation of religious meanings into established secular frames. On the other hand, one might assume that translation is an effort to find a common language that transcends particular discourses."[49] As she helpfully concludes, neither assumption holds. The struggle to create strategies to end gender violence is fundamentally shaped by pernicious histories of systemic cultural, political, and religious support for that violence. Because supports from transnational secular or Christian religious values are in some instances indistinguishable, an approach that stresses the translation of "religious meanings into established secular frames" would not suffice. Rather than pursuing a universal language for identifying gendered wrongs, the most useful transnational and intercultural translations require concern with the particularities of cultural generators of sexual exploitation and violence, especially as they relate to religion, race, and political economy.

In Salvador, when reminded of the parallel forms of gender violence in my U.S.-American context and expressions of Christian faith assumptions, questions, not orderly analogies, continually surfaced. A primary goal of engaging in transnational learning was to develop an expansive capacity to grasp the lessons of the truth-seeking encounters not to identify precisely corresponding values across global contexts or shared terms that transcend the particular. An emphasis on the role of religion and spirituality in antiviolence activism necessarily involves justice commitments sustained by the intangible roots of belief systems. This focus can offer a conceptual capacity that reserves space for valuing the untranslatable in intercultural exchanges. Even if awkwardness results, acknowledgment of the untranslatable yields a more trustworthy process. Oddly, I came to embrace the awkwardness of the intercultural connectedness I experienced in my listening process. While appreciative of the revelatory insights about the distinctiveness of Americanized blackness in Brazil that fed their antiviolence vision and practice, I yearned for further connections with other activist leaders beyond listening and learning how to translate what I heard.

"No arguments. You have to come out to the club tonight, hear some live music, drink some mojitos, and dance the samba with us," my host-friends said on the last evening we were together.

"Okay," I responded.

When we arrived at the small dance club, the dance floor was tightly packed. Several people including my friends and their friends made attempts to teach me samba. But I just could not get it. Once I got my hips going, I would forget about my feet. Even when I did get my feet moving, I looked like I was putting out burning cigarettes, with each foot simultaneously, vigorously, mashing them into the ground. But I loved the music. I tried to step, sway, bounce, and twitch. I just did my best to create my own version of the fast-paced movements the brown arms and hips and legs of my surrounding friends artfully formed in that cramped space.

Though I knew it was hardly the case, they encouraged me, saying, "Oooh, good, you're getting it Traci." I grew impatient with how my physical translation of their movements remained so clumsy. Frustratingly, no song was long enough for me to be able to declare "Yes, I got it," and then demonstrate that we were finally completely in sync by offering rhythmic bodily evidence.

PART III

Time for Solidarity

With South Africa

5

How Much Time Is Needed?

Night time. After six hours of waiting in the Washington, DC, airport for the "mild hurricane" to subside, four hours of unexpected delays in the Johannesburg airport, and a total of fourteen hours of flying time, I arrived in Pietermaritzburg, the capital city in the province of KwaZulu-Natal, South Africa. The trip had taken much longer than anticipated.

Velvety-quiet darkness and chilly South African air greeted me as my first visit to the country began. Other passengers on the tiny aircraft had scattered and disappeared. The small airport seemed to have closed almost immediately. I waited impatiently. Neither my promised hotel car service nor any taxis were in sight. I did not yet have a working cell phone and was unsure how long to wait. I experienced a familiar alertness—not fear, but a well-practiced heightened awareness—about being a woman alone at night, lingering in a dark lonely area. The feeling always arose in such situations, regardless of whether the setting was South Africa or the United States.

I fiddled with the ziplock plastic bag in my pocket that held a crown that had fallen off my back tooth while chewing rubbery chicken on the long flight to the African continent. The colored fabrics of my rain-drenched clothes had used that time productively to bleed all over each other in psychedelic patterns. Those clothes lay inside my suitcase on top of stained, swollen books that were supposed to have been gifts for colleagues. My water-resistant suitcase had failed to resist while apparently left outside for hours during the hurricane delay in Washington, DC.

In the Pietermaritzburg Airport parking lot, I broke the quiet with a shout directed at the young white woman I thought I had seen working behind the counter inside the airport building, now shuttered and locked. She was walking briskly, clearly eager to go home at the end of her workday. I hesitated before shouting again. Had she heard me? She kept walking toward the only car in the lot. I wondered if in South Africa it was any less likely than in the United States that a white stranger would want to help me. Should I expect the same toss-up risk of possible responses? If their racial dynamics mirrored those in the United States, her response would likely depend on how her views of blacks influenced her assessment of the dangers posed by a nearby middle-aged black woman stranger calling to her in a dark parking lot. Those views might fuel indifference, hostility, or a desire to help. Mulling over these possibilities and risks did not provoke any distress for me. Such racial calculations based upon historic patterns of prejudice and discrimination are ordinary aspects of most U.S.-American black and brown people's daily interactions with whites. Eventually, I got the woman's attention. She helped me with calling a cab and waited with me. The hotel clerk shrugged off my complaint about the missing car service, my clothes dried, and the badly stained ones were easily replaced. And throughout the weeks that followed, when I forgot to chew carefully, the exposed nerve of my tooth painfully reminded me not to repeat that mistake.

The sense of dissonance and need for translation that surfaced in my initial impressions of cultural and racial dynamics in Brazil were absent in South Africa. Instead, perhaps too automatically, I presumed the same shared attributes within U.S. and South African histories of white racism and black struggles against it. Both national histories are deeply influenced by Christianity-rooted British colonialism and centuries of official policies that upheld white superiority. However, the maintenance of white racial cultural and political power in the white-majority United States (approximately 62 percent at the beginning of the twenty-first century)[1] possesses marked differences from such patterns of racial dominance in the white-minority South African nation (approximately 20 percent in the late twentieth century to 6 percent in the early twenty-first century).[2] Political scientist Anthony Marx has mapped these complexities in his comparative study of racial politics in South Africa, the United States, and Brazil.[3] His historical analysis emphasizes the crucial role of anti-black white racism in nation building within each context. White racial domination prevailed as a unifying force in the late nineteenth and early twentieth centuries in South Africa after the crisis of the Boer wars. It did so with both the backing of the British Empire and agreement between white English-speaking British and (Dutch) Afrikaner elites. In the United States, white racial domination held sway during that same historical period after the crisis of a civil war over slav-

ery that dissolved the federal government, the reversal of federal policies of Reconstruction after the war, and imposition of Jim Crow, "with
blacks again paying the price for white reconciliation."[4]

As Marx has explained the similarities, "patterns linking nation-state
consolidation and formal racial domination were similar in the United
States and South Africa. In both, the nation-state was divided and policies of racial domination were designed to diminish such division. . . .
Legal exclusion of blacks helped gradually unify the core constituency
of whites. . . . Brazil was 'exceptional,' not in its lack of racial discrimination, but [in] failing to establish official racial domination."[5] Marx lik-
ened the political features of racism in Brazil to the post-Reconstruction
North in the United States where discrimination in community life was
imposed informally together with full complicity in and support for Jim
Crow state laws instituted in the South. Among other divergent patterns
of white political dominance across these nations, in South African history, the unifying of whites and solidifying of white control occurred
through centralized, strong state power. In contrast, in the United States
this was achieved through weakened central (federal) authority and increased states' rights, ceding "the issue of black rights to the states" for
the sake of national unity.[6]

In the late nineteenth and early twentieth centuries, therefore, the
literal creation of the nation-state in South Africa and re-creation of
the nation-state in the United States (after the Civil War) had similarly
depended upon the marshaling of anti-black white racism and socioeconomic control over vast territories of multiracial and multireligious
communities. In a focus on gender-based violence, a valuable resource
may be found in the extent to which those resonant racist histories produced comparable legacies of racial inequalities and, most importantly,
comparable forms of resistance in their antiracist social movements.[7]
As I reached out to South African antiviolence leaders, I hoped that perhaps the degree of similarity found in these collective narratives of our
two nations could provide a shortcut for envisioning antiracist activist
solidarity in opposing the violence. Shortcuts for strategizing were always welcome amid an ever-present impatient desire shared by gender
justice activists to decrease waiting times for ending violence. I anticipated finding unique black activist resources for resisting the habit of
reading one's self-worth through the lens of white perceptions. South

Africa's anti-apartheid struggle had just delivered, in the 1990s, a successful transfer of power to the black majority and the subsequent establishment of a radical constitution that contained clauses on gender and LGBTQ equality.

Elements of those initial moments in the Pietermaritzburg Airport parking lot could be metaphorically interpreted as prescient for my subsequent meetings in South Africa. Those minor travel annoyances symbolically foreshadowed fundamental themes about timing and transnational comparisons of antiracist consciousness and struggle that repeatedly emerged in my encounters. In discussions with interviewees about gender and racial justice movements, progress in addressing rape always seemed to involve a confrontation with the politics of timeliness: when is it a good time for public intervention, truth-telling, accountability, and intercultural and interreligious solidarity? Nuanced transnational comparisons of the history of anti-black racism and resistance could perhaps help lay the groundwork for contemporary gender justice solidarity across borders. But within those histories—including histories of antiracist resistance—attention must be paid to the distinctive ways in which black intragroup loyalties and betrayals of those victimized by the violence can obstruct change and thereby create costly delays for the implementation of gender justice practices (showcasing how resistance movements can fail to resist). Excruciatingly painful reminders of the consequences of forgetting that history of black intragroup struggle are embedded in the present political conditions of high rates of sexual assault. Additionally, I sought religious expressions of determination to stop waiting and create change in the face of doubt, not isolated to doubt about the existence of God—a common preoccupation of monotheistic religions—but doubt about human capacities in their practice of religion.

My discussions with Muslim and Christian religious scholars and community activist leaders in South Africa focused primarily on constructive communal responses to sexual assault of heterosexual and lesbian black women and linked to localized antirape services or organizing. My first interactions with religion scholar-activist colleagues in Pietermaritzburg introduced issues of race, religion, and sexual assault in the early twenty-first-century South African context and relevant comparisons to the United States. In the Cape Town setting, black and coloured intracommunal racial politics and antiviolence collaboration surfaced in conversations with leaders.[8] These examples evoke further U.S. comparisons concerning dynamics among activists of color and occasional competition over racial victim status. All of the encounters in South Africa are haunted by underlying questions about how to cross national, cultural, and religious differences for the sake of constructing solidarity. How expansively might we imagine possibilities for constructing it? For example, we might consider what it would mean to envision the differing religious backgrounds of Africana activist leaders across several national boundaries as a common spiritual resource. If such a vision of respectful, differentiated communality could be realized, how might leaders committed to antiracist methods for ending gender-based violence jointly draw upon this transnational spiritual resource?

My narrative reflections on the potential for solidarity suggestively draw attention to misperceptions littered throughout my interactions that uncomfortably mark cultural differences but do not negate evidence of deeply shared goals. These reflections contribute a running index of inquiries and notes pertinent to the conceptualization of solidarity-building practices.

Contradictory Values and Public Practices

The ethos of the country vibrated with political energy related to racism that was both awe-inspiring and agitating. During a ten-minute cab ride on my way to meet Religion and Theology Department faculty at Pietermaritzburg's University of KwaZulu-Natal campus, the driver angrily told me how badly the blacks in power are now "treating us—the Indians." I noticed the streets in Pietermaritzburg named Alan Paton Avenue (a tribute to a white anti-apartheid author), Chief Albert Luthuli Street (a black Christian anti-apartheid leader), and King Edward Avenue (the eldest son of Queen Victoria, who ruled the British Empire from 1837 to 1901, when South Africa was a part of it).

Even in those honorific street names the resilient interplay of racist and religious history demanded attention. White Christian British and Dutch missionaries had participated in the eighteenth- and early nineteenth-century enslavement of black Africans. Whites had united and consolidated their rule under the constitution of the South African

Republic in 1858. The formal establishment of apartheid took place in 1948. The Population Registration Act of 1950 required racial classifications of white, black, coloured, and Indian. Feminist religion scholars Nina Hoel and Sa'diyya Shaika note the significance of racist classifications in their study of contemporary issues of sexuality and gender among South African Muslim women. They summarize this twentieth-century apartheid history, explaining that under the 1950 act "Muslims of Indonesian and Malaysian ancestry were primarily classified coloured (of mixed ancestry), while Muslims from India were classified as Indian. Within the apartheid social architecture, residential areas were racially segregated, often by means of forced removals."[9] They note that some Muslim anti-apartheid activists also mobilized around gender justice in Islamic reform during the anti-apartheid struggle.[10] In South Africa, as Hoel and Shaika indicate, there was a readily available, recent tradition of struggle by some religious activists against the strictly enforced racial segregation policies of the state. That antiracist activism was conjoined with a struggle for gender justice and equality in religious and family life. Again, for some Muslim activists, the risk-taking act of questioning state-supported white racism amicably energized their commitment to question sexism within their religious tradition.

In references dating back to nineteenth-century colonialism, certain Christian anti-apartheid South African activist leaders refused to describe the state's racist policies without including Christianity's hypocritical role in morally justifying it. Before South African security police murdered him in a prison cell in Pretoria in 1977, black activist Steve Biko articulated a prominent expression of black consciousness for the anti-apartheid movement. In 1972, he asserted to a South African audience of black Christians that "because the white missionary described black people as thieves, lazy, sex-hungry etc., and because he equated all that was valuable with whiteness, our Churches through ministers see all vices I have mentioned above not as manifestations of the cruelty and injustice which we are subjected to by the white man but inevitable proof that after all the white man was right when he described us as savages. Thus if Christianity in its introduction was corrupted by the inclusion of aspects which made it the ideal religion for the colonisation of people, nowadays in its interpretation it is the ideal religion for the maintenance of the subjugation of the same people."[11] As Biko asserted, the black South African struggle for racial justice and freedom directly confronted the Christian religion's supportive role in white racist domination.

Moreover, Biko's activism featured a unique multiracialist facet. By advocating black consciousness that defined all of those subjugated by apartheid as black, he heralded an inclusive form of anti-apartheid resistance.[12] South Africa's brutal state-enforced apartheid had thrived on tightly interwoven Christian and white supremacist belief systems that justified an elaborate multitiered system of racial segregation. The anti-apartheid struggle, as articulated by Biko and others, envisioned a black consciousness that contradicted such subjugation with an alternative, expansive belief system about the political blackness of subjugated peoples across racial lines. Ultimately, the nonracial democratic state that replaced the apartheid regime also enacted policies that recognized equal rights related to gender and sexuality as an intrinsic component of the freedoms needed to unravel their racist history.

Unlike Ghana, Brazil, the United States, or any other country in the world, South Africa secured gender equality within their founding (post-apartheid) Constitution. The South African Constitution directly guarantees women's right to bodily safety. Their Constitution's Bill of Rights states, "Everyone has the right to bodily and psychological integrity which includes the right to make decisions over reproduction, security in and control over their body."[13] The "equal protection and benefit" clause includes "sexual orientation."[14] Although current South African gender justice activists struggle in the gap between state-promised freedoms and realized ones, they argue from the position of constitutional protections. For gender justice activists and feminist legal scholars in the United States who focus their efforts on state reforms, the achievement of the constitutional freedoms to which women in South Africa are already entitled may seem to be only a distant slim hope. After all, passage of the equal rights amendment to the U.S. Constitution, ensuring "equality of rights under the law shall not be denied or abridged by the United States or by any state on account of sex," has been halted for nearly a century.[15]

Although some Christian factions in South Africa had been unyielding in their opposition to it, the inclusion of sexual orientation in the final passage of the Equality Clause of the Bill of Rights received the explicit public support of Anglican Archbishop Desmond Tutu. In his 1995 letter to the Constitutional Assembly he underscored the importance of recognizing gay and lesbian people as equal citizens, demanding that the South African Constitution guarantee "the fundamental human right to a sexual life, whether heterosexual or homosexual."[16] This strand of antiracist religious activism insistent upon sexual and gender justice occupied a firm position in South Africa's securing of equal constitutional rights. It continues to be resilient in the struggle against contradictory realities of hate crimes and gender violence undermining the efficacy of those equality provisions.

As I sat down with Religion and Theology Department faculty members for the first time, they were gathered for their "daily tea" meeting. The Religion and Theology faculty and staff created the home for the Ujamaa Centre, which describes its work as "an interface between socially engaged biblical and theological scholars, organic intellectuals, and local communities of the poor, working-class, and marginalised. Together we use biblical and theological resources for individual and social transformation."[17] Several members of the faculty who hosted me had been active in the founding and ongoing leadership of the programs of the Centre.[18] The day I met with the Religion and Theology faculty, they were discussing a drawing by cartoonist Zapiro (Jonathan Shapiro) in the *Mail and Guardian*, which lay on the table.

The cartoonist had depicted one of the country's major political leaders, the head of the ruling party, Jacob Zuma, with his pants unzipped.[19] The drawing showed him in profile with one hand holding his pants open. A dripping shower above his head was attached to a pole that seemed to grow up out of the back of his lumpy, bald head. He had a smirk on his face and stood over a blindfolded, screaming woman. She lay on the ground, her dress hiked up, her knees together. A crumpled sash across her chest labeled her "Justice System." Four men held her down as one of them said: "Go for it, boss." The cartoon men had exaggerated large, puffy lips—I supposed to aid in identifying them as black. Almost instinctively, I pursed my own lips as I looked at it.

Sarojini Nadar, a faculty member who, at that time, directed the Gender and Religion Programme, explained how the drawing reflected the cartoonist's view of the current trial where corruption charges brought against Zuma were about to be dismissed. Years earlier, in 2006, he had been accused and acquitted of raping a young woman. The acquittal followed a trial in which Zuma claimed to have had consensual sexual intercourse with the young woman after she supposedly sexually tempted him. He claimed that her culturally traditional clothing was seductive and indicated a form of unspoken consent.[20] Zuma had also explained that he took a shower afterward as an HIV/AIDS prevention measure. Zuma was subsequently elected to two consecutive terms as president of South Africa and leader of the African National Congress (ANC), though a range of corruption allegations persisted throughout his presidency.[21]

I guessed that this sarcastic cartoon might spark politically polarizing public debates. A wide variety of strong advocacy organizations worked to address violence against women in South Africa. Because of their efforts, extensive legislative and judicial protections had been created, including fifty-two courts focusing only on sexual offense cases. The government funded several Thuthuzela Care Centres, where victims of sexual violence could access investigators, prosecutors, and counseling support. Mandates for such services and federal protections were built into South Africa's violence against women laws (the 1999 Domestic Violence Act and 2007 Sexual Offences Law). Unfortunately, at the same time, South Africa also had some of the highest incidents of rape as compared with other countries in the world.[22] Local activists struggled with these contradictions. South African feminist activist leader Mamphela Ramphele frankly asserts, "Rape has become a major epidemic that blots our post-apartheid track record as a society. . . . The rising levels of gender-based violence and rape involving not just women, but children as well, make a mockery of the human-rights foundations of our constitution."[23]

In 2002, in response to the national problem of sexual assault, Zuma invoked the history of apartheid in a moral formulation championing the restoration of healthier African family values.[24] Zuma, then deputy president of the ANC, had pointed to the culpability of apartheid for the crisis of child rape. Amid the internationally publicized crisis of sexual assaults targeting very young children, he said that "the apartheid history of this country left behind a legacy of a serious breakdown of the moral infrastructure of our society. . . . The molestation of children and infants is a symptom of this degeneration."[25] Zuma named the moral devastation that apartheid unleashed and its ongoing consequences as a major contributor to the high rate of sexual assault in South Africa.

However, the politics surrounding the high-profile trial increased the focus on current forms of cultural support for rape. Zuma's troubling attitudes about rape, sexuality, and young women subsequently revealed during his trial for rape undermined his credibility as a moral foe of sexual mores that nurtured sexual violence against women and girls.[26] Christian religion proved useful for reinforcing his skewed version of sexual morality espoused at the trial. His defense team called a parade of Christian church leaders as witnesses to impugn the character and reliability of his accuser's testimony.[27] Zuma's victim-blaming statements about gender and sexuality and the misogynistic extremism of some of his supporters generated a prolonged public spectacle centered on gender-based violence. Media coverage of these events together with Zuma's full acquittal had an ironic impact on antirape advocacy. Many South African HIV/AIDS activists, LGBTQ activists, and feminist activists were galvanized around a singular zealous concern with combating rape culture.

In the United States, activists opposed to gender-based violence have had to contend with other forms of racialized contradictions and the scarcity of meaningful consequences for sexual misconduct by political leaders at the highest level of government. President Bill Clinton's presidency survived when he was acquitted in 1998 impeachment proceedings. His lies about his sexual relationship with a twenty-two-year-old White House intern were featured in the charges brought against him. Unlike Zuma's case, the intern did not accuse Clinton of rape or nonconsensual sexual contact. Clinton had been caught in a lie. He appeared to assert that oral sex did not constitute sexual relations when he insisted, contrary to the intern's testimony, that he had not had sexual relations with her. The Clinton and Zuma cases illustrated contrasting forms of denial but similar forms of woman blaming. Clinton denied sexual intercourse had occurred and placed the blame on the intern for creating the drawn-out public scandal. Zuma denied sexual coercion or assault had occurred and placed the blame for the scandal on his accuser. He identified her as the sexual initiator who later lied about having been raped. Another version of heterosexual woman blaming made headlines decades later in U.S. presidential politics just before Donald

Trump's 2016 election. Trump was elected largely by white Christian supporters even after videotaped evidence revealed that he had bragged about his sexual assaults of women.[28] He claimed, "When you are a star they let you do it."[29] The politics of race and gender violence were explicitly linked in other moments in that election year's presidential primary. Trump launched his successful campaign for the presidency with a 2015 speech that identified Mexican immigrants in the United States as "bringing drugs . . . bringing crime. They're rapists. And some, I assume, are good people."[30] The prominence of these references to rape in the 2016 presidential campaign and Trump's victory did not deter support from his sizeable white Christian constituency.[31] He apparently found some kind of currency with them (or at least no hindrance) linked to his videotaped admissions of his heterosexual sexual assaults on women and invocation of racialized, xenophobic images of Mexican men as rapists who come to the United States to perpetrate their attacks.[32]

These South African and U.S. examples, of course, reference quite different late twentieth- and early twenty-first-century sociopolitical contexts and understandings of race. In South Africa's racial and gender politics, black presidential leadership had referenced white racism as an inescapable generator of child rape by black citizens. The reference may even have provided a handy shorthand assertion for unifying his black majority constituency. In U.S. racial and gender politics, the role of the president's whiteness (Clinton's) could be largely ignored in relation to his sexual misconduct. The media did not reference his whiteness as a factor in his dishonesty and inappropriate sexual contact with the young White House intern while he served as president.[33] Erasure of the significance of one's whiteness constitutes one characteristic of how white dominance—that is, whiteness as norm and center—inhabits U.S. culture. The erasure functions, as sociologist Joe Feagin argues, as a socially embedded "white racial frame."[34] In a white racial "frame assumption" in U.S. politics, mass media news reports usually leave the whiteness of white politicians unproblematized and unexamined while assuming news consumers possess a shared (white) racially framed perspective.[35] Through this often-hidden cultural pattern, whiteness may help destigmatize the sexual misconduct of a prominent white political leader. In the Clinton scandal, white racial identity upholds authority rather than stigmatizing and delegitimizing authority, perhaps assisting in allowing him to escape removal from office. Whiteness might also have lent a historically rooted authorizing influence to the acquittal. It may have tacitly provided the support of a historical tradition of impunity granted to politically powerful white males regarding their entitlement to sexual access to women that dates back to others such as President Thomas Jefferson (child rapist of his slave).[36] As he invoked the threat of invading brown men rapists, the white presidential candidate (Trump) appealed to white Christian U.S.-American voters utilizing what has been for centuries a means of stoking white racist fears about protecting white women. A stabilizing norm for maintaining rape culture was supported by various racially inflected public statements by these high-level political leaders when they publicly identified women as liars about sexual relations, boasted about their unfettered sexual access to women, and caricatured Mexican men as U.S.-invading rapists.

South African feminist activists seeking to dismantle rape culture in a nation struggling to recover from apartheid recognized the inextricable and urgent tasks of antiracism in ending gender-based violence. The faculty's discussion of the cartoon gave me a glimpse of the demands of their charged social context for antiviolence advocates and scholars, such as Sarojini Nadar. As in the U.S. context, dramatic political changes in their nation were continuously unfolding. The leadership struggles of the ANC, the ruling political party, have continued to evolve, especially the racial and ethnic tensions in their contemporary politics. The weighted post-apartheid dynamics between Asians (primarily of Indian descent) and blacks, between blacks and whites, and between black tribal groups such as the Xhosa and Zulu were all at issue in South African political life. The rape metaphor in the cartoon epitomized how the politics surrounding sexual violence against women took shape in their broader public discourse. The group discussion I witnessed illustrated the centrality of addressing the politics of rape and race in the work of the Religion and Theology faculty and the staff of the Ujamaa Centre.

In an essay on the Zuma trial, Sarojini analyzes a combination of personal, sociocultural, and religious dimensions in the confrontation of rape culture. Her approach incorporates her own emotional identification with Zuma's accuser while also utilizing gender studies and Christian feminist theological sources as analytical tools. Her essay begins with an assertion of solidarity among rape survivors. She explains that as a rape survivor, "accused of 'playing with' the family friend who raped me (at the grand age of 10), I cannot but get emotional when survivors are accused of 'seducing' their rapists through the example of wearing a 'kanga.'"[37] For her, the trial provided a case study to examine the "unholy trinity" of "religion, culture, and gender/social construction" and how they contribute to violence against women.[38]

When we met for a one-on-one discussion Sarajoni spoke about the challenge she found in the fact that South Africa had one of the most progressive constitutions in the world "and we still can't overcome gender violence. Because legislation alone will never achieve it, you must engage the worldviews of people in the villages and their cultures. And the Bible does this."[39] Sarajoni described her work on Bible study methods specifically relating stories about teaching the story in Judges 19 where the concubine was gang raped by the Benjaminite men. She stressed how "the communities with which I work, with which I want to work, take the Bible very seriously, which means that we have to take it seriously."[40] Sarajoni and the other leaders of Ujamaa Centre (faculty and local community partners) nurtured an approach to interpretation that invited analysis of community consciousness, starting with the community in the biblical text. In their study sessions she would ask the members of the women's groups if any of them knew a woman who had been raped like the woman in Judges. "And then the stories begin," Sarajoni said. "Oh, my goodness. You never have enough time" to get through all of the stories the women have to tell or to explore all of the insights that emerge.[41]

Her contentions about the meaning of Bible study for community members point to fertile possibilities offered by attention to religion in gender justice goals. Sarajoni's examples of working with Christian women in community groups give witness to how religion offers distinctive tools to enable communal conscientization about stopping rape and also in sustaining the commitment to do so. The focus on lay congregational Bible studies in the work of the Ujamaa Centre leaders relies on a democratized method. Studies of scripture such as Judges 19 allow spiritual, theological, and political reflection on rape of women and ethnic group domination. This method nurtures religious work by community members that could reinforce support for democratic legislative reforms focused on gender-based violence while critical engagement of their own faith traditions and understandings remains the impetus and sustaining practice.

In this community conscientization approach, the emphasis on contextualization drives toward political solidarity rather than polarization. Sarajoni worked mostly with Christian South African Indian communities.[42] South Africa has one of the largest Indian communities outside of India, mostly brought by British colonials to work as indentured servants and perform bureaucratic jobs denied blacks and too menial for whites. As she spoke of a broader notion of political blackness that included formerly colonized diasporic Asian Africans, her perspective highlighted the necessity to constructively mobilize post-apartheid multireligious and multiracial solidarity politics in opposition to rape. In addition, Sarajoni's ideas invited attention to how antiviolence solidarity must value emotional knowledge. As she had written in her article about the Zuma trial, "as a rape survivor I cannot but think emotionally about this issue. Khwezi's story is my story,[43] is the story of countless other women in this country."[44] Her conceptualization of the role of rape, religion, race, and cultural traditions in South Africa suggests a kind of shared thinking and feeling—the ability to "think emotionally"—that makes possible antirape solidarity.

Seeking Shared Faith Commitments

Zarina Majiet's leadership was impressively sustained by her South African Muslim faith. At least that was the nationalistic framing I had initially assumed. She had explained when we first met that her faith and work were deeply rooted in the teachings of the Prophet Muhammad. "Peace be upon him," she had intoned immediately after mentioning his name, and then she began to describe her faith in the context of her rape crisis work. From her decision to become a social worker thirty years ago, Majiet understood "the very qualities that our prophet had are qualities that social workers need. There is nothing that I am teaching or doing that contradicts my faith."[45] There were so many aspects of this perspective to explore, and I wanted to sit there doing so for days but needed to conclude the meeting.

When I had arrived earlier at the Simelela Centre where Majiet worked (at the time that we met) as the staff manager, I noticed the inviting bright orange "Simelela" above the doorway. The "i" was actually the red ribbon symbol for HIV and AIDS awareness. A big, brilliant-yellow colored sun hugged the "a" on the end. With its curvy lettering and vibrant colors, the sign resembled an artist's painting. *Simelela* means "to lean on" in Xhosa, one of South Africa's official languages. The word *Simelela* sat atop a fat orange line with "Supporting Survivors of Sexual Violence" below, also in orange lettering. At first it might have seemed as if the dual message it conveyed about bright, warm, sunlight-filled attention and the rape crisis needs of victim-survivors presented an oxymoron. As I learned, the work of the staff proved that it did not. When I entered and asked the Centre's receptionist if I could speak with her, Majiet had been in the middle of a lunch meeting with staff. I was there well before our scheduled appointment time but as soon as she saw me she stopped and warmly welcomed me by offering coffee, cookies, and all of her attention.

In her staff position, Majiet coordinated and supervised the medical staff who conducted initial forensic examinations on women and children who came for help after being assaulted as well as the staff responsible for on-site DNA testing of accused perpetrators police had located. Issues of race and religion showed up in her everyday conversations with staff colleagues as they responded to sexual and reproductive health concerns of their clients, including HIV testing and counseling for those who tested positive. She also oversaw the work of staff who advised the women and girls on how to navigate state social services, police, courts, or staff at the hospital (located directly across from the Centre) when physical injuries required their help.

I had considered Majiet as a member of a South African Muslim faith tradition in an attempt to sensitively acknowledge her identity. But I would not have given my own Christian faith tradition the same nationalist identification. I did not regard my faith as wholly shaped by U.S.-American Christianity, that is, as a Christianity comprising the influences in U.S.-American cultural and political history. In my view of my own political-spiritual identity, there were several ways in which the gender-violence-supporting values of my U.S.-Americanness clashed with the peace-waging aspirations of the black feminist Christian faith perspective I claimed. Yet I had assumed, without asking her, that Majiet's post-apartheid, South African national identity fully meshed with the qualities she cherished in her Islamic faith.

After her first reference to the Prophet Muhammad I experienced a heightened awareness that I could not be certain that I knew which terms were appropriate for comparing Majiet's religious inspiration to end rape with my own. Were there objectionably universalizing Christian terms in my condemnations of male-perpetrated sexual violence as sinful or my criticisms of how religion helped perpetuate tolerance for rape with teachings about women's inherently blameworthy sexual-temptress nature? Was the celebration of antirape activism as a prophetic witness an interreligiously viable acknowledgment? Interfaith dimensions of intercultural solidarity demanded an elementary concern with language that allowed respectful comparisons. Basic steps toward that respect should incorporate the unique ways differing faiths named the harm that the violence represented as well as our mutual, shared desire to stop it.

As we spoke, the dissonances and convergences that needed exploring included the topic of doubt. I could not deny my longing to know if doubts ever arose for her, as they sometimes did for me, about the effectiveness of mustering the spiritual power of religion to help end the gender-based violence. In monotheistic religious terms, why was God taking so long to ensure that the misogynist brutality and suffering ceased? Or instead of a focus on God, one might have doubts about the capacity of humans to genuinely desire to access the spiritual power of religion in order to stop the misogynist violence. Oddly, in listening to Majiet's clarity about how her Islamic faith centered on the Prophet Muhammad fed her antirape leadership, I found encouragement for developing and better articulating the connection between my Christian beliefs about the person of Jesus, especially as prophet, and my commitment to ending gender-based intimate violence.

With more guidance for making appropriate comparisons and attention to doubt, it might be possible to ferret out an expansive understanding of how our shared antiviolence passion was steeped in the peculiar gift of religious imagination. Religion at its best trains the believer to actively engage the world as it is while providing a lens for imagining what the world ought to be. Through ongoing religious nurturance, therefore, the believer might foresee woman-affirming human possibilities such as halting sexual assaults even while there is little evidence to suggest such a human possibility could ever exist. Again, this kind of formulation of imaginative religious potential for fueling political resistance must be tested for its interreligious applicability, not merely asserted as generalizable.

African American Muslim feminist scholar of Islam Amina Wadud has offered a related caution about gender rights solidarities among women of differing faith traditions. "For the sake of commonality, we focus on shared experiences because of gender disparities resulting from textual interpretations and religious practices," she states. "Our discussions must address whether similar experiences ameliorate distinctions, since it has been dramatically demonstrated that femaleness is configured in different ways because of other particularities like race, class, ethnicity, sexual orientation, or religious perspective."[46] Across faith communities there are similar experiences of religiously based gendered exclusions as well as privately and publicly repeated interpretations of religious texts that support gender-based violence. But those similar experiences must never be presumed as ameliorating other culturally and nationally reinforced differences in power and status. To her reveling in the freedoms that Islamic feminism can offer when one chooses Muslim faith, Wadud adds criticism of the constraints of a forced national identity embedded in a history of rape and racism: "I will always be American because my options to be something else were taken away once my fore-mothers were raped by white owners. . . . We became something altogether different from African and in this we become very particularly American."[47] In contrast to her freely chosen Muslim faith I do not share, Wadud names a forced aspect of my national-continental identity I carried to the South African Simelela Centre setting.

Yet Majiet explained the importance that she placed on being involved in an organization that "spoke to women's lives and the choices we make" and how certain realities of "the social and political context of our lives mean that there are some choices that it is just not possible for us to make."[48] As she referred to the choices "we make," the context of "our lives," and what is not possible "for us," she communicated parts of her vision of social change. She conveyed her certainty that wrapped together in a singular political plight she and I, the women and girls who were raped in Khayelitsha, and those raped in my U.S. context. Her description introduced a kind of gendered, communal solidarity. It contrasted with an accompaniment solidarity one might expect when bridging disparate communal interests or standpoints in relation to human inflicted suffering. In accompaniment solidarity often articulated in Christian liberationist visions, members of privileged groups walk with members of oppressed groups (or in this instance those who have been sexually assaulted).[49] Majiet's perspective seemed oppositional to the well-intentioned but individualistic presumptions about political agency represented in that privileged/oppressed binary. Her view bore no hint of nationalism. She unsettled my approach to solidarity-building across U.S. national borders that requires self-problematization for U.S.-Americans,[50] and challenges the ways in which we are steeped in a traditional U.S. imperialist gaze. Her political vision seemed to demand thoroughly imbricated positions of subjectivity and responsibility across groups of women.

Although Majiet did not label it this way, she went on to describe what a Christian narrative framing would identify as her vocation, explaining, "So, I chose domestic violence and sexual violence, because—no. They chose me."[51] After assisting women clients with mental health issues, and then focusing on women victimized by domestic violence, Majiet eventually shifted to support services exclusively for sexually assaulted women and girls. Her political activism began in high school and university in the uprisings of 1976 and 1982 against apartheid.[52] To Majiet, the building of a better South African society in the twentieth century represented an essential duty of respect, a debt owed because of the lethal costs activist members of her family and community had borne to end apartheid. Her time as a university student had been important for developing her faith even though her father had warned her before she left, "Don't start questioning the Qur'an, don't start questioning what your mother and I have taught you about your faith." In a confident tone, she told me "of course I did start questioning because my mind was expanding."[53] For her, there seemed to be an unambiguous consistency between questioning and preserving religious faith.

To comparatively probe the nature of sexual violence in our two nations, I noted a range of sexual violence categories and contexts experienced by women and girls in the United States, such as marital rape, familial and incestuous rape, stranger rape, and acquaintance rape in school settings such as high school and college campuses as well as sexual assaults within state-run institutions such as the mental hospitals, prisons, and immigrant detention centers. Sexual assaults could also be classified by the role of the perpetrator functioning as trusted, professional, caregiving doctor, therapist, or clergy member, or by the uniqueness of the business relations surrounding the sexual coercion and exploitation as in the human trafficking and pornography industries. I then asked her about the range they usually saw at the Simelela Centre.

After acknowledging my lists, Majiet explained that the most common complaints for the women and girls who came to the Centre involved incestuous rape, attempted rape by strangers and family members, and suspected rape. "When I say suspected rape, I mean the little ones," she clarified, "the little girls that are brought in because their moms suspect something either because it's itchy in the vaginal area or when mom washes them, it is sore to touch them there."[54] Less interested in pointing out the breadth in the categories and forms of the violence and violation as I had, she was intent on conveying the role of community decision making in perpetuating it, in ensuring that I understood exactly how "the personal is political" (she repeated the phrase several times) for the local crime of rape. Majiet explained that sexual assaults of women and girls were directly related to urban planning decisions that failed to address aspects of daily life in Khayelitsha (and other similar black areas). She gave examples of communal toilets where women were especially vulnerable, the lack of streetlights, and construction of streets too narrow for an ambulance to drive through in response to emergency calls.

Certain forms of disjuncture between our perspectives could usefully pry open space for solidarity to emerge. Her Islam-informed commitment to racial equality and women's bodily freedoms need not mirror my Christianity-informed approach. Our encounter instigated the outlines of a shared agenda that needed time to evolve. It held the promise of generative exchanges about how doubt and questioning of faith births antirape commitment and how traditions centered on ancient male prophets spur a stalwart justice orientation toward the equal human rights and well-being of black and coloured women and girls in South Africa as well as women of color in the United States.

Realizing that unfortunately we had to conclude, I glanced down at my watch. I was concerned about staying within the time frame I had requested of her that day since she had already generously shared so much of her time earlier in the week.

Intragroup Strategies and Harm

Prompted by my visit, Majiet had hosted a group of about ten local black and coloured women activist leaders. Their work addressed domestic and sexual violence against women in the Cape Town area through an array of religious, governmental, and nongovernmental community organizations. The majority of them grounded their antiviolence leadership in strong religious (Muslim and Christian) faith commitments. Majiet led our group of visitors, together with Nozwelo Ncube, Simelela's program manager, on a tour of the busy facility, taking us step by step through the process experienced by sexually assaulted clients who came there seeking help. I started to write down the information from Majiet and Nozwelo but became so absorbed in what they were sharing that I could not keep up. Carrying a tape recorder around the crowded building was not possible because of client confidentiality. My notes contained hastily scribbled phrases and truncated reminders: "... *everyone who is seen receives a paper bag kit to take home after the exam. All of the brown paper bag kits include???? Ask later. Police interview women at the Centre. Women are not sent to wait at police stations. . . . Only black and coloured women staff doctors. Stuffed animal pillows for little girls during their exams. . . . Most children seen at Centre were girls. A few boys as well.*"

Following the Centre tour, our group discussion generated a host of intense intersecting concerns related to sexual assault and race. As a prelude to inviting them to share some of the intracommunal issues among black and coloured groups, I commented on the political complexity in U.S. examples. I noted internal African American community taboos against criticizing certain black male religious leaders "in front of white people." This pressure intensified if one pointed out sexually inappropriate conduct or identified the problem of domestic violence committed by some of them. One must, for instance, figure out how to speak critically about the clergy sexual misconduct of Rev. Dr. Martin Luther King Jr. without reinforcing white racist stereotypes of black male sexuality.[55] King had a series of extramarital sexual affairs while serving as a clergy leader in the 1950s and 1960s civil rights movement. If current advocates of black women's equal rights publicly criticized King for his inappropriate private sexual conduct and public sexist treatment of women movement leaders, I explained, they risked being accused of black racial group betrayal. It was difficult to avoid entrapment in fighting off a perpetually shaming white gaze as one simultaneously both refused to tacitly condone these unethical sex/gender dimensions of King's leadership *and* insisted on claiming him as one of the most courageous and articulate U.S. leaders in the twentieth century.

Of course, some U.S. black feminists have criticized the exploitative sexual conduct of black male freedom movement leaders, but not without some opposition. Writer and activist documentary filmmaker Aishah Simmons has written about political roadblocks she encountered when seeking funding to complete her landmark film *NO! The Rape Documentary.* In response to its focus on heterosexual intraracial rape of black women, one opponent of the documentary questioned her right to offer this exposé because she is a lesbian.[56] Simmons filmed testimonies by black women activists that provided accounts of black-male-perpetrated sexual assault within twentieth-century U.S. black freedom movements—both the civil rights and black power movements. There were "Black women on the frontlines of revolutionary struggles," Simmons had argued, who we forget "were faced with death threats by the white establishment while simultaneously having to live with threats of rape and sexual assault by their Black male comrades."[57] She details the racial and sex/gender dynamics in both the support and rejection she received for this kind of truth-telling work.

As Simmons's analysis underscores, publicly identifying black intraracial sexual assaults in U.S. antiracist movements unravels multiple layers of threat and violence. Unfortunately, when black feminists raise this point it often means contending with an insidious, silencing logic of competing black loyalties: to the anti-white supremacy agenda of radical black advocacy groups, the political activist black heterosexual male perpetrators, or political activist black female victim-survivors. Heteropatriarchal assumptions can also contribute to upholding this warped framework of imposing a black racial loyalty test. In the case of Simmons, those assumptions relied on the targeting of the openly lesbian identity of the truth-teller as an additional means of discrediting the necessity for public criticism of sexual violence within black communities.

During my meeting with leaders in the Simelela Centre I also raised strategy questions about how to create more dialogue space among nonwhite activists whose work addresses intimate violence against women and girls. In the United States, it can be controversial to propose an exclusive gathering of activist leaders of color who identify themselves as South Asian, Asian American, Latina or Latinx, African American, American African, Caribbean American, and Native American, who purposely direct their work on gender-based violence toward serving those nonwhite communities. Unique assets and strengths might be found if such a collection of leaders could confer on common obstacles and agendas as well as conflicts and competition for resources that surround their joint commitment to fending off white racism in their antiviolence work. Might it nurture generative solidarities or reproduce destructive racial and ethnic parochialisms to be able to strategize without negotiating the differences in racial perspectives white women activist allies may bring? U.S. feminist cultural studies scholar Andrea Smith argues, for instance, for new models of women of color organizing, beyond recognition of shared victimhood of white supremacy. She suggests resistance strategies that "check our aspirations against the aspirations of other communities to ensure that our model of liberation does not become the model of oppression of others."[58] There are resonances to explore between what it means in post-apartheid South Africa to organize against gender-based violence without generalizing about a primary shared victimization by white supremacy that neglects differences in status between coloured and black women and what it would mean to create an ethical process for excluding whites in the negotiation of women of color alliances in the United States. However, through my continued interactions with the Cape Town leaders, it became clear that the cultural and political meaning of their references to coloured women in South African communities and of mine to women of color in the United States bore no resemblance to each other.

In their serious facial expressions and nods, I thought I saw recognition of some of the dynamics I had mentioned and confirmation of an emergent connection between our antiviolence concerns (theirs and mine). One of the black activist leaders disgustedly referred to her failed attempt to hold a sexually exploitative black male pastor accountable for his abusive treatment of women parishioners. The outsider vantage point that I brought seemed to function productively in this conversation with local leaders and activists. As our reflections sparked off of one another, the need for reciprocal learning became more identifiable as a crucial and fruitful dimension of the process of trust building for the practice of solidarity.

Their negative experiences of globally dominant U.S. influence also surfaced. The particularity of the foreign context—my context—that I referenced mattered. After my opening remarks one of the women leaders reminded the group how they (South Africans) were continually told about the superiority of everything in America. A regular church attendee, she described her frustration with U.S.-American black clergy who routinely visited her congregation and preached lengthy sermons containing neither a sufficient understanding of the South African context, nor even questions about it. For me, her candor bore hope. This articulation of distrust linked to previous experiences with arrogant U.S.-American black Christian visitors seemed a necessary precursor for developing common cause. Her expression of wariness cracked opened the possibility of recognizing ourselves (this participant and I) as linked in a related transnational struggle against male-perpetrated intimate violence.

There were also politically disconcerting gaps in my sense of connectedness to this group of leaders. I cited my unease with how U.S. gender violence activism and scholarship sometimes rigidly divide concerns with intimate male assaults targeting lesbians from those committed against heterosexual women. When assaults targeting lesbians were identified as hate crimes, activist concern with stopping them could be seen as most appropriately relegated to the arena of LGBTQ rights groups. The challenge of bringing attention to these crimes could be cordoned off from the agenda of a movement to end sexual and domestic violence that erroneously portrays all victimized women as heterosexual. Basic feminist claims that define the ongoing nature of the violence by asserting that women are at greater risk inside their homes than on the streets are usually predicated on the experiences of abused and assaulted heterosexuals.[59] This characterization carries inadequate consideration of both the public and private risks to gender-nonconforming lesbians and transgender community members. Compared to other examples that I had mentioned at this Simelela group meeting, there was minimal response to this U.S.-based concern about some of the heterosexist and transphobic dynamics that can stymie coalition building among committed antiviolence advocates. The targeting of gender-nonconforming lesbians for rape and murder was certainly a serious problem in the Khayelitsha community in which we were located. Because religion contains so many virulent heterosexist traditions, the centrality of religion in our meeting may have subtly stifled critiques of how and why the targeting of lesbians may be neglected on the agendas of their movement against gender-based violence. The kinds of divisions I described may have been too foreign to their South African antiviolence movement experience to provoke any comments. There may have been a casual, underlying homophobic desire to avoid this subject among some of the group members. I did not know. Regardless, the awkward moment was a reminder that the conceptualization and practice of solidarity had to allow mutual criticism and confrontation if needed. When the rape of lesbians resides at the center of religion-based gender justice activism, it can productively reveal the authenticity of a shared movement obligation to common gendered interests.

Tense racial dynamics unrelated to homophobia were discussed with less hesitation. One of the participants complained about hierarchical racial dynamics within their gender violence organizations. It appeared to be an uncomfortable topic among the racially mixed black and coloured group. She pointed out how the leadership structure of some gender violence organizations in Cape Town reinforced hierarchical racial dynamics favoring white women, coloured women, and black women, in that order. Tensions about racialized organizational dynamics signaled the continuing struggle against the legacy of apartheid, and they held the power to sabotage activist solidarity among black and coloured antiviolence activists. Racial group hierarchies of power and status undermine a counternarrative so crucial for interrupting rapist and rape culture logic denying the intrinsic worth of women's bodies and their entitlement to respect.

More analyses of racism and colorism are needed in feminist studies of U.S. sexual violence crisis and advocacy organizations with a similar mission to the Simelela Centre. Law and society scholar Rose Corrigan's extensive early twenty-first-century study of local rape crisis centers draws upon interviews with over 150 staff leaders across six states in differing regions of the United States. She explains the absence of analysis of issues of race in her study by noting, "despite my intention to focus more attention on the racial dimensions of institutional responses to rape, I heard very little talk about race from advocates." Therefore, more attention to race could not be included in her study, which she also asserts "of necessity sweeps broadly."[60] The recent late twentieth-century history of the U.S. rape crisis movement incorporates shifts to accommodate state bureaucratization and reliance on law enforcement interventions, as well as the ascendency of a social services definition of antirape work. These shifts aid in eroding any antiracism priorities that may have previously existed in feminist antirape activism and organizations.[61] A tenacious U.S.-American political retreat in which racial issues and sex/gender issues are split off from one another within social justice movements too often persists. In strategic conceptualizations of needed antiviolence initiatives, this default perspective bolsters the illusiveness of the public's capacity to make a direct link between the hierarchical racial labeling of bodies and cultural tolerance for the rape of women's bodies.

The willingness of South African local activists to engage the omnipresent implications of race within anti-gender violence organizations, and more broadly in their nation, likely reflects the freshness of the scars of apartheid. The legacy of brutally enforced racial categories and differential treatment in accord with those categories surrounded us as we sat in that meeting. The present-day fenced-in black neighborhoods that dotted the outskirts of Cape Town directly resulted from apartheid policies dating back to the 1913 Native Land Act. As mentioned earlier, in 1950 the apartheid program of the white minority's National Government Party obligated all South Africans to identify themselves as "white," "coloured," "Asian," or "Native/African" with multiple subcategories related to each.[62] A local Cape Town museum I visited vividly captured details of the 1960s destruction of the racially integrated District Six neighborhood when the apartheid government designated it as a "White Group Area." The shops and homes of Asians, coloureds, and Jews were demolished—over sixty thousand people displaced—to enforce racial segregation and allow only white Christians to live there. The government resettled over thirty-five thousand coloureds to "Cape Flats" in an outlying, barren area. The grand apartheid policy of the 1970s declared blacks (75 percent of the population) noncitizens to be removed from even the squatter camps surrounding the urban areas to so-called Homelands that were suffocating, overcrowded, and environmentally degraded wastelands.

Even when I stared hard at their multiple tones of brown skin, I could not recognize the difference between coloured and black citizens of Cape Town. My assumptions about the significance of phenotypic racial distinctions did not fit their context. In South Africa coloured residents were described as having racially mixed ancestry, some combination of Asian, European, and black African ancestry. Their immediate families usually spoke Afrikaans, and often, especially for those under thirty years old, English as well.

In one of my informal encounters at Robben Island maximum security prison (now a museum), a male tour guide of South Asian ancestry, formerly incarcerated for his anti-apartheid activism, glibly summarized the history of racial mixing. Under the apartheid government the prison had housed political prisoners such as Robert Sobukwe, Walter Sisulu, Nelson Mandela, and Jacob Zuma. As the guide explained it, "race mixing" resulted from how "the first European men came without their women and were naughty with the Native Africans." In popular parlance "mixed ancestry" euphemistically referenced the rape of Khoi-San women by Dutch invaders, documented by scholars of South African history.[63] The phenomenon of an obscured rape legacy is reminiscent of the history of enslaved African women in the slave castles of Ghana and the history of Brazil's enslaved domestic workers, as well as the history of other peoples of African and Native/Indigenous descent across the Americas. In South Africa, rape by Christian European settler-colonialists is nestled in the historical meaning of the term *coloured*.

Yet I was still caught inside my U.S. racial sensibilities where all African Americans are considered black, though most inherited some combination of European, African, and sometimes Native American ancestry. Even if one's biracial mixed parentage includes one black biological parent and one who is white, such as former President Barack Obama, one is still most often publicly identified as black. In an enduring feature of white racism too often given expression by black U.S.-Americans, colorism also maintains hurtful phenotypic biases that calibrate social status and influential notions of aesthetic beauty among blacks. According to colorist standards of personal appearance, skin, hair, or facial features closely resembling those of whites of Northern

European ancestry are preferable over those typically associated with black Africanness. These biases require activist attention in any freedom struggle concerned with how U.S. black women's bodies are in jeopardy of intimate assaults.

Combined issues of racism, colorism, and women's bodily freedom from public physical and sexual assault have been part of activist organizing debates dating back to early civil rights struggles against white segregationist policies. This confluence of justice issues arose when local organizers of the 1950s Montgomery bus boycotts had decided against allowing Claudette Colvin to be a test case for their desegregation campaign. Montgomery police yanked Colvin, as a teenage racial justice activist, off of the city bus for refusing to give up her seat to a white person. The white male police officers physically assaulted her as they removed her. She was terrified of being raped when one of the arresting officers made "a joke about her breasts and bra size" as they placed her in the back of the squad car.[64] Historian Danielle McGuire chronicles the sexual violence that black women faced during that civil rights era. She explains that because of the ongoing violence black women had endured in Montgomery "the bus boycott was more than a movement for civil rights," it was also "a women's movement for dignity, respect, and bodily integrity."[65] In the weeks after her unfair criminal conviction for refusing to give up her seat, Montgomery leaders ultimately rejected Colvin as a test case, in part because she became pregnant. In addition, McGuire notes, "Colvin's dark skin color and working-class status made her a political liability in certain parts of the black community."[66] The celebrated attributes of the activist finally selected by Montgomery movement leaders, Rosa Parks, included, as one of the key local black women leaders indicated, that she was "a medium sized, cultured mulatto woman."[67] Color and class biases can infiltrate strategic choices for mobilizing communities against white racism and sexual violation, even as activists seek protest responses from women and girls who risk bodily assaults by police when doing so.

Colorism, especially a belief in the superiority of white skin over dark brown skin, persisted among some African American children and adults in the United States over half a century after the struggle to end de jure segregation had been won.[68] In her study of the harms of colorism in the lives of contemporary black women, Sociologist JeffriAnne

Wilder documents prejudice and discrimination in social, institutional, and family life that can fuel a self-esteem-diminishing confirmation of innate black inferiority. [69] The resiliency of colorism adds another crucial agenda item for the formation of Africana transnational solidarity opposing violence. Colorist social messages translate the aesthetic meaning of certain bodily features of black women into currency for white supremacist shaming.[70] These social messages blend too easily with perpetrator reasoning that judges certain types of female bodily curves, breast sizes, swinging hips, or open-legged sitting postures as supposedly inviting sexual harassment and assault. As the 1950s Montgomery example prompts us to consider, colorism generates intracommunal toxicity that may even seep into activist organizing strategies on behalf of respect for women's bodily integrity in public spaces. Womanist Christian ethicist Emilie Townes argues for a sense of urgency about garnering African American spiritual and communal resources to combat colorist toxicity. African American people of faith, she warns, should not "underestimate what colorism and caste do to the soul and spirit."[71] Yet, as in Brazil, the imposition of a singular U.S. narrative about the social meanings of blackness and struggles to resist related subjugation could impede an understanding of the specific forms of post-apartheid South African racialism that the leaders there identified as impactful in their antirape work.

When Majiet described the motivations behind her antiviolence work in our one-on-one meeting she emphasized her allegiance to the black struggle against apartheid. "The history that I have gone through, the history of what happened in 1976, the uprisings, it is so clear to me, like it was yesterday," she told me.[72] Her declarations about the historical impetus for her antirape leadership conveyed the significance of her national context for grounding her work, but stressed the black freedom struggle, not nationalism. That history of black women's leadership in black freedom movement struggles involved particular forms of embodied protest that often risked sexualized bodily assault as a consequence.

Certain gendered, embodied dimensions of black women's participation in the 1950s and 1960s struggle against apartheid in South Africa parallel black women's history in the U.S. civil rights movement. In her comparative study of both movements, black feminist social theorist M. Bahati Kuumba notes the troubling of gender role norms in the deliberate strategy of submitting to arrest and jail in protest of white racist policies, sometimes with the refusal of bail, including by pregnant activist leaders.[73] She compares thousands of women jailed in 1956 anti-pass protests in South Africa to the actions of black women protesters jailed in 1950s and 1960s desegregation campaigns in the United States. Kuumba's documentation of these histories acknowledges both the suffering of the women activists, exemplified in sexual humiliation and assault by jailers, and their models of embodied courageous leadership tactics. Patriarchal organizational structures and narrow gender role understandings also imposed unfair limits for women movement leaders in both national contexts. In the U.S. Montgomery civil rights campaign political calculations of gendered respectability designated the activist teenager Colvin, as Kuumba asserts, a "less attractive representation of African American womanhood" and a less attractive movement symbol.[74]

"As much as I say I have forgiven. I have not forgotten," Majiet explained. "And so, my motto remains: never again. Never again. I am not completely over my anger and it does rear its head when I am confronted with issues of racism."[75] When I pressed for more details about her anger, she said, "Never again will a white person tell me what I can think. What's acceptable and what's not. Never again. I have not lost friends, I have not lost family members for nothing. If their deaths are to mean something we must remember never again to allow a white person to tell us what to think. You have to remember the past to make sure that it does not happen again."[76] Her discussion of this history elicited a portrait of how the costs of the black struggle to overcome the brutal apartheid regime directly motivated her antirape work. Each time she said "never again" the spirituality of social change work became almost viscerally apparent. This form of revitalizing spirituality seamlessly weaves together stubborn perseverance and visions of freedom. It reflects activist resistance to past centuries of white racist devaluation of black human dignity in South Africa and also propels forward the impulse to end the current rape of black girls and women by their black male relatives and neighbors. Majiet's invocation of memory declared a sustained indignation with even the slightest insinuation of attitudes that normalized the dehumanization of black and coloured peoples. Fighting to end rapes of black women and girls therefore constituted a refusal to accept colonial and apartheid logic of devalued black human worth.

The memory work summoned by Majiet constituted yet another form of spirituality that is not confined to the usual, compartmentalized, established traditions of religiosity. Her words point to a particular type of gender justice spirituality, sometimes nurtured by ancient organized religious traditions. But at other times this spirituality draws strength from a broader array of cultural and antiracist political sources that peculiarly equip advocates like Majiet to confront leaders of established religious traditions. For example, some iteration of this gender justice spirituality seemed to be operative when she urged Christian clergy to use their authority in local communities to support women who have been raped. Majiet confronted them on the specifics of women's empowerment, including a woman's right to have an abortion if she feels it is her only choice, particularly when impregnated by her rapist. Her earnest comment "more dialogue with clergy is needed" punctuated her description of these workshop sessions with clergy.

Certain activist expressions of spirituality can engage the religious worldview of clergy by inviting them to enter the context of women's lives in which rape and the threat of rape diminish their sense of empowerment. Support for bodily integrity in one's antirape commitments has to address reproductive freedoms and challenge religion's traditional role in exercising its moral influence to restrict those freedoms. The persistence of the rape of women and girls mandates the creation of pathways of escape from religious prohibitions on birth control and abortion that further the social erasure of this reality of violence.

After my meeting with Majiet concluded, I stood outside the Simelela Centre digging around in my overstuffed shoulder bag for my cell phone because I needed to call the taxi driver who was supposed to be waiting for me. I glanced up to see a little girl, six or seven years old, exiting with a woman I presumed to be her mother. As they pushed through the Centre's door, its dull-brown steel security bars contrasted with the bright multicolored fabric of her pants. When I waved hello, her entire chocolate-brown face radiated with a smile as she and her mother waved back, slightly startling me. I had not expected them to come to a full stop and greet me so warmly.

When I began to speak on my cell phone, shouting because of a bad connection, they turned around again, looking at me expectantly. I awkwardly offered another quick wave. As they moved away a second time, I noticed a long brown paper bag hanging from the little girl's shoulder by a drawstring handle. The bag that held the Centre's kit for rape survivors bounced off her small body as she walked. I stood still, silently staring at the bag and the beautiful brightly colored pants of the receding little girl. She held her mother's hand as they slowly made their way down the narrow street.

The encounter made the wrenching spiritual costliness of the violence obvious, communicating an immediacy not fully realizable in the meetings with the leaders. My brief, wordless exchange with the little girl carrying the rape kit exposed how morally misguided it is to harbor any inclination to concede the inevitability of intragroup power struggles among gender justice groups.

* * *

All of my Simelela Centre discussions pointed to productive frictions for building solidarity within and across national settings. Many of them invited interrogation of what racially unifies, why racial unity is pursued, and how. A goal of some sort of harmonious unity was politically inadequate and dangerously simplistic. Religious practices that are explicitly antirape-oriented can kindle solidarity-building habits as they encourage painful truth-telling about how the violence in patriarchal traditions reflects conditions in the everyday lives of community members. Ujamaa Centre pedagogy in Pietermaritzburg illustrated how this kind of Christian group study focused on depictions of rape and ethnic conflict in sacred scripture can allow for the development of both faith-based antirape attitudes and antiracist cultural critiques. These democratized communal practices hold potential to unleash the freeing power of tradition.

However, the destructive potential of racial discord continues to lurk in antirape social movement building. Usually the tensions can be traced to cultural and political protections that gender-based violence has historically enjoyed in the United States and South Africa. The legacies of state apparatuses for institutionalizing racial segregation systematically sowed disunity and distrust among subcultural groups. Together with informal attitudes for preserving cultural and political white dominance, they are implicated in the pervasiveness of the violence. These practices and attitudes are echoed in racial tensions found in the antiviolence advocacy agendas and organizing of racial and gender justice groups.

The anti-apartheid-rooted "never again" invoked by Zarina Majiet that also spurred her antirape work offers a lens for creatively envisioning responses to these corrosive dynamics. Majiet's Islamic feminist spirited resolve fundamentally rejected what apartheid taught about how to think and feel—a combination also stressed in Nadar's Christianity-based antirape analysis. This rejection demands consequences for woman-blaming, rape-culture-supporting public assertions by leaders who are involved in sexual assault or harassment scandals at the highest levels of government in South Africa and the United States. The "we" referenced by gender justice advocates must evidence a repudiation of any homophobic and transphobic assumptions about the sexual orientation and gender expression of those victimized by gender-based violence. In local organizing the spirited anger must be channeled toward insistence on the design of neighborhood living spaces for safety and freedom that helps to prevent the violence. A further enhanced examination of spirituality as a catalyst for activist methods of claiming time and space to reject rape culture and racisms that participate in it can make room for even more ideas about creative antiviolence conceptualizations and actions.

6

Defiant Spirituality

It was the first thing that I saw as we entered this group meeting: a sturdy cloth hanging on the wall, large and colored a deep shade of red. Members of the Free Gender black lesbian activist group that I came to meet had hung it there for our gathering. We sat in the Wetlands Park boardroom of the small community center located in the Makhaza section of Khayelitsha, not far from the Simelela Centre. Returning to the same area of Cape Town as the Simelela Centre generated a welcome sense of familiarity for me. The cars outside zipped along the smooth blacktop of a well-constructed, immaculately maintained highway. In tin-roofed sheds with hand-painted signs, some local businesses sold fruits and vegetables or furniture, and others sold services such as haircuts. The Simelela Centre's new building, with its clean gray concrete parking area, sat back from this main road behind a large Pentecostal church on the corner. Like most of the black and coloured communities on the outskirts of Cape Town, the terrain was mostly flat but with ever-visible gray mountains towering in the background.

I became acquainted with Funeka Soldaat, a founding leader of Free Gender, for the first time at that meeting. She wore a deep red cap that almost matched the fabric on the wall. A mature adult, Funeka had a round brown face the color of maple syrup. Her toned, large muscles peeked out from under her short-sleeved shirt when she gestured with her arms as she spoke. Free Gender was committed to ending violence against black lesbians as well as all forms of "stigma, exclusion, and discrimination in terms of sexual identities and gender expressions."[1]

My Cape Town host, Elizabeth Petersen, director of South African Faith and Families Institute (SAFFI), who had worked with Funeka to organize the meeting, drove me there that morning. SAFFI's primary mission was to mobilize faith leaders in South Africa to oppose gender-based violence through a wide array of local organizing strategies. In addition to Funeka's Free Gender group members, Cape Town Christian and non-Christian leaders who were activists for lesbian, gay, bisexual, transgender, queer, and intersex (LGBTQI) rights as well as heterosexual Christian church leaders also attended.[2]

Considering activist leadership examples from Free Gender and others can provide some clues for envisioning defiant spirituality in political resistance to violence against black lesbians in South Africa and the United States. Although I focus on violence against black lesbians, in both countries the perpetrators of this kind of gender violence target lesbians and gender-nonconforming persons across a spectrum of racial backgrounds and sex/gender identity minority groups. In 2015, for example, the U.S. National Coalition of Anti-Violence Programs documented a sampling of 1,253 incidents of hate violence against LGBTQ and HIV-affected people from a range of racial/ethnic backgrounds (e.g., Arab, Asian, multiracial, white), but in the twenty-four murders reported in the study, more than half the victims were black or Latino/a.[3]

Defiant spirituality as part of solidarity building can also thrive in organizational practices that depend on a combination of interfaith religious cooperation and antiracist commitments for addressing this form of gender-based violence. Activist examples related to ending homophobic gender-based violence spur appreciation of communally generated forms of defiant spirituality that accentuate the human-life-enhancing potential and connectivity generated by community leaders as they face off against the death-dealing opponents of black lesbian humanity. In discussing defiant spirituality here, I do not privilege the spirituality that arises from language and practices that reiterate the historic symbols and texts of organized religious traditions such as Christianity and Islam. Dependence upon divine revelation is decentered though not excluded in my investigation of the role of faith and spirit. To differing degrees, spiritual understandings of Christianity and/or African Traditional Religion inform the antirape perspectives of some of the leaders I met. My interactions with South African activist leaders in combination with U.S. black feminist and womanist analyses and other feminist antiviolence frameworks spark suggestions about how to define spiritually resourceful communal practices that are involuntarily tethered to abusive ones.

Defiant spirituality seemed to reside, for instance, as an underlying resource within Free Gender group demonstrations of their allegiance to violently victimized black lesbians. The expansiveness and defiance in this spirituality manifested a timeless quality upheld through their open-ended allegiance. Defiant spirituality also assumed a form that helped to ignite and support collective public demands for accountability, though there were dangerous risks for activist leaders who made such demands. Rooted in stubborn, shared political resolve, defiant spirituality lent sustaining energy to the task of creating space for honoring community members' intentional transgressions of certain coercive sex/gender norms of self-expression.

Solidarity as Strategic and Spiritual Practice

What is the spiritual significance of the ways in which gender-based violence enjoys cultural support for the targeting of a specific collective group of socially stigmatized women and girls? When the violence and the ongoing threat of it include the precise goal of terrorizing groups of black women and girls based upon their nonconforming gender expression and lesbian sexual identities, a wide array of accompanying spiritual costs result. The costliness resides in the daily trial of facing such a heightened sense of the precariousness of one's life due to one's group identity. As U.S. feminist philosopher Judith Butler explains, "precariousness implies living socially, that is, the fact that one's life is always in some sense in the hands of the other."[4] This notion of precariousness has spiritual implications alongside of the social ones Butler names. The targeting of black lesbians and gender-nonconforming queer women for violence weaponizes social precariousness in order to rob them of a primary spiritual dimension of human affirmation: a sense of communal belonging. The potential for communal solidarity under these circumstances rests upon how moral parameters are set when defining the violence and its costs.

In South Africa, the targeted assaults on lesbians had plagued many black township communities during recent years.[5] The male perpetrators, mostly young black men, believed themselves to be engaging in the practice of "corrective rape," supposedly raping to persuade lesbians to become heterosexuals. I had referred to this crime as "corrective rape" in a discussion with Free Gender activist leader Funeka Soldaat, and she stopped me immediately, clarifying that the perpetrators had coined the term and antiviolence activists there did not use it to describe the assaults. "There's nothing to correct," she asserted.[6] With her explanation, she guided me toward an understanding of how allies of those targeted for assault rejected the "corrective rape" terminology. Those who un-equivocally located their solidarity with the victimized lesbians there-fore refused to lend credibility to the term and the justification of the violence that it normalized. As South African feminist scholar-activist and filmmaker Zethu Matebeni argues, "the use of such language (or the reading of violence as curative) suggests an elevated status for the perpetrator who is seen as 'curing' and 'correcting' for the good of the dominant culture, while stigmatizing and branding the survivor."[7] If one uses terminology, even unwittingly, for defining the crime in a manner that championed the perpetrator's logic and supported his actions as a communal good, one participates in a kind of communal spiritual as-sault that aggressively disavows communal belonging for black lesbian identity.

Combined elements of sexuality and brutal violence targeting black lesbians bore the potential for sensationalized U.S.-American reactions, including perhaps desensitized titillation for imaginations well trained by mass media to revel in rape and murder as prime-time entertain-ment. This potential pointed to the urgency and delicacy of sorting out the meaning of positioning oneself as a U.S.-American transnational ally in relation to both those targeted and their advocates, rather than as a fascinated observer of their struggles. While the rates of occurrences of and political attention to this crime were distinctive in South Africa, such attacks were hardly unique to the country.

U.S.-American black feminist scholar Chandra Ford described wrenching, racialized cruelties of a sexual assault where she was tar-geted because she was a lesbian.[8] She recalled struggling with her rapist, a black student acquaintance on her U.S. college campus who wanted to teach her a lesson: "Laughing at me, he'd ask me questions like 'Are you a lesbian?' There was no right answer, for when I said 'Yes,' he physically assaulted me, and when I said 'No,' he sexualized the assault telling me I enjoyed what he was doing."[9] Ford's testimony also highlights how her racial isolation on the predominantly white Pennsylvania campus de-veloped in the aftermath of this assault. Additionally, she experienced betrayal by other black college students who had previously been her friends. Soon after the rape in her dorm room, Ford writes, "a group of about ten brothas from our shared circle of black activists barged into my dorm room and mock gang-raped me. . . . At the time, my desire to fit into the black community and my understanding of what it means to commit oneself to a movement made it difficult for me to blame them for the pain I experienced as a result of their actions . . . it seemed more appropriate to blame myself."[10] Years later she realized how deliberate and planned the assault by the group of men had been when she learned they had bragged to others about having "raped a black lesbian to teach her a lesson."[11] At the time of the incident a white feminist student sexual assault staff member had also betrayed her by supporting her perpetrator over her. When Ford successfully pursued criminal charges against her rapist, she desperately needed genuine communal sources of personal support, but they remained scarce.

As Ford characterized her post-rape recognition of her rapist's culpability, she understood that "it was not I who was wrong for being."[12] It seems apparent that the rapist used her social identity—beingness—as a woman and a lesbian as a tool useful for his attempt to drain away her entitlement to human dignity. Yet she resisted both a social and spiritual assault on her beingness. The assault was social, as the rapist drew from rape-legitimizing societal narratives of heterosexual superiority and black male sexist entitlement. It can also be construed as spiritual insofar as the rapist sought to disconnect her from assuming her moral right to exist, that is, to destroy her ties of rightful belonging to human community, because she was a lesbian. In counterclaiming the rightness of her beingness, Ford drew strength from radical writings of lesbian women of color who knew what it meant to choose, as she writes, to "Be across identity borders."[13] This is an act of summoning community for moral and spiritual support—community that was not physically present. The crossing of identity borders enriches and affirms the dignity of black lesbian beingness under assault. A collective witness to the goodness of crossed identity borders of race, gender expression, and sexuality may be seen as a spiritual witness to the moral process of beingness. It signals freedom. Lesbian or queer ways of being represented in the collective witness Ford summoned demonstrate movement across identity borders with a bold refusal to be controlled. Simultaneously, this collective witness defiantly rooted in certain boundaried communities of color whose borders lesbian writers of color choose to cross.

Therefore, to imagine defiant spirituality that constitutes a supportive response to this gender-based violence, affirmation of the crossing of identity borders is a crucial ingredient. The spirituality needs to align with the imbricated social dynamics embedded in this violence. Sociologist Doug Meyer conducted a qualitative study focusing on racial differences in sexual and physical assaults targeting LGBTQ persons in the United States. He found that respondents repeatedly described the distinctive roles of individual social markers such as their race, gender expression, and lesbian identity, as difficult to distinguish as they later tried to understand the nature of the attack. For instance, Meyer explains, "lesbian women of color sometimes found it difficult to distinguish between misogynistic and homophobic forms of violence. Judy, a 43 year-old Latina lesbian woman, encountered discourse that was simultaneously misogynistic and homophobic when she was sexually assaulted. . . . 'I can't be sure if it occurred because of my sexuality or just because I'm a woman. Both probably played a role.'"[14] Her attacker had told her, "All I want to do is fuck you and I bet you'll come back straight."[15] As illustrated here, perpetrator logic targets, confuses, and isolates the women by seizing upon gender and sexual identity markers as a source of vulnerability to be manipulated. In a relevant protective counterresponse, strategies of spiritual defiance should appreciatively reflect multiply located and overlapping social identities, such as Latina lesbian womanhood, and also claim the collective power of women of color scholar-activists publicly articulating what it means to, as Ford describes, "Be across identity borders."

The members of the Cape Town Free Gender group stressed collective action and cultivation of firm alliances among black lesbians, bisexuals, transgender, and intersex women as an essential aspect of their organizing. This solidarity-building work within their group and beyond was steeped in extreme circumstances of political recalcitrance and ongoing threats to their lives and bodily safety. Free Gender pressured politicians, police, courts, and other community leaders to address the ongoing targeting of black lesbians for assault, especially sexual assault, and hold perpetrators accountable.

The name of the group showcased its human rights goals and, in my interpretation, its liberation spirituality centered upon gender. Human Rights Watch issued a report, "We'll Show You're a Woman: Violence and Discrimination against Black Lesbians and Transgender Men in South Africa," discussing the gendered nature of the violence. It documents the circumstances of the violence and the how masculine gender identity and gender expression played a significant role.[16] The report defines a transgender man as a female-born person who identifies as male and often expresses his preferred gender through dress and mannerisms. The report includes interviews with black South African lesbian and transgender male victim-survivors of these assaults, as well as human rights activists and government officials in several communities, including police personnel at the Khayelitsha police station.

The Human Rights Watch report on South Africa describes the gender dynamics of the violence with references to an interview with Zebo, a black lesbian South African who lived in a former black township in Gauteng, South Africa, and provided examples of daily rape threats and taunts she endured. "Men who rape lesbians are known not only to boast of the criminal acts in public," the report explains, "but some assert their intent to rape again because, as they say, lesbians do not treat 'the guys' with due respect. Raping a lesbian can make men 'heroes' in their communities and fuel a climate in which more sexual assaults may occur. Zebo's close friend, also a lesbian, was brutally gang raped in late 2008 and left for dead by some men in her neighborhood.[17] Zebo said, 'The guys around treat [the rapists] like heroes. They applaud them.'"[18] The masculinity of the rapists seems to be at stake. Their brutality reinforces gender norms of deference that they apparently feel that lesbians in their communities deny them. Lesbians whose expressions of their gender are most commonly associated with masculinity have become especially vulnerable to being targeted. Attackers try to prohibit lesbians from sharing in their supposed exclusive entitlement to black masculine identity by utilizing violence and threats of it. Zebo's testimony points to collusion with the attackers by other cisgender black men who celebrate the violent protection of their exclusive claims on masculinity.

Lesbians do, unapologetically, contest such exclusivity. In their study of hate crimes against black lesbian South Africans, South African feminist scholars Nonhlanhla Mkhize, Jane Bennett, Vasu Reddy, and Relebohile Moletsane explain how "the question of 'lesbian masculinity' is taken up with vigor in the negotiation of several South Africans with their preferences for self-recognition, sexual orientation and gender identification" and how the eschewal of masculinity is not a useful assumption in the liberation politics of the LGBTQI movement.[19] Free Gender created an open and affirming space for gender expression by black lesbians, especially masculine expressions of gender. For black lesbians living under the conditions of being terrorized by the threat of gang rape and murder, the creation of *free gender* space involves a unique form of defiant spirituality.

Space and Time for Freedom

Inside the meeting room, that large red cloth loomed like a stain that refused to be ignored, taking up almost a third of one wall. With "Court Cases" printed at the top, a list of numbers and letters, handwritten in black marker, covered most of the cloth. The black lines of the marker had an uneven thickness. The sizes of the individual letters varied slightly so that each stroke had a highly personalized quality. Following every set of numbers, thicker black capital letters identified the circumstances that the numbers referenced. The first several items on the list included:

1. 132/5/2010 RAPE
2. 75/05/2009 RAPE
3. 306/05/2009 RAPE
4. 108/2001 RAPE
5. 105/2005 MURDER
6. 216/02/2006 MURDER
7. 982/12/2011 SUICIDE
8. 324/09/2008 MURDER
9. 553/12/2010 ASSAULT

An ominously empty red space of fabric was left below the last notation on the list. As the possibility entered my mind that more cases might be inserted in that space, I guiltily rushed it away, as if my thoughts could invite such tragedies.

The cloth linked differing types of violence together as it bore witness to the community's costs and losses. Acknowledgment of the suicides, assaults, murders, and rapes on the red cloth seemed to constitute a spirituality of politicized collective grieving. It claimed the space to grieve and the impetus to pursue justice in the courts. The cloth marked the group's timeless allegiance to the lives of the victimized black lesbians, confirming a spiritual and political tether that defied the final ending their torturers had sought. The spirituality generated a defiant continuity, that is, a refusal to accept neither the final breach in the mystery of death by murder or suicide, nor the perpetrator's last word to survivors in the psychic theft that accompanied the brutality and bodily invasion of the assaults. Feminist theorist Judith Butler writes about the immorality of state violence and torture that consigned others to a status of unworthiness to be grieved, explaining "grievability is a presupposition for the life that matters . . . without grievability, there is no life, or, rather, there is something living that is other than life."[20] In that Free Gender space, the losses of black lesbians victimized by violence were countered by the regard accorded them in ongoing collective grieving. Therefore, the spiritual defiance this regard produced had to be characterized by vehement insistence on the moral irreducibility of black queer existence in all spaces and throughout all of time. This form of intervention on the meaning of space and time was particularly crucial in the aftermath of violence intended to send a threatening, communal message about the reducibility of black lesbian humanity to objects vulnerable to attacks at any moment, in any public space.

At that Free Gender meeting the room gradually filled to about thirty people. We gathered in a wide circle. One of the Free Gender leaders called the meeting to order. Our dark-gray plastic chairs crowded the edges of the room and left a big space in the center that we had to talk across. In the circle of activists and religious leaders (mainly representatives of church groups), Free Gender members composed the largest number of attendees who came from the same activist organization. Several of the Free Gender members were energetic young adults who appeared to be twenty to thirty years old. Some were Christians, some not. Free Gender members started us off with singing. The unique sound of South African a cappella harmony filled the room. They sang "We Glorify Your Name" with the melodious wail of the lead voice followed by an echo response by the other singers: "We glor-rifyy." "We glo-rrrrify." "Your name." They sang in English, then in Xhosa, and then in English again.

With a slow, steady tempo, the tune slid up and down the scale in a heart-wrenching choral invocation of sacred spirit. The naked beauty of their voices enveloped the room, gripped me, and held me. The comfort their voices offered coexisted alongside my captivity to that red cloth hanging with its black handwritten numbers and letters. I swayed to the music, tried to sing with them, and swallow tears before they were seen. My Cape Town host and cosponsor of this meeting, Elizabeth, had lit a vanilla-colored candle and placed it in the center of the room. Almost everyone's attention seemed to gravitate toward that candle at some point during the singing.

The music of our collective voices led by Free Gender members effectively conveyed holiness and spirituality in the claiming of space to discuss resistance to the targeting of lesbians for assault, rape, murder, and social torment to the point of suicide. In the repeated line, "We glorify your name," the glory attributed to the unnamed one whose existence was honored in the lyric pointed to both a divine Spirit as well as the victimized lives of those also unnamed on the red cloth. Divine spirit and black lesbian humanity (in some cases, murdered or dead by suicide) were spiritually present. The intermingled sacredness of both seemed implicit with the words "your name."

Additionally, in this setting, glorifying signified an honoring of victimized black lesbian lives with not only communal grief but also political mobilization. The singing underscored the spiritual dimension of routinizing communal accountability on behalf of the assaulted and dead. It illustrated how social movement work of seeking political justice through the police and in the courts involved the spiritual work of refusal to allow the broader society to forget their deaths. The activists would not permit the assaults to dehumanize, isolate, or wreak bodily destruction with impunity. The words "we glorify" could be seen as proclaiming glory as appropriate for black lesbian bodies with nonconforming gender identities that were societally rendered inglorious. The lyric heralded the active, not quiescent, and the collective, not individualistic, struggle in which "we" must engage. There was no space for morally neutral bystanders.

That collective moment illustrated ritual innovation in its combination of the spiritual and the political. Yet it constituted only a glimpse of how the spiritual aspect of solidarity building in this antiviolence struggle might be manifest. Creation of space for freedom in the wake of homophobic gender-based violence could also emerge spontaneously. Black LGBTQ church groups, with their rootedness in their faith traditions as impetus, sometimes helped transform nonreligious spaces of antiviolence struggle into spirituality-in-action spaces of political witness. Transformation of public space occurred suddenly in a U.S. community response to the hate-motivated 2003 killing of Sakia Gunn, in which the Liberation in Truth Unity Fellowship Church participated. Reverend Jacqueline Holland, an out African American lesbian minister in the black, predominantly LGBTQ national Unity Fellowship Church Movement, founded the church in 1995.[21] Liberation in Truth was actively committed to serving LGBTQ members of the majority low-income African American city of Newark, New Jersey, where Sakia, a fifteen-year-old African American lesbian, was murdered. In her sex/gender expression, Sakia's preferred self-presentation of "baggy jeans, double XL white t-shirts, and a closely cropped afro" marked her black queerness as "Ag" (aggressive).[22] Two adult black males accosted Sakia and her teenage friends as they stood at a bus stop late at night after partying in Greenwich Village in New York City. The older black male attackers climbed out of their car, at first propositioning the teens, then escalating to anger. Sakia rebuffed their taunts and let them know that she and her friends were lesbians and not interested in dating men. A physical struggle ensued, and one of the men stabbed Sakia to death.

U.S. black feminist theorist Zenzele Isoke described the tense atmosphere between police and the hurt and angry group of black queer teenagers who attended the funeral for Sakia in Newark. The heavy police presence at the funeral, supposedly there to provide security, clashed with the teenagers who were often harassed and unprotected by city police. Isoke explained that Liberation in Truth leaders together with others reacted immediately and provided "a mediating zone between the traumatized young people and Newark's power structure."[23] Rev. Janyce Jackson, senior pastor of Liberation in Truth at that time, later explained how she and others "formed a human line between the young people who attended the funeral and the police."[24] In response to the murder of Sakia and other expressions of community homophobia, black queer activist leaders also organized other ongoing projects that focused on the needs of these youth.[25] In Isoke's analysis, the leaders created a geography of resistance by respatializing the city setting with activism to transform it for black queer people such that "even if one could not always be safe, they could still belong."[26] The activism of the black LGBTQ church demonstrated an embodied spirituality of solidarity with the murdered Gunn and the angry queer youth. With their leadership focused on the protection of the youth from the police, Jackson and other black lesbian Christian adult leaders displayed a unique means of being and doing church. Through a spontaneous street ritual of solidarity with the youths, the leaders made provisions affirming the rightfulness of their belonging at and access to the funeral for the murdered youth. Their Christian faith commitments grounded this active expression of collective spirituality through political negotiation with the police and bodily witness to the validation, belonging, and preciousness of the LGBTQ youth to their community.

Sometimes, spirituality infused the task of creating space for freedom from gender violence by defiantly nurturing long-lasting roots in a hostile community environment. While in Cape Town, I met an activist leader, Bulelwa Panda, manager for over thirteen years at a Christian safe house, iThemba Lam. The house offered refuge to black LGBTQ community members who had been raped, beaten, or kicked out of their family homes because of their sexual identity. The house provided residents with a place, as one international religious news report noted, "to integrate 'God's gift of faith with God's gift of sexuality.'"[27] As I spoke with her, Bulelwa chronicled the evolution of the neighbors' reactions to iThemba Lam's establishment. At first there were homophobic fears about what would be done to neighborhood children by Bulelwa and threats to destroy the house. Increasingly there was a bit more acceptance of it as "the gay house" in their community.[28] Neighbors gradually became willing to help strangers who were looking for the safe house and point the way to "the gay house." Yet Bulelwa had experienced considerable personal danger and threat. "If I was walking down the road, they would call me names, especially men," she explained, "because they think that I want to be a man, you see, that's how they see me, they perceive me . . . with men, they've got that fear that you are going to play their role and you make them feel inferior."[29] Through her leadership of the safe house and local residency for well over a decade, she claimed a form of black LGBTQI space in that neighborhood that directly challenged the coercive control of cisgender black masculinity. Far from being a hideaway secretly occupied by LGBTQI persons, the Christian safe house was well known for its preservation of gay home space in the community.

The spirituality referenced by Bulelwa and exemplified in her leadership assumed multiple forms. A spiritual boldness inhabited her defiance of the homophobic danger and threat attached to her openness about her sexuality and gender expression as she moved throughout her community on a daily basis. With this boldness Bulelwa performed a kind of missionary work to the Christians with homophobic views. As she explained, "When you live among them, you change the way that they see you."[30] Her leadership of the Christian safe house was endowed with a spirituality of hospitality that incorporated Africana transnational solidarity. Its expansive welcome extended to LGBTQI immigrants from elsewhere on the African continent, such as Angola and Zimbabwe, who fled persecution based on their sexual orientation. The welcome Bulelwa offered in her work applied even to heterosexual women fleeing abusive men who were intimate partners. After mentioning this point, Bulelwa had immediately added a clarification. She explained that she had to protect herself from any accusations of improper behavior that might be falsely made against her. So she ensured that when these women initially came and knocked on the door of her private residence they were taken directly to the Christian safe house. As part of her ethical leadership practices it remained her responsibility to preemptively integrate a cognizance of stereotypes of lecherous lesbians that homophobic heterosexuals routinely invoke. This precaution illustrated how the politics of solidarity with women victimized by heterosexual intimate partner violence could unfairly burden black lesbian antiviolence activism and demand expansive expressions of Christian hospitality that carried peculiar forms of costliness.

It became clear that a complex web of spiritual traditions could play a vital role in supporting the leaders' everyday defiance of the violence. Conveying a sense of pride and enthusiasm, Bulelwa described the significance that certain African Traditional Religious practices and understandings had for her. Noting that she went to church when she felt like it, she declared, "I'm more focused on my tradition" and the practices of her clan. She spoke of how important it was to her to introduce her newly purchased house to her ancestors. She sat down with local community elders and told them that she and her (same-sex) partner had bought a house and wanted to introduce it to her ancestors. In response, the all-male group of her local clan elders had thought "it was a great thing."[31] They praised her financial accomplishment. With this example, Bulelwa emphasized the distinctiveness of this spirituality of communicating with ancestors, of "never having been judged" as the church had judged her.[32] It displayed another instance of a boundary-breaking spirituality of solidarity that involved the claiming of space. Elders and spiritual ancestors provided collective spiritual affirmation of the home that she and her wife shared and seemed to generate a revitalizing, nurturing resource for Bulelwa. This situated African spiritual nurturing seemed essential within the challenging, sometimes hostile environment in which she maintained both her own home and a safe house home for LGBTQI persons and others victimized by abuse and violence who may have crossed national borders or just come from across the street.

The creation of spirituality-infused mechanisms to activate freedom from homophobic gender violence could also be centered in specific relational connections. In South Africa, the United States, and elsewhere, acute interpersonal relational damage leaves a long-lasting impact on those victimized by the violence and has to be addressed with reparative relational strategies. Black lesbian church leaders contributed relational antiviolence responses to situations where poisonous Christian teachings had helped fuel assaults targeting lesbians, including against lesbian youths still living with their parents. At the Free Gender meeting in Cape Town, I had mentioned one such example from the United States. I cited the work of a black lesbian pastor serving a North Carolina black LGBTQ congregation in the Metropolitan Community Churches (MCC) denomination.[33] Several MCC churches were also located in South Africa. Nokuthula Dhladla, for instance, a black lesbian MCC co-pastor of a predominantly black LGBTQI congregation in Johannesburg, routinely spoke out against sexual violence targeting black lesbians, citing her own experience of sexual violence.[34]

In the United States, I had interviewed the North Carolina MCC pastor, Wanda Floyd, for a previous research project. Floyd described her ongoing supportive meetings with a fifteen-year-old black girl who had been raped by her father when she told him that she was a lesbian. "Not only did he rape her," Floyd said, "he gave her an STD."[35] The pastor identified the challenge of countering the rigid Christian Pentecostal teachings with which the girl had been raised and taught that she was going to hell because she was a lesbian. Eventually, the girl was removed from the father's care and placed in a foster home, where she formed a positive bond with two white lesbian peers. The actions of Floyd in this situation directly opposed the condemning spiritual messages that this Christian girl had been taught and challenged the ways in which those messages elided with the emotional and physical damage of her father's violent response to her disclosure of her lesbian identity. But Floyd had explained that she was "not necessarily trying to take away all of the negative stuff that she grew up with, because that's so much a part of who she is right now, but I'm trying to give her another perspective."[36] The pastor's relationship with the girl opened up an emergent space of freedom from paternal rape and Christian spiritual abuse. This emergent relational space functioned as a means of generating alternative Christian spiritual and emotional territory for an affirming relationship to lesbian selfhood and new, trustworthy family connections. An antiviolence lesbian kinship developed through the supportive relationship with this black lesbian Christian pastor. The relationship restoratively demonstrated lesbian identity as a resource of kindness, respect, and nonviolence. It highlighted the capacity of Christian lesbian nurture to gradually replace Christian heterosexual shaming and degradation.

Kinship epitomizes the enduring spirituality and moral values needed for this struggle. In response to the violence, spaces of black queer kinship must be invented. U.S. black queer Christian scholar Thelathia Nikki Young offers a constructive articulation of family morality that stresses an innovativeness relevant to antiviolence goals. She describes black queers as "creative resisters [who] redact, improvise, and initiate community narratives as well as new practices of kinship and family, thereby transforming social realities."[37] "Creative resister" Christian lesbian leaders have invented practices of kinship to transform the reality of violence against lesbians and gender-nonconforming or queer persons as well as related Christian-fostered hostility to these community members.

Practices of kinship can produce variegated forms of solidarity-infused spirituality publicly staking out literal zones of belonging, whether it occurs with a group on the street navigating hostile police or through hospitality offered to individuals in a neighborhood home of refuge. Kinship practices generate spirituality that invents reparative freedom spaces composed of supportive relational connectedness. As evidenced by Bulelwa's example in Cape Town, Christianity does not function as a solitary traditional source of spiritual nurture for such activist leadership. Nonetheless the black queer Christianity exemplified by the U.S. black lesbian pastoral interventions of Wanda Floyd and Janyce Jackson provide an assertion of freedom from the abusers' controlling narrative that conflates Christian morality with the abasement of lesbians and gender-nonconforming or queer people. All of the lesbian Christian leaders mentioned above initiate a spirituality of solidarity in which kinship practices are exhibited in material spaces and timely disruptions.

How Is Spirituality for Antiviolence Solidarity Produced?

For some activist leaders, a rejection of Christianity represents the most appropriate antiviolence response. For those dubious of Christian religious claims because they view it as too deeply flawed by its hypocrisy, Christian theological and spiritual language lacks the moral capacity to characterize effective antiviolence responses. Particularly in activist political struggles to end homophobic gender violence, sex/gender justice values may incorporate such skepticism but still rely upon some vital non-Christian forms of spirituality. Might a defiant spiritual impetus constitute a shared antiviolence resource without covert Christian appropriation of the meaning of the spirituality?

At the Free Gender meeting, Funeka had complained about popular black homophobic Christian pastors with large Christian followings and extensive media access in South Africa. She decried the ways in which pastors were permitted to make such aggressively homophobic public statements on the radio, especially at a time when there was so much violence against lesbians. Funeka was adamant as she pointed out the societal impact of those public expressions. She encouraged Christian lesbians within her Free Gender networks to develop antiviolence strategies within their churches, but she had minimal interest in leading it as she was not a Christian. She noted the fact that many church leaders refuse to challenge the broad cultural tolerance for the violence. Instead, they actively choose to further stigmatize lesbian, gay, transgender, and all gender-nonconforming community members by publicly identifying them as moral degenerates. As rapes, murders, and assaults targeting black gender-nonconforming lesbians occur, many black church leaders use their considerable moral power to incite additional hostility to them by promoting the idea that lesbians do not possess any rightful belonging or connectedness to their communities. In the United States some black pastors have vigorously expressed their opposition to legal protections from violence for all LGBTQ persons. Some actively advocated for the defeat of federal hate crimes legislation that later passed.[38] In a full-page *USA Today* advertisement, over thirty black pastors publicly opposed the inclusion of "sexual orientation" and "gender identity" beside the categories of "race, color national origin, religion" in U.S. federal hate crimes law: "Don't allow misguided compassion to erode America's most basic freedoms of speech, conscience, and the free exercise of religion."[39] They misleadingly suggested that the legislation would restrict African American pastors and others from expressing "opposition to homosexual behavior."[40]

Under such circumstances, moral leadership that rejects Christianity as a reliable moral resource for ending homophobic gender-based violence exhibits integrity. Any expression of solidarity by Christians such as myself with activist leaders who are deeply skeptical of Christianity such as Funeka requires Christian admissions of Christianity's complicity in culturally supporting the violence. Honest Christian admissions are tricky to achieve. Christian admissions about aiding violence are insufficient if they exclusively dwell on Christian history such as Christian leadership in the rapes and enslavement of Africans in Africa and the Americas or mass killings of indigenous peoples and kidnapping of their children in the Americas. Contemporary Christianity, in its concerted lived expressions of antipathy to and thus cultural collusion in supporting rape and assaults of lesbians and all gender-nonconforming community members, also constitutes a form of evil. This admission of Christianity's perpetuation of societal evil, while not a comprehensive representation of Christianity, nonetheless truthfully depicts it. In addition, for cultivating the possibility of solidarity with activist leaders distrustful of Christianity, admissions of Christians' culpability in homophobic violence must be distinguishable from traditional Christian theological emphases on confession of sin and pursuit of forgiveness. These standard Christian theological declarations are too self-indulgently transactional, concentrating on Christians ridding themselves of discomfiting culpability rather than participation in change that ends violence. Yet, spiritual ingredients can still populate activist commitments to ending homophobic gender violence through joint production of a defiant Africana human spirit of resistance, claimed as a foundational, sustaining goal of solidarity among both Christians and skeptics of Christianity.

In the focus of her activist leadership, Funeka relentlessly worked to hold police accountable and pressure them to take the harassment, rape, physical assault, and murder of black lesbians seriously. She described the importance of certain traditional African religious beliefs related to reverence for ancestors. She emphasized her deceased grandmother's comforting presence in her spirituality, especially after she had been assaulted. As an outspoken activist lesbian who exhibited nonconforming gender expression, Funeka had been repeatedly targeted. She was brutally assaulted twice. Once she was beaten and stabbed in a hate-motivated attack so badly that her recovery required a lengthy hospital stay. And on another occasion she was raped by a group of young men also out to teach her a lesson. At the police station where she sought help afterward, the trauma was only intensified as the officers merely laughed and joked about her assault. "They didn't even take me to the hospital. They didn't do anything. It just was a laugh," she told me.[41] Long after her physical recovery, stress and panic had enveloped her when she first began working with the police in her activist leadership role. When she entered that same station for one of the first planning meetings, she initially froze as she was surrounded by police officers. It was emotionally overwhelming for her because, she told me, "it made me remember." Funeka recalled the trauma of their derision and humiliation when she had sought their help in the wake of having been attacked. "And now it's nothing" for me, she quickly added and then listed the routine meetings Free Gender and others continued to organize to compel the police to act.[42]

Her intense commitment to ending violence and discrimination was driven by a belief in a free, quality human experience of everyday life to which victimized peoples for whom she advocated were entitled. As she spoke of it, Funeka's faithfulness to this belief exhibited an obvious radical solidarity with her community. Her motivation was stoked by the fact that lesbians were chased from their homes because of their sexual orientation and from the health clinic when seeking help after being assaulted. They were sometimes mistreated after they informed health care workers that they were lesbians. As she had experienced firsthand, even police derided assaulted lesbians. Funeka asserted her goal of creating a community "where people can be human beings and then they can continue their lives."[43] Her description offered an activist model of liberation morality that was not simply centered on recognition of black lesbian worth and dignity. It stressed black lesbian human freedom to continue to live: to make one's own choices about one's daily life, free from the threat of humiliation, harassment, assault, and murder. The core intentions of this activist work are not concerned with spirituality, but fulfillment of the antiviolence goals unquestionably allows the human spirit to thrive.

The liberative approach of Free Gender's activism combined relentless pressure on the state for justice, particularly with regard to holding perpetrators accountable, together with an insistence on transformation of the local community ethos. It demanded that all local community leaders actively support lesbians' equal human freedom to live without being targeted for violence and discrimination. It designed a defense of the victimized yet actively engaged in reclamation of belonging. Black African queer scholars Zethu Matebeni and Jabu Pereira highlighted queer Afrikan reclamation in their introduction to *Reclaiming Afrikan: Queer Perspectives on Sexual and Gender Identities*.[44] "As sexual and gender nonconforming or queer persons," they wrote, "we have been alienated in Africa. We have been stripped of our belonging and our connectedness. For these reasons, we have created our own version of Afrika—a space that cuts across the rigid borders and boundaries that have for so many years made us feel disconnected and fractured."[45] To lay claim to collective belonging acknowledges the collective violation of being "stripped of" cultural identity. An adequate antiviolence response to the targeted assaults, therefore, entailed development of queer space, where one's rootedness in historic traditional Africannness and invention of new nonconformist Africanness cohered.

Spirituality can contribute to the cultivation of that kind of Afrikan space. A defiant form of spirituality supports freedom from rigid, damaging borders and boundaries policed by homophobic and transphobic violence and its threat. Defiant spirituality can undergird activist responses that demand the freeing of gender in social practices for the sake of enabling human thriving. As U.S. Christian womanist scholar Emilie Townes wrote, "The spiritual dimension of liberation concentrates on the acquisition of power that enables each person to be who she or he is . . . the challenge of spiritual liberation is choosing between wholeness and destruction."[46] Acquisition and transfer of power are indeed necessary for halting gender-based violence, but moral choices about the process of doing so inevitably involve the risk of further exploitation and harm to those most vulnerable to it. Liberation spirituality takes that risk when its aim of human wholeness and well-being focuses on defiance of cultural support for the targeting of black lesbian and gender-nonconforming identities for disbelonging, disconnection, and assault.

As the meeting hosted by Free Gender finally started to draw to a close, the honest and sometimes tense exchanges reverberated in the room. When one Free Gender member spoke up late in the meeting, she started out tentatively, then bravely admitted to wondering what Elizabeth and I might have been thinking during the opening "church songs." The young woman referred to me as one of "the pastors." When she recounted a past experience of rejection by Christian leaders, it provided some context for the expectation that she then stated in our meeting: Christian pastors think "homosexuals" should not be allowed to sing "church songs." Looking directly at me with increased self-assurance and assertiveness, she reminded me that a discussion linking Christianity and "homosexuality" introduced a very sensitive subject.

In that moment, my association with Christianity had engendered distrust and vulnerability. It had cast self-doubt upon whether she could or should openly express her Christian faith in my presence because she was lesbian and had delivered the opposite effect from what I had intended or desired as I participated in the meeting. Her consideration of how I might have been condemningly judging her as they sang could not have been further from the spirituality that I experienced. I felt the homophobic, terrorizing impact of our religion (mine and hers) and the impediments to solidarity it spawned between us. Once more, Christian spirituality could not be disconnected from its harmful political tentacles, especially for any conceptualization of spirituality that informed activist solidarity in working to end the violence. Even our shared values (between Christian Free Gender members and myself) and moral relatedness could not produce Christian religious spirituality with the capacity to rid itself of the poisonous qualities of publicly disseminated Christian messages that incubated the hate violence.

Before the meeting ended, one of the male heterosexual pastors found the space that had been created by the honest tenor of the discussion to admit his struggles with the topic of lesbian sexual orientation. He sympathized with the plight of the victimized but asked for help. While he despised the raping of lesbians and the murders, he required more time, personally, to learn and grow, time to better understand "this lifestyle." Varied responses followed, ranging from expressions of gratitude for the openness to flashes of anger at the equivocations, and the air in the room seemed to thicken with vulnerabilities, anger, distrust, and questions. To bring the meeting to a close because of our prior agreement on the time frame, I tried to offer a concluding thank-you statement that named the pain and openness of the meeting in summary fashion. My words fell flat in the charged atmosphere—even I could hear it as I spoke.

Then, in a calming yet challenging tone, Elizabeth reminded the group that as a nation, they had only recently emerged from apartheid. She encouraged everyone to recall how apartheid "taught us to be divided from each other. But this is the time," her voice increased in its intensity, "this is the time to change from what the colonizers have taught us." This is the time to change the "colonial thinking that operates in the church" and enables Christians to exclude their lesbian sisters from their faith communities, demean them, or silently tolerate their suicides and murders.

After she completed her final comment, I risked the awkwardness of expressing my genuine desire to close with music from the Free Gender choir. "We glor-rify . . ." began a young woman's solo voice in the now-familiar slow, melodic wail.

Confrontational Faith Response

Confrontation enables truthfulness in spiritual and political strategies to end homophobic gender-based violence. Confrontation of white racist realities in faith-based settings can be understood as helpfully disciplining activists in organizing against rape and murder of black lesbians as well as other forms of gender-based violence. My conversations with Elizabeth centered on her leadership of the Cape Town–based SAFFI evoked consideration of how confrontation might be a generative element in interfaith solidarity spirituality aimed at countering the violence. Elizabeth had cultivated the participation of SAFFI board members and stakeholders comprising local South African faith leaders who were Hindu, Muslim, Jewish, Catholic, Baháʼí, Anglican, Methodist, and others. Spiritual leadership of these communities, SAFFI insisted, had to include taking responsibility for the violence and coordinating efforts across their communities to end it. Therefore, spirituality born of interfaith solidarity held the potential to harness a unique form of collective political power to advocate on behalf of racial and sex/gender justice. SAFFI's faith-based activist leadership could fashion a defiant spirituality by using confrontation tactics that single out religious teachings, hypocrisies, and silences that imperil their community members.

Cultivation of the relevant skills could allow for more efficacious faith-based confrontations. Direct—but not violent—confrontation of the moral harm that homophobic violence produces might occur through the honing of antiracist consciousness. Elizabeth's reference to antiracist commitment and post-apartheid memory work at the end of that Free Gender meeting served as an example, demonstrating the deployment of racial justice solidarity to galvanize opposition to homophobic gender violence. In Cape Town, activist black religious faith community leaders constituted a valuable group for practicing the confrontation of their "colonial thinking" implicated in the violence against lesbians and gender-nonconforming community members. Faith-based activist advocates for ending the violence could draw upon the spirituality present in certain antiracist aspects of the legacies of religious and political struggle bequeathed to them. Advocates could be inspired by a legacy of antiracist confrontations in those liberation struggles steeped in a belief in the unseen possibility of human freedom. The courage found there combined organized collective political resistance and faith-based convictions about the capacity of spiritual power and vision.

Before Elizabeth founded SAFFI, her antiviolence leadership had been nurtured in faith-based organizing that included confrontation of racial barriers. For example, in the 1990s she had served as the first non-white director of an Anglican-church-based shelter for abused women and children, St. Anne's Homes, founded in 1904. She recalled how on her first day one of the residents, a coloured woman, had confrontationally told her, "I didn't want you. I wanted the white social worker."[47] The woman had reasoned, Elizabeth supposed, "that I wouldn't give her the quality of service" that she needed.[48] This encounter showcased the constraints and boundaries for measuring worth and status that white racism fomented. Social barriers that perpetuated white racist stigmatizing of her coloured identity was also systemically reinforced by historic support of apartheid in the cultural and institutional attitudes of the broader society.

As its pioneering director, Elizabeth had helped to break down racial barriers at the shelter, which had historically reserved leadership for whites. While Elizabeth committed herself to the demanding work of ensuring safety and shelter for women and children victimized by violence, the coloured woman resident's objections to Elizabeth's leadership sought to uphold traditional white racist barriers and stigma. Unfortunately, sometimes the social benefits of guarding white racist boundaries can appear to outweigh the costs and provide incentives for community members of groups who are historically victimized by racism to destructively undermine one another's opportunities for equality. In this case, a coloured woman rejected another coloured woman's leadership because she was not white.

Elizabeth's experiences of these challenges evidenced a kind of leadership training ground for learning what it means to swim in the complex political waters of confrontation. Such multilayered confrontations in faith-based settings could usefully school activists in how racial identity borders wreak harm. They expose the means by which supposedly moral institutions justified dehumanizing racial boundaries, hiding the harm within a larger mission of serving an ultimate good, such as sheltering abused women.

Violence and its threat penalized disobedience of self-appointed regulators of sex/gender standards and norms. It was precisely because lesbians and gender-nonconforming community members did not live within dominant borders and boundaries of sex/gender expression and identity that perpetrators targeted them and local authorities left them unprotected. Yet there is potential for activist leaders to draw upon confrontation skills gained from their practiced rejection of white supremacist racial identity borders, also traditionally upheld by the influence of white racist Christian religion. These antiracism skills may be applicable when confronting the border guardians of heteronormative sex/gender identity expression and their supposed moral aims that, at best, evade responsibility for stopping homophobic rapes, assaults, and murders, and, at worst, celebrate this violence.

For antiviolence activist faith leaders, attention to the problem of coerced identity borders would lack efficacy without an accompanying confrontation of the moral gaps in the faith traditions guiding their efforts. Spiritually engaged activism that seeks out interfaith and multifaith axes as part of its core antiviolence vision defies conventional respect for boundaried faith community concerns. This defiant spirituality has to be confrontational when creating collaborative interfaith and multifaith practices directed toward the root causes and systemic dimensions of gender-based violence.

For instance, as Elizabeth maintained, SAFFI had a challenging message for faith leaders: "You religious leaders have a sacred responsibility . . . [having] said 'yes,' you will serve your people spiritually . . . so what *exactly* is the responsibility that goes along with that?"[49] SAFFI's strategy to disrupt the root causes of the violence bypassed an emphasis on providing much-needed crisis services for those victimized. Indeed, finding agreement on a shared faith-based means to conduct mission projects that support the material needs of the victimized might have been easier. Instead, this SAFFI approach demanded a shared commitment to hold one's own traditions, scriptures, and leadership practices accountable for the conditions that enabled gender-based violence. To provide spiritual service to the people meant that faith leaders had to come out of the closets of their traditions to join others in ridding those traditions of gender messages that provided moral harbor for violence against all women and gender-nonconforming or queer members of the community.

Coordinated confrontation of faith practices related to gender justice had to diverge from standard goals usually prioritized in pluralistic faith-based collaboration. Often, multifaith approaches were internally focused on comparatively placing differing views of faith and spirituality side by side with one another. Similarly, interfaith conversations too often gave precedence to forging mutual understandings and friendships across their radically different expressions of faith and spirituality. Confrontation in the spirituality of faith-based gender justice activism spotlighted the debasing inconsistencies and exclusions related to sexual orientation and nonconforming gender expression. Rather than a proliferation of comparisons of differing established faith perspectives, this defiant work engendered spirituality that relished internal critiques linked to outwardly directed, coordinated antiviolence activism. It demonstrated the kind of cooperative influence religious faith communities could exert in support of thriving and freedom from the threat of violence for their black lesbian community members.

Defiant spirituality that emphasizes this commitment to faith-based confrontation needs to manifest concrete multifaith and interfaith practices that address the gaps between rhetoric and practices about human freedom. In one of our conversations with each other, Elizabeth offered examples of the gaps related to racism and religion that she encountered in her antiviolence work. She was drawn to address the urgency posed by seemingly hopeless distrust between groups that should be powerfully allied in addressing gender-based violence. One of the ongoing themes grounding her work appeared to be her impatience with how the distrust stalled the unrealized potential for solidarity. On a personal level, her motivation in founding SAFFI emerged, in part, from her quest to find space for her own voice among secular feminist activists working on issues of domestic and sexual violence. Amid an overwhelming Christian majority in South Africa, she found little acknowledgment of the importance of Christianity in the lives of so many women victim-survivors whose needs they all sought to address. On an organizational level, Elizabeth saw the need for more leadership that stepped into the breach of mutual alienation that too often existed between secular activists and religious leaders. Activists whose leadership concentrated on opposing gender-based violence frequently did not trust religious leaders; reciprocally, religious leaders who were committed social justice advocates often "did not know what to do with gender activists."[50]

In her conceptualization of SAFFI's work, Elizabeth wanted to ensure that a commitment to challenging all the cultural and political ideas supporting the abuse and violence against women and girls, especially religious ones, was demonstrably rooted in SAFFI's core self-definition. The organization of roundtables at the first conference launching SAFFI

(2010) illustrated this goal by emphasizing critical readings of sacred texts and religious teachings about gender. At that initial conference, a roundtable discussion of inclusive and affirming religious resources for LGBTI persons of faith who had experienced violence rooted SAFFI's commitment to the promotion of concrete antiviolence faith practices within its central mission. When faith leaders came together to create faith-based practices that align with inclusive and affirming faith values, their efforts demonstrated a theory-practice commitment to freedom from the violence.

To conceptualize the most nimble capacity possible for defiant spirituality in antiviolence activism, we must consider the dexterity of violence. Feminist philosopher Gail Mason reflects theoretically on homophobic gender violence and its characteristics in a manner that enables our understanding of another dimension of the role faith-based defiant spirituality can play.[51] Although spirituality is not incorporated in her study, her ideas still help to illuminate features of the violence that spiritual resources can help to defy. Mason studied lesbian perceptions and experiences of homophobia-related violence and hostility by drawing on an Australian-based research project. She points out the ways in which violence maintains social order, holding steady certain gaps in power relations by controlling the moral status of the targeted and the perpetrator. As Mason maps it, violence produces a reaction to it and forms our understanding of the vulnerability of those who are targeted as well as of heterosexual masculinity of perpetrators as dangerous to others.[52] In other words, violence wages its destructive influence as it burrows into this moral gap between the moral status of the targeted and that of the perpetrator. Violence works to maintain certain forms of social order that are threatened. Mason notes, "If certain types of violence—such as homophobic, gendered, or racist violence—emerge when power is in jeopardy, the very existence of such violence must function as a sign of the vulnerability or disintegration of that power."[53] In my conceptualization of it, defiant spirituality can be understood as stepping into a gap between the power of domination and resistance to that power.[54] Ironically, violence functions as a catalyst for both. Defiant spirituality with a faith-based impetus may be especially equipped to step into the moral gaps that violence maintains.

Moreover, opportunity awaits in confrontations focused on the vulnerability in an abusive social order that violence signals. As we have seen in the work of activist leaders, defiant spirituality emerges in advocacy and inventiveness. It is present in their strategies of resistance to violence and racial reinforcement of certain gendered forms of social order. Defiant spirituality may also flourish in the task of finding ways to erode the productivity of violence by infiltrating that place between the social power afforded violence and organized resistance to it.

SAFFI organized the Walk of Witness that illustrates how leaders might move into the painful spaces violence generates. For the Walk of Witness SAFFI invited religious leaders to spend time in the homes of those who had been targeted for rape because they were lesbians and with families of those who had been murdered for the same reason. The Walk of Witness required the clergy to tarry a while with the suffering people in their homes. There was a space left after the assaults had occurred and before any organized political resistance had achieved some measure of justice. It was a kind of communal gap or disconnect in which the raw brutality of homophobic violence against black lesbians and the power of cultural ideas stigmatizing their worth seemed to prevail.

"That's what I wanted," Elizabeth said. "I believe that we must allow our own humanity to be touched by the pain and the suffering, to be shocked" by the experience of torment of the victims and survivors. She mentioned a parent who had spoken about one of the perpetrators of the hate crimes against her daughter. "But we knew him," the parent had repeated. The parent struggled to make sense of the rape and murder of the parent's daughter by a young man who attacked her because she was a lesbian, even though as children they had played together and worshipped in the same church. The SAFFI clergy witness magnified the moral and human destruction that the violence created even as the perpetrators claimed to be regulators and upholders of moral order.

Besides witnessing within homes, the Walk of Witness strategy also incorporated Elizabeth's confrontation with faith leaders about the urgency of antiviolence public witness. "We were very intentional about trying to get some black clergy leaders to be part of that Walk of Witness," Elizabeth continued, "and it was a struggle." She had sought out, for example, a particularly committed social activist black pastor. He was a leader who had publicly campaigned against poverty and spoken out against ongoing white oppression, including sharp criticism of the hypocrisy of white South African Christianity. Even though he had attempted to excuse himself by referencing a prior commitment to an event concerned with the current government's neglect of the ongoing dire poverty conditions in black communities, Elizabeth had persisted, repeatedly calling him on his cellphone. "I told him, 'I need you, as a black leader, to say something.'"[55] Ultimately, this pastor did attend part of the concluding gathering of the Walk of Witness event.

SAFFI had also organized a culminating conversation between LGBTQ activists and faith leaders. An already emotionally grueling day only increased in intensity, Elizabeth told me, when one of the black lesbian speakers at the face-to-face discussion with clergy leaders spoke. This speaker tried to convey how much fear wells up in black lesbians' everyday lives because "they don't know whether they may be the next ones to be raped, or killed and disappear, only to have their bodies found after a couple of months or years," Elizabeth recounted. Clergy were then called upon to reply. In one of the most disappointing clergy responses in that emotionally raw moment, the black social justice activist pastor "said that he acknowledged what he had heard," Elizabeth relayed to me, "but was not prepared to make any statement, to take any position on this." But she added, a coloured Protestant bishop did make a clear statement against the hate crimes, declaring God's unequivocal opposition to it, as did a black Muslim sheikh she had invited to participate.

Witnessing to its wrongness after the fact could never be a sufficient response to the rapes, assaults, suicides, and murders, but witnessing did evidence solidarity. Clergy publicly deployed their social, spiritual, and moral authority, adding the weight of that authority on the side of declaring the sexual assaults and murders as intolerable violations against their God and undermining the morality of the entire community. But confrontation by confrontation, activist leaders such as Elizabeth Petersen and the black lesbian activist leaders at the event jointly produced spirituality that defied complacency or retreating acquiescence to faith-based recalcitrance.

* * *

The black activism I encountered in South Africa inspired a wide range of ideas about how to create, deploy, and practice spiritual defiance of violence. Faith-based components that offered promise included the model of Christian Bible study by Nadar and the other leaders at Umjamaa Centre in Pietermaritzburg on passages such as the gang rape of the woman in Judges 19 and the Muslim antirape activist leader Majiet confronting Christian leaders on the need for bodily freedoms for women including abortion rights of raped women and girls. The spirited, angry, anti-apartheid-based "never again" of Majiet signaled a grounding impetus for rebellious spatial and time interruptions in transnational geopolitical patterns and historical cycles of racist per-mission for gendered assaults and sexual violations. The U.S. and South African contexts provided meaningful contrasting lessons on how our sensibilities are trained in manipulative racial logics through public woman-blaming discourse about sexual assault articulated by certain figures found among each nation's highest levels of political leadership. Whether they involved multifaith and interfaith public witness in opposition to violence or Christian lesbian leaders' innova-tion of kinship, these strategies generated resilient forms of faith-based defiant spirituality.

Time for cultivating purposeful transnational and intercultural soli-darity would have to be taken. Months later after I had returned home to the United States from Cape Town, I met Funeka in New York City, where she was attending a U.N. summit on gender-based violence. As we spoke together and reflected on my visit to the Free Gender meeting, we discussed Christian pastors and their role in supporting violence. She reasserted her impatience with Christians who claimed they needed more time. Then she expressed exasperation with Christian leaders who were tepid at best in their reliability as a source of solidarity, and how "you Christians" always talk about taking your burdens to the Lord. "What does that mean?" she asked. I felt a bit defensive. Actually, "take your burdens to the Lord" was not anything I had ever said to anyone. But Funeka's candor helped to strengthen our mutual understanding. She was not at all hostile, just matter-of-fact in her tone. The confron-tation opened possibilities for a transnational Africana solidarity that could be truthful. Her spirituality motivated her to *do* something, she told me. That's why she had founded Free Gender, confronted the police about their lack of responsiveness to lesbians victimized by violence and inadequate zealousness in holding their attackers accountable, and why she continued doing her other Free Gender activist work.

"Christians. I just don't have the time or patience," she reiterated. Then, she gave me a considering look and a warm smile.

I smiled back, and she continued to talk with me about how to do the work of stopping the violence.

Conclusion

Hope as a Process

Defiant spirituality gives birth to hope. The birthing occurs in Africana activist leadership to end heterosexual marital abuse, sex trafficking, and the targeting of black lesbians for rape, assault, and murder. Defiant spirituality also fosters activist responses to other forms of gender-based violence against women and girls. It bubbles up from the creative endeavors of Africana activist leaders and activist-scholars. When we begin to recognize the ways in which defiant spirituality makes anti-violence creativity more possible, evident, and sustainable, hope surges outward. Defiant spirituality carries the hope-filled prospect of border-crossing solidarity to match the border-crossing politics and belief systems that abet the violence.

Although not necessarily synonymous with religious belief, defiant spirituality is often guided by it. Several but not all of the leaders I met intentionally drew upon their Christian, Islamic, Candomblé, or African Traditional religious beliefs as a wellspring for their antiviolence work. The hopefulness that the defiant spirituality of religiously based activist leaders unleashed reflects their justice-oriented practices. They found inexhaustible troves of spiritual nurture in religious symbols and involvement.

Even when we understand hope as wholly disconnected from the spirituality of an established religion or set of religious beliefs, we can still recognize it as spiritually motivating. Hope flows from the work of nonreligious activist leaders as well and is found in their vigorous defiance of cultural devaluations that make violence against women and girls of African descent and others seem socially tolerable. The nonreligiously rooted defiant spirituality the leaders displayed—inspired by an amalgamation of antiviolence cultural and political resources—can ignite hope among victim-survivors, advocates, and other leaders no matter what their religious affiliation or lack thereof. This amalgamation also represents an inexhaustible source of spiritual support for political transformation needed to end violence—inexhaustible partly because its capacity is left unregulated by sexist norms of established traditions.

In a related description of a nonreligious form of politicized spirituality, feminist Chicana theorists Irene Lara and Elisa Facio summarize their focus on spiritual activism as it is given voice by Chicana, Latina, and Indigenous women in the Americas. "Spirituality often plays a decolonizing role in creating meaning, inspiring action, and supporting healing and justice in our communities," Lara and Facio explain. The task of analyzing it contributes to a "body of knowledge focused on voicing and understanding spirituality through an intersectional, interdisciplinary, and nonsectarian lens."[1] Defiant Africana spirituality relies on this kind of expansive conceptualization of spirituality for the vitality of its antiviolence contributions to be fully apparent. However, as I have stressed, sectarian religious resources and abuses must also be counted as part of the knowledge needed in the decolonizing "meaning, inspiring action . . . healing and justice" creation in which defiant Africana spirituality engages.

The birthing of hopefulness for antiviolence transformation that signals potential for transnational solidarity can evolve through a process of learning. In this book, I have investigated how such a learning process might be manifest in a black U.S.-American outsider's dialogue with Africana activist ideas and practices. I have described a series of inquiries about what the embrace of culturally distinctive, non-U.S. political tools of resistance to gender-based violence might entail. One might regard my inquiries, in part, as a spiritual quest launched out of a deep thirst for encountering ideas of religious and nonreligious Africana leaders that offer insights for the defiance of dangerously insular expressions of U.S.-American Christianity. My pursuit thrived on a fundamental sense of hopefulness about the potential for learning that could occur through transnational encounters.

When one considers the ingenuity of widely varied activist leaders in Ghana, Brazil, and South Africa together with my complicated intercultural encounters with them, the transnational capacity of the hopefulness comes into view. Said differently, when made tangible through lived examples, a spirit of defiance introduces the possibility of transnational solidarity. This quest is focused on acts of defiance expressed through leadership practices. Contemplating how activists in differing Africana contexts work to end gender-based violence can spur defiance in other geopolitical settings such as the United States. But additional consideration must be incorporated about how hypocritical, paternalistic, or predatory regard for Africana humanity (and African natural resources) can impede solidarity formed out of those common commitments. The result helps to generate hopeful yearning for creating genuinely antiracist starting points for connecting our gender justice struggles.

My analysis has presumed that oral witness about leadership practices is a comparable knowledge-bearing resource to written scholarly textual sources. The experiential narratives about and oral witness of Africana leaders are interwoven with scholarly sources and directly contribute to our grasp of a spirituality that decolonizes as it creates meaning.[2] Analyzing these disparate "texts" and contextualized encounters provides glimpses of promising ingredients of Africana political knowledge and spiritual stamina needed for contesting and ending gender-based violence. Indeed, a transnationally conceptualized infusion of such Africana hope functions like spiritual yeast, amplifying antiviolence innovation with the capability to cultivate more defiance and new pathways for devising bonds of solidarity.

Defiant Africana spirituality's geopolitical situatedness functions as key to the formation of that hope. Drawing on varied antiviolence approaches, the activist and scholar-activist leaders I met in Ghana, Brazil, and South Africa crafted ideas and practices to enable women and girls' freedom of gender expression. They did so even as they confronted diverse forms and degrees of permission for gender-based violence that have allowed constricting and sexually exploitative valuations of femaleness. Comparing U.S. examples of gender-based violence with those in other countries revealed both sharp differences and some overlaps in antiracist strategies to counter cultural and political tolerance, forming a useful transnational black feminist agenda for recognizing how antiblack racism, religious spirituality, and communal moral equivocation collaborate in violence. My Christian assumptions and U.S.-American cultural perspective shape my contentions about defiant Africana spirituality, and undoubtedly deserve even more criticism than I have leveled. Yet hopefully my engagement of Christianity provokes rather than stymies feminist thought and activism with a desire to take seriously spiritual sustenance in the crafting of culturally diverse but synergistic tools to end gender-based violence.

To name the ways in which defiant Africana spirituality and hope can be understood as a process of learning from and about strategic responses to violence that invite intercultural and transnational solidarity, we must deliberately linger on the topic of method, on *how* learning might transpire through unconventional sources, dissonance, and other characteristics that mark this perspective.

Basics of Defiant Spirituality

To some degree, the spirituality of activist and scholar-activist antiviolence leadership occupies a space beyond reasoned arguments for equality. At the same time, again borrowing from Lara and Facio's conceptualization, comprehension of activist spirituality "insists on the intellectual and political significance of analyzing spirituality and activism within transcultural and historical contexts."[3] Defiant Africana spirituality explicitly contests the role of racist historical patterns that have anchored political hindrances to freedom from gender violence, bodily violation, and sexual exploitation. In response to gender-based violence, spirituality has multiple functions as a source of comfort, affirmation of worth and dignity, and meaning making in the midst of crisis for the assaulted or abused victim-survivor. Activist and activist-scholar goals of justice-oriented cultural transformation are always mindful of the need for spirituality-based responses within immediate crisis interventions. But spirituality can also function less reactively as something that evokes, summons, and invites the kind of human connectedness and belonging that creates hope for widespread solidarity in broad cultural transformations.

Defiant Africana spirituality cannot assist in opposing violence by reproducing naïve hopefulness about the innate virtuousness of any particular faith tradition, spiritual practice, or civil religion. Too many established faith communities and civil religion adherents already claim hopefulness about antiviolence change that relies on select forms of political amnesia. For example, U.S. civil religion narratives pridefully and erroneously claim that U.S.-American identity is imbued with an ongoing, naturally generated progressive movement toward freedom and equality. In contrast, contemporary transnational constructions of defiant Africana spirituality demand attention to the memory of past centuries of sexual violence against women and girls of African descent by European and American Christians as well as male African traders who played a key role in selling them to the European Christians. The recovery of that history provides a means for remembering how religiously based spiritualties and socioeconomic ideologies bequeathed a legacy of systematically preying upon human precarity across national borders and reframed kidnapping as salvific and gender violence as a blessed transactional entitlement.

Defiant Africana spirituality and Africana hope are interdependent. Together, they counter the role of anti-black racism in gender-based violence and sexual exploitation. As discussed above, defiant Africana spirituality births Africana hope for solidarity in ending gender violence, which in turn fosters a solidarity within which hope can be found. Thus, defiant Africana spirituality relies upon Africana hope in a constructive feedback loop. Defiant Africana spirituality becomes apparent because of the alternative valuing of human relatedness that hope reveals. Antiracist commitments signal hope, for example, because of decolonial analyses of marital rape in Ghana or critical attention to how popular images of black Brazilian women as hot and ready for sex embolden traffickers and international sex tourists. Such antiracist commitments make a spirit of countercultural courage, stamina, and creativity more perceivable. The commitments give practical expression to how hope emerges and can be manifest in multiply located sites of resolve proclaiming that black cisgender and transgender women's mind-body-spirit safety, dignity, and freedom will no longer be threatened.

Spirituality that builds hopeful alliances flourishes when immersed within the politics of intercultural dynamics. For U.S. Christians such as myself, it is not easy to discover Africana hope that revitalizes opposition to gender violence in the United States and elsewhere. A sense of it can be gained only with the precondition of truth-telling about how core U.S. cultural, racial, and dominant Christian religious values systemically support violence. Guideposts for defiant spirituality that encourage solidarity are also located in the development of skills to translate the knowledge—when possible—learned from Africana activist leaders in culturally diverse global settings.

The hopefulness of defiant spirituality culminates in the process of climbing the slippery steps of inventing or reclaiming shared Africana activist antiviolence commitments to unseating heteropatriarchal arrogance. Indeed, U.S.-American arrogance poses a major challenge to how defiant Africana spirituality enables comprehension of transnational possibilities for solidarity. Even grasping the *potential* for solidarity becomes feasible only when one eschews the idea of U.S.-American exceptionalism. The process of building antiviolence solidarity interculturally and transnationally compels ongoing probing and admissions of what U.S.-Christian participants cannot fully know or culturally translate. To reject our virtuous status attributed simply to being Christian or from the United States requires consideration of how our imperiousness has activated solidarity-building missteps, reoccurring over and over again, and how we might interrupt some of that reoccurrence.

Defiant Africana spirituality must be understood as a reliable resource for instigating nonviolent conflict within established forms of religious spirituality. In particular, its influence dwells where beliefs supporting gender inequality and stark gender polarities comfortably resonate with such racial hierarchies as colorism. Confrontational truthtelling can make transparent, for instance, the sexually exploitative ways in which certain U.S. male tourists of African descent seek out black Brazilian settings for exploitative sexual encounters, sometimes including Candomblé *terreiros*. Ghanaian activist leaders seeking liberation of the girls who were enslaved through sacred communal practices in certain Ghanaian indigenous religious shrines displayed the respectful but resolute quality of defiant Africana spirituality. We desperately need this standard of confrontation in contemporary U.S. public policy debates about gender and sexuality justice, such as, for instance, when the U.S. group of Christian black homophobic pastors publicly opposed proposed U.S. legislation classifying as hate crimes the assault or murder of LGBTQ community members.

Alongside its encouragement of oppositional practices and ideas, defiant spirituality invites a conjoined affirmation of the value of black womanhood. This spirituality reserves defiant space—a space that might be construed in imaginary, aspirational, and experiential terms as "peaceful like Africa" (as Sandra dos Santos, Afro-Brazilian Candomblé practitioner and antiviolence activist, expressed). This space exists wherever equality and freedom in religion, spirituality, and affirmation of black women's sexual embodiment are recognized as essential to maintaining antiviolence gender values.

Learning Defiantly Yields Hope

An itemized list of what I learned about the work of antiviolence activist and scholar-activist leaders I met would press my conclusions into the wrong shape. A side-by-side comparison of what leaders said or did in each national context would not adequately capture the lessons about spirituality and politics that emerged. An attempt to build a comparative list would risk creating a conclusion too skewed toward isolating individual outcomes and too reductive of the process of intercultural encounter. There was distinctiveness in the content of the ideas mentioned to me in Accra, Ghana, for example, by Audrey Gadzekpo about how gendered Christian European colonialisms are linked there to contemporary debates about outlawing marital rape. We might compare Gadzekpo's insights to the manner in which dos Santos's African-based Candomblé religious faith shaped her drive as an outreach worker teaching about the Maria da Penha Law in Salvador, Brazil. In contrast, there was an evolutionary process of development in how Zarina Majiet's deeply held Islamic faith commitments and the legacy of anti-apartheid struggles contributed to her advocacy work on sexual assault in Cape Town, South Africa. Collectively, they illustrate multiple, complicated views of the role of faith traditions and issues of racism in the politics of ending gender violence. But I do not want to merely collect them.

How do we, particularly U.S.-Americans, move beyond appreciative observations of these culturally and politically imbricated antiviolence strategies? What are the characteristics of an intercultural method that might create the opportunity for learning that inspires transnational antiviolence vision and, perhaps, mutual support, in working toward that vision? Characteristics must include unconventional resources, a capacious imagination, and a method that mines inspiration for conceptualizing the particular role of defiant Africana spirituality with tools ranging from concrete contextualized examples of practices to unusual, sometimes even startling, metaphors.

Defiant Africana spirituality functions as a participatory method of learning that intellectually, emotionally, and spiritually equips us for the visionary praxis of ending gendered assault and murder and sexual exploitation. Metaphorically speaking, this learning must productively *blacken*—and in doing so flout the standard associations of evil, sin, and ignorance with darkness in need of whitening Christian purification. *Blackening* repudiates the legacy of disparaging European labeling of Africa as the Dark Continent and names a spiritually invigorating process of learning about the political struggle for gendered equality and non-exploitative interpersonal relations, a view attainable from encountering African and African diaspora sources. Blackening can symbolize how defiant spirituality is revealed in the process of antiviolence learning from a U.S.-American-based cultural perspective. Blackening equips by enlivening the ethical relations needed to constitute alternative attitudes, practices, and historical critique that help to prevent violence.

Unconventional sources of knowledge help stimulate the moral imagination necessary for recognizing those alternatives. For U.S.-Americans already allied in their commitment to addressing gender-based violence in the United States and elsewhere, adopting Africana-centered approaches to conceptualizing antiviolence can be advantageously disconcerting. The emotional and intellectual challenges that unfamiliar knowledge and approaches raise coupled with the implicit stereotypes most U.S.-Americans have imbibed about black African inferiority can elicit fresh inquiries with beneficial effects. The results may include an unanticipated awakening—chiefly an appreciation of the role cultural plurality (with a rejection of stereotypes) can play in antiviolence strategies—and an interruption of those internally directed cultural practices that protect both U.S. perpetrators and U.S.-American gender-violence norms.

As Christian Ghanaian activist leaders and scholars stressed, cultural plurality of religious traditions and backgrounds in local communities could form a valuable resource rather than, as conventionally regarded, a competitively territorial, conflict-ridden problem. As Ghanaian scholar Rose Mary Amenga-Etego asserted, Christian church settings can offer a communal capacity within which to draw a plurality of cultural strengths to devise woman-affirming freedoms. So too South African activist leader Elizabeth Petersen drew upon a multifaith foundation for alliance-building practices to counter homophobic rapes and murders of lesbians and gender-nonconforming community members. These African feminist approaches support the contention that a cultural home space free from even the threat of abuse and violence can be nurtured through the presence of a multiplicity of gender expressions and respectful, consensual intimate relations. Moreover, the strategies described by Amenga-Etego, Petersen, and others highlight how cultural and religious plurality can effectively contribute to a spiritually grounding antiviolence response. To combat hydra-headed cultural support for gender-based violence, the maintenance of pluralistic cultural home space demands continuously reproducing communal investment in perpetuating woman-affirming gender freedoms, connectedness, and belonging.

Conversations with Salvador, Bahia, activists who addressed sex trafficking and sex tourism that targeted black girls (and some boys) point to the need for antiracist strategies that incorporate mind-body-spirit wholeness. Anti-trafficking organizing illustrates necessary transnational dimensions in confronting insidious cultural factors. In that matrix of freedom, connectedness, and belonging (key elements of human spiritual thriving), the work to end sexual exploitation and violence reinforces unconventional knowledge confirming the preciousness of gendered bodies socially marked by queer, fluid, nonconforming gender identities and erotic blackness.

Even apprehension about eliciting xenophobia can function as an unconventional motivational resource. In focusing on how Ghanaian activist leaders took on certain cultural issues in their local context, I was fearful about generating disrespect among my U.S.-American colleagues who may be unfamiliar with such local cultural issues. But open examinations of fearfulness can expand our moral imaginations. Confronting fears about exposing contextualized Africana knowledge that may further U.S.-American racist stereotypes of and paternalism toward black Africans can actually stimulate valuable U.S. public conversations.

Analyses by activist and activist-scholar leaders of Ghanaian public debates of marital rape raised my fears about how to describe their leadership to U.S. audiences without reinscribing simplistic and pejorative views of the influence of cultural traditions in Ghanaian legislative politics. Yet consideration of the Ghanaian public conversation about cultural values encourages investigation of which "authentic" cultural values contribute to a stubbornly enduring resistance to enacting uniform federal laws outlawing marital rape in the United States.

Fears of inciting racist understandings of perpetrators in public campaigns to stop gendered violence illustrate how knowledge about culture, race, and gender is inextricably linked to the crafting of prevention strategies. For example, I observed the depiction of black male perpetrators in the poster campaign in Ghana, including one that featured the statement "You will go to jail for sexual abuse." Some U.S. antiracist allies who oppose gender violence would likely consider this kind of campaign incendiary racist shaming in the U.S.-American context. Yet interrogating how such fears about racial shaming do or do not surface could help develop an understanding of how racist shaming by Europeans or Euro-Americans functions in the politics and histories of race in each global context. Consideration of the Ghanaian public strategy alongside of the constraints of U.S. racial dynamics for such public campaigns may be informative for building Africana connections on antiracist approaches to violence. Doing so exposes contrasting communal moral narratives that shape public responsiveness to shaming strategies featuring black male faces in an effort to hold perpetrators of gender violence accountable.

In Brazil, I had to admit my fears of objectifying black Salvadoran men when viewing accused perpetrators incarcerated at the women's police stations. I felt ashamed when even contemplating the possibility that I would participate in staring at those black male incarcerated bodies as if they were an exhibit in a Brazilian museum. The dynamics of the scene displayed the uncomfortable juxtaposition between the Brazilian black feminist police officer proudly pointing to the arrested men detained in the *delegacia* jail and my role as a U.S.-American outsider being beckoned to see them. In this case, apprehension may function as a catalyst that compels scrutiny of the differences outsiders and insiders bring to measuring how accountability, humanization, and judgments applied to black men's acts and beings function in criminal justice remedies.

Certain expressions of explicitly religious spirituality in antiviolence strategies can additionally require creative attention to apprehensions that differences in power and status inject. The distrust of me that one member of Free Gender expressed clarified how our shared Christian religious faith and my status as a faith leader could actually hamper solidarity building. The metaphor of blackening captures the deliberate quality of counterintuitive learning in these encounters. When they assault and emotionally torment victim-survivors, perpetrators of intimate violence *denigrate*, a term conventionally defined as blackening. Supposedly because of their fears about bringing shame to their racially and/or religiously marginalized groups, some U.S. community leaders protect male abusers at the expense of victim-survivors who need help and protection. Breaking with conventions, therefore, the blackening manifested in this kind of intercultural and transnational process of learning assertively engages shame, fear, and distrust to repel religious community leaders' role in shielding perpetrators, deepening the anguish of victim-survivors, or discouraging their outspoken protests against violence.

Somatic learning supplies another unconventional resource that can hold and elicit revelatory insights about how spiritual and political resistance join with bodily experience. Instigations from somatic knowledge might, for instance, take the form of scientific medical truths about bodily functions that Rev. Helena Opoku-Sarkodie sought when she countered certain myths in her Ghanaian church community that supported heterosexual male sexual abuse of girls. My encounter with her account of these bodily myths initiated uncomfortable cultural dissonance and fears about reinforcing derisive U.S.-American stereotypes of Africans. Somatic learning that illustrates defiant spirituality was present in her Christian leadership, which featured medical and communal body-centered strategies to stop sexual violence against girls. I experienced somatic learning through nature in the Brazilian context of trying to translate the meaning of embodied African-based Candomblé rituals and the antiracist contours of the leadership by unionized domestic workers to end sexual assaults by their employers. My own bodily experience of the ocean provided a reminder of how spirituality inhabits sensuality. Amid the binding consequences of bodily invasion, humiliation, and spiritual theft that can accompany sexual assault for victim-survivors, spirituality can offer a mind-freeing, body-affirming countersensation. Sometimes certain physical encounters with the nonhuman environment can transmit somatic learning about conceptualizing antiviolence resources.

In South Africa, Funeka Soldaat mentioned how she had felt sick and panicky when, as an activist-leader, she entered the same police station in which she had been treated with disdain after being criminally targeted and brutally assaulted. Her somatic reaction may have not only signaled the harm done to her in that space but also indicated how much her organized political opposition to the harm mattered. Funeka's account demonstrated how both the courage of her leadership and the painful consequences of the police abuse in the wake of the homophobic violence she had experienced manifested as emotional, physical, and political knowledge. By occupying that police space as an activist-survivor, she refused to cede that space to her tormenters. She did so because of her belief in her rights. That is, her refusal was rooted in her conviction about her right (and the rights of Free Gender members) to openly live and thrive as black lesbian women without being targets for assault and with full access to justice if they were.

The spirit of defiance that comes from somatic knowledge and learning can hold psychic, physical, and political space for the transformation of rape cultures. It can support fluid gender freedoms and expressions and energize the claiming and reclaiming of space for them. Defiance can also open conceptual and public policy spaces to interrupt the religious and political mores that nurture gender-based violence. The process of opening up spaces by Muslim antiviolence activist-leaders in Ghana and South Africa dramatically differs from the same process in the U.S. context. The public project of fending off anti-Muslim political rhetoric and policies looms imposingly on the conceptual space needed by U.S. Muslim activist and activist-scholar leaders to address gender violence in U.S. Muslim communities and beyond. Opening up conceptual space demands learning from political dissimilarity in a manner that expands the meaning of solidarity.

Reclaiming spatial freedom makes room for remembering how Christian theology and practices have historically created white racist space for the rape of women of African descent. As exhibited in the architectural design of the Elmina slave castle—which placed the Christian chapel and the Christian governor's bedroom (where he raped slave women) in close proximity—the significance of rape tolerance has been securely compartmentalized within the influential foundations of global Christian mission and capitalist commerce. Freedom demands memory, not forgetfulness. Memory expands our capacity to be conscious of the moral consequences of these patterns. Abandoning the project of this painful decolonial memory work does not free up cultural space as some might suppose. When unexamined, the patterns of racist and religious support for gendered violence and the threat of it monopolize cultural space and morally discipline public attitudes. Reclaiming the space of political memory by engaging in a critical excavation of support for violence broadens our collective community consciousness. It allows us to recognize the necessary role of transformational power dynamics where alternative, innovative realities of racial and gender relations rebuff gender violence.

Incongruities aid the process of intercultural and transnational learning about antiviolence and underscore the value of certain forms of awkwardness and dissonance that epitomize defiant Africana spirituality. Although many religious teachings and practices uphold intimate violence against women and girls, an emphasis on religion and spirituality also offers unique elements for welcoming unconventional resources. The substance of religion and spirituality always incorporates some embrace of mystery—of unseen realities and possibilities. An appreciation of the unforeseen potential for good that is intrinsic to religion and spirituality may reserve a conceptual space of hospitality for accepting untranslatable cultural differences that form the context of violence and are related to race, religion, and political economy. For example, Patience, the Christian activist in Ghana, worked to end sexual exploitation of girls at certain Troxovi shrines. She asserted her love for her Ghanaian culture and her refusal to condemn another's religion as a basic ingredient in her approach to negotiating with the leadership of the shrines. I experienced something untranslatable about the loyalties she tried to convey in her assertions. Of course when discovering the untranslatable, awkwardness is often heightened rather than diminished. However acknowledgment of the awkwardness might spur more reliable truth seeking and appreciation of how sociohistorically divergent antiviolence approaches can cohabitate supportively with one another in an otherwise shared set of gender justice commitments.

In the spirituality of such traditional religions as Christianity, defiant methods of reclaiming cultural spaces of gender freedoms must incorporate inventiveness. As Christian ethicist Thelathia Young conceptualizes in her discussion of queer family ethics, the invention of kinship inculcates freedom.[4] The inventive aspect of defiant Africana spirituality can be recognized in how Christian activist members of Free Gender constructed communal relatedness through their political organizing and musical expression. To counter homophobic gender-based violence that targets lesbian black women and girls, indeed all of the members of the group (Christian and non-Christian) claimed cultural space within their own black communities for spiritually garnering resistance. Their innovations ranged from crafting mourning rituals for lesbians who were murdered or committed suicide to finding ways to pressure local police and faith leaders for more just and compassionate institutional responses.

To invent transnational and intercultural spaces of kinship involves bearing witness to the necessity to defy Africana claims that celebrate any form of black kinship unconcerned with the perpetuation of gender-based violence. Romanticized depictions of the organic existence of some kind of seamless spirit of Africana connection for all peoples of African descent deserve our suspicion and distrust. As examples in Salvador exhibit, white racist understandings can travel with sex tourists. As part of *their* Africana transnational encounters, black U.S.-American sex tourists engage in gendered exploitation and degradation of foreign black women and girls abroad, sometimes partially motivated by an unquenchable pursuit of social status they are denied at home. Similarly, U.S. black church mission and outreach projects in local African contexts do not reflexively bring antipathy to gender-based violence because of shared black African ancestry. Some U.S.-American black Christian leaders join together with certain South African black Christian leaders, for example, in supporting homophobic messages that stigmatize black gender-nonconforming or queer community members targeted for rapes, beatings, and murder. A defiant invention of antiviolence Africana ties of kinship unmasks dangerous, in some instances lethal, consequences of heteropatriarchal customs given cover by hollow assertions of ontological Africana unity.

Defiant Africana spirituality's capacity to evoke hope also relies on other defections from religiously held yet questionable loyalties. As mentioned above, learning from the standpoint of U.S.-American cultural perspectives demands emphatic objections to myths of exceptionalism, notions of Christian paternalistic superiority, and capitalist-driven savior syndrome mission work. We should consider a commitment to nurturing antiviolence dissonance to be a specific methodological tool that can support such objections and give them staying power. A blackening immersion in dissonant knowledge or risk-taking quest in support of antiviolence solidarity can leave a mark of hope. However, a caution is in order about erroneously equating defiant spirituality with some notion of Christian love, especially for U.S.-based Christians.

Defiant Africana spirituality has to cultivate a degree of uneasiness with standard articulations of Christian love. Theological declarations about love regularly serve as Christians' default formula for an adequate antidote to all forms of violence—except in cases of wars where our God is purportedly on our side and violent means are seen as justifying the ends. Attempting to grasp the dissonant aspect of defiant Africana spirituality may prove especially difficult for Christians wedded to such generalized assertions of Christian love as a panacea. Specifically, heterosexual Christians too often reflexively interpret the major Christian moral tenet "love your neighbor as yourself" as deeply caring about those who most resemble themselves. This interpretation of neighborly love typically involves Christians making an intense, compassionate effort to aid others in becoming more like themselves—that is, culturally, racially, economically, and in sexual orientation and gender expression more like the Christians who are reaching out to love those others. Sung, prayed, preached, and missionized Christian love rhetoric has traditionally enjoyed an unperturbed attachment to transphobic and misogynist denials of gender equality such as the exclusion of femaleness from the patriarchal Christian godhead composed of Father, Son, and Holy Spirit. Especially since abusers so often manipulatively use the language of love (for God and family) in their emotional, physical, and sexual coercion of their intimate partners, the moral implications of Christian use of the language of love demands particular attention in the context of dismantling support for gender violence.

Christian religious gender and sexuality values crudely reinforce forbearance with heteropatriarchal gender values embedded in Christianity and gender violence, even as Christians call for the perpetual, salvific Christian work of love as a response to violence. An understanding of harm-free Christian love as the most authentic representation of Christianity denies the prevalent, *authentic* reality of the Christian gender-based violence and spiritual abuse interwoven throughout Christian practices of love. The complacency so often generated by Christian love rhetoric obscures political and cultural choices that could be made to halt violence and abuse. Schooled in the moral gymnastics of Christian "love your neighbor as yourself" hypocrisy, U.S.-American Christians (and people in any society where Christianity is culturally dominant) may delete the core meaning of the commitments to antiviolence in defiant Africana spirituality by misguidedly absorbing it into that problematic love framework.

The discordant relationship among intersecting violence-supporting cultural values stokes an understanding of the role of trustworthy intercultural and transnational knowledge that also contains dissimilar elements. Focusing on this form of dissonance usefully highlights political differences surrounding gender-based violence. Appreciation of divergent forms of antiviolence knowledge can further a spirit of defiance that attends to the particularities of those differences. As previously discussed with regard to highly influential early twenty-first-century politicians, we can see dramatic differences in the racial and cultural dynamics of black former anti-apartheid freedom fighter and a long-term political leader in South African, Jacob Zuma, using his power and status during his rape trial to make victim-blaming references to his black accuser and the impact of victim-blaming statements by white billionaire and top U.S. political leader Donald Trump. Trump aimed his attack at white women who accused him of sexual harassment or assault.[5] But appreciatively making such distinctions can be a spiritual gift that bolsters the possibility of solidarity building among antiviolence activists. It can provide release from any presupposition that common cause and trustful alliance must be formed out of political sameness and cross-culturally homogenized universal truths that sound like a monotone echo standardizing the definition of cultural support for gender violence. Instead, the incongruity functions as a reminder of the benefits of recognizing competing, dissimilar knowledge about cultural patterns in public discourse that solidify resignation to ongoing patterns of violence and acceptance of the gender values that support it.

Dissonance facilitates the process of recognizing such knowledge and serves as a kind of alarm bell about the usefulness of uncertainty. An enlivening possibility for building intercultural and transnational solidarity stems from acknowledgment of uncertainties that arise from dissimilar knowledge about racism, religion, and antiviolence solidarity. Although potentially constructive, such acknowledgment can also bring a deeply personal uneasiness. For U.S.-Americans such as myself, it involves certain risks of making mistakes or having to grasp uncomfortable differences in the tone of black feminisms such as at the Salvador *delegacia*. A mistake might include, for example, how I failed to recognize a protocol in Accra—a protocol well known to me in the United States—that prohibits disclosing the location of shelters for abused women and children. Listening intently for unfamiliar cultural differences that require respectful consideration does not preclude (embarrassing) mistakes.

To be steeped in social justice movement morality usually means highly valuing the virtuousness of consistently being right about what constitutes holistic and equitable social practices. Unfortunately, it can also leave little room in which to admit one's ignorance and misjudgments about what is politically necessary or for responding generously to others' genuinely repentant admissions of their strategy mistakes—even in response to one's antiviolence movement allies. But admitting one's mistakes can allow constructive responses to conflict and disappointment to surface among activist allies. Examining the incongruity of sometimes being wrong about the means for doing right and good can serve the interests of building gender-justice solidarity.

In an intense form of sounding an alarm bell about uncertainty, dissonance also calls out irreconcilable status differences that undermine solidarity and offers a warning about exploitation concealed in well-meaning efforts. South African scholar Zethu Matebeni gives voice to this kind of confrontational approach when assessing international concern for homophobic gender violence in Africa. In "How NOT to Write about Queer South Africa," she offers a stinging critique of stereotyping by well-meaning outsiders. She sarcastically suggests that when supposed allies with good intentions write about queer South Africa they should "always paint a picture that lesbians, particularly the Black ones, are from poor townships, are victims of rape and murder, and your writing and the money you will raise, will save them."[6] Matebeni's rebuke should produce a pause of uncertainty for outsiders such as myself who seek antiviolence solidarity. Matebeni's representation of black South

African lesbians illustrates how a defiant spirit that refuses to play the role of objectified mission project supports building authentic solidarity. Acknowledgment of the systemic inequalities related to race, sex/gender, and economics should never presume to encapsulate the realities of people's lives with descriptive categories of inequality, nor should the vulnerability of violently victimized black lesbians (in South Africa, the United States, and elsewhere) ever be reduced to a problem to be fixed. From uncertainty about how to formulate analyses that do not objectify victims emerges the potential for greater accountability to the vulnerable and an opening for conjoined activist solidarity through such accountability.

Blackening a way forward, packed with truth-telling and life-giving lessons about Africana activist thought and practice, the fluidity of defiant Africana spirituality can seep into cultural crevices and gaps to disrupt deeper, systemic, violence-sanctioning patterns. Its pulsating hope materializes through our mutually reinforcing yet culturally and politically distinctive struggles to end gender-based violence for good.

ACKNOWLEDGMENTS

It is simply a fact that without the spiritual nourishment of encouragement and concrete gifts of time and expertise that I received from friends and strangers this project would not have started and it certainly would never have been completed.

I owe an immeasurable debt of gratitude to the leaders who generously shared their insights, energy, and commitments with me. Even though they did not know me beforehand they allowed me into their workspaces, communities, and lives for in-depth conversations. There are too many of them to name here, and I fear that I will accidentally omit someone if I try to do so. But they provided the catalytic glue that held this project together by offering me contact information on other local colleagues and/or directly encouraging those colleagues to trust and meet me, hosting me as a speaker or preacher, and giving me directions on how to safely travel around their communities. They gave me books, articles, reports, and websites on gender violence. They gave me coffee, tea, and cookies, and asked me helpful questions about my work and goals. To you, the advocates, activists, NGO staff, government officials, legislators, clergy, faith leaders, scholars, and professors in Accra, Ghana, Salvador, Brazil, and Pietermaritzburg, Johannesburg, Durbin, and Cape Town, South Africa, I humbly and enthusiastically thank you for teaching me how the work of ending gender-based violence can be accomplished.

I must express my utmost gratitude to the interviewees who are featured: Fatimatu N-Eyare Sulemanu, Helena Opoku-Sarkodie, Dorcas Coker-Appiah, Mercy Amba Oduyoye, Angela Dwamena-Aboagye, Audrey Gadzekpo, Patience, Sandra Maria dos Santos, Creuza Oliveira, Tânia Mendonça, Jacinta Marta and Taveres Leiro, Débora Cristina da Silva Aranha, Leide Manuela Santos, Isabella Santos de Jesus, Sarojini Nadar, Zarina Majiet, Funeka Soldaat, Bulelwa Panda, Elizabeth Hoorn Petersen. I am grateful for the myriad of ways that their ideas and leadership commitments as well as my interactions with them helped to provoke the learning that I have discussed.

Like other researcher-dreamers, in the beginning I was not at all sure how to design my project and I received tremendous formative help and encouragement in each of the international settings to which I traveled. For the initial on-the-ground assistance that allowed me to get started with this project in Ghana, I offer deep thanks to Lillie Edwards, Obiri Addo, Rose Mary Amenga-Etego, Elizabeth Amoah, Audrey Gadzekyo, Agnes Quansah, E. Gyimah-Boadi, Sarah Ashley, Fiifi Ampong. For help as I started out in Salvador, Bahia, Brazil, I offer profound gratitude to Nessette Falu, who mentored me, translated for me, and debriefed each interview with me, Erica Rocha whose extensive networks of activist contacts, detailed arrangements of meetings with the ideal interviewees, unconditional welcome, and savvy political insights were invaluable to me, and Rachel Harding, Sandra dos Santos, Tania Palma, and Vilma Reis. For assistance in getting started in South Africa I offer my heartfelt thanks to Cheryl Anderson, Cookie Edwards, Gerald West, Beverley Haddad, Sarojini Nadar, Isabel Apawo Phiri, Bongi Zengele, Linda Naiker, Shahana Rasool Bassadien, Thula Hlongwane, Musa Ngubane, Mpumi Mathabela, Emily Craven, Lisa Vetten, Elizabeth Petersen, Lungiswa Memela, Miranda N. Pillay, and Mpho Tutu. After the initial period of scrambling to get started, I received needed guidance and resources for which I offer my thanks from many more individuals in each of those settings who gave me mini-tours, transportation, materials, advice, encouragement, hospitality, and their valuable time for conversations about my research interests as well as mundane matters of everyday community life.

My research assistants graciously contributed an enormous amount of labor and efficiency by helping to organize materials from my research trips, locating scholarly resources, and transcribing some of my interview tapes. Charon Hribar, Natalie Williams, Jean Felipe de Assis, Elyse Ambrose, Tejai Beulah, Ericka Dunbar, Nicole Hoskins, and Lisa Cunningham, I thank you for your diligence, skill, and patience with me.

I wish to express my gratitude for the assistance that I received on translation and transcription of interviews, especially from Julia Landau, Jordan Mendes, Sandra Almeida, Lorelei Williams, Kanyere Eaton,

Helen LaKelly Hunt, Sisterfund, CONNECT: Safe Families, Peaceful Communities.

I have friends who believed in me and walked with me each step—from start to finish—of the long journey of completing this project. I thank Jennifer Wriggins for her concrete help with supporting my trips, interpreting and finding legal scholarly resources, editing some of my manuscript, and listening to me complain. I thank Althea Spencer-Miller for being my faithful, caring writing partner, reading (and re-reading) and offering feedback on every word of this book throughout its many iterations. I thank Amy Ballin for her daily (literally) loving prodding and empathizing, for providing me with a place to study and resources for writing, and, most importantly, for keeping me alive during several tough months.

My thinking has been shaped by feedback, resources, ideas, and support from a host of colleagues, friends, and family members who directly enabled me to do this work on gender-based violence, especially Nina Schwarzschild, Elias Ortega-Aponte, Kesha Moore, Kate Ott, Laurel Kearns, Jonathan Reader, Nancy Noguera, Sally MacNichol, Sarah Azaransky, Bil Wright, Karen Amore, Robynne West; my conversation partners on gender, religion, and decoloniality: Kwok Pui-Lan, Susan Abraham, Wonhee Anne Joh, Mayra Rivera, Laurel Schneider, Stephanie Mitchem; my summer program conversation partners on issues of sexuality and religion: Rebecca T. Alpert, Ellen Armour, Sharon Groves; my summer research colloquium partners: Charles Henderson, Lisa Anderson, J. C. Austin, Annemarie Mingo, Melissa Snarr, Kelly Frances Fenelon Snarr, Jay Smith, Ann Kaloski-Naylor, Louis Porter; and my teachers and writing group colleagues at Sackett Street Writers (in Brooklyn, New York, and Montclair, New Jersey), When Words Count (in Vermont), and Wellspring (in Massachusetts); my professional and personal advocates: Laurie Ferguson and Tom Johnson.

I received support for this book that I truly appreciate from Drew University leaders and reference librarians, particularly Dean Maxine Beach, Ernest Rubenstein, Jesse Mann, and Center for Conflict and Culture directors Terry Todd and Jonathan Golden. For assistance with editing, I thank Natalie Williams, Leah Thomas, and particularly Heather Lee Miller whose generosity and expertise meticulously assisted me with the entire final manuscript and made it much better.

I would like to thank my NYU editor Jennifer Hammer for her steady guidance of and wonderful attentiveness to this project as well as her compassionate support of me. I am also grateful for the thorough, proficient work of the NYU Press staff on the production of this book.

Finally, I still find his sloppily scribbled notes giving me pointed, critical feedback on the sides of early drafts of some of my chapters. I reread his long emails (sent while I was away on my research trips) encouraging me to persevere past a particular disappointment about which I had just written to him, coaching me to be sure to "write-up" and save an insight that I mentioned on the phone, and cajoling me by punctuating each message with silly comments to get me to smile instead of worrying. I relied on him to make arrangements to send me crucial items I had accidentally forgotten back home, take me to get medical help when I arrived home ill, argue with me about ideas, magically produce books I needed at exactly the right moment, and lift my spirits when I was dejected about my slow progress. There may be words to express appreciation for the vastness of the role my spouse and life-partner Jerry G. Watts played in enabling me to travel, research, write, and think. But I cannot find adequate ones. I cannot find them right now because the desperate ache of his shocking departure from this earth still continues to overwhelm me. Half of my heart is gone and will never be restored.

NOTES

INTRODUCTION

1 The corporate name Young Women's Christian Association of the United States of America, Inc. was changed subsequent to this 2012 speech to YWCA USA, Inc., effective December 15, 2015 (YWCA, "History," www.ywca.org).

2 The Violence Against Women Act (VAWA), enacted in 1994, addresses domestic violence, dating violence, sexual assault, stalking, and human trafficking. After the failure by Congress to renew it in 2012, the reauthorization of VAWA occurred in 2013. Violence Against Women Act of 2013, Pub. L. No. 113-4 (2013, available at www.gpo.gov). For a critical assessment of the changes in the law in the 2013 authorization, see Weissman, "Law, Social Movements, and the Political Economy of Domestic Violence."

3 "Vice President Biden Speaks on Reauthorizing the Violence Against Women Act," April 18, 2012, www.youtube.com/watch?v=ohbz99Ug7vI. See also C-SPAN, User-Created Content, "Clip of Vice President Biden on Violence Against Women Act," May 4, 2012, www.c-span.org.

4 "Vice President Biden Speaks."

5 The term *U.S.-American* identifies the United States and the continent in which it is located. Unlike the more common labeling of the residents and influence of the United States as *American*, *U.S.-American* more accurately indicates belonging to one nation—the United States—located in proximity to many others on the American continent.

6 "Vice President Biden Speaks."

7 Ibid.

8 Pew Forum on Religion and Public Life, "U.S. Religious Landscape Survey," 5.

9 See, for example, Davis, "Rape, Racism, and the Capitalist Setting"; Collins, *Black Sexual Politics*, 32–33; McClintock, *Imperial Leather*; and Stoler, *Carnal Knowledge and Imperial Power*. See also nonfeminist discussions of the use of rape by colonizers in Fanon, *Dying Colonialism*.

10 See Fortune, *Sexual Violence*; Cooper-White, *Cry of Tamar*; Brown and Bohn, *Christianity, Patriarchy and Abuse*; and Scholz, *Sacred Witness*.

11 See, for example, Yancy, *Christology and Whiteness*.

12 Merry, *Human Rights and Gender Violence*, 10.

13 Ibid., 10–11.

14 See discussions of rape of slaves in White, *Ar'n't I a Woman?*, 34, 63; Roberts, *Killing the Black Body*, 29–33; and Martin, *More Than Chains and Toil*, 91–92. See also Deer, *Beginning and End of Rape*; Smith, "Sexual Violence and American Indian Genocide"; and Weaver, "Colonial Context of Violence."

15 See Taves, *Religion and Domestic Violence in Early New England*; Pleck, *Domestic Tyranny*; Smith, *Sex without Consent*; and Block, *Rape and Sexual Power in Early America*. Intragroup sexual coercion and assaults also occurred among African slaves, especially in the breeding practices on plantations and among indigenous native groups.

16 Winthrop, "We Shall Be as a City upon a Hill," 63–65.

17 Jefferson fathered six children with Sally Hemings, three of whom lived beyond infancy. See Bay, "Love, Sex, Slavery, and Sally Hemings," and Gordon-Reed, *Thomas Jefferson and Sally Hemings*. On how to interpret this history, see Tillet, *Sites of Slavery*.

18 I am indebted to the discussion of these intersections by Nayak, "Geography, Race, and Emotions."

19 For example, the 1662 Virginia law stipulated that children of enslaved-free unions inherited the status of their mothers, "making unions with African girls and women all the more attractive to white men, in that any resulting offspring became the man's property." Botham, "'Purity of the White Woman,'" 252. On ownership of slave women's children by white masters, see Roberts, *Killing the Black Body*, 33–34.

20 Earl, *Dark Symbols, Obscure Signs*, 16. For a womanist Christian ethics discussion of this sexual violence, see Copeland, *Enfleshing Freedom*, esp. 35.

21 William Gilmore Simms—a strong nineteenth-century public proponent of slavery and the necessity of violence in U.S. expansionism—declared, "War is the greatest element of modern civilization, and our destiny is conquest," and the *Southern Quarterly Review* noted that "Negro slavery is one of the greatest of moral goods & blessings" (quoted in Horsman, *Race and Manifest Destiny*, 167).

22 For discussions of how the history of anti-black racism in European colonial practices has been incorporated into Christian theology, see Jennings, *Christian Imagination*; and Copeland, *Enfleshing Freedom*.

23 For discussion of breeding and slave women's bodies, see Roberts, *Killing the Black Body*, 24–28; and Smithers, *Slave Breeding*.

24 See discussion in Weaver, "Colonial Context of Violence," 1552–63.

25 Amnesty International, *Maze of Injustice*.

26 See, for example, Cappriccioso, "House VAWA Bill." Also note that the House of Representatives passed a bill deleting the Native American right to bring nonnative attackers to tribal courts, which had been a provision in the Senate bill. Grant, "House Passes Violence Against Women Act, Grudgingly."

27 Alexander, *Pedagogies of Crossing*, 272.

28 Ibid., 281.

29 Ibid.

30 Swarr and Nagar, *Critical Transnational Feminist Praxis*, 5.

31 Craven and Davis, *Feminist Activist Ethnography*, 2.

32 Berger and Quinney, *Storytelling Sociology*, 10.

33 Fine and Weis, "Writing the 'Wrongs' of Fieldwork."

34 See extensive discussion of such cultural negotiations in the history of Christian theology in Carter, *Race*.

35 Gates, *Black in Latin America*.

36 Ibid., 12.

37 Jackson, "Between Biography and Ethnography." See also Jackson, *Politics of Storytelling*.

38 Jackson, "Between Biography and Ethnography," 378.

39 Jackson relies on Gloria Anzaldúa for the lens and terms of this analysis: Anzaldúa, *Borderlands/La Frontera*.

40 Scharen and Vigen, *Ethnography as Christian Theology and Ethics*, 17.

41 Ibid., xxi.

42 Behar, *Vulnerable Observer*.

43 Ibid., 14.

44 Berman, "Critical Reflection"; Temple, "Crossed Wires"; Temple, "Watch Your Tongue"; Temple and Edwards, "Interpreters/Translators and Cross-Language Research"; and Temple, Edwards, and Alexander, "Grasping at Context."

45 Lawrence-Lightfoot, "Reflections on Portraiture," 7.

46 Ibid., 11. See also Lawrence-Lightfoot and Hoffman Davis, *Art and Science of Portraiture*.

47 I offer details on this topic in my book *Wounds of the Spirit*.

48 Twenty-two million women in the United States have been raped in their lifetime. Of the women who reported being raped, physically assaulted, and/or stalked since age eighteen, 63.8 percent were victimized by a current or former husband, cohabiting partner, boyfriend, or date (Black et al., "National Intimate Partner and Sexual Violence Survey (NISVS)," 41).

49 Madison, *Acts of Activism*.

50 Ibid., 171.

51 Ibid., 171.

52 Michael Jackson offers a concise summary of the constraints and empowerment of this method. Though there is disagreement "over the extent to which our lives are actually configured by the stories we tell, there is no denying that storytelling gives us a sense that though we do not exactly determine the course of our lives we at least have a hand in defining their meanings" (*Politics of Storytelling*, 16).

53 Richie, *Arrested Justice*, 4.

54 Ibid.

55 Townes, *Womanist Ethics*, 2.

56 Only trips for which this project was the exclusive purpose are included in this number. I made additional trips for other professional purposes in which initial

contacts for future interviews were made or follow-up conversations with interviewees took place.

CHAPTER 1. CONSTRICTED RELIGIOUS RESPONSES

1 Philip Read, "Scared Mom's Farewell: 'If You're Reading This . . .': At Funeral,
   Woman's Children Hear the Words She Wrote Before She Was Killed," *Star-
   Ledger*, July 4, 2008, 1; Philip Read and George Berkin, "Woman Is Shot to Death
   at Montclair YMCA Pool; Violence Erupted during Children's Swimming Class,"
   Star-Ledger, June 27, 2008, 15. In a nearby brutal killing involving a black couple
   that occurred after Paul's murder, Stacey Ann Guillette was gunned down by her
   estranged husband, Ewart Guillette, while taking her two children to a shelter
   in Elizabeth, New Jersey, on August 30, 2010. Guillette shot her sixteen times in
   the back before fleeing the scene. See Ryan Hutchins, "Hillside Man Suspected of
   Wife's Slaying Captured Authorities: Victim, Who Had Fled Domestic Dispute,
   Was Shot Dead in Elizabeth," *Star-Ledger*, September 1, 2010; Hutchins, "Man Accused of Fatally Shooting Wife Captured. Woman Had Plans to Become a Nurse,"
   Star-Ledger, September 1, 2010; and Hutchins, "Victim's Kids Safe with Family as
   Father Is Charged in Killing," *Star-Ledger*, September 2, 2010.

2 Paul Cox, "How Manhunt Led to YMCA Slaying Suspect," *Star-Ledger*, July 9,
   2008; Juri Carmen, "Alleged Murder Pleads Not Guilty to Killing Wife," *Star-
   Ledger*, July 16, 2008; Brian T. Murray, "YMCA Murder Suspect Returned from
   New York," *Star-Ledger*, July 15, 2008; Alexi Friedman, "Man Accused of Fatally
   Shooting Girlfriend at Montclair YMCA Was Passion Driven, Lawyer Says,"
   Star-Ledger, December 1, 2010; Alexi Friedman, "Man Is Convicted of Slaying
   Estranged Girlfriend at Montclair YMCA," *Star-Ledger*, December 23, 2010; Alexi
   Friedman, "N.J. Man Convicted of Fatally Shooting Ex-Girlfriend at Montclair
   YMCA Is Sentenced to Life," *Star-Ledger*, February 1, 2011; Alexi Friedman, "Two
   Jurors in Montclair YMCA Shooting Case Say That They Felt Pressured to Reach
   Guilty Verdict," *Star-Ledger*, February 1, 2011; and Alexi Friedman, "N.J. Judge De-
   clines Motion for New Trial in Montclair YMCA Slaying," *Star-Ledger*, February 2,
   2011.

3 Read, "Scared Mom's Farewell."

4 As Carolyn West has stated: "Because Black women live at the intersection of
   oppressions, they are vulnerable to a broad range of violence in all areas of their
   lives, including their intimate relationships, their communities, and their work-
   places" (West, "I Find Myself at Therapy's Doorstep," 195). See also West, *Violence
   in the Lives of Black Women*.

5 Cannon and Buttell, "Illusion of Inclusion"; Ristock, "Understanding Violence in
   Lesbian Relationships," 129–50; Smith, "Women Who Abuse"; Kaschak, "Intimate
   Betrayal"; Robinson, "There's a Stranger in This House"; Butler, "African Ameri-
   can Lesbian Women"; and Dorothy M., "When the Hand That Slaps Is Female."

6 Catalano, "Intimate Partner Violence, 1993–2010."

7 Ibid.

8 Catalano et al., "Female Victims of Violence."

9 Black et al., "National Intimate Partner and Sexual Violence Survey (NISVS)."
Multiple government websites continually disseminate the most up-to-date
national and state reports of the growing or fluctuating numbers of incidents.
For example, see the websites of the Centers for Disease Control and Prevention
(www.cdc.gov), National Coalition Against Domestic Violence (http://ncadv.org),
and Office on Violence Against Women (www.justice.gov).

10 According to a 2015 study published in the *Journal of Interpersonal Violence*,
"Compared with other racial and ethnic groups, African American women are
disproportionately more likely to experience intimate partner violence (IPV).
In the United States, more African American (44%) than European American
(35%) or Hispanic (37%) women report IPV during their lifetime, and African American women experience recurrent IPV at a rate 6 times higher than
that of European American women." The authors emphasize that "rates of
reported IPV victimization among African American women are dispropor-
tionally higher than reported rates among women of other races and ethnicities" (Fincher et al., "Effect of Face-to-Face Interview," 819, 831). According
to the 2011 National Intimate Partner and Sexual Violence Survey, "In the
United States, an estimated 32.3% of multiracial women, 27.5% of American
Indian/Alaska Native women, 21.2% of non-Hispanic black women, 20.5% of
non-Hispanic white women, and 13.6% of Hispanic women were raped during
their lifetimes" (Breiding, Smith, and Basile, "Prevalence and Characteristics
of Sexual Violence," 5). With the recent addition of the category "multiracial,"
violence rates for black women are sometimes reported as lower than those
for white women. For example, the 2017 NISVS reports that for contact sexual
violence "half of multiracial women in the U.S. (49.5%), 45.6% of American
Indian/Alaska Native women, 38.9% of non-Hispanic White women, 35.5% of
non-Hispanic Black women, 26.9% of Hispanic women, and 22.9% of Asian/
Pacific Islander women experienced some form of contact SV during their
lifetime" (Smith et al., "National Intimate Partner and Sexual Violence Survey,"
20). According to a 2013 *Homicide Studies* report on domestic violence fatalities, "Overall, black females were murdered by males at a rate (2.61 per 100,000)
more than two and a half times higher than white females (0.99 per 100,000)."
Violence Policy Center, "When Men Murder Women." Also see Bent-Goodley,
"Domestic Violence Fatality Reviews"; Bhandari et al., "Comparison of Abuse
Experiences"; Goldscheid et al., *Responses from the Field*; Catalano, "Intimate
Partner Violence."

11 Bent-Goodley, "Domestic Violence Fatality Reviews," 376.

12 Catalano et al., "Female Victims of Violence."

13 Tjaden and Thoennes, "Stalking in America," 1–20. A later study on the global
problem of intimate partner homicides found a strong link between domestic
violence and homicides. Stöckl et al., "Global Prevalence of Intimate Partner
Homicide." See also Campbell, *Assessing Dangerousness*.

14 Violence Policy Center, "When Men Murder Women."

15 Mary Houtsma, "Victims of Domestic Violence Can't Wait for Help; Rash of Deaths Shows That the Government Must Do More," *Star-Ledger*, July 9, 2008, 13. And according to the 2010 U.S. census, the population of New Jersey is approximately eight to nine million people, half of whom were women, and 15 percent of whom were African American (www.census.gov).

16 See Russell and Van de Ven, *Crimes against Women*; Radford and Russell, *Femicide*; and Della Giustina, *Why Women Are Beaten and Killed*.

17 See Fregoso and Bejarano, *Terrorizing Women*. On religion and femicide, see Pineda-Madrid, *Suffering and Salvation*; and O'Donovan, *Rage and Resistance*.

18 Jones, *Next Time She'll Be Dead*, 81. See also Taylor, "Slain and Slandered."

19 Pineda-Madrid, *Suffering and Salvation*, 12.

20 These crimes are indicative of an alarming crisis of murders of women by their husbands and boyfriends that occur in many communities throughout the country. Violence Policy Center, "When Men Murder Women."

21 New Jersey Department of Law and Public Safety, Division of State Police, "Domestic Violence in New Jersey: Twenty-Sixth Annual Domestic Violence Report" and "Domestic Violence in New Jersey: Twenty-Eighth Annual Domestic Violence Report."

22 Stewart, "Relationship Violence Strikes Campuses."

23 Carpenter, "Father's Shadow."

24 Graham, "Secret Shame."

25 Sahgal and Greg Smith, "Religious Portrait." See also Taylor, Chatters, and Jackson, "Religious and Spiritual Involvement."

26 Sahgal and Smith, "Religious Portrait," 1–5; and Frederick, *Between Sundays*.

27 Bent-Goodley, St. Vil, and Hubbert, "Spirit Unbroken," 53.

28 Crumpton, *Womanist Pastoral Theology*, 39.

29 Ibid., 39.

30 See Neighbors, Musick, and Williams, "African American Minister"; Ward, Clark, and Heidrich, "African American Women's Beliefs"; and Thompson, Sanders, and Akbar, "African Americans' Perceptions."

31 Bent-Goodley and Fowler, "Spiritual and Religious Abuse," 292.

32 Brade and Bent-Goodley, "Refuge for My Soul," esp. 441.

33 Rotunda, Williamson, and Penfold, "Clergy Response to Domestic Violence." Most but not all of the clergy in this study were Christian.

34 Kelley, "What Is It about the Walls?," 11.

35 Ibid., 10.

36 Potter, *Battle Cries*, 160. Also see Potter, "Battered Black Women's Use of Religious Services"; Bent-Goodley and Fowler, "Spiritual and Religious Abuse," 282–95; and Popescu et al., "'Because of My Beliefs.'"

37 See discussion of black women victim-survivors' cognizance of their supposed obligation to protect black men in the study by Nash, "Through Black Eyes." See also Davis, *Battered African American Women*.

38 See Crenshaw et al., *Say Her Name*; Crenshaw, Ocen, and Nanda, *Black Girls Matter*; and Morris, "Race, Gender and the School-to-Prison Pipeline."

39 As I have argued elsewhere, black women victim-survivors may receive an array of mutually reinforcing messages of blame, shame, sacrifice, and submission from religion, racist attitudes in society, and the abuser. See West, *Wounds of the Spirit*.

40 In their study of African American religious and spiritual community responses to domestic violence, Bent-Goodley and Fowler found that "many participants acknowledged that the methods that an abuser uses to keep a woman in an abusive relationship are often similar to those used by the church to maintain the relationship." See Bent-Goodley and Fowler, "Spiritual and Religious Abuse," 291.

41 See discussion of the trial of Reverend Bishop Terry Lee Hornbuckle of Dallas, Texas. Shupe and Eliasson-Nannini, *Pastoral Misconduct*, 86.

42 Ibid. See also Jackson, *For the Souls of Black Folks*; and Matthews, *Sexual Abuse of Power*.

43 See discussion in Walton, *Watch This!*, 225–26. Walton gives the example of a Maryland black pastor, minister of men, who conducted men-only events "that focused on marriage and family" at the ten-thousand-member church he served. He was charged with battery of his own wife, and later with rape of a woman with whom he admitted to having been sexually active while leading this ministry. Only after extensive media coverage did the church finally place him on paid administrative leave and the senior pastor publicly comment with a call for prayer.

44 For critical discussions of Jakes, see Walton, *Watch This!*, 113–14, 119–21; Lee, *America's New Preacher*, 123–39; Cole and Guy-Sheftall, *Gender Talk*, 125–26; and McGee, "Wal-Martization of African American Religion." For more general or laudatory summaries of the ministries, business enterprises, and influence of T. D. Jakes, see Lee and Sinitiere, *Holy Mavericks*, 53–75; and Pappu, "Preacher."

45 T. D. Jakes, "Domestic Abuse Is Unholy," *Atlanta Constitution-Journal*, September 4, 2007, Opinion.

46 Jakes, *Woman, Thou Art Loosed!*, 67.

47 Jakes, *God's Leading Lady*,165. Jakes repeatedly admonishes women for failing to take responsibility for their actions. He lists examples of women he "constantly" meets "who wear the mantle of victim," including those who say, "I know I shouldn't be so promiscuous, but I was abused as a child and I'm just looking for some love" (145).

48 Ibid., 165.

49 Crumpton, *Womanist Pastoral Theology*, 165.

50 Ibid., 101.

51 Most Muslims in the United States are foreign-born immigrants (approximately 65 percent), but of the remaining U.S.-born Muslims (35 percent), approximately 56 percent are African American. See Pew Research Center, "Muslim Americans," 17. See also McCloud, *African American Islam*.

52 Majeed, "Khalidah's Story."

53 Ibid.

54 Potter, "Battered Black Women's Use of Religious Services," 276.

55 Berns, *Framing the Victim*; Martinez et al., "Analysis of Dr. Phil's Advice"; and Henson and Parameswaran, "Getting Real."

56 Berns, "Domestic Violence and Victim Empowerment Folklore," 111.

57 Ibid., 121.

58 The same kind of advice giving was mirrored in the popular black movie character created by Tyler Perry: Madea. Perry dressed up as an older black woman who counseled and scolded couples, especially in relation to situations of abuse and violence. Most often, Madea recommended that the men properly assert themselves as authorities in the home and that the women respectfully submit themselves to the authority of the right kind of heterosexual male partner. For detailed critical discussions of Perry's depictions of black women and domestic violence that highlight the role of religion and black church culture, see Manigault-Bryant, Lomax, and Duncan, *Womanist and Black Feminist Responses*.

59 Consalvo, "Hegemony, Domestic Violence, and Cops"; Fishman and Cavender, *Entertaining Crime*; and Liebler, Hatef, and Munno, "Domestic Violence as Entertainment."

60 See discussions in Projansky, "Rihanna's Closed Eyes"; Rodier and Meagher, "In Her Own Time"; Patterson and Sears, "Letting Men Off the Hook?," 1; Rothman et al., "U.S. Tabloid Magazine Coverage"; Leonard and Casper, "Rotten to the Core"; and Shoos, "Representing Domestic Violence."

61 Bushman et al., "Gun Violence Trends in Movies."

62 Wintemute, "Epidemiology of Firearm Violence."

63 Ferguson, "Does Media Violence Predict Societal Violence?"; Markey, French, and Markey, "Violent Movies and Severe Acts of Violence"; Bushman, Romer, and Jamieson, "Distinguishing Hypotheses from Hyperbole"; and Markey et al., "Lessons from Markey et al. (2015)."

64 Violence Policy Center, "When Men Murder Women."

65 Wintemute, "Epidemiology of Firearm Violence," 5–19.

66 The "When Men Murder Women" report (6) states: "Compared to a black male, a black female is far more likely to be killed by her spouse, an intimate acquaintance, or a family member than by a stranger. Where the relationship could be determined, 92 percent of black females killed by males in single victim/single offender incidents knew their killers (384 out of 417). . . . As with female homicide victims in general, firearms—especially handguns—were the weapon most commonly used by males to murder black females in 2012. In the 433 homicides for which the murder weapon could be identified, 57 percent of black female victims (245 victims) were shot and killed with guns. And when these females were killed with a gun, it was most often a handgun (187 victims or 76 percent). The number of black females shot and killed by their husband or intimate acquaintance (111 victims) was more than three times as high as the total number murdered by male strangers using all weapons combined (33 victims) in single victim/single offender incidents in 2012."

67 See Britto et al., "Does 'Special' Mean Young, White and Female?"; Kahlor and Eastin, "Television's Role"; and Mason and Magnet, "Surveillance Studies."

68 See Easteal, Judd, and Holland, "Enduring Themes and Silences"; Kahlor and Eastin, "Television's Role"; and Gillespie et al., "Framing Deadly Domestic Violence."

69 Morgan, Shanahan, and Signorielli, "Cultivation Processes," 36.

70 Domestic Violence Act 2007, Act 732, Parliament of the Republic of Ghana, www.africalegalaid.com.

71 As noted in the introduction, in the United States, there is only one federal law, initially passed in 1994, that focuses on the problem, the Violence Against Women Act (VAWA); it expires every five years unless Congress votes to renew it. See Modi, Palmer, and Armstrong, "Role of Violence Against Women Act."

72 For a history of Kwanzaa, see Mays, *Kwanzaa.*

73 A total of 71.2 percent are Christian. Ghana Statistical Service, "2010 Population and Housing Census."

74 For discussion of disputes about the 2000 Ghana census count of Muslims, see Weiss, *Between Accommodation and Revivalism,* 359–70.

75 For discussion of African Traditional Religion in Ghana see Rose Mary Amenga-Etego's study of northern Ghanaian communities in *Mending The Broken Pieces.* For a helpful scholarly overview defining the study of African Traditional Religion, see Ezra Chitando, "Phenomenology of Religion and the Study of African Traditional Religions," *Method and Theory in the Study of Religion* (2005) 17, no. 4: 299-316.

76 Gaines, *American Africans in Ghana,* 80. See also Azaransky, *This Worldwide Struggle,* 199–204.

77 Gaines, *American Africans in Ghana,* 80.

78 Ibid.

79 Murray, *Song in a Weary Throat,* 318–43; Gaines, *American Africans in Ghana,* 114–15; and Azaransky, *Dream Is Freedom,* 52–53.

80 Gaines, *American Africans in Ghana,* 122.

81 Klein, "African Women in the Atlantic Slave Trade." See also Perbi, *History of Indigenous Slavery;* and Kankpeyeng, "Slave Trade in Northern Ghana."

82 Hartman, *Lose Your Mother,* 63; and Ryder, *Benin and the Europeans,* 55.

83 Austin, *African Muslims in Antebellum America;* Mirzai, Montana, and Lovejoy, *Slavery, Islam, and Diaspora.* On Islam as the religion of thirteenth-century ancient Ghanaian rulers, court officials, merchants, and townspeople, see Clarke, *West Africa and Islam.* On gender and sexual violence in the history of Islam and slavery, see Ali, "Slavery and Sexual Ethics in Islam" and *Marriage and Slavery in Early Islam.*

84 See Asante, "Henry Louis Gates Is Wrong"; Gates, "Ending the Slavery Blame-Game"; and Ransby, "Henry Louis Gates' Dangerously Wrong Slave History."

85 For an intellectual history of how Europeans invented the idea of Africa, see Mudimbe, *Idea of Africa.*

86 Sulemanu, "Situation of Muslim Women." See also Sulemanu, "Mitigating Violence Against Women."

87 Ammah-Koney, "Violence Against Women," 179.

88 See Ammah-Koney, "Violence Against Women"; and Issaka Toure, "Contesting the Normative." For further discussion of religion and female circumcision, see Nyangweso, *Female Circumcision*.

89 For example, see O'Conner and Jahan, "Under Surveillance and Overwrought"; Al Baker and Rick Rojas, "Police Broke Surveillance Rules after 9/11, Inquiry Finds," *New York Times*, August 24, 2016; and ACLU, "Raza v. City of New York—Legal Challenge to NYPD Muslim Surveillance Program" (August 3, 2017), www.aclu. org.

90 Courts outlawed this ban in Oklahoma in 2013, but other attempts to ban the implementation of sharia law were considered in over thirty states. See Pew Research Center, Religion and Public Life, "State Legislation Restricting Use of Foreign or Religious Law," April 8, 2013, http://features.pewforum.org.

91 Ayyub, "Many Faces of Domestic Violence," 24.

92 Very Rev. Helena Opoku-Sarkodie, Methodist clergy and director of religious programming, Ghana Broadcasting Corporation, interview by author, Accra, Ghana, June 6, 2008.

93 Ibid.

94 Ibid. See also Mansaray, "Girl-Child Sexual Abuse."

95 Opoku-Sarkodie interview.

96 Ibid.

97 Ibid.

98 Amenga-Etego, "Violence Against Women in Contemporary Ghanaian Society," 40.

99 See Herman, *Father-Daughter Incest*; Sacco, *Unspeakable*; Stone, *No Secrets, No Lies*; and Feuereisen and Pincus, *Invisible Girls*.

100 See Bhuyan, Shim, and Velagapudi, "Domestic Violence Advocacy." More generally, dramatic variations in ethnicity and national origin exist in urban hubs such as New York City, where, in the early twenty-first century, public schools educated children from over two hundred countries who spoke over one hundred twenty languages. See Ellen et al., "Immigrant Children and New York City Schools," 184. Comparable cultural variation was also evident in Houston and Los Angeles. See Gates, "Houston Surpasses New York and Los Angeles."

CHAPTER 2. AUTHENTIC CULTURAL VALUES

1 Dorcas Coker-Appiah, director of Gender Studies and Human Rights Documentation Centre, interview by author, Accra, Ghana, June 10, 2008.

2 Ibid.

3 Convention on the Elimination of All Forms of Discrimination Against Women (CEDAW, 1979), www.un.org. See also: Merry, Human Rights and Gender Violence.

4 Meyersfeld, *Domestic Violence and International Law*, 37-38; Declaration on the Elimination of Violence Against Women (DEVAW), UNGA Res 48/104 (December 1993) UN Doc A/RES/48/104.

5 Meyersfeld, *Domestic Violence and International Law*, 30.

6 See discussion in Heyman, "Time Has Come," esp. 195.

7 Quoted in Powell, "Lifting Our Veil of Ignorance," 331. She discusses the explicit claims defending U.S. cultural values made during the Senate hearings on CEDAW.

8 Coker-Appiah and Cusack, "Breaking the Silence."

9 For a fuller discussion of this controversy, see Ampofo, "Collective Activism," 413–16; and Stafford, "Permission for Domestic Violence."

10 Isabella Gyau, "Politics-Ghana: Domestic Violence Bill Focuses on Marital Rape," Interpress Service, July 3, 2003, www.ipsnews.net; and Public Agenda, "Asmah Suggests Alternative to Marital Rape," Africa News Service, June 2, 2003, https://business.highbeam.com.

11 Ampofo, "Collective Activism."

12 Ibid., 414.

13 Mercy Amba Oduyoye, interview by author, Guilford, CT, September 26, 2014. Although Oduyoye lives and works in Ghana, this interview, unlike all others presented in the book, occurred in the United States.

14 Some people defended the bill's impact on families. See Public Agenda, "Domestic Violence Bill Will Help Weed Out Outmoded Customs," Africa News Service, November 11, 2005, http://allafrica.com.

15 Angela Dwamena-Aboagye, executive director, Ark Foundation, interview by author, Accra, Ghana, June 5, 2008.

16 For more information, see the Ark Foundation's Facebook page at www.facebook.com.

17 Dwamena-Aboagye interview.

18 Ibid.

19 Audrey Gadzekpo, senior lecturer at the School of Communication Studies, University of Ghana, interview by author, Accra, Ghana, June 5, 2008.

20 Gadzekpo, "Invigorating Activism," 329.

21 Merry, *Human Rights and Gender Violence*, 12.

22 Ibid., 13.

23 For further feminist and womanist critical discussions of these scriptures, see Weems, *Battered Love*; Yee, *Poor Banished Children of Eve*; and Scholz, *Sacred Witness*.

24 See Schroeder, *Dinah's Lament*, 101–52.

25 Ibid., 121–23.

26 Ampofo, "Collective Activism," 421; Archampong, "Marital Rape."

27 Ampofo, "Collective Activism," 421.

28 For an in-depth discussion of the legal status of marital rape in Ghana, see Archampong and Sampson, "Marital Rape in Ghana"; Stafford, "Permission for Domestic Violence," 63–75; and Adinkrah, "Criminalizing Rape within Marriage."

29 As quoted in Martin, Taft, and Resick, "Review of Marital Rape."

30 Klarfeld, "Striking Disconnect," 1831; and Jackson, "State Contexts and the Criminalization of Marital Rape."

31 Klarfeld, "Striking Disconnect," 1820.

32 Adams, "'I Just Raped My Wife!,'" 61.

33 On marital rape and South Asian immigrant women's experiences, see Mazumdar, "Marital Rape"; and Abraham, "Sexual Abuse in South Asian Immigrant Marriages."

34 Craumer and Schuster, "Legal Recognition of Same-Sex Relationships." These state bans were overturned by the Supreme Court ruling in *Obergefell v. Hodges* on June 26, 2015. www.scotusblog.com.

35 Reportedly, millions of dollars of church member funds were spent to secure their Christian positions in state law. See Sara Gates, "Roman Catholic Church Leadership Poured $2 Million into Fight Against Marriage Equality," *Huffington Post*, November 15, 2012, www.huffingtonpost.com; Kevin Miller, "Question 1 Fueling a Fundraising Fight," *Bangor Daily News*, September 30, 2009, http://bangordailynews.com; and Jesse McKinley and Kirk Johnson, "Mormons Tipped Scale in Ban on Gay Marriage," *New York Times*, November 14, 2008, www.nytimes.com.

36 See my discussion in West, "Civil Rights Rhetoric in Media Coverage."

37 Walter Fauntroy, quoted in West, "Naming the Problem," 186. See also Griffin, *Their Own Receive Them Not*, 95–97.

38 See Keim, *Mistaking Africa*.

39 See Bonsu, "Colonial Images in Global Times"; and Mayer, *Artificial Africas*. See also Hawk, *Africa's Media Image*; and Repo and Yrjölä, "Gender Politics of Celebrity Humanitarianism in Africa."

40 For example, Kevin Macdonald, dir., *The Last King of Scotland* (Fox Searchlight Pictures, 2006); Edward Zwick, dir., *Blood Diamond* (Warner Brothers, 2006); Terry George, dir., *Hotel Rwanda* (United Artists, Lionsgate, 2004); and Billy Ray, dir., *Captain Phillips* (Sony Pictures, 2013).

41 Patience (abbreviation of name requested by interviewee), director of Gender Program, International Needs Network, interview by author, Accra, Ghana, June 9, 2008.

42 Now called International Needs Network Ghana (INNG), http://internationalneedsgh.org. According to their website, INNG's Troxovi project advocates for the emancipation and rehabilitation of young virgin girls and women enslaved in ritual cult slavery. These girls are sent to shrines to serve and worship in atonement for offenses committed by their family members. This practice is mostly found in the Volta Region, some parts of Greater Accra, and the Eastern Region of Ghana. As part of the system, the girls are forced to marry the priests of the shrines. The girls can suffer all forms of abuse, including rape, and are not taught any skills. In one of the most intensive periods of this campaign (2003), INNG reported that they were able to liberate and rehabilitate thirty-five hundred of the estimated five thousand Trokosi girls believed to be incarcerated in shrines. See also http://internationalneedsgh.org.

43 Greene, "Modern 'Trokosi.'"

44 Madison, "Narrative Poetics and Performative Interventions," 393. Also see the extensive discussion of Madison's work with activist women leaders in Ghana including Patience and Angela Dwamena-Aboagye: Madison, *Acts of Activism*. In this tradition, Trokosi refers to the child or girl that the Troxovi deity accepts in the transactional arrangement with the families.

45 "Troxovi/Trokosi Evil or Force of Good," *Accra Daily Mail*, Africa News Service, June 6, 2012, http://allafrica.com. Also see Nicholas, "Legal Immanence."

46 Patience interview.

47 See Madison's discussion of defenders of the shrines and African traditions in "Narrative Poetics and Performative Interventions," esp. 238–39.

48 There are many other forms of slavery in the contemporary United States involving farm and factory labor and elsewhere in the U.S. economy. See Bowe, *Nobodies*; and Bales and Soodalter, *Slave Next Door*.

49 Carter, *Call to Action*, 125.

50 See Blackmon, *Slavery by Another Name*; Alexander, *New Jim Crow*.

51 President Jimmy Carter, *The Colbert Report*, March 25, 2014, http://thecolbertreport.cc.com.

52 Kara, *Sex Trafficking*.

53 Ibid., 179.

54 Based on discussion in Wilson, "Common Religion in American Society."

55 Bellah, "Civil Religion and the American Future"; and Bellah, "Civil Religion in America." See critique of Bellah by Fenn, *Beyond Idols*, 111–13.

56 Senator John Cornyn (R-TX) in his 2004 opening statement at a Senate hearing, quoted in Hua, *Trafficking Women's Human Rights*, 98. Hua gives several other similar examples of the slavery rhetoric of high-level politicians including President George W. Bush. In my discussion here, I am indebted to Hua's cogent analysis of the race and gender assumptions invoked by politicians and activists who address sex trafficking public policy.

57 Ibid., 101.

58 Inspired by the passage of the Arizona law SB 1070, a trend emerged in several states that required local and state law enforcement to question suspects about their immigration status, including Indiana, Alabama, South Carolina, Georgia, and Utah. See Ian Gordon and Tasneem Raja, "164 Anti-Immigration Laws Passed since 2010? A MoJo Analysis," *Mother Jones*, April 2012, www.motherjones.com; Randal C. Archibold, "Arizona Enacts Stringent Law on Immigration," *New York Times*, April 24, 2010, www.nytimes.com; Jimenez, "Immigration, Crime, and Neo-segregation"; Sandoval, "Race and Immigration Law"; and Behrends, "Immigration Reform."

59 See Ditmore, *Kicking Down the Door*; Brennan, "Competing Claims of Victimhood?"; and Women's Commission for Refugee Women and Children, "U.S. Response to Human Trafficking."

60 Ditmore, *Kicking Down the Door*.

61 Ibid., 8.

62 Patience interview.

63 Oduyoye, "Catalyst, Resource, or Roadblock?," 154.

64 For this point about the conceptualization of black women, I am indebted to the discussion of the legacy of slavery and black women's sexuality in Roberts, "Paradox of Silence and Display," 48.

CHAPTER 3. VULNERABILITY

1 On August 7, 2006, President Lula da Silva signed the Lei de Enfrentamento à Violência Doméstica e Familiar contra a Mulher (Federal Law No. 11.340), known as Lei Maria da Penha (Maria da Penha Law), which took effect later that year.

2 Sandra Maria dos Santos, Bahia Secretraria de Promocio da Igualdade, CDDM Conselho Estadual de Defesa dos Direitos da Mulher, interview by author, Salvador, Bahia, Brazil, August 8, 2008.

3 Ibid.

4 See Pasinato, "Maria da Penha Law"; Spieler, "Maria da Penha Case"; and for a feminist critique of it, see Santos, "Da delegacia da mulher."

5 One Salvador, Brazil, website for tourists ("Salvador Central Music and Arts Discovery Matrix," www.salvadorcentral.com) includes a map that identifies the sites of over eleven hundred *terreiros* in Salvador ("Mapeamento dos Terreiros de Salvador," www.terreiros.ceao.ufba.br).

6 Stefania Capone offers a detailed description of Afro-Brazilian Candomblé and how it has been studied by anthropologists, including specific discussions of Casa Branca *terreiro* (*Searching for Africa in Brazil*, 8, 213–14).

7 Harding, *Refuge in Thunder*, 38.

8 Historian E. Bradford Burns explains, "The African origins of Brazil's slaves were extremely varied. They came from Guinea, Dahomey, Nigeria, Ghana, Cape Verde, São Tomé, Angola, the Congo, Mozambique and many other parts of Africa" (*History of Brazil*, 43).

9 Horton, "Slavery in American History"; Sweet, "Teaching the Modern African Diaspora"; and Thornton, "Teaching Africa."

10 According to Anthony W. Marx, the total slave populations remained comparable in both Brazil and the United States, but much lower domestic mortality rates than those in Brazil reduced the need for imports to the United States. Marx, *Making Race and Nation*, 57. See also Eltis and Richardson, "New Assessment of the Transatlantic Slave Trade"; Eltis and Lachance, "Estimates of the Size and Direction of Transatlantic Slave Trade"; Riberio, "Transatlantic Slave Trade to Bahia."

11 As quoted in Brooten, "Introduction," 16.

12 Marx, *Making Race and Nation*, 50, For a discussion on the particular role of the Jesuits, see Burns, *History of Brazil*, 31. See also Raboteau, *Fire in the Bones*.

13 Jordan, *White over Black*, 24.

14 Ibid., 94. See also a discussion of this process of racialization of slavery in Patterson, *Slavery and Social Death*, 7. For a discussion that includes a comparison of

North American and Latin American attitudes and practices, see Davis, *Problem of Slavery.*

15 See, for example, Davis, *Problem of Slavery*, esp. 262–88; Marx, *Making Race and Nation*, esp. 65–76.

16 Howard Winant discusses religion and gender in slavery in the Americas but stresses the unique role of white supremacy, asserting that "when Europe came to America, it brought with it comprehensive, fundamental, permanent slavery: *racial* slavery" (Winant, *World Is a Ghetto*, 55, 60–62).

17 See also McCallum, "Women Out of Place?"; da Silva, Benjamin, and Mendonça, *Benedita da Silva*; and Perry, *Black Women Against the Land Grab.*

18 Caldwell, *Negras in Brazil*, 150. See also Carneiro, *Racismo, Sexismo e Desigualdade em Brasil.*

19 For critical discussions of nonracialism in Brazil, see essays in Hamilton et al., *Beyond Racism*, especially Abdias Do Nascimento and Elisa Larkin Nascimento, "Dance of Deception: A Reading of Race Relations in Brazil" (105–56) and Antonio Sérgio Guimarães, "The Misadventures of Nonracialism in Brazil" (157–85).

20 Caldwell, *Negras in Brazil*, 152.

21 For a discussion of black women leaders in NGOs functioning within a range of communities in Brazil, see dos Santos, "As ONGs de mulheres negras no Brasil."

22 For discussion of the politics of memorializing this history in museums, see Sansone, "Challenges to Digital Patrimonialization."

23 See early comparison by Du Bois, *The Negro*, 76, or the influential study of Degler, *Neither Black nor White*; Skidmore, "Racial Mixture and Affirmative Action."

24 Frazier, "Negro Family in Bahia, Brazil," 469. See also Frazier, "Some Aspects of Race Relations in Brazil," *Negroes in Brazil*, "Comparison of Negro-White Relations," and "Brazil Has No Race Problem," in which Frazier insisted that race prejudice against blacks in Brazil was not legal or institutionalized and therefore afforded blacks in Brazil a sense of dignity and stated, "in Brazil, there is no stigma attached to Negro blood" (123).

25 Frazier was deeply influenced by Gilberto de Mello Freyre's understanding of racial democracy just starting to gain a wider audience at the time of Frazier's study. For a good summary of the views of many other U.S. blacks of Brazil as a racial paradise compared to the United States, see Hellwig, "Racial Paradise or Run-Around?"

26 See, for example, discussion of racial attitudes of Afro-Brazilians and their belief in racial democracy in spite of their experiences of racism by Twine, *Racism in a Racial Democracy*. In their study of youth culture in Bahia, Carol Sansone and Livio Sansone stated, "In Salvador 28% of those who say they like candomblé very much state that in Brazil there is no racial discrimination" (*Blackness without Ethnicity*, 100). For a comprehensive discussion of attitudes about race in Brazil, see Telles, *Race in Another America.*

27 Caldwell, *Negras in Brazil*, 9.

28 Alvarez, "Introduction to the Project," 1.

29 Ibid., 8.
30 See discussion of gender and the significance of female deities and black women leaders in Candomblé in Bahia in pioneering work by feminist anthropologist Landes, *City of Women*, and subsequent discussions of her claims: Cole, "Ruth Landes and the Early Ethnography of Race and Gender"; Healey, "'Sweet Matriarchy of Bahia'"; and Healey, "Os desencontros da tradição."
31 Pinho, *Mama Africa*, 33.
32 Motta, "Enchantment, Identity, Community, and Conversion"; and Selka, "Morality in the Religious Marketplace."
33 Matory, *Black Atlantic Religion*, 161.
34 Harding, *Refuge in Thunder*, xvi. For an argument with Harding about whether or not Candomblé represents a space of resistance, see Parés, *Formation of Candomblé*, 88. For an in-depth study of Afro-Brazilian Candomblé with specific discussions of Casa Branca *terreiro*, see Capone, *Searching for Africa in Brazil*.
35 Dos Santos interview. In Candomblé, Oxum is an orixá associated with fresh waters and fecundity. For a discussion of related traditions of water deities, see Drewal, "Mami Wata."
36 Dos Santos interview.
37 Between 1941 and 1943, Melville Herskovits and E. Franklin Frazier argued about this subject. See Frazier's "Negro Family in Bahia, Brazil"; Herskovits, "Negro in Bahia, Brazil"; and Frazier, "Rejoinder to Melville J. Herskovits." For discussion of this Frazier-Herskovitz debate by a Brazilian scholar, see Sansone, "Estados Unidos e Brasil no Gantois." See also Matory, *Black Atlantic Religion*; Dawson, *In Light of Africa*; Capone, *Searching for Africa in Brazil*; Hall, *Slavery and African Ethnicities*; and Romo, *Brazil's Living Museum*.
38 Pinho, "African-American Roots Tourism in Brazil."
39 Pinho, *Mama Africa*, 4.
40 See also Matory's discussion of the importance of the imagined senses of community produced by Afro-Brazilian Candomblé beliefs and practices in *Black Atlantic Religion*, 71.
41 Bernardino-Costa, "Destabilizing the National Hegemonic Narrative," 33–35, esp. 34.
42 Pinho and Silva, "Domestic Relations in Brazil," esp. 95.
43 Bernardino-Costa, "Destabilizing the National Hegemonic Narrative," 34.
44 Diallo gave an in-depth interview to *Newsweek* explaining that "he pushed her to her knees, her back to the wall. He forced his penis into her mouth, she said and he gripped her head on both sides. . . . The report from the hospital where Diallo was taken later for examination notes that 'she felt something wet and sour come into her mouth and she spit it out on the carpet'" (Christopher Dickey and John Solomon, "The Maid's Tale," *Newsweek*, August 8, 2011, 26. ; and Christopher Dickey, "'DSK Maid' Tells of Her Alleged Rape by Strauss-Kahn: Exclusive," *Newsweek*, July 25, 2011, www.newsweek.com).

45 For example, she was falsely accused of "doing double duty as a prostitute, collecting cash on the side from male guests," when she made her accusation against Strauss-Kahn (Laura Italiano, "Maid Cleaning Up as Hooker," *New York Post*, July 2, 2011, 4), and she was accused of inviting the assault (Tracy Connor, "New Bio: Seductive Glance Set Off Le Perv," *New York Daily News*, December 2, 2011, 22). Diallo admitted that she had previously lied about having been gang raped by two soldiers on her 2003 application for asylum from Guinea. In a largely sympathetic *Newsweek* story, the reporter concludes that this error would have made it difficult for her to win her trial: "Her fictionalized narrative worked to get her a green card and allow her to bring her child to America. But her past misstatements may make it impossible to win a criminal case against DSK based on her testimony" (Dickey, "'DSK Maid'"). See also Jim Dwyer, "With False Tale about Gang Rape, Strauss-Kahn Case Crumbles," *New York Times*, August 23, 2011, www.nytimes.com.

46 Fine, "Troubling Calls for Evidence," 9. See also Lomax, "Strauss-Kahn, Domestic Immigrants and Money, Power, Respect"; Jayawardane, "Maid in Public"; and Brenner, "Beyond Seduction."

47 See Ordóñez, "Circuits of Power."

48 Pinho and Silva, "Domestic Relations in Brazil," 109.

49 Creuza Oliveira, interview by author, Salvador, Bahia, Brazil, February 21, 2008.

50 Pinho and Silva, "Domestic Relations in Brazil," 92.

51 Savas, "Social Inequality at Low-Wage Work."

52 See Frymer, *Black and Blue*, 28–29; Katznelson, Geiger, and Kryder, "Limiting Liberalism"; Nadasen, "Citizenship Rights"; and Nadasen, *Household Workers Unite*.

53 Eileen Boris and Jennifer Klein explained that domestic workers omitted in 1935 did fare better in 1974 in one of the largest expansions of the Fair Labor Standards Act: "Congress finally included private household workers in the wage and hour law"; although workers in nursing homes became eligible for overtime pay, "those doing the same care work in individual homes were left out" (*Caring for America*, 130). President Barack Obama added federal labor protections in Labor Department rules for minimum wage and overtime that are applicable "to workers who do domestic service work, including home health aides, nannies, and housekeepers," which took effect in 2015 (see Cassandra Leveille, "Wage Rules to Affect Health Aides Sent by Agencies," *Women's eNews*, December 23, 2013, http://womensenews.org); and for an example of a global treaty, see Jason DeParle, "For Domestic Workers, Vast Global Labor Pool Challenges Treaty's Aim," *New York Times*, October 9, 2011, A6.

54 See Middaugh, "Lessons from the 'Unorganizable' Domestic Workers Organizing"; Lerner, "Labor of Love"; Goldberg, "Domestic Worker Organizing in the United States"; and for examples of official measures in the city of New York, see Patrick McGeehan, "For Hotel Staff, Panic Buttons and Big Raises," *New York Times*, February 8, 2012, A1.

55 Schwarzenegger with Petre, *Total Recall*, 592, 595. Schwarzenegger wrote about their sexual encounter: "My whole life I never had anything going with anyone who worked for me. . . . Mildred had been working in our household for five years, and all of a sudden we were alone in our guest house. When Mildred gave birth the following August, she named the baby Joseph and listed her husband as the father" (ibid., 592). See a discussion of the treatment of the women in both the Schwarzenegger case and the Strauss-Kahn case in Kate Zernike, "With a Harsh Light on Two Men, Much of the Scrutiny Falls on the Women," *New York Times*, May 19, 2011.

56 See National Domestic Workers Alliance, "California Bill of Rights" (2016), www.domesticworkers.org; and news coverage of the veto in Hannah Dreier, "Domestic Workers Bill of Rights in California, AB889, Vetoed by Gov. Jerry Brown," *Huffington Post*, October 1, 2012, www.huffingtonpost.com. See also Sheila Bapat, "Finally Domestic Workers Get Basic Labor Protections," *Rewire*, September 18, 2013.

57 Selka, "Morality in the Religious Marketplace."

58 Gebara, *Out of the Depths*, 36–37.

59 See "Trabalho Doméstico: Direitos e Deveres, Orientações," Edição revista em conformidade com as alterações, trazidas pela Lei n.º 11.324, de 19 de julho de 2006 (Brasília: Ministério do Trabalho e Emprego, 2007). See also Direitos e deveres, ministério do trabalho, www.mte.gov.br.

60 For examples, see Longazel, "Moral Panic as Racial Degradation Ceremony."

61 See Boris and Nadasen, "Domestic Workers Organize!"

62 For a discussion of the internationalization of black music, see de Souza and Oliveira Montardo, "Music and Musicalities in the Hip Hop Movement." They argue, "Rap enters the musical scene as a result of cultural encounters in the United States. Although it has spread through a wide variety of contexts, rap is a music that thinks locally. In the diaspora, among immigrant populations, in religious contexts, in the peripheries, rap becomes a form of updating practices of protest, which are aestheticized by subjectivities that give form and content to this music" (11). Carol Sansone and Livio Sansone also argue that there has been an "internationalization of black culture" strongly influenced by the United States, "aided by the development of English as a world language and by the growth of the music industry, certain cultural products of English-speaking black culture, like soul music, reggae music, Rasta paraphernalia, and the hip-hop youth style, have reached and influenced over the last two decades large numbers of blacks. . . . The impact on Brazil and especially Bahia has been quite pronounced" (Sansone and Sansone, *Blackness without Ethnicity*, 98). See also Sansone, "Localization of Global Funk."

63 Reports available from Centro de Planificación y Estudios Sociales: Jubb et al., "Access to Justice for Women in Situations of Violence"; and Camacho Z and Hernández, "Women's Police Stations," 204. See also David and Jubb, "Access to Justice for Women."

64 Esqueda and Harrison, "Influence of Gender Role Stereotypes"; Harrison and Esqueda, "Myths and Stereotypes." See also *Private Violence*, dir. Cynthia Hill (HBO Documentary Films, 2014).

65 Iyengar and Sabik, "Dangerous Shortage of Domestic Violence Services."

66 Ibid., w1058. See also Lucea et al., "Factors Influencing Resource Use."

67 Abramovitz, "Feminization of Austerity."

68 Graetz, "Trusting the Courts."

69 Abramovitz, "Feminization of Austerity," 35. See also A. G. Sulzberger, "Facing Cuts, a City Repeals Its Domestic Violence Law," *New York Times*, October 11, 2011, www.nytimes.com.

70 Brad Plumer, "America's Staggering Defense Budget, in Charts," *Washington Post*, January 7, 2013, www.washingtonpost.com.

71 Enloe, *Maneuvers*; Barstow, *War's Dirty Little Secret*, esp. Butler, "Militarized Prostitution"; Moon, *Sex among Allies*; Bierria, "Way We Do Things in America"; and Sturdevant, "Who Benefits?"

72 Enloe, *Maneuvers*.

73 Tânia Mendonça, interview by author, Salvador, Bahia, Brazil, February 22, 2008.

74 See Alvarez, *Engendering Democracy in Brazil*.

75 Sardenberg and Alcantara Costa, "Contemporary Feminisms in Brazil."

76 Ibid., 258.

77 She was referencing 2007–8 cases.

78 In her study of women's police stations in Salvador, Bahia, Sarah Hautzinger described Tânia Mendonça's distinctive leadership as "ambitious about new goals, and enduringly, energizingly outraged about men's violence against women" (*Violence in the City of Women*, 268).

79 As Andrea J. Ritchie summarizes, "To date, public debate, grassroots organizing, litigation strategies, civilian oversight, and legislative initiatives addressing police violence and misconduct have been almost exclusively informed by a paradigm centering on the young Black and Latino heterosexual man as the quintessential subject, victim, or survivor of police brutality," and, I would add, of mass incarceration ("Law Enforcement Violence Against Women of Color," 139). For a discussion of how procriminalization domestic violence policies have contributed to mass incarceration, see Gruber, "Feminist War on Crime," esp. 741.

80 Richie, *Arrested Justice*, 3, 7.

81 Davis, *Battered Black Women and Welfare Reform*.

82 Brito, "Fear as the Commodity Blacks Own Most."

83 Jacinta Marta and Taveres Leiro, interview by author, Salvador, Bahia, Brazil, August 15, 2008.

84 For additional feminist evaluations of this policy, see Hautzinger's criticisms in *Violence in the City of Women*; and Santos, *Women's Police Stations*.

85 Sardenberg et al., "Domestic Violence and Women's Access to Justice in Brazil," 8–9.

86 Ibid.

87 Ibid., 9. Also see Santana, "Roda de Conversa entre mulheres."

88 As quoted in Sardenberg et al., "Domestic Violence and Women's Access to Justice in Brazil," 28.

89 Kim Geiger, "Indiana Senate Candidate Mourdock Calls Rape Pregnancy God's Will," *Los Angeles Times*, October 23, 2012, http://articles.latimes.com.

90 See Santos, "En-gendering the Police"; Nelson, "Constructing and Negotiating Gender"; and Hautzinger, "Criminalizing Male Violence."

CHAPTER 4. PRECIOUS BODIES

1   Débora Cristina da Silva Aranha (Gerente, CATCH—Combatendo o Abuso e o Trafico de Criancas, Winrock International Brasil), interview by author, Salvador, Bahia, Brazil, June 28, 2011.

2   Winrock International (www.winrock.org) is a nonprofit international development organization that focuses on local economic empowerment (particularly of the most disadvantaged) and environmental sustainability at project sites in the United States, Asia, Latin America, and Africa.

3   Winrock International, "Empowerment and Civic Engagement."

4   Aranha, Souza, and de Castro, *Pesquisa*.

5   The U.S. State Department notes that in Brazil "child sex tourism remains a problem, particularly in resort and coastal areas" ("Trafficking in Persons Report," 98).

6   Velasco, "Loan Proposal"; and Institute of Economic Research Foundation and Ministry of Tourism, "Characterization and Sizing of Domestic Tourism."

7   See Williams, *Sex Tourism in Bahia*, 28–29.

8   Pinho, *Mama Africa*.

9   Gary Duffy, "Brazil Markets Its African Culture," *BBC News*, November 29, 2007.

10 Leide Manuela Santos (staff, Winrock International Brasil), interview by author, Salvador, Bahia, Brazil, June 28, 2011.

11 See U.N. General Assembly, Protocol to Prevent, Suppress and Punish Trafficking in Persons, Especially Women and Children, Supplementing the United Nations Convention Against Transnational Organized Crime (2000); U.N. Office on Drugs and Crime (UNODC) in cooperation with the International Labour Organization (ILO), et al., United Nations Global Initiative to Fight Human Trafficking (UN.GIFT) (2009); United Nationals Office on Drugs and Crime (UNODC), "Global Report on Trafficking in Persons" (2013); U.N. Office on Drugs and Crime (UNODC), "The Abuse of a Position of Vulnerability and Other 'Means' within the Definition of Trafficking in Persons" (2013); De Heredia, "People Trafficking."

12 Lima de Pérez, "Criminological Reading of the Concept of Vulnerability," 24.

13 Williams, "Moral Panic," 197.

14 Aranha interview.

15 Ibid.

16 See the U.S.-based "Travel and the Single Male" club referenced in Davidson and Taylor, "Fantasy Islands," 335.

17 Zimmerman, *Other Dreams of Freedom*, 127.

18 Ibid. See also Zimmerman, "From Bush to Obama" and "Christianity and Human Trafficking"; Bernstein and Jakobsen, "Sex, Secularism, and Religious Influence"; Kapur, "'Faith' and the 'Good' Liberal"; Peach, "'Sex Slaves' or 'Sex Workers'?," esp. 119–20.

19 See the example of the Joyce Meyer Ministries video described in "Wedding Bells Ring for Human Trafficking Survivors," in Zimmerman and Campbell, "Christian Ethics and Human Trafficking Activism," esp. 161.

20 Aranha interview.

21 On September 23, 2001, President George W. Bush made a speech stating, "When they struck, they wanted to create an atmosphere of fear. And one of the great goals of this nation's war is to restore public confidence in the airline industry. It's to tell the traveling public: Get on board. Do your business around the country. Fly and enjoy America's great destination spots. Get down to Disney World in Florida. Take your families and enjoy life, the way we want it to be enjoyed" ("At O'Hare, President Says 'Get On Board,'" Office of the Press Secretary, White House Archives, September 27, 2001, https://georgewbush-whitehouse.archives. gov). This response was offered a few weeks after the September 11 terrorist attacks in Pennsylvania, Washington, DC, and New York. See also Robert J. Shiller, "Spend, Spend, It's the American Way," *New York Times*, January 14, 2012; and Gonzalez, *Shopping*.

22 Zimmerman and Campbell, "Christian Ethics and Human Trafficking Activism," esp. 158–59. They cite an assertion by Kevin Bales, a leading expert on modern slavery and human trafficking, championing the goal of helping freed slaves to become consumers (158).

23 Bernstein and Jakobsen, "Sex, Secularism, and Religious Influence," 1033.

24 Ibid.

25 Santos interview.

26 Aranha interview.

27 Santos interview.

28 Ibid.

29 One activist I interviewed described the vulnerability of some black lesbian youth to sexual exploitation by European tourists. Barbara E. Dos R. Alves, LGBTQ rights activist leader, interview by author, Salvador, Bahia, Brazil, June 24, 2011. See also Martinez and Kelle, "Sex Trafficking of LGBT Individuals."

30 Williams, "Moral Panic," 198. See also Williams, *Sex Tourism in Bahia*, 149–56; and Piscitelli, "Transnational Sex Travels." Gebara discusses how the young girls are sexually exploited and their "dream of a prince, a hero who will save them" (Gebara, *Out of the Depths*, 36). For a strong critique of research on sex trafficking in Brazil, see Blanchette and Da Silva, "On Bullshit and the Trafficking of Women."

31 Davidson and Taylor, "Fantasy Islands"; see also Davidson, *Children in the Global Sex Trade*; Davidson, "Sex Tourist"; and Kempadoo, *Sexing the Caribbean*. For further examples of African American heterosexual sex tourists, see Williams, *Sex Tourism in Bahia*, 91–95.

32 Davidson and Taylor, "Fantasy Islands."

33 Williams, *Sex Tourism in Bahia*, 57.

34 Santos interview.

35 Ibid.

36 Ibid.

37 Aranha interview.

38 Ibid.

39 According to the National Coalition of Anti-Violence Programs (NCAVP), a U.S.-based coalition of local member programs and affiliate organizations who work to end violence against and within LGBTQ and HIV-affected communities, "As of August 23rd, 2017, NCAVP has recorded reports of 36 hate violence related homicides of LGBTQ and HIV affected people, the highest number ever recorded by NCAVP. . . . So far in 2017, there has been nearly one homicide a week of an LGBTQ person in the U.S. . . . For the last five years NCAVP has documented a consistent and steadily rising number of reports of homicides of transgender women of color, which continued in 2017. . . . New York and Texas had the most anti-LGBTQ homicides, with 5 victims from each state" (Waters and Yacka-Bible, "Crisis of Hate," 6). In 2016 Grupo Gay da Bahia, which tracks hate-motivated deaths in Brazil through news articles, reported an upsurge in hate crimes, "By its tally, a gay or transgendered person is killed almost every day in this nation of 200 million." These numbers are "only the tip of the iceberg," according to the group's data manager, Eduardo Michels, who adds that "the Brazilian police often omit anti-gay animus when compiling homicide reports" (Andrew Jacobs, "Brazil Is Confronting an Epidemic of Anti-gay Violence," *New York Times*, July 5, 2016, www.nytimes.com). According to Rede Trans, a Brazilian website that tracks attacks on transgender people, "a record 144 transgender people were murdered in 2016, compared with 57 in 2008, when the site began recording cases" (Dom Phillips, "Torture and Killing of Transgender Woman Stun Brazil," *New York Times*, March 8, 2017, www.nytimes.com; Maggie Astor, "Violence Against Transgender People Is on the Rise, Advocates Say," *New York Times*, November 9, 2017, www.nytimes.com).

40 Alves interview.

41 Isabella Santos de Jesus (staff, Centro Humanitário de Apoio à Mulher), interview by author, Salvador, Bahia, Brazil, June 29, 2011.

42 Ibid.

43 Ibid.

44 Ibid.

45 Ibid.

46 Alvarez, "Beyond NGOization?"

47 As previously referenced in chapter one, the U.N. Declaration on the Elimination of Violence Against Women (DEVAW) defines "violence against women" as "any act of gender-based violence that results in, or is likely to result in, physical, sexual or psychological harm or suffering to women, including threats of such

acts, coercion or arbitrary deprivation of liberty, whether occurring in public or in private life" (U.N. General Assembly, Resolution 48/104, Declaration on the Elimination of Violence Against Women, A/RES/48/104 [December 20, 1993], www.un.org).

48 See Bloom, *Against Empathy*.

49 Butler, *Parting Ways*, 8.

CHAPTER 5. HOW MUCH TIME IS NEEDED?

1 Hixson, Hepler, and Kim, "White Population." The 2010 census form asked people to choose one or more of fifteen options that make up five race categories—white, black, American Indian/Alaska Native, Asian, or Native Hawaiian/Other Pacific Islander. Jens Manuel Krogstad and D'Vera Cohn, "U.S. Census Looking at Big Changes in How It Asks about Race and Ethnicity" (Pew Research Center, March 14, 2014), www.pewresearch.org. In a 2015 report issued by the U.S. Department of Commerce of the U.S. Census Bureau, titled "Projections of the Size and Composition of the U.S. Population: 2014 to 2060," the white race category is divided into "White" and "Non-Hispanic White." In the 2010 census "Hispanic origin" was not a race category but a separate question to identify "Hispanic, Latino, or Spanish origin." This 2015 report describes the white population ("non-Hispanic white alone") as 62.2 percent in 2014. By 2044, the white population ("non-Hispanic white alone") is projected to compose less than 50 percent of the nation's total population. Colby and Ortman, "Projections of the Size."

2 According to Robert Ross, "Until 1948, the proportion of whites in the population remained more or less constant, at around 21 percent, but then began to decline sharply, until by 1988 it was only around 14 percent" (*Concise History of South Africa*, 144). Based on the 1996 census, Donald Treiman estimated South Africa's four official racial groups as follows: "'Whites,' 11 percent of the population in 1996; 'Asians,' 3 percent; 'Coloureds,' 9 percent; and 'Blacks,' 77 percent" ("Legacy of Apartheid," 404).

3 Marx, *Making Race and Nation*.

4 Ibid., 179.

5 Ibid., 179.

6 Ibid., 181.

7 For examples of comparative studies of anti-black racism and opposition to it in the United States and South Africa, see Fredrickson, *Black Liberation* and *White Supremacy*; Winant, *World Is a Ghetto*; and Ansell, "Casting a Blind Eye."

8 These are examples of a much wider range of racial and ethnic identities claimed in South Africa, and they include intermingled and evolving experiences of communal identity.

9 Hoel and Shaika, "Sex as Ibadah," 72.

10 Ibid.

11 Biko, *I Write What I Like*, 57.

12 Marx, *Making Race and Nation*, 201.

13 The Constitution of the Republic of South Africa, Act No. 108 of 1996.

14 The Constitution of the Republic of South Africa, 1996, Bill of Rights, Equality, 9. See Jacklyn Cock, "Engendering Gay and Lesbian Rights".

15 Patterson, "New Directions in the Political History of Women"; Boles, "Building Support for the ERA"; and Soule and King, "Stages of the Policy Process."

16 Hoad, Martin, and Reid, *Sex and Politics in South Africa*, 222.

17 University of Kwazulu-Natal, "Ujamaa Centre," http://ujamaa.ukzn.ac.za.

18 In the early twenty-first century it included: Gerald West, senior professor of biblical studies, School of Religion, Philosophy and Classics, University of Kwazulu-Natal; Beverley Haddad, associate professor in theology and development, School of Religion, Philosophy and Classics, University of Kwazulu-Natal; Isabel Apawo Phiri, professor of African theology, School of Religion, Philosophy and Classics University of Kwazulu-Natal; and Sarojini Nadar, associate professor of gender and religion, School of Religion, Philosophy and Classics, University of Kwazulu-Natal.

19 Zapiro (Jonathan Shapiro), *Mail and Guardian* (Johannesburg), September 7, 2008. See also Imke Van Hoorn, "Zapiro in Zuma Cartoon Uproar," *Mail and Guardian* (Johannesburg), September 8, 2008, https://mg.co.za.

20 Charles Molele, Moipone Malefane, and Ndivhuho Mafela, "The World According to Jacob Zuma," *Johannesburg Sunday Times*, April 9, 2006.

21 Jacob Zuma became president of the ANC in 2007 and president of the Republic of South Africa in May 2009.

22 Sigsworth, "'Anyone Can Be a Rapist'"; and Bruce et al., "State of Tyranny."

23 Ramphele, *Laying Ghosts to Rest*, 106–7.

24 Thabo Mokgola, "South Africa: Zuma Calls for Strong Family Values," September 11, 2002, http://allafrica.com. See also Moral Regeneration Movement, "The History of MRM," http://mrm.org.za; Swartz, "Long Walk to Citizenship"; Rauch, "Crime Prevention and Morality."

25 Quoted in Okyere-Manu, "'When the Community I Know Is No Longer a Safe Haven,'" 92.

26 See Motsei, *Kanga and the Kangaroo Court*. See also Ashley Currier's discussion of how, "Zuma had claimed that the garment Khwezi was wearing at the time constituted a request to have sex; not to honor her unspoken request to have sex would have amounted to rape." *OUT in Africa*, 68. See also Hassim, "Democracy's Shadows"; Waetjen and Maré, "Tradition's Desire"; and Robins, "Sexual Politics and the Zuma Rape Trial."

27 Fikile-Ntsikelelo Moya, "Can JZ Rise Again?," April 13, 2006, *Mail and Guardian* (Johannesburg), https://mg.co.za/.

28 Robert P. Jones, "Donald Trump and the Transformation of White Evangelicals," *Time*, November 19, 2016, http://time.com; and Public Religion Research Institute (PRRI), "The High Correlation between Percentage of White Christians, Support for Trump in Key States," November 17, 2016, www.prri.org.

29 David A. Fahrenthold, "New Clips Show Trump Talking about Sex, Rating Women's Bodies, Reminiscing about Infidelity on Howard Stern Show," *Washington Post*, October 14, 2016; Sean Sullivan, "Women Accuse Trump of Forcible Groping and Kissing," *Washington Post*, October 13, 2016; and Rosalind S. Helderman, "The Accusations against Trump and His Campaign's Responses," *Washington Post*, October 18, 2016.

30 See C-SPAN, "Donald Trump Presidential Announcement," June 16, 2015, www.c-span.org.

31 Gregory A. Smith, "Among White Evangelicals, Regular Churchgoers Are the Most Supportive of Trump" (Pew Research Center, April 26, 2017), www.pewresearch.org; Gregory A. Smith, "Most White Evangelicals Approve of Trump Travel Prohibition and Express Concerns about Extremism" (Pew Research Center, February 27, 2017), www.pewresearch.org; and PRRI, "One Nation, Divided, under Trump: Findings from the 2017 American Values Survey," December 5, 2017, www.prri.org.

32 This was similar to Trump's public refusal to admit his error of condemning the black teenagers who were convicted of raping a white woman jogger after they were found to be innocent and exonerated. See Donald J. Trump, "Central Park Five Settlement Is a 'Disgrace,'" *New York Daily News*, June 21, 2014, www.nydailynews.com.

33 In an instance of racialized public discourse in defense of Clinton, black novelist Toni Morrison compared him to a black man, noting how "the President's body, his privacy, his unpoliced sexuality became the focus of the persecution, when he was metaphorically seized and body-searched." Toni Morrison, Janet Malcolm, James Salter, and Lorrie Moore, "The Talk of the Town," *New Yorker* 74, no. 30 (October 5, 1998): 31–39, www.newyorker.com. See McElya, "Trashing the Presidency."

34 Feagin, *White Racial Frame*.

35 Ibid., 98–99.

36 For a discussion of white maleness and presidential politics, see Warren, "Presidential Wounds." In an article written prior to the election of Obama, Warren commented: "Those women and nonwhites who pursue the White House must take on masculine traits and 'white' characteristics, while, paradoxically, a white president can behave 'blacker' than 'actual' black politicians. More than any other elected position in America, then, the presidency reinforces traditional white masculinity while at the same time providing an all-important public stage on which the boundaries of white male identity are repeatedly explored and shifted" (559). The issue of race was examined in the press but only with regard to black support for Clinton. See Brooks and Rada, "Constructing Race in Black and Whiteness," esp. 113.

37 Nadar, "Toward a Feminist Missiological Agenda."

38 Ibid., 92.

39 Sarojini Nadar, interview by author, Pietermaritzburg, South Africa, September 12, 2008.

40 Ibid.

41 Ibid.

42 Also see Radhakrishnan, "'Time to Show Our True Colors.'"

43 Khwezi is the pseudonym given to Zuma's accuser by the media.

44 Nadar, "Toward a Feminist Missiological Agenda," 91.

45 Zarina Majiet, manager, Simelela Centre, Cape Town, interview by author, Cape Town, South Africa, February 13, 2012.

46 Wadud, "Qur'an, Gender and Interpretive Possibilities," 317.

47 Wadud, "American by Force, Muslim by Choice," 703.

48 Majiet interview.

49 See Slessarev-Jamir, Prophetic Activism, 88. See also Peters, Solidarity Ethics.

50 See Medina, Epistemology of Resistance, 22.

51 Majiet interview.

52 See Marx, Lessons of Struggle. Hoel and Shaika note that "during the anti-apartheid struggle, Muslim activists also mobilized around gender justice as a central category of Islamic reform" ("Sex as Ibadah," 72).

53 Majiet interview.

54 Ibid.

55 See my discussion in West, "Gendered Legacies of Martin Luther King Jr.'s Leadership."

56 Simmons, "War Against Black Women," 174.

57 Ibid., 172.

58 Smith, "Heteropatriarchy and the Three Pillars of White Supremacy," 69.

59 Mason, Spectacle of Violence, 39.

60 Corrigan, Up Against a Wall, 56.

61 See Matthews, Confronting Rape, 127–28; Whalley, "Rape Crises in Rape Cultures," 55.

62 Hamilton et al., Beyond Racism, 31–32.

63 See Adhikari, Anatomy of a South African Genocide.

64 McGuire, At the Dark End of the Street, 70–71.

65 Ibid., 43.

66 Ibid., 75.

67 Robinson, Montgomery Bus Boycott, 43.

68 Black children were given brand-new dolls, some with white complexions and others with very dark brown complexions. The children consistently pointed to the white dolls as pretty and clean and identified the black dolls as ugly and dirty. See Clark and Clark, "Racial Identification and Preference in Negro Children"; Jordan and Hernandez-Reif, "Reexamination of Young Children's Racial Attitudes"; Bagby-Young, "Mirror, Mirror on the Dresser"; Dark Girls, dir. Bill Duke and D. Channsin Berry (2011, Duke Media and Urban Winter Entertainment). See also Banks et al., "Intersection of Colorism and Racial Identity."

69 JeffriAnne Wilder, *Color Stories.*

70 See my discussion of how racism-inspired black inferiority complexes can reinforce self-blame in intimate violence against black women in West, *Wounds of the Spirit*, 73.

71 Townes, *In a Blaze of Glory*, 119.

72 Majiet interview.

73 Kuumba, *Gender and Social Movements*, 102, and Kuumba, "'You've Struck a Rock.'"

74 Kuumba, "'You've Struck a Rock,'" 518.

75 Majiet interview.

76 Ibid.

CHAPTER 6. DEFIANT SPIRITUALITY

1 "About," *Free Gender*, accessed April 8, 2017, https://freegender.wordpress.com.

2 I deliberately reference *LGBTQI* in this setting (rather than *LGBTQ*) to reflect the language of several of the activist leaders I met in South Africa.

3 Waters, Jindasurat, and Wolfe, "Lesbian, Gay, Bisexual, Transgender, Queer, and HIV Affected Hate Violence in 2015."

4 Butler, *Frames of War*, 14.

5 Mkhize et al., *Country We Want to Live In*; Human Rights Watch, "We'll Show You're a Woman."

6 Funeka Soldaat, interview by author, Cape Town, South Africa, October 22, 2015.

7 Matebeni, "Deconstructing Violence towards Black Lesbians."

8 Ford, "Standing on *This* Bridge."

9 Ford, "Standing on *This* Bridge," 307.

10 Ibid., 307–8.

11 Ibid., 308.

12 Ibid., 305.

13 Ibid., 311, author's capitalization.

14 Meyer, "Interpreting and Experiencing Anti-queer Violence," 273.

15 Ibid., 274.

16 Human Rights Watch, "We'll Show You're a Woman."

17 Zebo is a black lesbian South African who lived in a former black township in Gauteng, South Africa, and was interviewed in the Human Rights Watch report about the daily rape threats and taunts she endured.

18 Human Rights Watch, "We'll Show You're a Woman," 29.

19 Mkhize et al., *Country We Want to Live In*, 13.

20 Butler, *Frames of War*, 14–15.

21 Bates, "Religious Despite Religion"; Unity Church Fellowship Church Movement, http://ufcmlife.org/.

22 Isoke, *Urban Black Women*, 97.

23 Ibid., 109.

24 As quoted in ibid., 108.

25 LIT donated the physical space of the church's Social Justice Center, which provides drop-in services such as showers, needle exchange, and condoms, addressing the needs of the poor and homeless in the city, especially persons with HIV and AIDS, transpersons, and sex workers.

26 Isoke, *Urban Black Women*, 120.

27 Brian Pellot, "South Africa's Safe House Offers Gay Community Refuge and Hope," *Religion News Service*, January 6, 2017, http://religionnews.com.

28 Bulelwa Panda, interview by author, Cape Town, South Africa, October 22, 2015.

29 Ibid.

30 Ibid.

31 Ibid.

32 Ibid.

33 Metropolitan Christian Churches (MCC) is an international organization founded in the United States in 1968 that now has over forty thousand members, including churches in South Africa. As its website explains, it is the "world's first church group with a primary, positive ministry to gays, lesbians, bisexual, and transgender persons." http://mcchurch.org.

34 Reid, *Above the Skyline*, 195.

35 As quoted in West, *Disruptive Christian Ethics*, 166.

36 Ibid., 167.

37 Young, *Black Queer Ethics*, 111.

38 "Don't Muzzle Our Pastors" (a message from the High Impact Leadership Coalition, paid for by High Impact Leadership Coalition, Bishop Harry R. Jackson, founder and chairman), *USA Today*, July 13, 2007.

39 Ibid. See also Bill Berkowitz, "Conservative Black Preacher Leads Crusade Against Hate Crimes Legislation," *Religion Dispatches*, June 18, 2009, http://religiondispatches.org.

40 They claim that they do not support violence but do not believe that violence against lesbians and gay men can constitute a "real" hate crime. Bishop Jackson, one of the leaders of the opposition to the hate crimes bill, stated that the number of incidents involving gays does not "rise to the level of murder and lynchings that happened to black people." Oren Dorell, "Ministers Say Hate Crimes Could Muzzle Them," *USA Today*, June 15, 2007, https://usatoday30.usatoday.com.

41 Soldaat interview.

42 Ibid.

43 Ibid.

44 Matebeni and Pereira, "Preface." They explain: "We deliberately use 'k' in Afrikan to emphasise the need to *reclaim* our existence and being in this continent" (7).

45 Ibid., 7.

46 Townes, "Ethics as an Art," 39–40.

47 Elizabeth Hoorn Petersen, interview by author, Cape Town, South Africa, February 10, 2012.

48 Ibid.

49 Ibid.

50 Ibid.

51 Mason, *The Spectacle of Violence.*

52 Ibid., 124.

53 Ibid., 134.

54 Mason argues that Foucauldian and feminist theories agree that "violence is the outcome or the result of the struggle between power and resistance" (ibid., 131).

55 Petersen interview.

CONCLUSION

1 Lara and Facio, "Introduction," 3.

2 Ibid.

3 Ibid., 7.

4 Young, *Black Queer Ethics.*

5 For example, see Megan Twohey and Michael Barbaro, "Two Women Say Donald Trump Touched Them Inappropriately," *New York Times*, October 12, 2016, www.nytimes.com; Michael Tackett, "Trump's Combative Denials Again Draw Him into the Sexual Harassment Debate," *New York Times*, December 12, 2017, www.nytimes.com.

6 Matebeni, "How NOT to Write about Queer South Africa," 61.

BIBLIOGRAPHY

Abraham, Margaret. "Sexual Abuse in South Asian Immigrant Marriages." *Violence Against Women* 5, no. 6 (June 1999): 591–618.

Abramovitz, Mimi. "The Feminization of Austerity." *New Labor Forum* 21, no. 1 (Winter 2012): 30–39.

Adams, Carol J. "'I Just Raped My Wife! What Are You Going to Do about It, Pastor?' The Church and Sexual Violence." In *Transforming Rape Culture*, edited by Emilie Buchwald, Pamela Fletcher, and Martha Roth. Minneapolis: Milkweed, 1993.

Adhikari, Mohamed. *Anatomy of a South African Genocide: The Extermination of the Cape San Peoples*. Athens: Ohio University Press, 2011.

Adinkrah, Mensah. "Criminalizing Rape within Marriage: Perspectives of Ghanaian University Students." *International Journal of Offender Therapy and Comparative Criminology* 55, no. 6 (September 2011): 982–1010.

Alexander, Michelle. *The New Jim Crow: Mass Incarceration in the Age of Colorblindness*. Jackson, TN: New Press, 2012.

Alexander, M. Jacqui. *Pedagogies of Crossing: Meditations on Feminism, Sexual Politics, Memory, and the Sacred*. Durham, NC: Duke University Press, 2006.

Ali, Kecia. *Marriage and Slavery in Early Islam*. Cambridge, MA: Harvard University Press, 2010.

———. "Slavery and Sexual Ethics in Islam." In Brooten and Hazelton, *Beyond Slavery*.

Alvarez, Sonia E. "Beyond NGOization? Reflections from Latin America." *Development* 52, no. 2 (2009): 175–84.

———. *Engendering Democracy in Brazil: Women's Movements in Transition Politics*. Princeton, NJ: Princeton University Press, 1990.

———. "Introduction to the Project and the Volume/Enacting a Translocal Feminist Politics of Translation." In Alvarez et al., *Translocalities/Translocalidades*.

Alvarez, Sonia E., Claudia de Lima Costa, Verónica Feliu, Rebecca Hester, Norma Klahn, and Millie Thayer, eds. *Translocalities/Translocalidades: Feminist Politics of Translation in the Latin/a Américas*. Durham, NC: Duke University Press, 2014.

Amenga-Etego, Rose Mary. *Mending The Broken Pieces: Indigenous Religion and Sustainable Rural Development in Northern Ghana*. Trenton, NJ: Africa World Press, 2011.

———. "Violence Against Women in Contemporary Ghanaian Society." *Theology and Sexuality* 13, no. 1 (2006): 23–46.

Ammah-Koney, Rabiatu. "Violence Against Women in Ghanaian Muslim Communities." In Cusack and Manuh, *Architecture of Violence Against Women in Ghana*.

Amnesty International. *Maze of Injustice: The Failure to Protect Indigenous Women from Violence in the USA*. New York: Amnesty International USA, 2007. www. amnestyusa.org.

Ampofo, Akosua Adomako. "Collective Activism: The Domestic Violence Bill Becoming Law in Ghana." *African and Asian Studies* 7, no. 4 (September 2008): 395–421.

Ansell, Amy E. "Casting a Blind Eye: The Ironic Consequences of Color-Blindness in South Africa and the United States." *Critical Sociology* 32, nos. 2–3 (2006): 333–56.

Anzaldúa, Gloria. *Borderlands/La Frontera: The New Mestiza*. San Francisco: Aunt Lute, 1999.

Aranha, Débora, Frederico Fernandes de Souza, and Katia Martins de Castro. *Pesquisa: Tráfico de Crianças e Adolescentes Para Fins de Exploração Sexual No Estado Da Bahia Salvador, Bahia: Outubro, 2008*. Salvador, Bahia: Winrock International Brasil, 2008.

Archampong, Elizabeth A. "Marital Rape—A Women's Equality Issue in Ghana." Kumasi, Ghana: KNUST, 2010. www.theequalityeffect.org.

Archampong, Elizabeth, and Fiona Sampson. "Marital Rape in Ghana: Legal Options for Achieving State Accountability." *Canadian Journal of Women and the Law / Revue Femme et Droit* 22, no. 2 (December 2010): 505–34.

Asante, Molefi Kete. "Henry Louis Gates Is Wrong about African Involvement in the Slave Trade." *Asante.net*, May 6, 2010. www.asante.net.

Austin, Alan D. *African Muslims in Antebellum America: Transatlantic Stories and Spiritual Struggles*. New York: Routledge, 1997.

Ayyub, Ruksana. "The Many Faces of Domestic Violence in the South Asian American Muslim Community." In *Body Evidence: Intimate Violence Against South Asian Women in America*, edited by Shamita Dasgupta. New Brunswick, NJ: Rutgers University Press, 2007.

Azaransky, Sarah. *The Dream Is Freedom: Pauli Murray and American Democratic Faith*. New York: Oxford University Press, 2011.

———. *This Worldwide Struggle: Religion and the International Roots of the Civil Rights Movement*. New York: Oxford University Press, 2017.

Bagby-Young, Valencia. "Mirror, Mirror on the Dresser, Why Are Black Dolls Still Viewed as Lesser? When Black Children Turn a Blind Face to Their Own Race: The Doll Study Revisited." PhD dissertation, American International College, 2008.

Bales, Kevin, and Ron Soodalter. *The Slave Next Door: Human Trafficking and Slavery in America Today*. Berkeley: University of California Press, 2009.

Banks, Kira Hudson, Richard D. Harvey, Tanisha Thelemaque, and Onyinyechi V. Anukem. "The Intersection of Colorism and Racial Identity and the Impact on Mental Health." In *Meaning-Making, Internalized Racism, and African American Identity*, edited by Jas. M. Sullivan and William E Cross. Albany: State University of New York Press, 2016.

Bapat, Sheila. "Finally, Domestic Workers Get Basic Labor Protections." *Rewire*, September 18, 2013. https://rewire.news.

Barstow, Anne Llewellyn, ed. *War's Dirty Little Secret: Rape, Prostitution, and Other Crimes Against Women*. Cleveland: Pilgrim, 2001.

Bates, Aryana F. "Religious Despite Religion: Lesbian Agency, Identity, and Spirituality at Liberation in Truth, Unity Fellowship Church, Newark." PhD dissertation, Drew University, 2001.

Bay, Mia. "Love, Sex, Slavery, and Sally Hemings." In Brooten and Hazelton, *Beyond Slavery*.

Behar, Ruth. *The Vulnerable Observer: Anthropology That Breaks Your Heart*. Boston: Beacon, 1996.

Behrends, Sonny. "Immigration Reform: A Reflection on Arizona Bill 1070 and Beyond." *Regent Journal of International Law* 9, no. 1 (2012): 75–103.

Bellah, Robert N. "Civil Religion and the American Future." *Religious Education* 71, no. 3 (May–June 1976): 235–43.

———. "Civil Religion in America." *Daedalus* 96, no. 1 (December 1967): 1–21.

Bent-Goodley, Tricia B. "Domestic Violence Fatality Reviews and the African American Community." *Homicide Studies* 17, no. 4 (2013): 375–90.

Bent-Goodley, Tricia B., and Dawnovise N. Fowler. "Spiritual and Religious Abuse Expanding What Is Known about Domestic Violence." *Affilia* 21, no. 3 (2006): 282–95.

Bent-Goodley, Tricia B., Noelle St. Vil, and Paulette Hubbert. "A Spirit Unbroken: The Black Church's Evolving Response to Domestic Violence." *Social Work and Christianity* 39, no. 1 (2012): 52–65.

Berger, Ronald J., and Richard Quinney, eds., *Storytelling Sociology: Narrative as Social Inquiry*. Boulder, CO: Lynne Rienner, 2005.

Berman, Rachel C. "A Critical Reflection on the Use of Translators/Interpreters in a Qualitative Cross-Language Research Project." *International Journal of Qualitative Research Methods* 10, no. 1 (2010): 178–90.

Bernardino-Costa, Joaze. "Destabilizing the National Hegemonic Narrative: The Decolonized Thought of Brazil's Domestic Workers' Unions." *Latin American Perspectives* 38, no. 5 (2011): 33–45.

Berns, Nancy. "Domestic Violence and Victim Empowerment Folklore in Popular Culture." In The Media and Cultural Attitudes, Vol. 4, Stark and Buzawa, *Violence Against Women in Families and Relationships*, edited by Evan Stark and Eve S. Buzawa. Santa Barbara, CA: Praeger/ABC-CLIO, 2009.

———. *Framing the Victim: Domestic Violence, Media, and Social Problems*. Piscataway, NJ: Transaction, 2004.

Bernstein, Elizabeth, and Janet R. Jakobsen. "Sex, Secularism, and Religious Influence in U.S. Politics." *Third World Quarterly* 31 (2010): 1023–39.

Bhandari, Shreya, Linda F. C. Bullock, Jeanita W. Richardson, Pamela Kimeto, Jacquelyn C. Campbell, and Phyllis W. Sharps. "Comparison of Abuse Experiences of Rural and Urban African American Women during Perinatal Period." *Journal of Interpersonal Violence* 30, no. 12 (2015): 2087–2108.

Bhuyan, Rupaleem, Woochan Shim, and Kavya Velagapudi. "Domestic Violence Advocacy with Immigrants and Refugees." In *Domestic Violence: Intersectionality and*

Culturally Competent Practice, edited by Lettie L. Lockhart and Fran S. Danis. New York: Columbia University Press, 2010.

Bierria, Alisa. "The Way We Do Things in America: Rape Culture and the American Military." In Ochoa and Ige, *Shout Out*.

Biko, Steve. *I Write What I Like*. Johannesburg: Heinemann, 1978.

Black, Michele C., Kathleen C. Basile, Matthew J. Breiding, Sharon G. Smith, Mikel L. Walters, Melissa T. Merrick, Jieru Chen, and Mark R. Stevens. "National Intimate Partner and Sexual Violence Survey (NIPSVS): 2010 Summary Report." Atlanta: Centers for Disease Control and Prevention, National Center for Injury Prevention and Control, 2011. www.cdc.gov.

Blackmon, Douglas A. *Slavery by Another Name: The Re-enslavement of Black Americans from the Civil War to World War II*. New York: Anchor, 2009.

Blanchette, Thaddeus Gregory, and Ana Paula Da Silva. "On Bullshit and the Trafficking of Women: Moral Entrepreneurs and the Invention of Trafficking of Persons in Brazil." *Dialectical Anthropology* 36 (2012): 107–25.

Block, Sharon. *Rape and Sexual Power in Early America*. Chapel Hill: University of North Carolina Press, 2006.

Bloom, Paul. *Against Empathy: The Case for Rational Compassion*. New York: Ecco, 2016.

Boles, Janet K. "Building Support for the ERA: A Case of 'Too Much, Too Late.'" *PS: Political Science & Politics* 15, no. 4 (1982): 572–77.

Bonsu, Samuel K. "Colonial Images in Global Times: Consumer Interpretations of Africa and Africans in Advertising." *Consumption Markets and Culture* 12, no. 1 (February 2009): 1–25.

Boris, Eileen, and Jennifer Klein. *Caring for America: Home Health Workers in the Shadow of the Welfare State*. New York: Oxford University Press, 2012.

Boris, Eileen, and Premilla Nadasen. "Domestic Workers Organize!" *WorkingUSA* 11, no. 4 (2008): 413–37.

Botham, Fay. "The 'Purity of the White Woman, Not the Purity of the Negro Woman': The Contemporary Legacies of Historical Laws Against Interracial Marriage." In Brooten and Hazelton, *Beyond Slavery*.

Bowe, John. *Nobodies: Modern American Slave Labor and the Dark Side of the New Global Economy*. New York: Random House, 2007.

Brade, Kesslyn A., and Tricia B. Bent-Goodley. "A Refuge for My Soul: Examining African American Clergy's Perceptions Related to Domestic Violence Awareness and Engagement in Faith Community Initiatives." *Social Work and Christianity* 36, no. 4 (2009): 430–48.

Breiding, Matthew J., Sharon G. Smith, and Kathleen C. Basile. "Prevalence and Characteristics of Sexual Violence, Stalking, and Intimate Partner Violence Victimization." Atlanta: Centers for Disease Control and Prevention, 2011.

Brennan, Denise. "Competing Claims of Victimhood? Foreign and Domestic Victims of Trafficking in the United States." *Sexuality Research and Social Policy* 5, no. 4 (December 2008): 45–61.

Brenner, Hannah. "Beyond Seduction: Lessons Learned about Rape, Politics, and Power from Dominique Strauss-Kahn and Moshe Katsav." *Michigan Journal of Gender and Law* 20 (2013): 225–90.

Brito, Dyane. "Fear as the Commodity Blacks Own Most: An Essay on Police Violence Against Black People and the Poor in Salvador, Bahia, Brazil." In *Race and Democracy in the Americas*, edited by Georgia A. Persons. New Brunswick, NJ: Transaction, 2003.

Britto, Sarah, Tycy Hughes, Kurt Saltzman, and Colin Stroh. "Does 'Special' Mean Young, White and Female? Deconstructing the Meaning of 'Special' in *Law and Order: Special Victims Unit*." *Journal of Criminal Justice and Popular Culture* 14, no. 1 (2007): 39–57.

Brooks, Dwight E., and James A. Rada. "Constructing Race in Black and Whiteness: Media Coverage of Public Support for President Clinton." *Journalism and Communication Monographs* 4, no. 3 (September 2002): 51–58.

Brooten, Bernadette J. "Introduction." In Brooten and Hazelton, *Beyond Slavery*.

Brooten, Bernadette J., and Jacqueline L. Hazelton, eds. *Beyond Slavery: Overcoming Its Religious and Sexual Legacies*. New York: Palgrave Macmillan, 2010.

Brown, Joanne Carlson, and Carole R. Bohn, eds. *Christianity, Patriarchy and Abuse: A Feminist Critique*. New York: Pilgrim, 1989.

Bruce, David, Romi Fuller, Collet Ngwane, and Angelica Pino. "A State of Tyranny: The Prevalence, Nature, and Causes of Sexual Violence in South Africa." Johannesburg: Centre for the Study of Violence and Reconciliation and Secretariat for Safety and Security, November 2008. www.csvr.org.za.

Burns, E. Bradford. *A History of Brazil*. New York: Columbia University Press, 1993.

Bushman, Brad J., Patrick E. Jamieson, Ilana Weitz, and Daniel Romer. "Gun Violence Trends in Movies." *Pediatrics* 132, no. 6 (2013): 1014–18.

Bushman, Brad J., Daniel Romer, and Patrick E. Jamieson. "Distinguishing Hypotheses from Hyperbole in Studies of Media Violence: A Comment on Markey et al. 2015." *Human Communication Research* 41, no. 2 (2015): 174–83.

Butler, Jennifer. "Militarized Prostitution: The Untold Story (USA)." In Barstow, *War's Dirty Little Secret*.

Butler, Judith. *Frames of War: When Is Life Grievable?* New York: Verso Books, 2016.

———. *Parting Ways: Jewishness and the Critique of Zionism*. New York: Columbia University Press, 2013.

Butler, Lola. "African American Lesbian Women Experiencing Partner Abuse." In *A Professional's Guide to Understanding Gay and Lesbian Domestic Violence: Understanding Practice Interventions*, edited by Joan C. McClennen and John Joseph Gunther. Lewiston, NY: Edwin Mellen, 1999.

Caldwell, Kia Lilly. *Negras in Brazil: Re-envisioning Black Women, Citizenship, and the Politics of Identity*. New Brunswick, NJ: Rutgers University Press, 2007.

Camacho Z, Gloria, and Kattya Hernández. "Women's Police Stations: A Path towards Justice? Case Study: Cuenca, Ecuador." Quito: CEPLAES, 2010. www.ceplaes.org.ec.

Campbell, Jacquelyn. *Assessing Dangerousness: Violence by Batterers and Child Abusers*. New York: Springer, 2007.

Cannon, Claire, and Frederick Buttell. "Illusion of Inclusion: The Failure of the Gender Paradigm to Account for Intimate Partner Violence in LGBT Relationships." *Partner Abuse* 6, no. 1 (2015): 65–77.

Capone, Stefania. *Searching for Africa in Brazil: Power and Tradition in Candomblé*. Durham, NC: Duke University Press, 2010.

Capriccioso, Rob. "House VAWA Bill to Strip Native American Protections." *Indian Country*, May 8, 2012. http://indiancountrytodaymedianetwork.com.

Carneiro, Sueli. *Racismo, Sexismo e Desigualdade em Brasil: Consciencia Em Debate*. São Paulo: Selo Negro, 2011.

Carpenter, Les. "A Father's Shadow." *Washington Post Magazine*, May 25, 2008, 16–21, 29–33.

Carter, J. Cameron. *Race: A Theological Account*. New York: Oxford University Press, 2008.

Carter, Jimmy. *A Call to Action: Women, Religion, Violence, and Power*. New York: Simon & Schuster, 2014.

Catalano, Shannan. "Intimate Partner Violence, 1993–2010." Washington, DC: U.S. Department of Justice, November 2012. www.bjs.gov.

Catalano, Shannan, Erica Smith, Howard Snyder, and Michael Rand. "Female Victims of Violence." Washington, DC: U.S. Department of Justice, Office of Justice Programs, October 23, 2009. www.bjs.gov.

Centro de Planificación y Estudios Sociales. "Nadine Jubb, Gloria Camacho, and Almachiara D'Angelo, Access to Justice for Women in Situations of Violence: A Comparative Study of Women's Police Stations in Latin America (NGO)." Quito: CEPLAES, 2008. www.ceplaes.org.ec.

Chitando, Ezra. "Phenomenology of Religion and the Study of African Traditional Religions." *Method and Theory in the Study of Religion* (2005) 17, no. 4: 299–316.

Clark, Kenneth B., and Mamie P. Clark. "Racial Identification and Preference in Negro Children." In *Readings in Social Psychology*, 3rd ed., edited by Eleanor Maccoby, Theodore Newcomb, and Eugene Hartley. New York: Holt, Rinehart & Winston, 1958.

Clarke, Peter B. *West Africa and Islam: A Study of Religious Development from the 8th to the 20th Century*. London: Edward Arnold, 1982.

Cock, Jacklyn. "Engendering gay and lesbian rights: The equality clause in the South African Constitution." *Women's Studies International Forum*, vol. 26, no. 1 (2003): 35-45.

Coker-Appiah, Dorcas, and Kathy Cusack. "Breaking the Silence and Challenging the Myths of Violence Against Women in Ghana: A Report of a National Study on Violence." Accra, Ghana: Gender Studies and Human Rights Documentation Centre, 1999.

Colby, Sandra L., and Jennifer M. Ortman. "Projections of the Size and Composition of the U.S. Population: 2014 to 2060." Washington, DC: U.S. Census Bureau, 2015.

Cole, Johnnetta B., and Beverly Guy-Sheftall. *Gender Talk: The Struggle for Women's Equality in African American Communities*. New York: One World/Ballantine, 2003.

Cole, Sally Cooper. "Ruth Landes and the Early Ethnography of Race and Gender." In *Women Writing Culture*, edited by Ruth Behar and Deborah A. Gordon. Berkeley: University of California Press, 1995.

Collins, Patricia Hill. *Black Sexual Politics: African Americans, Gender, and the New Racism*. New York: Routledge, 2004.

Consalvo, Mia. "Hegemony, Domestic Violence, and Cops: A Critique of Concordance." *Journal of Popular Film and Television* 26 (1998): 62–70.

Cooper-White, Pam. *The Cry of Tamar: Violence Against Women and the Church's Response*. 2nd ed. Minneapolis: Fortress, 2012.

Copeland, M. Shawn. *Enfleshing Freedom: Body, Race, and Being*. Minneapolis: Fortress, 2010.

Corrigan, Rose. *Up Against a Wall: Rape Reform and the Failure of Success*. New York: New York University Press, 2013.

Craumer, Davia, and Kirsten Schuster, eds. "Legal Recognition of Same-Sex Relationships." *Georgetown Journal of Gender and the Law* 14, no. 2 (2013): 517–51.

Craven, Christa, and Dána-Ain Davis, eds. *Feminist Activist Ethnography: Counterpoints to Neoliberalism in North America*. Lanham, MD: Lexington, 2013.

Crenshaw, Kimberlé W., Priscilla Ocen, and Jyoti Nanda. *Black Girls Matter: Pushed Out, Overpoliced and Underprotected*. New York: African American Policy Forum, 2015. https://static1.squarespace.com.

Crenshaw, Kimberlé W., Andrea J. Ritchie, Rachel Anspach, Rachel Gilmer, and Luke Harris. *Say Her Name: Resisting Police Brutality Against Black Women*. New York: African American Policy Forum, 2015. http://static1.squarespace.com.

Crumpton, Stephanie M. *A Womanist Pastoral Theology Against Intimate and Cultural Violence*. New York: Palgrave Macmillan, 2014.

Currier, Ashley. *Out in Africa: LGBT Organizing in Namibia and South Africa*. Minneapolis: University of Minnesota Press, 2012.

Cusack, Kathy, and Takyiwaa Manuh, eds. *The Architecture of Violence Against Women in Ghana*. Accra, Ghana: Gender Studies and Human Rights Documentation Centre, 2009.

da Silva, Benedita, Medea Benjamin, and Maisa Mendonça. *Benedita da Silva: An Afro-Brazilian Woman's Story of Politics and Love*. Oakland, CA: Institute for Food and Development Policy, 1997.

David, Stephanie, and Nadine Jubb. "Access to Justice for Women Survivors of Violence in Latin America: Concepts, Paths, and Outcomes." *CERLAC* [Centre for Research on Latin America and the Caribbean] *Bulletin* 7, no. 1 (2009): 1–2. http://cerlac.info.yorku.ca.

Davidson, Julia O'Connell. *Children in the Global Sex Trade*. Cambridge, MA: Polity, 2005.

———. "The Sex Tourist, the Expatriate, His Ex-Wife and Her 'Other': The Politics of Loss, Difference and Desire." *Sexualities* 4 (2001): 5–24.

Davidson, Julia O'Connell, and Jacqueline Sanchez Taylor. "Fantasy Islands: Exploring the Demand for Sex Tourism." In *Sexualities: Identities, Behaviors, and Society*, edited by Michael S. Kimmel and Rebecca F. Plante. New York: Oxford University Press, 2004.

Davis, Angela Y. "Rape, Racism, and the Capitalist Setting." *Black Scholar* 9, no. 7 (April 1978): 24–30.

Davis, Dána-Ain. *Battered Black Women and Welfare Reform: Between a Rock and a Hard Place*. Albany: State University of New York Press, 2006.

Davis, David Brion. *The Problem of Slavery in Western Culture*. Ithaca, NY: Cornell University Press, 1966.

Davis, Sharon Ellis. *Battered African American Women: A Study of Gender Entrapment*. Lewiston, NY: Edwin Mellen, 2014.

Dawson, Allan Charles. *In Light of Africa: Globalizing Blackness in Northeast Brazil*. Toronto: University of Toronto Press, 2014.

Deer, Sarah. *The Beginning and End of Rape: Confronting Sexual Violence in Native America*. Minneapolis: University of Minnesota Press, 2015.

Degler, Carl N. *Neither Black nor White: Slavery and Race Relations in Brazil and the United States*. Madison: University of Wisconsin Press, 1971.

De Heredia, Marta Iniguez. "People Trafficking: Conceptual Issues with the United Nations Trafficking Protocol 2000." *Human Rights Review* 9, no. 3 (2008): 299–316.

Della Giustina, Jo-Ann. *Why Women Are Beaten and Killed: Sociological Predictors of Femicide*. Lewiston, NY: Edwin Mellen, 2010.

De Souza, Angela Maria, and Deise Lucy Oliveira Montardo. "Music and Musicalities in the Hip Hop Movement: Gospel Rap." *Vibrant: Virtual Brazilian Anthropology* 8, no. 1 (2011): 7–38.

Dewey, Susan, and Patty Kelly. "Moral Panic: Sex Tourism, Trafficking, and the Limits of Transnational Mobility in Bahia." In Dewey and Kelly, *Policing Pleasure*.

———, eds. *Policing Pleasure: Sex Work, Policy, and the State in Global Perspective*. New York: New York University Press, 2011.

Ditmore, Melissa. *Kicking Down the Door: The Use of Raids to Fight Trafficking in Persons*. New York: Sex Workers Project at the Urban Justice Center, 2009.

Dorothy M. "When the Hand That Slaps Is Female: Fighting Addiction." In *African Americans Doing Feminism: Putting Theory into Everyday Practice*, edited by Aaronette M. White. Albany: State University of New York Press, 2010.

dos Santos, Sônia Beatriz. "As ONGs de mulheres negras no Brasil." *Sociedade e cultura* 12, no. 2 (2010): 275–88.

Drewal, Henry John. "Mami Wata: Arts for Water Spirits in Africa and Its Diasporas." *African Arts* 41, no. 2 (2008): 60–83.

Du Bois, W. E. B. *The Negro*. 1915. Reprint, New York: Oxford University Press, 2007.

Earl, Riggins R. *Dark Symbols, Obscure Signs: God, Self and Community in the Slave Mind*. Maryknoll, NY: Orbis, 1993.

Easteal, Patricia, Keziah Judd, and Kate Holland. "Enduring Themes and Silences in Media Portrayals of Violence Against Women." *Women's Studies International Forum* 48 (January 2015): 103–13.

Ellen, Ingrid Gould, Katherine O'Regan, Amy Ellen Schwartz, Leanna Stiefel, Derek Neal, and Thomas Nechyba. "Immigrant Children and New York City Schools: Segregation and Its Consequences." Brookings-Wharton Papers on Urban Affairs. Washington, DC: Brookings Institution Press, 2002.

Eltis, David, and Paul F. Lachance. "Estimates of the Size and Direction of Transatlantic Slave Trade." Voyages: The Trans-Atlantic Slave Trade Database, 2010. www.slavevoyages.org.

Eltis, David, and David Richardson, eds. Extending the Frontiers: Essays on the New Transatlantic Slave Trade Database. New Haven, CT: Yale University Press, 2008.

———. "A New Assessment of the Transatlantic Slave Trade." In Eltis and Richardson, Extending the Frontiers.

Enloe, Cynthia. Maneuvers: The International Politics of Militarizing Women's Lives. Berkeley: University of California Press, 2000.

Esqueda, Cynthia Willis, and Lisa A. Harrison. "The Influence of Gender Role Stereotypes, the Woman's Race, and Level of Provocation and Resistance on Domestic Violence Culpability Attributions." Sex Roles 53, nos. 11–12 (2005): 821–34.

Fanon, Frantz. A Dying Colonialism. New York: Grove, 1965.

Feagin, Joe R. The White Racial Frame: Centuries of Racial Framing and Counterframing. New York: Routledge, 2013.

Fenn, Richard K. Beyond Idols: The Shape of a Secular Society. New York: Oxford University Press, 2001.

Ferguson, Christopher J. "Does Media Violence Predict Societal Violence? It Depends on What You Look At and When." Journal of Communication 65, no. 1 (2015): E1–22.

Feuereisen, Patti, and Caroline Pincus. Invisible Girls: The Truth about Sexual Abuse. Emeryville, CA: Seal Press, 2005.

Fincher, Danielle, Kristin VanderEnde, Kia Colbert, Debra Houry, L. Shakiyla Smith, and Kathryn M. Yount. "Effect of Face-to-Face Interview versus Computer-Assisted Self-Interview on Disclosure of Intimate Partner Violence among African American Women in WIC Clinics." Journal of Interpersonal Violence 30, no. 5 (2015): 818–38.

Fine, Michelle. "Troubling Calls for Evidence: A Critical Race, Class, and Gender Analysis of Whose Evidence Counts." Feminism and Psychology 22, no. 1 (February 2012): 3–19.

Fine, Michelle, and Lois Weis. "Writing the 'Wrongs' of Fieldwork: Confronting Our Own Research/Writing Dilemmas in Urban Ethnographies." Qualitative Inquiry 2, no. 3 (September 1996): 263–64.

Fishman, Mark, and Gray Cavender, eds. Entertaining Crime: Television Reality Programs. Piscataway, NJ: Transaction, 1998.

Ford, Chandra. "Standing on This Bridge." In This Bridge We Call Home: Radical Visions for Transformations, edited by Gloria E. Anzaldúa and Analouise Keating. New York: Routledge, 2002.

Fortune, Marie M. Sexual Violence: The Sin Revisited. Cleveland: Pilgrim, 2005.

Frazier, E. Franklin. "Brazil Has No Race Problem." *Common Sense* 11 (November 1942): 363–65. Reprinted in *African-American Reflections on Brazil's Racial Paradise*, edited by David Hedwig. Philadelphia: Temple University Press, 1992.

———. "The Negro Family in Bahia, Brazil." *American Sociological Review* 7, no. 4 (1942): 465–78.

———. "Negroes in Brazil: A Study of Race Contact at Bahia. Donald Pierson," *American Journal of Sociology* 48, no. 3 (Nov., 1942): 434-435.

———. *On Race Relations: Selected Writings.* Chicago: University of Chicago Press, 1968.

———. "Rejoinder to Melville J. Herskovits, 'The Negro in Bahia, Brazil: A Problem in Method.'" *American Sociological Review* 8 (August 1943): 402–4.

———. "Section of Anthropology: A Comparison of Negro-White Relations in Brazil and in the United States." *Transactions of the New York Academy of Sciences*, series II, 6, no. 7 (1944): 251–69.

———. "Some Aspects of Race Relations in Brazil." *Phylon* 3, no. 3 (1942): 287–49.

Frederick, Marla. *Between Sundays: Black Women and Everyday Struggles of Faith.* Berkeley: University of California Press, 2003.

Fredrickson, George M. *Black Liberation: A Comparative History of Black Ideologies in the United States and South Africa.* New York: Oxford University Press, 1996.

———. *White Supremacy: A Comparative Study in American and South African History.* Oxford: Oxford University Press, 1981.

Fregoso, Rosa-Linda, and Cynthia Bejarano, eds. *Terrorizing Women: Feminicide in the Americas.* Durham, NC: Duke University Press, 2010.

Frymer, Paul. *Black and Blue: African Americans, the Labor Movement and the Decline of Democratic Party.* Princeton, NJ: Princeton University Press, 2008.

Gadzekpo, Audrey. "Invigorating Activism to End Gender Based Violence." In Cusack and Manuh, *Architecture of Violence Against Women in Ghana.*

Gaines, Kevin K. *American Africans in Ghana: Black Expatriates and the Civil Rights Era.* Chapel Hill: University of North Carolina, 2006.

Gates, Henry Louis. *Black in Latin America.* New York: New York University Press, 2011.

———. "Ending the Slavery Blame-Game." *New York Times*, April 10, 2010.

Gates, Sara. "Houston Surpasses New York and Los Angeles as the 'Most Diverse in Nation.'" *Huffington Post*, March 5, 2012. www.huffingtonpost.com.

Gebara, Ivone. *Out of the Depths: Women's Experience of Evil and Salvation.* Minneapolis: Fortress, 2002.

Ghana Statistical Service. "2010 Population and Housing Census: Summary Report of Final Results." Accra, Ghana: Sakoa Press, 2012. www.statsghana.gov.gh.

Gillespie, Lane Kirkland, Tara Richards, Eugena Givens, and M. Dwayne Smith. "Framing Deadly Domestic Violence: Why the Media's Spin Matters in Newspaper Coverage of Femicide." *Violence Against Women* 19, no. 2 (February 2013): 222–45.

Goldberg, Harmony. "Domestic Worker Organizing in the United States: Reports from the Field." *International Labor and Working-Class History* 88 (2015): 150–55.

Goldscheid, Julie, Donna Coker, Sandra Park, Tara Neal, and Valerie Halstead. *Responses from the Field: Sexual Assault, Domestic Violence, and Policing.* New York: American Civil Liberties Union, 2015.

Gonzalez, Michelle. *Shopping.* Minneapolis: Fortress, 2010.

Gordon-Reed, Annette. *Thomas Jefferson and Sally Hemings: An American Controversy.* Charlottesville: University of Virginia Press, 1997.

Graetz, Michael J. "Trusting the Courts: Redressing the State Court Funding Crisis." *Daedalus* 143, no. 3 (Summer 2014): 96–104.

Graham, Renée. "The Secret Shame of Prince George's County." *Essence* 37, no. 6 (October 2006): 217–22.

Grant, David. "House Passes Violence Against Women Act, Grudgingly." *Christian Science Monitor,* May 16, 2012. www.csmonitor.com.

Greene, Sandra E. "Modern 'Trokosi' and the 1807 Abolition in Ghana: Connecting Past and Present." *William and Mary Quarterly* 66, no. 4 (October 2009): 959–74.

Griffin, Horace. *Their Own Receive Them Not: African American Lesbians and Gays in Black Churches.* Cleveland: Pilgrim, 2006.

Gruber, Aya. "The Feminist War on Crime." *Iowa Law Review* 92, no. 3 (2007): 741–833.

Hall, Gwendolyn Midlo. *Slavery and African Ethnicities in the Americas: Restoring the Links.* Chapel Hill: University of North Carolina Press, 2005.

Hamilton, Charles V., Lynn Huntley, Neville Alexander, Antonio Sérgio Alfredo Guimarães, and Wilmot James, eds. *Beyond Racism: Race and Inequality in Brazil, South Africa, and the United States.* Boulder, CO: Lynne Rienner, 2001.

Harding, Rachel E. *A Refuge in Thunder: Candomblé and Alternative Black Spaces.* Bloomington: Indiana University Press, 2000.

Harrison, Lisa A., and Cynthia Willis Esqueda. "Myths and Stereotypes of Actors Involved in Domestic Violence: Implications for Domestic Violence Culpability Attributions." *Aggression and Violent Behavior* 4, no. 2 (1999): 129–38.

Hartman, Saidiya. *Lose Your Mother: A Journey along the Atlantic Slave Route.* New York: Farrar, Straus & Giroux, 2013.

Hassim, Shireen. "Democracy's Shadows: Sexual Rights and Gender Politics in the Rape Trial of Jacob Zuma." *African Studies* 68, no. 1 (2009): 57–77.

Hatef, Azeta, and Greg Munno. "Domestic Violence as Entertainment: Gender, Role Congruity, and Reality Television." *Media Report to Women* 44, no. 1 (2016): 6–20.

Hautzinger, Sarah. "Criminalizing Male Violence in Brazil's Women's Police Stations: From Flawed Essentialism to Imagined Communities." *Journal of Gender Studies* 11, no. 3 (2002): 243–51.

———. *Violence in the City of Women: Police and Batterers in Bahia, Brazil.* Berkeley: University of California Press, 2007.

Hawk, Beverly G., ed. *Africa's Media Image.* New York: Praeger, 1992.

Healey, Mark Alan. "Os desencontros da tradição em A Cidade das Mulheres: raça e gênero na etnografia de Ruth Landes" [Mistranslations of tradition in *The City of Women*: Race and gender in the ethnography of Ruth Landes]. *Cadernos Pagu* 6–7 (1996): 153–200.

————. "'The Sweet Matriarchy of Bahia': Ruth Landes' Ethnography of Race and Gender." *Dispositio* 23, no. 50 (1998): 87–116.

Hellwig, David J. "Racial Paradise or Run-Around? Afro-North American Views of Race Relations in Brazil." *American Studies* 31, no. 2 (1990): 43–60.

Henson, Lori, and Radhika E. Parameswaran. "Getting Real with 'Tell It Like It Is' Talk Therapy: Hegemonic Masculinity and the Dr. Phil Show." *Communication, Culture, and Critique* 1, no. 3 (2008): 287–310.

Herman, Judith. *Father-Daughter Incest.* Cambridge, MA: Harvard University Press, 2013.

Herskovits, Melville. "The Negro in Bahia, Brazil: A Problem in Method." *American Sociological Review* 8 (July 1943): 394–404.

Heyman, Michael G. "The Time Has Come for the United States to Ratify the Convention on the Elimination of All Forms of Discrimination Against Women." *Washington University Global Studies Law Review* 9, no. 2 (January 2010): 195–223.

Hixson, Lindsay Kae, Bradford B. Hepler, and Myoung Ouk Kim. "The White Population: 2010." Washington, DC: U.S. Department of Commerce, Economics, and Statistics Administration, U.S. Census Bureau, 2011. www.census.gov.

Hoad, Neville, Karen Martin, and Graeme Reid, eds. *Sex and Politics in South Africa.* Cape Town: DoubleStory, 2005.

Hoel, Nina, and Sa'diyya Shaika. "Sex as Ibadah: Religion, Gender, and Subjectivity among South African Muslim Women." *Journal of Feminist Studies in Religion* 29, no. 1 (2013): 69–91.

Horsman, Reginald. *Race and Manifest Destiny: The Origins of American Racial Anglo-Saxonism.* Cambridge, MA: Harvard University Press, 1981.

Horton, James Oliver. "Slavery in American History: An Uncomfortable National Dialogue." In *Slavery and Public History: The Tough Stuff of American History*, edited by James Oliver Horton and Lois E. Horton. Chapel Hill: University of North Carolina Press, 2006.

Hua, Julietta. *Trafficking Women's Human Rights.* Minneapolis: University of Minnesota Press, 2011.

Human Rights Watch. "We'll Show You're a Woman: Violence and Discrimination Against Black Lesbians and Transgender Men in South Africa." December 5, 2011. www.hrw.org.

Incite! Women of Color Against Violence. *Color of Violence: The Incite! Anthology.* Cambridge, MA: South End, 2006.

Institute of Economic Research Foundation and Ministry of Tourism. "Characterization and Sizing of Domestic Tourism in Brazil—2010/2011." São Paulo, 2011.

Isoke, Zenzele. *Urban Black Women and the Politics of Resistance.* New York: Palgrave Macmillan, 2013.

Issaka Toure, Fulera. "Contesting the Normative." *CrossCurrents* 63, no. 2 (2013): 198–21.

Iyengar, Radha, and Lindsay Sabik. "The Dangerous Shortage of Domestic Violence Services." *Health Affairs* 28, no. 6 (November/December 2009): 1052–65.

Jackson, Aubrey L. "State Contexts and the Criminalization of Marital Rape across the United States." *Social Science Research* 51 (May 2015): 290–306.

Jackson, Cari. *For the Souls of Black Folks: Reimagined Black Preaching for the Twenty-First Century*. Eugene, OR: Pickwick, 2013.

Jackson, Michael D. "Between Biography and Ethnography." *Harvard Theological Review* 101, nos. 3–4 (October 2008): 377–97.

———. *The Politics of Storytelling: Violence, Transgression, and Intersubjectivity*. Copenhagen: Museum Tusculanum Press, 2002.

Jakes, T. D. *God's Leading Lady: Out of the Shadows and into the Light*. New York: Penguin, 2003.

———. *Woman, Thou Art Loosed! Healing the Wounds of the Past*. Shippensburg, PA: Destiny Image, 2005.

Jayawardane, Manori Neelika. "Maid in Public: Negotiating 'Authenticity' via Public Confessionals, or A Question of Agency: Narrative, Power, and the 'Maid from Guinea.'" *JENdA: A Journal of Culture and African Women Studies* 2 (2015): 132–41.

Jennings, Willie James. *The Christian Imagination: Theology and the Origins of Race*. New Haven, CT: Yale University Press, 2010.

Jimenez, Lilian. "Immigration, Crime, and Neo-segregation: America's Legacy of Xenophobia: The Curious Origins of Arizona Senate Bill 1070." *California Western Law Review* (2012): 279–315.

Jones, Ann. *Next Time She'll Be Dead: Battering and How to Stop It*. Boston: Beacon, 2000.

Jordan, Phillip, and Maria Hernandez-Reif. "Reexamination of Young Children's Racial Attitudes and Skin Tone Preferences." *Journal of Black Psychology* 35, no. 3 (August 2009): 388–403.

Jordan, Winthrop. *White over Black: American Attitudes toward the Negro, 1550–1812*. Chapel Hill: University of North Carolina Press, 1968.

Jubb, Nadine, Gloria Camacho, Almachiara D'Angelo, Gina Yáñez De la Borda, Kattya Hernández, Ivonne Macassi León, Cecília MacDowell Santos, Yamileth Molina, and Wânia Pasinato. "Access to Justice for Women in Situations of Violence: A Comparative Study of Women's Police Stations in Latin America." Quito: CEPLAES, 2008. http://citeseerx.ist.psu.edu.

Kahlor, LeeAnn, and Matthew S. Eastin. "Television's Role in the Culture of Violence toward Women: A Study of Television Viewing and the Cultivation of Rape Myth Acceptance in the United States." *Journal of Broadcasting and Electronic Media* 55, no. 2 (2011): 215–31.

Kankpeyeng, Benjamin W. "The Slave Trade in Northern Ghana: Landmarks, Legacies, and Connections." *Slavery and Abolition* 30, no. 2 (2009): 209–21.

Kapur, Ratna. "'Faith' and the 'Good' Liberal: The Construction of Female Sexual Subjectivity in Anti-trafficking Legal Discourse." In *Sexuality and the Law: Feminist Engagements*, edited by Vanessa E. Munro and Carl F. Stychin. New York: Routledge, 2007.

Kara, Siddharth. *Sex Trafficking: Inside the Business of Modern Slavery*. New York: Columbia University Press, 2009.

Kaschak, Ellyn. "Intimate Betrayal: Domestic Violence in Lesbian Relationships." *Women and Therapy* 23, no. 3 (2001): 1–5.

Katznelson, Ira, Kim Geiger, and Daniel Kryder. "Limiting Liberalism: The Southern Veto in Congress, 1933–1950." *Political Science Quarterly* 108, no. 2 (1993): 283–306.

Keim, Curtis. *Mistaking Africa: Curiosities and Inventions of the American Mind.* Boulder, CO: Westview, 1999.

Kelley, Venita. "What Is It about the Walls? A Summary Report of African American Women's Experiences of Domestic Violence in Lincoln Nebraska." In Ochoa and Ige, *Shout Out.*

Kempadoo, Kamala. *Sexing the Caribbean: Gender, Race, and Sexual Labor.* New York: Routledge, 2004.

Klarfeld, Jessica. "A Striking Disconnect: Marital Rape Laws Failure to Keep Up with Domestic Violence Law." *American Criminal Law Review* 48, no. 4 (Fall 2011): 1819–40.

Klein, Herbert S. "African Women in the Atlantic Slave Trade." In *Women and Slavery in Africa,* edited by Claire C. Robertson and Martin Klein. Madison: University of Wisconsin Press, 1983.

Kuumba, M. Bahati. *Gender and Social Movements.* Walnut Creek, CA: Altamira, 2001.

———. "'You've Struck a Rock': Comparing Gender, Social Movements, and Transformation in the United States and South Africa." *Gender and Society* 16, no. 4 (2002): 504–23.

Landes, Ruth. *City of Women.* Albuquerque: University of New Mexico Press, 2005.

Lara, Irene, and Elisa Facio. "Introduction: Fleshing the Spirit, Spiriting the Flesh." In *Fleshing the Spirit: Spirituality and Activism in Chicana, Latina, and Indigenous Women's Lives,* edited by Elisa Facio and Irene Lara. Tucson: University of Arizona Press, 2014.

Lawrence-Lightfoot, Sara. "Reflections on Portraiture: A Dialogue between Art and Science." *Qualitative Inquiry* 11, no. 1 (2005): 3–15.

Lawrence-Lightfoot, Sara, and Jessica Hoffman Davis. *The Art and Science of Portraiture.* San Francisco: John Wiley, 1997.

Lee, Shayne. *America's New Preacher, T. D. Jakes.* New York: New York University Press, 2005.

Lee, Shayne, and Phillip Luke Sinitiere. *Holy Mavericks: Evangelical Innovators and the Spiritual Marketplace.* New York: New York University Press, 2009.

Leonard, David J., and Monica J. Casper. "Rotten to the Core: The NFL and Domestic Violence." *Feminist Wire,* September 8, 2014. www.thefeministwire.com.

Lerner, Sharon. "Labor of Love." *Stanford Social Innovation Review,* Summer 2013, 66–71.

Leveille, Cassandra. "Wage Rules to Affect Health Aides Sent by Agencies." *WeNews,* December 23, 2013. http://womensenews.org.

Liebler, Carol M., Azeta Hatef, and Greg Munno. "Domestic Violence as Entertainment: Gender, Role Congruity, and Reality Television." *Media Report to Women* 44, no. 1 (2016): 6–20.

Lima de Pérez, Julie. "A Criminological Reading of the Concept of Vulnerability: A Case Study of Brazilian Trafficking Victims." *Social and Legal Studies* 25 (2016): 23–24.

Lomax, Tamura A. "Strauss-Kahn, Domestic Immigrants and Money, Power, Respect." *JENdA: A Journal of Culture and African Women Studies* 2 (2013): 161–65.

Longazel, Jamie G. "Moral Panic as Racial Degradation Ceremony: Racial Stratification and the Local-Level Backlash Against Latino/a Immigrants." *Punishment and Society* 15, no. 1 (January 2013): 96–119.

Lucea, Marguerite B., Jamila K. Stockman, Margarita Mana-Ay, Desiree Bertrand, Gloria B. Callwood, Catherine R. Coverston, Doris W. Campbell, and Jacquelyn C. Campbell. "Factors Influencing Resource Use by African American and African Caribbean Women Disclosing Intimate Partner Violence." *Journal of Interpersonal Violence* 28, no. 8 (May 2013): 1617–41.

Madison, D. Soyini. *Acts of Activism: Human Rights as Radical Performance.* New York: Cambridge University Press, 2010.

———. "Narrative Poetics and Performative Interventions." In *Handbook of Critical and Indigenous Methodologies*, edited by Norman K. Denzin, Yvonna S. Lincoln, and Linda Tuhiwai Smith. Los Angeles: Sage, 2008.

Majeed, Debra. "Khalidah's Story: An African American Muslim Women's Journey to Freedom." Seattle: FaithTrust Institute, 2010. www.faithtrustinstitute.org.

Manigault-Bryant, LeRhonda S., Tamura A. Lomax, and Carol B. Duncan, eds. *Womanist and Black Feminist Responses to Tyler Perry's Productions.* New York: Palgrave Macmillan, 2014.

Mansaray, Mariama Ahmeda. "Girl-Child Sexual Abuse as a Public Health Issue in Accra, Ghana." Master's thesis, Lakehead University, 2009.

Markey, Patrick M., Juliana E. French, and Charlotte N. Markey. "Violent Movies and Severe Acts of Violence: Sensationalism versus Science." *Human Communication Research* 41, no. 2 (2015): 155–73.

Markey, Patrick M., Mike A. Males, Juliana E. French, and Charlotte N. Markey. "Lessons from Markey et al. (2015) and Bushman et al. (2015): Sensationalism and Integrity in Media Research." *Human Communication Research* 41, no. 2 (2015): 184–203.

Martin, Elaine K., Casey T. Taft, and Patricia A. Resick. "A Review of Marital Rape." *Aggression and Violent Behavior* 12, no. 3 (May–June 2007): 329–47.

Martin, Joan M. *More Than Chains and Toil: A Christian Work Ethic of Enslaved Women.* Louisville: Westminster John Knox, 2000.

Martinez, Omar, and Guadalupe Kelle. "Sex Trafficking of LGBT Individuals: A Call for Service Provision, Research, and Action." *International Law News* 42, no. 4 (2013): 1–6.

Martinez, Sara B., Toni Schindler Zimmerman, Jennifer Matheson, and James Banning. "An Analysis of Dr. Phil's Advice about Relationships." *Journal of Couple and Relationship Therapy* 10, no. 1 (2011): 53–68.

Marx, Anthony W. *Lessons of Struggle: South African Internal Opposition, 1960–1990.* New York: Oxford University Press, 1992.

———. *Making Race and Nation: A Comparison of South Africa, the United States, and Brazil.* Cambridge: Cambridge University Press, 1998.

Mason, Corinne Lysandra, and Shoshana Magnet. "Surveillance Studies and Violence Against Women." *Surveillance and Society* 10, no. 2 (2012): 105–18.

Mason, Gail. *The Spectacle of Violence: Homophobia, Gender, and Knowledge.* London: Routledge, 2002.

Matebeni, Zethu. "Deconstructing Violence towards Black Lesbians in South Africa." In *Queer African Reader,* edited by Sokari Ekine and Hakima Abbas. Nairobi, Kenya: Pambazuka, 2013.

———. *Reclaiming Afrikan: Queer Perspectives on Sexual and Gender Identities.* Athlone, South Africa: Modjaji Books, 2014.

———. "How NOT to Write about Queer South Africa." In Matebeni, *Reclaiming Afrikan.*

Matebeni, Zethu and Jabu Pereira.. "Preface." In Matebeni, *Reclaiming Afrikan.*

Matory, J. Lorand. *Black Atlantic Religion: Tradition, Transnationalism, and Matriarchy in the Afro-Brazilian Candomblé.* Princeton, NJ: Princeton University Press, 2005.

Matthews, Donald. *Sexual Abuse of Power in the Black Church: Sexual Misconduct in the African American Churches.* Bloomington, IN: WestBow, 2012.

Matthews, Nancy. *Confronting Rape: The Feminist Antirape Movement and the State.* New York: Routledge, 1994.

Mayer, Ruth. *Artificial Africas: Colonial Images in the Times of Globalization.* Hanover, NH: University Press of New England, 2002.

Mays, Keith A. *Kwanzaa: Black Power and the Making of the African American Holiday Tradition.* New York: Routledge, 2009.

Mazumdar, Rinita. "Marital Rape: Some Ethical and Cultural Considerations." In *A Patchwork Shawl: Chronicles of South Asian Women in America,* edited by Shamita Das Dasgupta. New Brunswick, NJ: Rutgers University Press, 1998.

McCallum, Cecilia. "Women Out of Place? A Micro-historical Perspective on the Black Feminist Movement in Salvador Da Bahia Brazil." *Journal of Latin American Studies* 39, no. 1 (2007): 55–80.

McClintock, Anne. *Imperial Leather: Race, Gender, and Sexuality in the Colonial Contest.* New York: Routledge, 1995.

McCloud, Aminah Beverly. *African American Islam.* New York: Routledge, 2014.

McElya, Micki. "Trashing the Presidency: Race, Class, and the Clinton/Lewinsky Affair." In *Our Monica, Ourselves: The Clinton Affair and the National Interest,* edited by Lauren Berlant and Lisa A. Duggan. New York: New York University Press, 2001.

McGee, Paula L. "The Wal-Martization of African American Religion: T. D. Jakes and Woman Thou Art Loosed." PhD dissertation, Claremont Graduate University, 2012. http://scholarship.claremont.edu.

McGuire, Danielle L. *At the Dark End of the Street: Black Women, Rape, and Resistance—A New History of the Civil Rights Movement from Rosa Parks to the Rise of Black Power.* New York: Vintage, 2010.

Medina, José. *The Epistemology of Resistance: Gender and Racial Oppression, Epistemic Injustice, and the Social Imagination.* London: Oxford University Press, 2013.

Merry, Sally Engle. *Human Rights and Gender Violence: Translating International Law into Local Justice.* Chicago: University of Chicago Press, 2006.

Meyer, Doug. "Interpreting and Experiencing Anti-queer Violence: Race, Class, and Gender Differences among LGBT Hate Crime Victims." *Race, Gender & Class* 15, no. 3 (2008): 262–82.

Meyersfeld, Bonita. *Domestic Violence and International Law.* Portland, OR: Hart, 2010.

Middaugh, Laine. "Lessons from the 'Unorganizable' Domestic Workers Organizing." *Kennedy School Review* 12 (2012): 12–13.

Mirzai, Behnaz A., Ismael Musah Montana, and Paul E. Lovejoy, eds. *Slavery, Islam, and Diaspora.* Trenton, NJ: Africa World Press, 2009.

Mkhize, Nonhlanhla, Jane Bennett, Vasu Reddy, and Relebohile Moletsane. *The Country We Want to Live In: Hate Crimes and Homophobia in the Lives of Black Lesbian South Africans.* South Africa: HSRC, 2010.

Modi, Monica, Sheallah Palmer, and Alice Armstrong. "The Role of Violence Against Women Act in Addressing Intimate Partner Violence: A Public Health Issue." *Journal of Women's Health* 23, no. 3 (2014): 253–59.

Moon, Katharine H. S. *Sex among Allies: Military Prostitution in U.S.–South Korean Relations.* New York: Columbia University Press, 1997.

Morgan, Michael, James Shanahan, and Nancy Signorielli. "Cultivation Processes." In *Media Effects: Advances in Theory and Research*, edited by Jennings Bryant and Mary Beth Oliver. New York: Routledge, 2008.

Morris, Monique W. "Race, Gender, and the School-to-Prison Pipeline: Expanding Our Discussion to Include Black Girls." New York: African American Policy Forum, 2012. https://static1.squarespace.com.

Motsei, Mmatshilo. *The Kanga and the Kangaroo Court: Reflections on the Rape Trial of Jacob Zuma.* Sunnyside, South Africa: Jacana, 2007.

Motta, Roberto. "Enchantment, Identity, Community, and Conversion: Catholics, Afro-Brazilians, and Protestants in Brazil." In *Conversion in the Age of Pluralism*, edited by Guiseppe Giordan. Boston: Brill, 2009.

Mudimbe, Valentin Yves. *The Idea of Africa.* Bloomington: Indiana University Press, 1994.

Murray, Pauli. *Song in a Weary Throat: An American Pilgrimage.* New York: Harper & Row, 1987.

Nadar, Sarojini. "Toward a Feminist Missiological Agenda: A Case Study of the Jacob Zuma Rape Trial." *Missionalia: Southern African Journal of Mission Studies* 37, no. 1 (2009): 85–102.

Nadasen, Premilla. "Citizenship Rights, Domestic Work, and the Fair Labor Standards Act." *Journal of Policy History* 24, no. 1 (2012): 74–94.

———. *Household Workers Unite: The Untold Story of African American Women Who Built a Movement.* Boston: Beacon, 2015.

Naidoo, Kogieleum. "Rape in South Africa—A Call to Action." *SAMJ: South African Medical Journal* 103, no. 4 (2013): 210–11.

Nash, Shondrah Tarrezz. "Through Black Eyes: African American Women's Constructions of Their Experiences with Intimate Male Partner Violence." *Violence Against Women* 11, no. 11 (2005): 1420–40.

Nayak, Anoop. "Geography, Race, and Emotions: Social and Cultural Intersections." *Social and Cultural Geography* 12, no. 6 (2011): 548–62.

Neighbors, Harold W., Marc A. Musick, and David R. Williams. "The African American Minister as a Source of Help for Serious Personal Crises: Bridge or Barrier to Mental Health Care?" *Health Education and Behavior* 25 (1998): 759–77.

Nelson, Sara. "Constructing and Negotiating Gender in Women's Police Stations in Brazil." *Latin American Perspectives* 23, no. 1 (1996): 131–48.

New Jersey Department of Law and Public Safety, Division of State Police. "Domestic Violence in New Jersey: Twenty-Sixth Annual Domestic Violence Report." 2008. www.njsp.org.

———. "Domestic Violence in New Jersey: Twenty-Eighth Annual Domestic Violence Report." 2010. www.njsp.org.

Nicholas, Bastine A. "Legal Immanence: Religion, Mythology and the Influence of the Divine." *US–China Law Review* 8, no. 5 (May 2011): 483–98.

Nyangweso, Mary Wangila. *Female Circumcision: The Interplay of Religion, Gender, and Culture in Kenya*. Maryknoll, NY: Orbis, 2007.

Ochoa, María, and Barbara K. Ige, eds. *Shout Out: Women of Color Respond to Violence*. Emeryville, CA: Seal Press, 2007.

O'Conner, Alexander, and Farhana Jahan. "Under Surveillance and Overwrought: American Muslims' Emotional and Behavioral Responses to Government Surveillance." *Journal of Muslim Mental Health* 8, no. 1 (2014): 95–106.

O'Donovan, Theresa M. *Rage and Resistance: A Theological Reflection on the Montreal Massacre*. Waterloo, ON: Wilfrid Laurier University Press, 2006.

Oduyoye, Mercy Amba. "Catalyst, Resource, or Roadblock? A Critical Examination of the Christian Religion and Violence Against Women and Children in Ghana." In *The Architecture for Violence Against Women in Ghana*, edited by Kathy Cusack and Takyiwaa Manuh. Accra, Ghana: Gender Studies and Human Rights Documentation Centre, 2009.

Okyere-Manu, Beatrice. "'When the Community I Know Is No Longer a Safe Haven': A Dangerous Masculinity Exposed." *Journal of Gender and Religion in Africa* 20, no. 1 (July 2014): 85–101.

Ordóñez, Maria-Belén. "Circuits of Power, Labour, and Desire: The Case of Dominique Strauss-Kahn." In *Reworking Postcolonialism: Globalism, Labor and Rights*, edited by Pavan Kumar Malreddy, Birte Heidemann, Ole Birk Laursen, and Janet Wilson. London: Palgrave Macmillan, 2015.

Pappu, Sridhar. "The Preacher: Bishop TD Jakes Wants His Flock Not Only to Do Good but to Do Well, and His Brand of Entrepreneurial Spirituality Has Made Him

Perhaps the Most Influential Black Leader in America Today." *Atlantic Monthly* 297, no. 2 (2006): 92–103.

Parés, Luis Nicolau. *The Formation of Candomblé: Vodun History and Ritual in Brazil.* Chapel Hill: University of North Carolina Press, 2013.

Pasinato, Wânia. "The Maria da Penha Law: 10 Years On." *Sur: International Journal on Human Rights* 13, no. 24 (December 2016): 155–63.

Patterson, Cynthia M. "New Directions in the Political History of Women: A Case Study of the National Woman's Party's Campaign for the Equal Rights Amendment, 1920–1927." *Women's Studies International Forum* 5, no. 6 (1982): 585–97.

Patterson, Natasha, and Camilla A. Sears. "Letting Men Off the Hook? Domestic Violence and Postfeminist Celebrity Culture." *Genders*, no. 53 (January 2011). www.colorado.edu.

Patterson, Orlando. *Slavery and Social Death: A Comparative Study.* Cambridge, MA: Harvard University Press, 1985.

Peach, Lucinda Joy. "'Sex Slaves' or 'Sex Workers'? Cross-Cultural and Comparative Religious Perspectives on Sexuality, Subjectivity, and Moral Identity in Anti–Sex Trafficking Discourse." *Culture and Religion* 6 (2005): 107–34.

Perbi, Akosua Adoma. *A History of Indigenous Slavery in Ghana from the 15th to the 19th Century.* Legon, Accra: Sub-Saharan Publishers, 2004.

Perry, Keisha-Khan Y. *Black Women Against the Land Grab: The Fight for Racial Justice in Brazil.* Minneapolis: University of Minnesota Press, 2013.

Peters, Rebecca Todd. *Solidarity Ethics: Transformation in a Globalized World.* Minneapolis: Fortress, 2014.

Pew Forum on Religion and Public Life. "U.S. Religious Landscape Survey." Washington, DC: Pew Research Center, 2008. http://religions.pewforum.org.

Pew Research Center. "Muslim Americans: Middle Class and Mostly Mainstream." May 22, 2007. www.pewresearch.org.

Pineda-Madrid, Nancy. *Suffering and Salvation in Ciudad Juárez.* Minneapolis: Fortress, 2011.

Pinho, Patricia de Santana. "African-American Roots Tourism in Brazil." *Latin American Perspectives* 35, no. 3 (May 2008): 70–86.

———. *Mama Africa: Reinventing Blackness in Bahia.* Durham, NC: Duke University Press, 2010.

Pinho, Patricia de Santana, and Elizabeth B. Silva. "Domestic Relations in Brazil: Legacies and Horizons." *Latin American Research Review* 45, no. 2 (2008): 90–113.

Piscitelli, Adriana. "Transnational Sex Travels: Negotiating Identities in a Brazilian 'Tropical Paradise.'" In Alvarez et al., *Translocalities/Translocalidades.*

Pleck, Elizabeth. *Domestic Tyranny: The Making of Social Policy Against Family Violence from Colonial Times to the Present.* New York: Oxford University Press, 1987.

Popescu, Marciana, René Drumm, Sylvia Mayer, Laurie Cooper, Tricia Foster, Marge Seifert, Holly Gadd, and Smita Dewan. "'Because of My Beliefs That I Had Acquired from the Church . . .': Religious Belief-Based Barriers for Adventist Women in

Domestic Violence Relationships." *Social Work and Christianity* 36, no. 4 (2009): 394–414.

Potter, Hillary. "Battered Black Women's Use of Religious Services and Spirituality for Assistance in Leaving Abusive Relationships." *Violence Against Women* 13, no. 3 (2007): 262–84.

———. *Battle Cries: Black Women and Intimate Partner Abuse*. New York: New York University Press, 2008.

Powell, Catherine. "Lifting Our Veil of Ignorance: Culture, Constitutionalism, and Women's Human Rights in Post–September 11 America." *Hastings Law Journal* 57, no. 2 (2005): 331–83.

Projansky, Sarah. "Rihanna's Closed Eyes." *Velvet Light Trap* 65 (Spring 2010): 71–73.

Raboteau, Albert J. *A Fire in the Bones: Reflections on African American Religious History*. Boston: Beacon, 1995.

Radford, Jill, and Diana E. H. Russell. *Femicide: The Politics of Woman Killing*. New York: Maxwell Macmillan International, 1992.

Radhakrishnan, Smitha. "'Time to Show Our True Colors': The Gendered Politics of 'Indianness' in Post-Apartheid South Africa." *Gender and Society* 19, no. 2 (2005): 262–81.

Ramphele, Mamphela. *Laying Ghosts to Rest: Dilemmas of the Transformation of South Africa*. Cape Town: Tafelberg, 2008.

Ransby, Barbara. "Henry Louis Gates' Dangerously Wrong Slave History." *Colorlines*, May 3, 2010.

Rauch, Janine. "Crime Prevention and Morality—The Campaign for Moral Regeneration in South Africa." *Institute for Security Studies Monographs* 2005, no. 114 (2005): 9–13.

Reid, Graeme. *Above the Skyline: Reverend Tsietsi Thandekiso and the Founding of an African Gay Church*. Pretoria: University of South Africa, Unisa Press, 2010.

Repo, Jemima, and Riina Yrjölä. "The Gender Politics of Celebrity Humanitarianism in Africa." *International Feminist Journal of Politics* 13, no. 1 (June 2011): 44–62.

Riberio, Alexandre Vieria. "The Transatlantic Slave Trade to Bahia, 1582–1851." In Eltis and Richardson, *Extending the Frontiers*.

Richie, Beth E. *Arrested Justice: Black Women, Violence, and America's Prison Nation*. New York: New York University Press, 2012.

Ristock, Janice. "Understanding Violence in Lesbian Relationships." In Victimization and the Community Response, Vol. 1. Stark and Buzawa, *Violence Against Women in Families and Relationships*.

Ritchie, Andrea J. "Law Enforcement Violence Against Women of Color." In Incite!, *Color of Violence*.

Roberts, Dorothy. *Killing the Black Body: Race, Reproduction, and the Meaning of Liberty*. New York: Pantheon, 1997.

———. "The Paradox of Silence and Display: Sexual Violation of Enslaved Women and Contemporary Contradictions in Black Female Sexuality." In Brooten and Hazelton *Beyond Slavery*.

Robins, Steven. "Sexual Politics and the Zuma Rape Trial." *Journal of Southern African Studies* 34, no. 2 (June 2008): 411–27.

Robinson, Amorie. "There's a Stranger in This House: African American Lesbians and Domestic Violence." *Women and Therapy* 25, nos. 3–4 (2002): 125–32.

Robinson, Jo Ann Gibson. *The Montgomery Bus Boycott and the Women Who Started It: The Memoir of Jo Ann Gibson Robinson.* Knoxville: University of Tennessee Press, 1989.

Rodier, Kristin, and Michelle Meagher. "In Her Own Time: Rihanna, Post-feminism, and Domestic Violence." *Women: A Cultural Review* 25, no. 2 (2014): 176–79.

Romo, Anadelia A. *Brazil's Living Museum: Race, Reform, and Tradition in Bahia.* Chapel Hill: University of North Carolina Press, 2010.

Ross, Robert. *A Concise History of South Africa.* Cambridge: Cambridge University Press, 1999.

Rothman, Emily F., Anita Nagaswaran, Renee M. Johnson, Kelley M. Adams, Juliane Scrivens, and Allyson Baughman. "U.S. Tabloid Magazine Coverage of a Celebrity Dating Abuse Incident: Rihanna and Chris Brown." *Journal of Health Communication: International Perspectives* 17, no. 6 (2012): 733–44.

Rotunda, Rob J., Gail Williamson, and Michelle Penfold. "Clergy Response to Domestic Violence: A Preliminary Survey of Clergy Members, Victims, and Batterers." *Pastoral Psychology* 52, no. 4 (2004): 353–65.

Russell, Diana E. H., and Nicole Van de Ven, eds. *Crimes Against Women: Proceedings of the International Tribunal.* Rev. ed. 1976. Reprint, East Palo Alto, CA: Frog in the Well, 1984.

Ryder, A. F. C. *Benin and the Europeans: 1485–1897.* New York: Humanities, 1969.

Sacco, Lynn. *Unspeakable: Father-Daughter Incest in American History.* Baltimore: Johns Hopkins University Press, 2009.

Sahgal, Neha, and Greg Smith. "A Religious Portrait of African Americans." Pew Forum on Religion and Public Life, January 30, 2009. www.pewforum.com.

Sandoval, Lisa. "Race and Immigration Law: A Troubling Marriage." *Modern American* 7, no. 1 (2011): 42–58.

Sansone, Carol, and Livio Sansone. *Blackness without Ethnicity: Constructing Race in Brazil.* Gordonsville, VA: Palgrave Macmillan, 2003.

Sansone, Livio. "Challenges to Digital Patrimonialization: Heritage.org / Digital Museum of African and Afro-Brazilian Memory." *Vibrant: Virtual Brazilian Anthropology* 10, no. 1 (2013). www.scielo.br.

———. "Estados Unidos e Brasil no Gantois: o poder e a origem transnacional dos estudos Afro-brasileiros." *Revista Brasileira de Ciências Sociais* 27, no. 79 (2012): 9–29.

———. "The Localization of Global Funk in Bahia and in Rio." *Brazilian Popular Music and Globalization* (2001): 136–60.

Santana, Taveres Márcia. "Roda de Conversa entre mulheres: denúncias sobre a Lei Maria da Penha e descrença na justiça / Wheel Conversation between Women: Complaints about the Inapplicability of the Maria da Penha Law in Salvador/BA and Disbelief in Justice." *Estudos Feministas* 23, no. 2 (August 2015): 547–59.

Santos, Cecília MacDowell. "Da delegacia da mulher à Lei Maria da Penha: Absorção/ tradução de demandas feministas pelo Estado." *Revista Crítica De Ciências Sociais*, no. 89 (2010): 153–70.

———. "En-gendering the Police: Women's Police Stations and Feminism in São Paulo Brazil." *Latin American Research Review* 39, no. 3 (October 2004): 29–55.

———. *Women's Police Stations: Gender, Violence, and Justice in São Paulo Brazil*. New York: Palgrave Macmillan, 2005.

Sardenberg, Cecilia M. B., and Ana Alice Alcantara Costa. "Contemporary Feminisms in Brazil: Achievements, Shortcomings, and Challenges." In *Women's Movements in the Global Era: The Power of Local Feminisms*, edited by Amrita Basu. New York: Westview, 2010.

Sardenberg, Cecilia, Márcia Gomes, Márcia Tavares, and Wânia Pasinato. "Domestic Violence and Women's Access to Justice in Brazil." OBSERVE—Observatório da Lei Maria da Penha, Pesquisa sobre condições de funcionamento das DEAMS e Juizados/Varas de Violência Doméstica e Familiar nas capitais brasileiras. Salvador: Observe, 2010.

Savas, Gokhan. "Social Inequality at Low-Wage Work in Neo-liberal Economy: The Case of Women of Color Domestic Workers in the United States." *Race, Gender & Class* 17, nos. 3–4 (2010): 314–26.

Scharen, Christian, and Aana Marie Vigen, eds. *Ethnography as Christian Theology and Ethics*. New York: Bloomsbury, 2011.

Scholz, Susanne. *Sacred Witness: Rape in the Hebrew Bible*. Minneapolis: Fortress, 2014.

Schroeder, Joy. *Dinah's Lament: The Biblical Legacy of Sexual Violence in Christian Interpretation*. Minneapolis: Fortress, 2007.

Schwarzenegger, Arnold, with Pete Petre. *Total Recall: My Unbelievably True Life Story*. New York: Simon & Schuster, 2012.

Selka, Stephen. "Morality in the Religious Marketplace: Evangelical Christianity, Candomblé, and the Struggle for Moral Distinction in Brazil." *American Ethnologist* 37, no. 2 (2010): 291–307.

Shoos, Diane. "Representing Domestic Violence: Ambivalence and Difference in What's Love Got to Do with It." *NWSA Journal* 15, no. 2 (2003): 57–77.

Shupe, Anson, and Janelle M. Eliasson-Nannini. *Pastoral Misconduct: The American Black Church Examined*. New Brunswick, NJ: Transaction, 2012.

Sigsworth, Romi. "'Anyone Can Be a Rapist': An Overview of Rape in South Africa." Johannesburg: Centre for the Study of Violence and Reconciliation, November 2009. www.csvr.org.za.

Simmons, Aishah. "The War Against Black Women and the Making of *NO!*" In Incite!, *Color of Violence*.

Skidmore, Thomas E. "Racial Mixture and Affirmative Action: The Cases of Brazil and the United States." *American Historical Review* 108, no. 5 (December 2003): 1391–96.

Slessarev-Jamir, Helene. *Prophetic Activism: Progressive Religious Justice Movements in Contemporary America*. New York: New York University Press, 2011.

Smith, Andrea. "Heteropatriarchy and the Three Pillars of White Supremacy: Rethinking Women of Color Organizing." In Incite!, *Color of Violence.*

———. "Sexual Violence and American Indian Genocide." In *Remembering Conquest: Feminist/Womanist Perspectives on Religion, Colonization, and Sexual Violence,* edited by Nantawan Lewis and Marie Fortune. Binghamton, NY: Haworth, 1999.

Smith, Carrol. "Women Who Abuse Their Female Intimate Partners." In *Intimate Partner Violence in LGBTQ Lives,* edited by Janice Ristock. Oxford: Routledge, 2011.

Smith, Merril D., ed. *Sex without Consent: Rape and Sexual Coercion in America.* New York: New York University Press, 2001.

Smith, Sharon G., Jieru Chen, Kathleen C. Basile, Leah K. Gilbert, Melissa T. Merrick, Nimesh Patel, Margie Walling, and Anurag Jain. "The National Intimate Partner and Sexual Violence Survey (NISVS): 2010–2012 State Report." Atlanta: Centers for Disease Control and Prevention, National Center for Injury Prevention and Control, 2017.

Smithers, Gregory D. *Slave Breeding: Sex, Violence, and Memory in African American History.* Gainesville: University Press of Florida, 2012.

Soule, Sarah A., and Brayden G. King. "The Stages of the Policy Process and the Equal Rights Amendment, 1972–1982." *American Journal of Sociology* 111, no. 6 (2006): 1871–1909.

Spieler, Paula. "The Maria da Penha Case and the Inter-American Commission on Human Rights: Contributions to the Debate on Domestic Violence Against Women in Brazil." *Indiana Journal of Global Legal Studies* 18, no. 1 (2011): 121–43.

Stafford, Nancy Kaymar. "Permission for Domestic Violence: Marital Rape in Ghanaian Marriages." *Women's Rights Law Reporter* 29, nos. 2–3 (Winter/Spring 2007–8): 63–75.

Stark, Evan, and Eve S. Buzawa, eds. *Violence Against Women in Families and Relationships.* 4 vols. Santa Barbara, CA: Praeger/ABC-CLIO, 2009.

Stewart, Pearl. "Relationship Violence Strikes Campuses." *Diverse Issues in Higher Education,* March 20, 2008, 12–15.

Stöckl, Heidi, Karen Devries, Alexandra Rotstein, Naeemah Abrahams, Jacquelyn Campbell, Charlotte Watts, and Claudia Garcia Moreno. "The Global Prevalence of Intimate Partner Homicide: A Systematic Review." *Lancet* 382, no. 9895 (2013): 859–65.

Stoler, Ann Laura. *Carnal Knowledge and Imperial Power: Race and the Intimate in Colonial Rule.* Berkeley: University of California Press, 2002.

Stone, Robin D. *No Secrets, No Lies: How Black Families Can Heal from Sexual Violence.* New York: Broadway, 2004.

Sturdevant, Saundra. "Who Benefits? U.S. Military, Prostitution, and Base Conversion." In *Frontline Feminisms: Women, War, and Resistance,* edited by Marguerite R. Waller and Jennifer Rycenga. New York: Routledge, 2000.

Sulemanu, Fatimatu N-Eyare. "Mitigating Violence Against Women in the Ghanaian Muslim Community: The Role of the Federation of Muslim Women's Associations in Ghana (FOMWAG)." In *Religion and Gender-Based Violence: West African Expe-*

rience, Legon Theological Studies, edited by Rose Mary Amenga-Etego and Mercy Amba Oduyoye. Legon, Ghana: Legon Theological Studies Series in collaboration with Asempa Publishers, 2013.

———. "Situation of Muslim Women in Ghana Today," 2009. http://shaaninzongo.com/index.php/womens-corner/9-womens-corner/8-situation-of-muslim-women-in-ghana-today.

Swarr, Amanda Lock, and Richa Nagar, eds. *Critical Transnational Feminist Praxis*. Albany: State University of New York Press, 2010.

Swartz, Sharlene. "A Long Walk to Citizenship: Morality, Justice, and Faith in the Aftermath of Apartheid." *Journal of Moral Education* 35, no. 4 (2006): 551–70.

Sweet, James H. "Teaching the Modern African Diaspora: A Case Study of the Atlantic Slave Trade." *Radical History Review* 77 (2000): 106–22.

Taves, Ann, ed. *Religion and Domestic Violence in Early New England: The Memories of Abigail Abbot Bailey*. Bloomington: Indiana University Press, 1989.

Taylor, Rae. "Slain and Slandered a Content Analysis of the Portrayal of Femicide in Crime News." *Homicide Studies* 13, no. 1 (2009): 21–49.

Taylor, Robert Joseph, Linda M. Chatters, and James S. Jackson. "Religious and Spiritual Involvement among Older African Americans, Caribbean Blacks, and Non-Hispanic Whites: Findings from the National Survey of American Life." *Journals of Gerontology, Series B: Psychological Sciences and Social Sciences* 62, no. 4 (2007): S238–50.

Telles, Edward E. *Race in Another America: The Significance of Skin Color in Brazil*. Princeton, NJ: Princeton University Press, 2014.

Temple, Bogusia. "Crossed Wires: Interpreters, Translators, and Bilingual Workers in Cross Language Research." *Qualitative Health Research* 12 (2002): 844–54.

———. "Watch Your Tongue: Issues in Translation and Cross-Cultural Research." *Sociology* 31 (1997): 607–18.

Temple, Bogusia, and Rosalind Edwards. "Interpreters/Translators and Cross-Language Research: Reflexivity and Border Crossings." *International Journal of Qualitative Methods* 1, no. 2 (2002): 1–12.

Temple, Bogusia, Rosalind Edwards, and Claire Alexander. "Grasping at Context: Cross Language Qualitative Research as Secondary Qualitative Data Analysis." *Forum Qualitative Sozialforschung/Forum: Qualitative Social Research* 7, no. 4 (2006): art. 10. www.qualitative-research.net.

Thompson, Vetta L., Anita Bazile Sanders, and Maysa Akbar. "African Americans' Perceptions of Psychotherapy and Psychotherapists." *Professional Psychology: Research and Practice* 35, no. 1 (February 2004): 19–26.

Thornton, John. "Teaching Africa in an Atlantic Perspective." *Radical History Review* 77 (2000): 23–134.

Tillet, Salamishah. *Sites of Slavery: Citizenship and Racial Democracy in the Post–Civil Rights Imagination*. Durham, NC: Duke University Press, 2012.

Tjaden, Patricia, and Nancy Thoennes. "Stalking in America: Findings from the National Violence against Women Survey." Washington, DC: U.S. Department of Justice Programs, National Institute for Justice, 1998.

Townes, Emilie M. "Ethics as an Art of Doing the Work Our Souls Must Have." In *Womanist Theological Ethics: A Reader*, edited by Katie Geneva Cannon, Emilie Maureen Townes, and Angela D. Sims. Louisville: Westminster John Knox, 2011.

———. *In a Blaze of Glory: Womanist Spirituality as Social Witness*. Nashville: Abingdon, 1995.

———. *Womanist Ethics and the Cultural Production of Evil*. New York: Palgrave Macmillan, 2006.

Treiman, Donald. "The Legacy of Apartheid: Racial Inequalities in the New South Africa." California Center for Population Research, 2005. https://escholarship.org.

Twine, France Winddance. *Racism in a Racial Democracy: The Maintenance of White Supremacy in Brazil*. New Brunswick, NJ: Rutgers University Press, 1998.

U.S. Department of State. "Trafficking in Persons Report." July 2015. www.state.gov.

Velasco, Mercedes. "Loan Proposal: Inter-American Development Bank-National Tourism Development Program in Bahia." Washington, DC: Inter-American Development Bank, 2013.

Violence Policy Center. "When Men Murder Women: An Analysis of 2015 Homicide Data." Washington, DC: Violence Policy Center, September 2017. www.vpc.org.

Wadud, Amina. "American by Force, Muslim by Choice." *Political Theology* 12, no. 5 (2011): 699–705.

———. "Qur'an, Gender and Interpretive Possibilities." *Hawwa* 2, no. 3 (2004): 316–36.

Waetjen, Thembisa, and Gerhard Maré. "Tradition's Desire: The Politics of Culture in the Rape Trial of Jacob Zuma." *Theoria: A Journal of Social and Political Theory* 56, no. 118 (Spring 2009): 63–81.

Walton, Jonathon L. *Watch This! The Ethics and Aesthetics of Black Televangelism*. New York: New York University Press, 2009.

Ward, Earlise C., Le Ondra Clark, and Susan Heidrich. "African American Women's Beliefs, Coping Behaviors, and Barriers to Seeking Mental Health Services." *Qualitative Health Research* 19, no. 11 (2009): 1589–1601.

Warren, Craig A. "Presidential Wounds: The JFK Assassination and the White Male Body." *Men and Masculinities* 10, no. 5 (2008): 557–82.

Waters, Emily, Chai Jindasurat, and Cecilia Wolfe. "Lesbian, Gay, Bisexual, Transgender, Queer, and HIV Affected Hate Violence in 2015." New York: New York City Gay and Lesbian Anti-Violence Project, National Coalition of Anti-Violence Programs, 2016. https://avp.org.

Waters, Emily, and Sue Yacka-Bible. "A Crisis of Hate: A Mid-year Report on Homicides Against Lesbian, Gay, Bisexual, and Transgender People." New York: National Coalition of Anti-Violence Programs, 2017.

Weaver, Hilary N. "The Colonial Context of Violence: Reflections on Violence in the Lives of Native American Women." *Journal of Interpersonal Violence* 24, no. 9 (2009): 1552–63.

Weems, Renita. *Battered Love: Marriage, Sex, and Violence in the Hebrew Prophets*. Minneapolis: Augsburg Fortress, 1995.

Weiss, Holger. *Between Accommodation and Revivalism: Muslims, the State, and Society in Ghana from the Precolonial to the Postcolonial Era.* Studia Orientalia vol. 105. Helsinki: Finnish Oriental Society, 2008.

Weissman, Deborah M. "Law, Social Movements, and the Political Economy of Domestic Violence." *Duke Journal of Gender Law and Policy* 20 (2012): 221–54.

West, Carolyn M., ed. "I Find Myself at Therapy's Doorstep: Summary and Suggested Readings on Violence in the Lives of Black Women." *Women and Therapy* 25, nos. 3–4 (2002): 193–201.

———. *Violence in the Lives of Black Women: Battered, Black, and Blue.* New York: Routledge, 2002.

West, Traci C. "Civil Rights Rhetoric in Media Coverage of Marriage Equality Debates: Massachusetts and Georgia." In *From Every Mountainside: Black Churches and the Broad Terrain of Civil Rights*, edited by R. Drew Smith. Albany: State University of New York Press, 2013.

———. *Disruptive Christian Ethics: When Racism and Women's Lives Matter.* Louisville: Westminster John Knox, 2006.

———. "Gendered Legacies of Martin Luther King Jr.'s Leadership." *Theology Today* 65, no. 1 (2008): 41–56.

———. "Naming the Problem: Black Clergy, U.S. Politics, and Marriage Equality." In *Our Family Values: Same-Sex Marriage and Religion*, edited by Traci C. West. Westport, CT: Praeger, 2006.

———. *Wounds of the Spirit: Black Women, Violence, and Resistance Ethics.* New York: New York University Press, 1999.

Whalley, Elizabeth Ellen. "Rape Crises in Rape Cultures: Transnational Dehumanization within Sexual Assault Response Complexes." PhD dissertation, University of Colorado Boulder, 2017. https://scholar.colorado.edu.

White, Deborah Gray. *Ar'n't I a Woman? Female Slaves in the Plantation South.* 1985. Reprint, New York: Norton, 1999.

Wilder, JeffriAnne. *Color Stories: Black Women and Colorism in the 21st Century.* Santa Barbara, CA: Praeger, 2015.

Williams, Erica Lorraine. "Moral Panic: Sex Tourism, Trafficking, and the Limits of Transnational Mobility in Bahia." In Dewey and Kelly, *Policing Pleasure.*

———. *Sex Tourism in Bahia: Ambiguous Entanglements.* Champaign: University of Illinois Press, 2013.

Wilson, John F. "Common Religion in American Society." In *Civil Religion and Political Theology*, edited by Leroy S. Rouner. Notre Dame, IN: University of Notre Dame Press, 1986.

Winant, Howard. *The World Is a Ghetto: Race and Democracy since World War II.* New York: Basic, 2001.

Winrock International. "Empowerment and Civic Engagement: Empowering Individuals." Salvador, Bahia: n.p., 2010.

Wintemute, Garen J. "The Epidemiology of Firearm Violence in the Twenty-First Century United States." *Annual Review of Public Health* 36 (2015): 5–19.

Winthrop, John. "We Shall Be as a City upon a Hill." In *Speeches That Changed the World*, edited by Owen Collins. Louisville: Westminster John Knox, 1999.

Women's Commission for Refugee Women and Children. "The U.S. Response to Human Trafficking: An Unbalanced Approach." New York: Women's Commission for Refugee Women and Children, 2007. www.womenscommission.org.

Yancy, George, ed. *Christology and Whiteness: What Would Jesus Do?* New York: Routledge, 2012.

Yee, Gale A. *Poor Banished Children of Eve: Women as Evil in the Hebrew Bible*. Minneapolis: Augsburg Fortress, 2003.

Young, Thelathia Nikki. *Black Queer Ethics, Family, and Philosophical Imagination*. New York: Palgrave Macmillan, 2016.

Zimmerman, Yvonne C. "Christianity and Human Trafficking." *Religion Compass* 5 (2011): 567–78.

———. "From Bush to Obama: Rethinking Sex and Religion in the United States' Initiative to Combat Human Trafficking." *Journal of Feminist Studies in Religion* 26 (2010): 79–99.

———. *Other Dreams of Freedom: Religion, Sex, and Human Trafficking*. New York: Oxford University Press, 2013.

Zimmerman, Yvonne C., and Letitia M. Campbell. "Christian Ethics and Human Trafficking Activism: Progressive Christianity and Social Critique." *Journal of the Society of Christian Ethics* 34 (2013): 145–72.

INDEX

Abramovitz, Mimi, 126

Abuse of women and girls, 38–40, 125–26; activism against, 25, 58–59; and advice for, 46; alternatives to, 31; black communities in, 43; Christian responses to, 22, 46, 53; and deception, 142; doubt and religious opposition to, 186; and European Christian men, 6; forms of, 5; gender-based violence, 223; in government institutions, 12; as horrors foreign to United States, 2; isolation of, 126; and LGBTQ persons, 150, 183; public responses to, 21–22, 85; racist shaming of women in, 232. *See also* Black women; Children; Domestic violence; lgbtq/lgbtqi

Accra, Ghana, 22, 24, 29, 36, 57–58, 64, 70, 76, 77, 96, 229, 239, 241. *See also* Ghana

Active listening, 84, 93, 95

Adams, Carol, 80

Africa, 4, 29, 55, 56, 225; convert to Christianity, 61; multicultural nature of, 78; and slave trade in West Africa, 60; U.S. views about, 61–62, 83; *See also* Ghana; South Africa

African American women: and intimate violence in the U.S., 39–51, 196–97, 206–7; activists collaborate with Ghanaian activists in Ghana in 1960, 58; and intimate partner violence, 35–37, 42–43, 46, 50–51, 66, 68, 249n10. *See also* Ghana; South Africa, United States and Ghana. *See also* Black lesbians; Black women

African Americans, 43, 50–51, 180–81, 230. *See also* African American women;

Black clergy; Black lesbians; Black men; Black women

African traditional religions, 86; and anti-violence, 27–28, 70

Africana, activist leadership of, 12, 17, 165, 223–25, 228, 240; approaches defy gendered violence, 16; problems with unity on, 236; spirituality against violence in, 30; transnational perspective on, 4–5. *See also* Spirituality

Alexander, M. Jacqui, 11–12

Alvarez, Sonia, 108

Alves, Barbara E. Dos R., 265n29

Amenga-Etego, Rose Mary, 66, 230–31

Americas, 224; and slavery in, 24, 29–31, 59–60, 79, 103–5, 112, 114, 186, 209. *See also* Colonialism in the Americas; Decolonization

Ammah, Rabiatu, 62–63

Ampofo, A. Adomako, 74

Ancestors, connection to, 49, 109, 205–6

Antiblack racism: in Brazil, 4, 24, 29, 105, 135; and church response to violence, 52; and colorism, 194; and crossing national borders, 65, 107; and Ghana, 227; historical patterns of, 68, 266; and intimate coercion 155; and intimate violence, 130, 225, 272n70; people of African descent, 55–56; and sex/gender expression, 215–16; and socioeconomic control, 163; and U.S. society, 3, 43, 46–47, 52. *See also* Brazil; Colorism; South Africa; United States; White/Whites

ABOUT THE AUTHOR

Traci C. West is Professor of Christian Ethics and African American Studies at Drew University Theological School. She is the author of *Disruptive Christian Ethics: When Racism and Women's Lives Matter* and *Wounds of the Spirit: Black Women, Violence, and Resistance Ethics.*